D1596657

AMERICAN TAX RESISTERS

AMERICAN
TAX RESISTERS

Romain D. Huret

Harvard University Press

*Cambridge, Massachusetts, and
London, England*

2014

Publication of this book has been supported through
the generous provisions of the Maurice and Lula Bradley Smith
Memorial Fund.

LIBRARY OF CONGRESS CATALOGING-IN-PUBLICATION DATA
Huret, Romain.
American tax resisters / Romain D. Huret.
pages cm
Includes bibliographical references and index.
ISBN 978-0-674-28137-0 (alk. paper)
1. Taxation—United States—History.   2. Income tax—United States—
History.   3. Tax evasion—United States—History.   4. Finance, Public—
United States—History.   5. Equality—United States—History.   I. Title.
HJ2362.H87   2014
336.200973—dc23   2013032961

*To Ariane, Emilien,
Melvil, and Raphaël*

CONTENTS

AMERICAN TAX RESISTERS

Prologue

In this world nothing can be said to be certain,
except death and taxes.

—*Benjamin Franklin (1789)*

Bᴇɴᴊᴀᴍɪɴ Fʀᴀɴᴋʟɪɴ's witty remark is familiar today to most American citizens. Each year, on April 15, many share his fatalistic sentiment when they rush to fill in their tax return and send it to the Internal Revenue Service. There is no doubt that Poor Richard was right about death. He forgot, however, that one could resist taxation. Citizens may refuse to sign the 1040 form, fail to send it to federal tax authorities, and organize political and social movements to protest against tax collection. By focusing on the uncertainty of taxes, this book offers an addendum to Franklin's famous statement. It highlights resistance to progressive taxation in the United States. As the country became one of the richest nations on earth, the idea of a redistribution of income through federal taxation appeared and raised one straightforward question: should rich citizens and big corporations pay more taxes than the poor man? In most democratic countries, progressive taxation emerged in the shadow of capitalism in an attempt to stabilize a social order deeply affected by corporate expansion and the extraordinary enrichment of a few citizens at the expense of many. Everywhere such redistribution provoked opposition and opened a debate about inequality, solidarity, and social contracts. From the American Revolution to the present, the exceptional accumulation of wealth in the United States lent greater intensity to the tax debates that had begun in the early days of the republic.[1]

In October 1785 a young Thomas Jefferson wrote to James Madison to describe his meeting with a poor woman in Fontainebleau, a small village a few miles from Paris. His main concern for her was the issue of equity and taxation in the French Ancien Régime. "Another means of silently lessening the inequality of property," he contended, was "to exempt all from taxation below a certain point, and to tax the higher portions or property in geometrical progression as they rise." Before bringing forward the idea of progressive taxation, however, the nation, born of revolution, needed institutions. Two years later, during the passionate constitutional discussions in Philadelphia revolving around federal power, important decisions were made.[2]

The motto "No taxation without representation" epitomized the consensus reached by delegates and was an answer to the unfair taxes that had been levied by the British Crown. The founders decided that federal taxes could be justified in light of the military and fiscal crises facing the republic. Article 1, Section 8 of the Constitution listed the powers of Congress and started with the power of the purse. Congressmen could "lay and collect Taxes, Duties, Imposts and Excises" in order "to pay the Debts and provide for the common Defence and general Welfare of the United States." These taxes had to be "uniform" throughout the country. Furthermore, direct taxation was strictly limited by the Constitution. Article 1, Section 9 contended that "no capitation, or other direct, tax shall be laid, unless in proportion to the Census or enumeration herein before directed to be taken." The Constitution opened unlimited, though unclear, possibilities for tax. In his *Notes on the Debates in the Federal Convention* of 1787, James Madison contended that nobody attempted to answer when one delegate asked his colleagues for the precise meaning of direct taxation. The blurred definition complicated the task of the ruling elite.[3]

During the 1790s, when the Federalists decided to use the new fiscal power, they only managed to weaken the young nation by sparking local revolts. Their taxes on alcohol and property were denounced in harsh terms by citizens and embittered opponents. The tax assessment on whisky barrels or the number of windows in a property ignited two major revolts: the Whiskey Rebellion in 1793, and the revolt against the window tax led by American Revolutionary War veteran John Fries in the winter of 1798. Two years later, Congress decided to repeal the infamous window tax, and in 1802 it repealed all internal taxes in the country. Customs duties soon appeared as the most efficient way to collect revenue for a small federal government. The tariff policy enabled Americans to avoid increasing sectional and social tensions by not taxing properties, especially the ones owned by slaveholders. With the exception of the War of 1812, this marked the end of internal taxation in the United States until the American Civil War.[4]

In his second inaugural address delivered on March 4, 1805, Thomas Jefferson was pleased to present his fellow Americans with an exceptional and limited system of federal taxation. He promised that it would be "the pleasure and pride of an American to ask, what farmer, what mechanic, what laborer ever sees a tax-gatherer of the United States?" Once he arrived in the White House and far from the argument he had made eighteen years earlier in France, he championed a retrenchment policy that called for a reduction in public expenditures and taxation. Without federal tax gatherers, Jefferson believed, Americans would inhabit a republic without taxpayers, as no citizen would pay a federal tax. It was the price to pay to save the fragile union. The only exception was taxes on luxury products and customs duties. Many Americans believed, however, that such taxes were voluntarily paid by customers, not taxpayers. In other words, citizens were free not to pay them by not buying taxed goods such as alcohol and tobacco. As a consequence, federal taxation was strongly regressive as rich and poor paid the same hidden tax. Even in the individual states, uniformity clauses that required different forms of property to be assessed in the same way and taxed at the same rate were adopted to limit the progressivity of local taxes. As Thomas Jefferson had promised, until the American Civil War, neither income nor property was taxed at the federal level.[5]

This book starts with the first gunshot at Fort Sumter in April 1861. With the coming of the war, the federal government increasingly expanded its powers and every corner of the nation was suddenly filled with visible taxation. Debates on the fairness of taxes grew, along with various forms of resistance against the intrusion of the new federal power. In the postbellum era, many Americans still believed they paid taxes in exchange for benefits received from institutions. In his treatise on taxation, published in 1876, famous Michigan jurist and lawyer Thomas M. Cooley perfectly captured such reciprocity when he contended that citizens and property owners received as "proper and full compensation" of their payments "the protection which the government affords to his life, liberty and property, and in the increase to the value of his possessions by the use to which the money contributed was applied." Yet, although federal taxes were accepted as a form of legitimate exchange in a time of war, they were still believed to be temporary and were soon to disappear once the benefits for citizens ceased.[6]

As a predominantly rural nation gave way to an industrial one, a new view of taxation appeared. Industrialization and the market revolution gave rise to vigorous debates on equality and poverty. The emergence of large corporations and the attacks against robber barons reinforced the legitimacy of progressive taxation as both a way to regulate corporations and to promote equality in the new industrial nation. The problem was that the Constitution required Congress to levy direct taxes in proportion to each state's population, not in proportion to each citizen's income. In 1910, as the ratification of the

Sixteenth Amendment that would legitimize the taxation of income was debated in the states, Edwin R. A. Seligman, a social reformer and probably the best tax expert in the country, staunchly supported progressive taxation and urged Americans to amend the Constitution, contending that "the conditions which existed when the constitution was framed are no longer existent." He added that "the development of the underlying economic and social forces had created a nation, and this development called for uniform national regulation of many matters which were not dreamed of by the founders." For him, the idea of reciprocity was nothing but a "selfish and narrow" doctrine, and taxes should be levied upon each citizen's ability to pay. Following that piece of advice, many Americans, especially in the South and the West, posited that the fairest tax was one that extracted from each taxpayer a proportionate "sacrifice."[7]

At the end of the nineteenth century, progressives explained that tax reform, including tax on personal and corporate income, was not a threat to prosperity and welfare. Their belief was based upon the popular theory in academic circles of the marginal utility of money. In other words, the more money one earned, the less utility was derived from the last dollar earned. Poor immigrants living in tenement houses in New York City spent all their money to pay for essentials, while rich men could spend their excess income on luxury goods. Claiming to be the "richest man in the world," William Henry Vanderbilt, the son of the "Commodore," had an annual tax-free income of over $10 million. Would a tax on the upper bracket of his astounding income affect his way of living? Tax reformers did not believe so, contending that the sacrifice of rich taxpayers would not jeopardize economic incentives.[8]

Eventually, progressives contended that this sense of fiscal citizenship should be made public. In an ideal republic, they argued, it should be the pride of the wealthiest citizens to pay more taxes in the name of equality and to divulge their tax returns. Furthermore, rich taxpayers would not try to reduce their tax liability or, in the event

they did so, it should be relatively easy for Congress to close tax loopholes. Publicity was part of the progressive agenda as it would enable
all citizens to know the precise amount sacrificed by each taxpayer.
During the civil war, taxes paid by the wealthiest were published in
the press. Why not pursue such disclosure in the name of tax fairness and social justice?[9]

The story, however, turned out to be more complicated. In 1935
one Harvard professor, Mason Hammond, deplored the progressivity
scheme imposed by President Franklin Delano Roosevelt. In a letter
he sent to Congress to protest against the public disclosure requirement for income tax returns, Hammond characterized the whole tax
system as unconstitutional and "un-American." "Quite apart from
the practical dangers of undesirable publicity and solicitation to which
such a policy will expose taxpayers," he asserted, "the income tax itself works sufficient hardship upon a minority of the citizens of this
country by subjecting their earnings to expenditures voted by representatives of the very large proportion of citizens who does not pay
this, or, often, any other direct tax." Hammond pointed out that "with
all the talk about the rights of minorities, it seems to me that this minority of income taxpayers might be protected in a right guaranteed
to every citizen by the Constitution." The Harvard professor of literature then detailed the main grievances against progressive taxes: arbitrary rates, inept redistribution, and dangerous publicity.[10]

Tax resisters tried to instill in the nation the idea that progressive
taxation was a fundamental mistake. From the civil war to the present, they have assumed the same mantle of principles and considered the household, the community, and the free market sanctified
places. They believed that the Constitution protected such rights as
inalienable. Defended by misguided idealists who carried out heavy-
handed economic and social reforms, the stated purpose of progressive taxes, they warned citizens, was to corrupt from within these
sacred elements of the American way of life. They vehemently opposed what they considered an attempt to undermine the founda-

tions of American exceptionalism. Most of the time, the ideology that infused their speeches and orations was not a coherent set of theories, guided by high intellectual principles, but more a set of beliefs based on common sense, historical precedents, and empirical analysis. Although tax resisters read academic treaties legitimating their disputes, they drew inspiration from tapping into a popular antitax literature comprised of newsletters, popular books, and conservative pamphlets.

For them, the very concept of sacrifice was nothing but "class legislation." Referring to the situation in Europe at the end of the nineteenth century, many businessmen and laissez-faire advocates denounced as soon as the civil war ended the socialistic idea of taxing personal and corporate incomes. In 1888 economist David A. Wells warned citizens against "the communism of a discriminating income-tax" that would inflict "spoliation" on a small class of citizens. The idea of sacrifice did not make any sense, Wells added, if a majority of citizens avoided the payment of federal taxes.[11]

As a consequence, graduated tax rates were pure and simple "confiscation." The federal government had no right to decide how rich people should spend their money, and it had no right to redistribute money to other citizens. It was an attack against the right of ownership and an odious intrusion into the management of corporations. Contrary to what tax reformers affirmed, progressive taxation would destroy incentive and demoralize the most energetic and entrepreneurial citizens. Tax resisters' praise of industriousness and laissez-faire economics became a distinguishing characteristic of the nation and unproductive citizens were targeted by angry militants. In such a Manichean view, tax transfer from one class to another appeared as nothing but inept and wasteful legislation.[12]

From the civil war onward, attacks against publicity, redistribution, and sense of sacrifice dovetailed seamlessly. Tax resisters denounced the public disclosure of taxes as an unconstitutional invasion of privacy and a dangerous attack on corporations. They feared that businesses would be ruined when competitors discovered corporate secrets. Furthermore, they argued, the public disclosure provision challenged the professionalism of businessmen for whom secrecy reigned supreme and it would give citizens a wrong sense of social justice and actually jeopardize businesses.

This book examines white upper- and middle-class Americans who resisted the advance of progressive taxation. Resistance should not be confused with individuals' dislike of taxes. Very few people like to pay taxes, but the vast majority of citizens do not turn into tax resisters. Resistance should also not be limited to violent and illegal actions against the Internal Revenue Service, which tend to be exceptional. More importantly, it was a legal and political form of protest that taxpayers used to defend their interests and their worldview against federal tax authorities. Wealthier citizens had access to financial resources and political opportunities, which gave them the clout to curtail democratic pressures for income redistribution and corporate regulation. Indeed, their goal was to maximize individual and collective capital accumulation and minimize federal intrusion through petitions, lobbying, and public meetings.[13]

Tax resistance was always much more than an economic matter. Resisters did not fight only to protect their money; they were defending their own conceptions of politics, power, and social hierarchies. Moral, racial, and social beliefs had a direct impact on resisters' taxation tolerance thresholds and their evolution as a movement. Resisters' crusades were rife with symbols, values, and passions about the role of elites and what resisters considered as their legitimate power in the country. They questioned the boundary between public good and private wealth, federal government and individuals, and legitimate and illegitimate forms of power.[14]

As a consequence, and despite their antistatist rhetoric, their resistance has always been a social and political act of negotiation with the federal government. By dissecting the relationship between tax resisters and federal intervention, this account offers a more nuanced vision of antistatism. Although their campaigns took a strong stance against the federal government, tax resisters did not live in an anarchist vacuum. From the civil war to the present, taxes have been from time to time necessary to finance federal action in times of crisis. When confronted with them, especially in wartime, militants eagerly sought to promote regressive taxes paid by everybody equally, rather than progressive ones that taxed the wealthy the most. Once the crisis was over, they worked steadily to erode the tax system that had been built.

Although French philosopher Michel Foucault was right to remind social scientists that resistance to power has been a central feature of modern societies, he forgot to mention that powerful men and women have often been the most active resisters. A linear and teleological view of history tends to see tax protests as the result of backward and traditional social groups in ancient and early modern societies. Such a framework implies that opposition was soon to disappear with the creation of the modern Weberian nation-state. It also conveys the notion of a relentless advance of democracy, taxation being a powerful social force of equalization. Once again, the story appears more complex. Although it has roots in the premodern contentious repertoire, tax resistance in the United States has grown with the emergence of capitalism and has been defended by both local and national elites. Since the civil war, their action has shaped the architecture of federal taxation and limited democratic pressures in favor of progressive taxation.[15]

Far from describing tax resistance as a life-or-death choice, this book describes reciprocal interactions between resisters and their institutions. Institutional procedures enabled American citizens to influence the design of the tax code and often gave tax resisters what they wanted. Such interactions explain the central role played by petitions in this narrative. Debates about tax reforms have always been public and have enabled resisters to anticipate and to curtail changes in the tax code. Petitions sent to the House Committee on Ways and Means

and the Senate Finance Committee, the two congressional committees in charge of revenue laws, have been very helpful to track the
size of the movement, especially since taxpayers' organizations left
few membership records. If the petitions explain the reasons for resistance, the lists of names and signatures provide much important
information about the petitioners. Petitions were used not only to
make citizens tax conscious but also to propose the reduction or the
repeal of a specific tax. Furthermore, in the fiction of a republic without taxpayers, petitions helped cement political coalitions, sometimes
even invent constituencies, and always perpetuate the glorious actions of the founding fathers. In other words, they had to convey the
idea that tax resisters were the spokespeople for a beleaguered populace of taxpayers.[16]

Since the civil war, resistance against progressive taxation has not
been a linear story because of changing social, political, and economic conditions. The development of capitalism, the transformation of the federal government, and the incremental expansion of
federal taxation radically reconfigured both the rhetoric and actions
of tax resisters. As the twentieth century dawned, the United States
had become the world's most productive industrial nation. Such a
development had momentous effects not only on standards of living
and everyday life of Americans but also transformed the federal government from a limited institution to an increasingly used tool for
market regulation and social engineering. Debates on progressive taxation became crucial in the nation as taxes derived from the success of industrialization financed the growth of federal power and
its bureaucracy.[17]

In the mid-nineteenth century, the view of limited taxation based
on tariffs prevailed. The civil war altered the consensus and raised
the question of the tax burden. Demographic and economic changes
made obsolete the rule of apportionment of direct taxes as wealth
was more concentrated in the northeastern states and the population
tended to move in the western part of the nation. It was no coinci-

dence that rich citizens and businessmen started to mobilize against the income tax as soon as the war ended. Their crusade soon turned to the repeal of all internal taxes, which were seen as the Trojan horse of tax reform and government expansion. In a postslavery society, the abolition of taxes became the rallying cry for opponents to any form of taxation of personal and corporate incomes. The severe economic crisis of 1893 and the enrichment of businessmen, however, pushed more and more citizens to endorse a limited income tax. Thanks to their stronghold on institutions, tax resisters were able to circumvent progressive forces in the nation. In 1895, with the *Pollock* decision, the Supreme Court declared unconstitutional the federal taxation of income in the republic.

Yet, the victory turned out to be a Pyrrhic one. From the adoption of the Sixteenth Amendment in 1913 to World War II, progressive taxation gained a new legitimacy. In the taxpayers' nation, resisters were compelled to negotiate. Calls for abolition or repeal segued into calls for a reduction of the burden of federal taxes for rich taxpayers. In order to limit federal spending on women, soldiers, and poor citizens, they tried to defend the notion of a taxpayers' right to oppose federal expenditures. Such taxpayers' standing could have enabled them to refuse the use of their money for a purpose that they disliked. At the forefront of tax resistance in the 1930s were businessmen who were especially eager to curtail the expansion of progressive taxation as public disclosure of tax returns and high-end progressivity were being proposed as the best way to control corporations. The mass-based income tax adopted during World War II marked the victory of progressive views in the country, and tax resisters were left with very little space to express their grievances. Even businessmen who had previously been eager to criticize the federal tax system accepted a limited form of progressive taxation to finance the Cold War and the globalization of markets.

In the postwar years the tax resistance movement was reinvigorated by conservative men and women living in the suburbs. In their white middle-class world, they made federal taxes a life-or-death choice that energized every aspect of life. Although tax resisters had always stated their case mainly in economic terms, a new moral imperative was soon to emerge in the discourse of white middle-class conservatives. The growth of the welfare state prompted them to call for the "abolition" or the "killing" of federal taxes that came to embody all the evils of the leviathan state. For many years, Americans scoffed at them, and tax resisters were labeled mavericks or "Neanderthal" men and women. In the 1970s the economic crisis and the triumph of neoliberal ideas made tax cuts the new priority of a coalition of middle-class resisters, corporate executives, and conservative intellectuals. The myth of a tax-free world cascaded into the ensuing decades. As conservatives in power revived the idea of reciprocity of taxation and refused to pay for people on welfare, they contributed to the demise of many tenets of progressivity, especially the idea of sacrifice and income transfers.

By going beyond the myth of a republic without taxpayers and examining the role of citizens who opposed the increase of progressive taxation, this book is also about citizenship. The enduring resistance movement offered the opportunity to ponder American democracy. Since the civil war, the contentious issue of taxation has raised the question of wealth and social justice in modern nations. By focusing on tax resisters, this book is not only about taxes; it is first and foremost a book about social justice and democratic values in the United States.[18]

1

Unconstitutional War Taxes

William Backhouse Astor had paid more
income tax than the State of Vermont.

—Elihu Spencer Miller and
William Maxwell Evarts (1871)

AFTER THE CIVIL WAR, Philadelphia lawyer Elihu Spencer Miller worked with his prominent colleague William M. Evarts to defend the interests of taxpayers against the U.S. Department of the Treasury. The two men were involved in a case challenging the constitutionality of the new federal income tax and informed readers of the *New York Times* on January 14, 1871, of their own reading of its constitutionality. By then, many discussions revolved around the Astor family, one of the richest in the nation. In order to vindicate his support in favor of the tax, Republican representative John Sherman wondered in 1870 why congressmen were afraid to "touch" the Astors' income. Contrary to what businessmen contended, Sherman believed that it was necessary to retain a peacetime income tax to reduce the federal debt and to promote a sense of equality in the nation after four years of bloody warfare. One year later, referring to the rule of apportionment of direct taxation, Miller and Evarts disagreed with him and offered what they believed was an important constitutional

objection: whether it was fair that William Backhouse Astor, during
the civil war, had paid more income tax than all taxpayers in the
state of Vermont. Furthermore, they cited the example of Alexander
Turney Stewart, the wealthy department store owner and the third
richest man in America, who paid more taxes than were collected
in any one of twenty-seven states and territories—more indeed than
the aggregate amounts paid by Florida, Arizona, Colorado, Dakota,
Washington, New Mexico, Utah, Idaho, and Montana combined.
The resisters claimed that the wartime income tax was, without
doubt, unconstitutional because it was not apportioned to the states'
population but to individuals' incomes. For many rich citizens who
lived in the industrial states of the Northeast, a progressive apportionment based upon each citizen's ability to pay betrayed the ruling
principles of the founding fathers, and war taxes had to be repealed.[1]

From the outset of the civil war, Northerners and Southerners
turned to war bonds and customs duties to avoid tax resistance and
endlessly constitutional debates. However, they were soon forced to
levy direct taxes. As federal expenditures rose, it was necessary to
find new sources of revenue to prosecute the war without dividing
the nation. From the first time since the War of 1812, internal taxes
were levied, including a small, graduated income tax. Once the soldiers came back home, the taxes were believed not to be necessary
anymore. The novelty of federal taxes and the hasty mechanisms of
collection slowly shaped the ideology of tax resistance around constitutional arguments. Industrialists and bankers who benefited greatly
from government contracts were the first to promote the repeal of
the war tax system. The wartime experience reinforced the idea that
progressive taxation was merely accidental. Although the energies of
an industrializing society had been harnessed to serve the cause of
the Union, they were no longer supposed to finance the leviathan
that the war had helped build up.[2]

A few months after the beginning of the civil war, on March 5, 1862,
119 citizens from Pike County, Ohio, warned Congress of "another

rebellion" that was brewing in the country due to tax increases. Petitioners were deeply concerned by the bill under discussion that would levy a host of new internal taxes to finance the war against the Confederate State. First and foremost, tapping into constitutional arguments, it was proclaimed that such new taxes "violated the broad principle of equal rights and justice to all men, special privileges to none." As petitioners further argued, "the poor laboring man has to pay as much as the rich nabob, because he eats, drinks and wears as much, or more as the millionaire." The creation of a bureaucratic apparatus raised strong concerns. Petitioners estimated that the federal government would have to pay "at least 30,000 new officers, who will eat up at least half of the money that is collected, and if a revenue [*sic*] of $100,000,000 is required, you will have to take $200,000,000 from the people's brackets." Such a costly tax system would even discourage the good will of immigrants as "the honest and industrial German and Irishman" would not come to this country if he met the same opposition here which he had suffered in his "fatherland." In the set of letters and petitions that were sent to Congress in the spring of 1862, citizens' grievances were based upon the Constitution to denounce the right to levy such a sweeping array of internal taxes, the power of the newly formed Bureau of Internal of Revenue (BIR), and the fairness of the whole tax system. If direct taxes had to be imposed in proportion to the population of each state, was it fair to put the tax burden on ordinary citizens while the rich industrialists and the rebellious Southerners remained untaxed?[3]

At that time, such concerns were not unusual. After the unexpected rout at Bull Run on July 21, 1861, hopes for a short war faded away, and for many citizens, war loomed large on the horizon. In a country profoundly transformed by war conditions, President Abraham Lincoln asked Salmon P. Chase, a former governor and senator from Ohio, to run the difficult task of creating a wartime tax system that would not provoke protests. Born in 1808 in Cornish, New Hampshire, Salmon Portland Chase moved to Ohio as a young boy. Trained as a lawyer, he became a senator in 1848 before becoming governor in 1856. After a brief return to the Senate from 1860 to 1861, he served as treasury secretary. Both Lincoln and Chase were strong advocates of tariff as the sole source of revenue for the government. In 1843 the Campaign Circular of Whig Meeting, which Lincoln helped to write, contended that the tariff was the cheaper system, because the duties, "being collected in large parcels at a few commercial points, will require comparatively few officers in their collection." As a consequence, a young Abe Lincoln hoped citizens would not be "perpetually haunted and harassed by the tax-gatherer." Chase shared Lincoln's desire to create a system that would avoid the encumbering presence of tax agents on the doorsteps of American men and women.[4]

In July 1861, from his office in the southeast corner of the third floor of the Treasury building, Chase sent Congress a report estimating that the federal government would need roughly $320 million to finance the war. He hoped that tariffs, bonds, and loans would provide the essential revenue and would remain hidden, obviating the need to hire tax collectors, thus imposing the federal government on the daily lives of citizens. Most businessmen were eager to help. The wealthy Philadelphia banker Jay Cooke accepted to convince both big investors and citizens to invest money. Symbolically, Cooke had an office across the street from the Treasury and orchestrated a campaign to sell war bonds through advertisements, patriotic speakers, and brass bands. During the war, Cooke & Company sold hundreds of millions of dollars in Union government bonds and earned hefty commissions.[5]

Bonds, however, were not enough to finance the war cost. Furthermore, it was important to reassure the business community that bond interest would be paid through new taxes. Chase suggested collecting $30 million dollars in new excise levies and a direct tax on real estate which would be apportioned to each state's population. Legislators in the House of Representatives, led by the powerful chairman of the Committee on Ways and Means, Thaddeus Stevens, crafted the bill. Expressing the fear of his constituents, Ohio congressman Samuel Shellabarger passed a wise piece of advice to his fellow congressmen when he remarked that "no financial measure will be sustained ultimately and permanently as a war measure, by the country, which does not have as its basis an equitable apportionment of the burdens of taxation upon all interests of the country." The problem was that the population distribution no longer corresponded with that of wealth. In the 1860s the population was growing in the western states, while the market revolution had profoundly altered income distribution. Between 1840 and 1860, per capita income grew at an annual rate of around 1.5 percent. Wealth and capital were mainly concentrated in the northeastern states, and by 1860 the top 5 percent of wealthiest families owned more than half of the nation's wealth. Choices made by congressmen would inevitably provoke tensions.[6]

As a consequence, most debates revolved around the proposed land tax, which was denounced as "obnoxious" and "unfair" by many citizens, especially in the midwestern states. It was proclaimed that an apportioned land tax would be highly inequitable and put the tax burden on farmers' shoulders. Ohio congressman Sidney Edgerton contended that "a more odious bill can't be devised, and one which the people will more promptly discard." His colleague from Illinois, Owen Lovejoy, added that it was not a good idea "to tax agricultural lands and not tax merchandise, bank notes, bonds, and mortgages," and Schuyler Colfax from Indiana refused to vote "for a bill that would allow a man, a millionaire, who has put his entire property in stock to be exempt from taxation, while a farmer who lives by his side must pay the tax." Hostile to such taxation, Illinois representative John Alexander McClernand deplored that the tax would fall upon the great agricultural states of the West and Southwest. For many representatives, it was necessary to avoid such an unfair allocation of the tax burden and the idea of taxing incomes appeared based upon the British experience during the Crimean War (1853–1856).[7]

For the first time since the Philadelphia Convention in 1787, a small income tax was proposed as a way to equalize the revenue burden. Illinois representative and staunch abolitionist Owen Lovejoy referred to the market revolution that had profoundly altered American society. "The wealth of this country," he insisted, "is in the East—in New England, in the great Empire State of New York, and in the great Keystone States of Pennsylvania; and yet by this bill, there, where the wealth is, the burden of taxation is made to fall lightest." Although he warned congressmen of the danger of a tax on income, New York representative Roscoe Conkling voted for it on the assumption that it would help "throttle the rebellion." Thaddeus Stevens agreed that the tax was the most unpleasant one but, he believed, the country had no choice. Rhode Island senator James Fowler Simmons, a Republican member of the Senate Finance Committee, defended an income tax that would make the wealthy pay their share. At the end of July, the House and Senate passed the first revenue law that included both a small income tax and a direct tax on land.[8]

On August 5, 1861, the *New York Herald* admired the fairness of the revenue law and the fact that "millionaires like Mr. W. B. Astor, Commodore Vanderbilt . . . and others, will henceforth contribute a fair proportion of their wealth to support of the national government." Resistance was limited because little changed for the wealthiest citizens. As a matter of fact, the income tax was never enforced since Treasury Secretary Chase feared that it would cause strong opposition in a nation at war. Indeed, he used many excuses for delay, notably the lack of accurate statistics, and eventually argued that it was not useful to proceed with the income tax as it was projected to yield less revenue than the cost of collection.[9]

As a consequence, the sum collected proved insufficient to cover the new expenses and payouts on the loans. Thus, the Union had to contemplate an expanded system of internal taxation in the early days of 1862. By then, Secretary Chase had requested fifty million dollars in additional revenues. During debates, petitions and letters were sent to tone down Congress's tax demands. Many came from the "middling classes" that had developed during the antebellum period. Using constitutional arguments, petitioners used a highly deferential tone to persuade their opposition. In this world of small merchants and manufacturers, landowning farmers, professionals, and self-employed artisans, fears increased that their businesses would decline because of wartime conditions and new federal taxation.[10]

In Ohio, 151 citizens signed a petition to protest against the tax on tobacco; in Missouri, another 97 spoke bluntly against the federal levy, even though they proclaimed to be "true and loyal citizens." The novelty of taxation prompted businessmen to warn Congress of the danger caused by its action. The Board of Trade of Pennsylvania feared the impact of federal taxes on businesses that had already been affected by the loss of southern markets. In Massachusetts, small businesses criticized the new tax on gas; in Brooklyn, manufacturers engaged in the "express business" opposed the impact of the new tax on their activities.[11]

Some congressmen tried to bring up these grievances in debates. John Stratton, a Princeton alumnus elected in New Jersey, did not mince his words when he argued that whatever the circumstances, "a Federal Tax is always odious to the people." Facing so many protests, Congress decided to sprinkle the tax burden by imposing a 3 percent excise tax on all manufactured goods. Carl Von Hock, an Austrian traveler in the United States, observed that "the citizen of the Union pays a tax every hour of the day, either directly or indirectly, for each act of his life; for his movable and immovable property, either directly or indirectly; for his income as well as his expenditure; for his business as well as his pleasure." On July 19, 1862, a New York weekly, the *Frank Leslie's Illustrated Newspaper*, pursued the same tone by publishing a cartoon lampooning Congress's tax policy. In the quiet home of a middle-class family, furnished with curtains, fine wallpapers, walls hangings, and a dressing table, the

THE HOME OF THE AMERICAN CITIZEN AFTER THE TAX BILL HAS PASSED.

N.B.—*Scroggs says he is ready and willing to pay any amount of tax, but he would like them to leave his wife's crinoline and other domestic trifles alone.*

Figure 1.1. "The Home of the American Citizen after the Tax Bill Has Passed," *Frank Leslie's Illustrated,* July 19, 1862. Courtesy of the Library of Congress.

civil war has caused an unexpected disturbance. Four tax collectors have invaded the house, and are searching under the spouse's dress and even beneath the bed. In front of revenue agents, the husband tries to explain that he is "ready to pay any amount of tax," but he asks them "to leave his wife's crinoline and other domestic trifles alone."[12]

To limit further protests, proposed income-tax legislation applied a mildly progressive scale of 3 percent on incomes of between $600 and $10,000, 5 percent on incomes above $10,000 and 7.5 percent on incomes in excess of $10,000. It also added a small inheritance tax. On July 1, 1862, President Abraham Lincoln signed the bill into law.

From his office in the Treasury, the first commissioner of internal revenue, George S. Boutwell, set up an office to collect new internal taxes.

Though few people contested the necessity of taxes to fight the Confederate rebellion, the number of tax resisters slowly grew as they began to perceive both the nature of the taxes and the process of collection to be unfair. As the federal government started to standardize financial and commercial transactions, difficulties arose. When the Union sought to define and to collect "income," for example, it had to create a definition where none had previously existed. In reference to the Jeffersonian tax creed, *The Crisis* newspaper instructed its readers that "it would be wrong to tax a mechanic, farmer, or other person of the gross amount that might come to him, without considering and deducting his outgoes, and call that 'gains, profits and incomes' subject to taxation." Eventually, the newspaper feared, such a construction would "repress industry" and "prevent improvement." The 3 percent tax soon came to symbolize the difficult and necessarily biased definition of both incomes and tax rates. In January 1863, Boston merchant tailors complained about their integration as "manufacturers of clothing," because by then they had to pay the tax imposed upon manufacturers, which they considered both "oppressive" and "unjust."[13]

Tailors' grievances against the general 3 percent tax were not isolated. For many businessmen, the tax, which was based on sales rather than profits, would be "utterly ruinous" to them and amounted to "triple and quadruple taxations" as it was already imposed through excise taxes on raw materials. As many tailors complained, the addition of this tax to ordinary expenses and losses would affect their activities. During a convention held in Chicago in June 1863, some manufacturers wrote a memorandum pushing the commissioner of revenue to either ignore or repeal the law. The BIR, however, refused to suspend fiscal operations. It was all too easy to neglect such protests in the wake of the growing cooperation between businesses and the federal government.[14]

As many politicians argued, most businessmen reaped great profits from the war and, day after day, new federal contracts were signed. In many states, government intrusion saved many firms from ruin. As more and more enterprises made healthy profits, it seemed inappropriate to hammer on the federal government. Only the scope and duration of the war made tax consent more complicated, especially in midwestern states.[15]

In a speech delivered in the House of Representatives on January 14, 1863, two weeks after Abraham Lincoln's Declaration of Emancipation, Clement Laird Vallandigham achieved national recognition when he warned his fellow citizens to oppose "the enslavement of the white race by debt and taxes and arbitrary power." Born in Lisbon, Ohio, in 1820, Vallandigham was the U.S. representative for the Third Congressional District of Ohio. A staunch supporter of states' rights with a stridency that lived up to his name, he objected in harsh terms to the increasing power of the federal purse. Furthermore, he expressed the conviction that the federal government had no constitutional right to regulate or abolish slavery. By doing so, he challenged the reciprocal views of taxation. Although most northerners agreed to pay the soldiers and war expenses, he cast doubts on the legitimacy of the war itself. The protest staged by the outspoken Vallandigham gained traction among Peace Democrats who were eager to portray Lincoln as a "dictator." Vallandigham believed that the only "trophies" for those who supported the war would be "defeat, debt, taxation."[16]

Vallandigham's influence was particularly strong in midwestern states where economic hardship plagued inhabitants in the early months of the war. Inflation rose, and shortages became apparent, especially of cotton goods and household staples. The large number of Southern-born citizens explained reservations about the war. In the southern part of Indiana, Illinois, and Ohio, between 10 and 12 percent of the population had been born in the South; in Ohio, it amounted to 6 percent of population. Furthermore, many German and Irish immigrants did not consider the war as their fight. Eventually, the nascent military-industrial sector was seen as corrupt, and many people criticized the "middlemen" in charge of government contracts. Accusations against "shoddy aristocrats" targeted the contractors and blamed the government for financing such a corrupt and wasteful system. It was all the more acute as midwesterners were convinced that taxes were unequally distributed. The internal taxes adopted in 1861 and 1862, which levied duties on tea, coffee, sugar, spices, and other items to support the war effort, were particularly criticized.[17]

As a consequence, protests grew after the summer of 1862 and took a more organizational turn. In December 1862 the first United States Brewers' Association was created in New York City to defend brewers' interests, and the association was particularly strong in the Midwest. In January 1863, in the city of Cincinnati, brewers opposed the "unlimited power" of the commissioner of internal revenue. When tax collectors wanted to assess their incomes, they refused to let assessors see their books because they had the constitutional right to keep "their doors unlocked" and their houses "not exposed to the public." As it became a regular target, tax collection was seen as a threat to both their religious and moral beliefs and something that should be amended "to the relief of our conscience." Most criticisms stemmed from antebellum debates about uniformity clauses. These clauses required that different types of property be treated "uniformly" and assessed in the same way and taxed at the same rate. In Milwaukee, petitioners transferred arguments of uniformity to the new tax structure adopted by the civil war Congress and hoped to have the taxes levied "equitably upon capital and labor alike" and "may be just to all and oppressive to none." Without such careful plans, Americans would have no choice but to criticize the tax system as "unfair," "unequal," and "unjust in its operation."[18]

Doubts about the war system escalated in the months following Abraham Lincoln's Emancipation Proclamation and spread out well beyond the midwestern states. "The fire in the rear," as the president himself portrayed it, grew in the North after both the emancipation of slaves in January 1863 and the new draft law. In March the government adopted a stricter federal draft procedure. By then all male citizens between twenty and thirty-five years of age and all unmarried men between thirty-five and forty-five years of age were subject to military duty. The federal government entered all eligible men in a lottery. Those who could afford to hire a substitute or pay the government $300 might avoid enlistment. All these measures were designed to sap the Confederacy but unexpectedly embittered class and racial tensions in the North. As a consequence, many rich people were able to pay to avoid the draft and poor people felt they bore the brunt of the war. In New York City immigrants were outraged by such blatant discrimination. They criticized the federal government's intrusion into local affairs on behalf of the "nigger war" and compared their value unfavorably to that of Southern slaves. Furthermore, they stated that the price of a soldier was $300 while "they pay $1,000 for Negroes." On July 13, 1863, in the early morning, riots began on the streets of New York and sparked off a fierce debate about war support. Other riots occurred in Indiana, Illinois, Pennsylvania, Wisconsin, and Ohio.[19]

To avoid such class conflicts and limit the influence of Peace Democrats, many congressmen pushed for a more progressive system that would impose some sacrifice on rich people as well. It was all the more needed as the public debt grew to more than $1 billion—the federal debt stood only at $64 million before the war. In the spring of 1864, during debates in Congress, Josiah Bushnell Grinnell, an Iowa representative, advocated for a 10 percent rate on all income without any exemptions. Otherwise, he explained, it would be another privilege for "the Astors and Stewarts and other rich men of the country." By then, as New York tax collector William Orton complained, tax evasion was rampant among the wealthiest. To reinforce social and political cohesion among Unionists, Congress adopted both higher and graduated rates for the income tax: 5 percent on incomes between $600 and $5,000 and 10 percent on incomes over $5,000. Congress also included corporate profits in the income tax base. Furthermore, false or fraudulent statements would be more severely punished with a fine of 100 percent of the tax.[20]

To make the sacrifice of wealthy citizens more visible, a public disclosure provision was added, and newspapers were allowed to publish the names of taxpayers and the amount of money they paid to the Treasury. By 1865 the *New York Times* had a front-page feature titled "Our Internal Revenue" that listed the names of New Yorkers who paid their income taxes. On July 8, 1865, the newspaper informed its readers that William B. Astor had paid $1.3 million, Cornelius Vanderbilt, $576,000, and Samuel Ward, $183,000. Thaddeus Stevens was one of the few congressmen who strongly opposed the graduated income tax system and its publicity. During debates, he lamented the fact that it was a strange "way to punish men" because they were rich. Such attacks against the graduated taxation of incomes remained limited; most citizens endorsed the idea of sacrifice to finance the war and to preserve the nation's unity.[21]

The novelty of the system, however, continued to raise concerns among citizens. In Portland, Oregon, a bookseller named S. J. McCormick proposed the Citizen's Edition of the New Tax law to explain how tax collection worked and what citizens had to do to fulfill their civic duty. The disclosure of taxes paid had an unexpected impact as it showed that some taxpayers were not paying their share. As an anonymous citizen lamented in the *New York Times*, "The full list has been published in only one district to this city; but that made it evident that the most glaring and shameless frauds are practiced in the return of incomes, and in the assessment of taxes upon them." The numerous letters sent to the *New York Times* showed that some people felt that tax collectors were not doing their jobs and were avoiding auditing some taxpayers. One reader wondered whether rich women were audited the same way as men. Moreover, in many states, cases of fraud and corruption among tax collectors were numerous.[22]

The *Inspector's Book of the Bureau of Internal Revenue*, which detailed inspections of tax assessors in the field, revealed a high number of cases implying unfair practices for the years 1864 and 1865. On June 2, 1864, a citizen named Joseph Karned, living in Steubenville, Ohio, charged some of the officers of the eleventh district with various irregularities and stated that the income of certain individuals and establishments had not been returned in full. In the same state, an impostor named Thomas H. Glanner pretended to be a tax collector and borrowed money on the strength of his alleged position. Local newspapers denounced such cases and hoped that the federal authorities would soon launch investigations into the alleged misdemeanors. The new commissioner, Joseph Lewis, decided to improve tax collection and establish investigations in tax districts to limit cases of tax abuse. In a letter sent to many inspectors, he urged them to report all wrongdoings. Otherwise, they would contribute to undermining the credibility of the whole tax system. For many Americans, tax collectors were similar to the middlemen who took advantage of government contracts at the expense of ordinary citizens.[23]

In spite of such difficulties, most Americans paid their share in order to save the Union and to win the war despite subterranean tensions that would resurface once the conflict was over. The fiscal regime was not just a financial machine designed to consolidate the coercive power of the government by funding military expenditures; nor may it be sufficiently characterized as a battle between

Republicans and Peace Democrats. Federal taxation was the product of discussions and negotiations and a new, temporary social contract emerged that gave power to the federal government to extract wealth from American society. Resistance to the new internal revenue system was more widespread in the Confederacy because of the long-held and deep-seated antitax ideology of Southern planters.

In December 1863 President Jefferson Davis asked his secretary to read a long, detailed letter about the financial and political situation after more than two and a half years of bloody warfare. Economic difficulties plagued the Confederacy with a disastrous impact on war operations. Willing to make Southerners aware of the desperate situation, Davis evoked "the long exemption from direct taxation by the General Government" that had created "an aversion to its raising revenue by any other means than by duties on imports." He urged his fellow citizens to accept new internal taxes and regretted the growing protests and the "obvious difficulty" in tax collection. He deplored such resistance as a subversion of "the whole intention of the framers of the Constitution," and the cause of "the most revolting injustice, instead of that just correlation between taxation and representation which it was their purpose to secure." In other words, poor people paid more taxes than rich planters to finance war expenditures. As Jefferson Davis sadly noted, aversion to the taxing power of the federal government was deeply rooted in the Southern ideology defended by wealthy inhabitants.[24]

States' rights had always been a central ideology in the antebellum years. The view of John C. Calhoun still found an echo among Southerners. Known for his adamant refusal of both high-tariff duty and powerful federal government, Calhoun became a household name. In his anonymously published *South Carolina Exposition and Protest* (1828), he developed a strong constitutional argument that drew from the point of view expressed in the Virginia and Kentucky resolutions of 1798–1799. His speeches were imbued with the idea that the states had a right to judge the constitutionality of federal actions. Interestingly, only taxes raised for revenue for such common purposes as defense were deemed constitutional. By endorsing a reciprocal and exceptional view of federal taxation, he helped frame the point of view of Southerners. If the federal government levied taxes in peacetime, Calhoun argued, only nullification could protect the minority against the majority's tyranny. His views gained political clout among governors and planters, even during a war that jeopardized the very foundation of the racial and political order of the "Old South."[25]

Beyond ideological claims, economic conditions under the slave regime reinforced the power of the white ruling class. In comparison to the ones in the North, Southern factories were small and were closely tied to agriculture. Lack of industry kept the region rural and explained the hegemonic power of planters. At the onset of the war, slaveholders concentrated the wealth. By 1860 the richest 1 percent owned 27 percent of the wealth. Planters controlled state politics in the South and used it to further their own interests. For Confederate authorities, enacting a fair tax system would be a difficult task as they would have to cope with strong ideological and political antitax forces.

Accordingly, with the exception of tariff duties, antebellum Southerners only paid state and local taxes. In February 1861 the new treasury secretary, Christopher Gustavus Memminger, published an anonymous draft to explain his view on tax policy, deploring the fact that the bureaucracy needed to collect a large amount of taxes did not exist. His options were then limited. In a speech delivered after the war broke out, the vice president of the Confederacy, Alexander Stephens, promised not to increase internal taxes. As the Union blockade of Confederate ports drastically reduced tariff revenues, bonds and loans were used to avoid direct taxation just as Northerners had done in the first months of the war.[26]

However, optimism of the early days soon gave way to the harsh reality of war and its financial aftermath. Bonds were not enough to pay war expenses, and the Confederacy had to rely on internal taxes. Memminger's main challenge was to convince rich planters to accept a limited system of taxation. Initially, he proposed to rely on a direct tax on real and personal property. To limit tax resistance, he tried to decentralize tax collection, hoping that the citizens of each state would "in all probability" be satisfied with the assessments and modes of collections established by their respective states. As a matter of fact, most states did not even try to implement taxation for fear of planters' anger. Echoing rhetoric honed by Calhoun, one planter in Alabama asserted that "this government belongs to the people, and not to a little self-assuming Congress, who had no more right to levy such a tax than you and I." On October 28, 1861, Alabama governor Andrew Barry Moore articulated the same arguments by explaining to the Confederate congressmen that the state should never "concede" to the government the exercise of powers not delegated in the Constitution, even in wartime. Furthermore, he added, the collection of a direct tax would be an onerous and unpleasant "duty," because it compelled state authorities to enforce the laws of the Confederate government against their own citizens. As a consequence, most Southerners did not pay the new internal taxes. Over the two years of tax collection, only $20 million were collected.[27]

By relying mainly on bonds to pay for war expenditures, the Confederacy had to face growing social tensions. In the few months after the war broke out, Secretary Memminger came to realize that bonds created a strong inflation that fell heavily on the poorest citizens. Economic hardship resulted for most people, and food shortages and subsequent rising prices plagued Southern states. Debates about war exemptions, for some professional occupations and for rich planters who owned at least twenty slaves, reinforced strong concerns among poor whites. Many of them felt that they paid a heavy war tribute, while rich people could escape both the draft and taxation. In

Southern cities such as Atlanta, Macon, and Columbus, food riots occurred in the spring of 1863. Many people feared the Union would collapse from within. In the face of such profound tensions even a states' rights advocate such as Georgia governor Joseph E. Brown urged the government to do something and "for God's sake, please tax us." On April 24, 1863, the Confederate congress decided to levy direct taxes, including a graduated income tax, a corporate tax, and a profits tax.[28]

New internal taxes provoked great dissatisfaction among businessmen and farmers. The *Richmond Enquirer* informed its readers that the tax bill brought "consternation" to the whole mercantile community. Merchants were so afraid, it added, that half of them talked of discontinuing their businesses. In the *Richmond Whig*, one southern businessman posted an advertisement to explain that "in consequence of the very heavy taxes, we have deemed it to close our business." The tithe tax—a 10 percent tax in kind, soon nicknamed TIK—provoked great "murmuring and discontent among the people" as a clerk warned Treasury Secretary Memminger. Many farmers sold their goods before collection time; others attacked the so-called TIK men. Public meetings against the tax and the "licensed thieves" who enforced it were held in the summer of 1863. Memminger received an increasing number of reports of robberies and violence due to the tax. The chief clerk of the Treasury asked him to abandon its collection as it was both too wasteful and expensive to collect. In February 1864 tax authorities decided to enact exemptions for small farmers and for soldiers' families in order to alleviate social tensions.[29]

Military difficulties reinforced the bad reputation of tax collection, and led many Southerners to equate "direct taxation" with corruption. As Jefferson Davis complained about it in his December 1863 letter, "with large portions of some of the States occupied by the enemy, what justice would be there in imposing on the remainder the whole amount of the taxation of the entire State in proportion to its representation?" In occupied territories, the Union collected a federal direct tax through the sales of lands that belonged to delinquent taxpayers. In July 1862 the Confiscation Act made it legal to confiscate the property of anyone who supported the rebellion, even those who paid Confederate taxes. In the sea islands of South Carolina, in the Mississippi Valley, and southern Louisiana, direct tax commissions were created to assess individual parcels of land and to sell them with the owners' consent. Many Southerners considered commissions as part of a Yankee plot to expand the government and to create an oligarchy of party officials paid by taxpayers' money. The corruption was blatant in Florida, where Salmon Chase's friend and political ally Lyman D. Stickney was chosen to become tax commissioner. With his brother, he confiscated the property of anyone who supported the rebellion, and created a newspaper, *The Peninsula*, to announce the sale of lands. Many people criticized the Stickneys for being nothing but adventurers who were trying to make money with the sale of land and create a patronage system in Florida for Chase. Following a series of letters denouncing their actions, a Treasury investigation was launched to figure out what exactly the brothers did. Such corrupt practices reinforced resistance against members of direct tax commissions, and, more generally speaking, against taxation.[30]

In the face of difficulties this profound, Treasury Secretary Memminger decided to resign. He blamed congressmen for adopting a system of taxation so "cumbersome and intricate" that it proved unable to collect enough revenue for war expenditures. In April 1864, of the 471 tax collection districts he helped establish, 133 were still not administered because of military operations or enemy occupation. In other districts, tax collection remained difficult. As a matter of fact, few states collected any tax at all, choosing instead to issue their own treasury notes. Memminger was strongly disillusioned by his four years at the head of revenue collection. First and foremost, he deplored "the frauds and evasions" that could not be uncovered under the present system and were "a perpetual drain upon the tax." Such distrust led to a vicious circle as more and more officers were needed and their presence increased tax resentment.[31]

Over the long four years of the civil war, political and social mobilization altered southern states beyond all expectations, but Southerners remained reluctant to levy internal taxes to pay for war expenditures. Despite Jefferson Davis's hope, the tax system proved inadequate for the South's war effort. The Confederacy borrowed over $2 billion but lost far more in the destruction of properties. To compound the problem, the Confederacy raised less than 5 percent of its wartime revenue from taxes compared to 21 percent in the North. In the Southern states, direct taxation was a hit-or-miss proposition that eventually missed its target because of the strong ideological opposition of rich white planters. In 1865 the idea prevailed both in the North and the South that the new fiscal policy was only a war measure, and peacetime required a shift in fiscal perspective.[32]

A few months after the end of the civil war, commissioner of Internal Revenue Joseph Lewis sent a letter to D. C. Whitman, a revenue agent living in Newark, New Jersey, on the subject of income tax collection: "Sir, it has been represented to this office that the assessment of the income tax in the village of Mahwah [sic], N.J. and vicinity has been a broad farce." To illustrate his case, Lewis referred to a photographer, some wealthy farmers, and other residents who "support family in excellent style" but "paid no income tax." Federal taxes levied during the war were then strongly criticized. Many shared the point of view of New York congressman Henry J. Raymond, who objected in harsh terms against war taxes. "Until a few years ago," he asserted, "we were the most lightly taxed nation on the earth." After four years of bloody warfare, he lamented, the country had become "the most heavily burdened of them all." Tensions brewing during the conflict escalated after it. The business community that largely benefited from government contracts took the lead to assail federal taxes. By going back to the antebellum system, it argued, the country would be able to pay off the war debt without endangering prosperity and freedom. As the soldiers returned home, it was necessary to repeal internal war taxes, especially the income tax and the 3 percent excise tax.[33]

Thus, after General Robert E. Lee surrendered in Appomattox on April 9, 1865, in a modest farmhouse, tax resisters quickly voiced their concerns about the tax burden. Through petitions, letters, and meetings, a coherent antitax ideology emerged, based upon constitutional arguments. Businessmen, many of whom had been pushed by the war to join new professional organizations including the American Bureau of Shipping, the National Association of Wool Manufacturers, and the National Paper Manufacturers Association, capitalized on their new organizational capacities. To broadcast their vision of federal taxation, industrialists sent petitions to the Committee on Ways and Means and the Senate Finance Committee urging congressmen to act as soon as possible. In January 1867, manufacturers from Detroit gathered 1,161 signatures to dismiss the 3 percent excise tax that would jeopardize the economy in peacetime. A committee was created to propagate ideas and to collect as many signatures as possible. One year later, iron and steel businessman and first Detroit's millionaire, Eber Brock Ward, sponsored another petition that did not condemn a specific tax but addressed the tax system as a whole. By enlarging their grievances, businessmen wanted to warn citizens of the serious threats posed by taxation to the future of the republic.[34]

In most petitions, the analysis of governmental tax operations still tended to be negative, deploring both fraud and inefficiency. The antebellum period was depicted as a golden age of politics. During a national convention in December 1867, businessmen highlighted their admiration for "all the ablest and most sagacious statesmen of our country including Jefferson, Calhoun, Clay, Morehead, Benton, Webster, and hosts of others." With the increase of federal power in many fields, opponents of federal taxation deplored, and Radical Republicans challenged, the fiscal consensus that emerged in the early days of the republic. During a meeting in Cleveland, a delegate of the National Convention of Manufacturers provided an apocalyptic description of the dangerous machinery he had observed firsthand in Washington, D.C. Listing growing government expenditures ("$95,000,000 for the War Department, $47,000,000 for the Navy Department and $50,000,000 for the Civil Service"), he took a strong stance against the dangerous autonomy of the federal bureaucracy, "each department vieing with the other to aggrandize itself at the expense of the producing class of the country." Such relentless expansion of federal power had to be interrupted in peacetime, and the income tax specifically came under attack.[35]

In the months following the civil war, businessmen tried to instill in the nation the idea that the income tax was "unnecessary, unfair, and inquisitorial." Petitioners from Delaware insisted that internal taxation had been a child of necessity, a temporary expedient enacted in the face of wartime revenue needs. In New York, the same arguments were used to dismiss the tax. Even though it was paid by the richest citizens, industrialists contended that it was "universally" felt to be "unnecessary and oppressive." Furthermore, the public disclosure provision and the method of collection were accused of creating a "universal public discontent." Tax assessors' corruption was perceived by many taxpayers as another major problem. Citizens of Detroit argued that tax rates were too "onerous" to be borne any longer by the population. In the end, the income tax came to symbolize all the flaws of federal power. Tax repeal, however, posed a serious threat to public finance.[36]

After the war, the national debt was enormous, and amounted to $2,677,929,012 in 1865. In his book, *The Public Debt of the United States* (1867), J. S. Gibbons explained that it was "the subject, above all others, which fills the thought and claims the anxieties of every serious mind in the country." It put strong financial constraints on policymakers and everybody agreed that it should be paid off by the generation that had created it. After the war, Jay Cooke claimed that 90 percent of the 3 million subscribers to wartime loans belonged to the "middling classes" and most of them were wealthy individuals. Thus the wartime debt was inextricably intertwined with the question of taxation. The vicious circle of tax and debt was well described by the new Treasury secretary, Hugh McCulloch, when he challenged the public to scrutinize the "anti-republican" influences of indebtedness. Debts rendered federal taxation necessary and explained why, as McCulloch put it, the country was "filled . . . with informers and tax-gatherers." Appointed chairman of the U.S. Revenue Commission in 1865, economist David A. Wells warned citizens that he had no choice but to pursue internal revenue collection in peacetime until the debt was paid off. Even if he disapproved of internal taxes, he recommended the duration of the war tax system.[37]

For businessmen, however, it was possible to play it both ways: debt payment and tax repeal through a tariff policy as the only source of revenue. Their criticisms were heard by some congressmen; many of them were moderate Republicans who propagated the idea of a blatant discrimination in the tax code. Wisconsin representative Halbert E. Paine focused on tax rates that made a difference between a man earning more than $1,000 and another earning less. Among the Republican Party, however, there was a split between those who wanted to remove the income tax completely and Republicans, elected in rural states, who wanted to keep a limited tax. In April 1866, the chairman of the Committee on Ways and Means, Justin Morrill, sought to find a compromise and urged congressmen to remove the graduated provisions adopted two years earlier. Progressive taxation, he contended, was unfair because it distributed the tax burden unevenly among the population. Instead, he proposed a flat 5 percent tax on all incomes over $1,000. Radical Republicans and Democrats opposed a reduction of the tax burden for the upper

income brackets. The battle for the repeal of war taxes was only beginning and soon took a radical turn in Southern states.[38]

During the civil war, North Carolina was at the forefront of tax resistance. After the first tax reform of 1861, the *Asheville News* editorial was furious at the collection of new taxes. With a clear reference
to the founding fathers, the headline summed up this discontent in
capital letters that expressed indignation: "DIRECT TAXATION IS
TYRANNY." The only consolation, the *News* instructed its readers,
was that Northerners would have to pay a similar tax. After the war,
the newspaper kept on protesting against federal taxation, and the
defeat of the Confederacy only exacerbated calls for repeal of all
internal taxes. Federal taxation provoked more suspicion as Radical
Republicans wanted to use them to promote African Americans'
emancipation. Political and social tensions caused the restoration of
military rule in the South. In 1868 a new headline of the *Asheville
News* deplored the destruction of the old Southern order and the tyrannical action of Unionists and carpetbaggers: "WHITE MEN OF
BUNCOMBE, your political and social rights are invaded." What
resisters feared the most was the transfer of white taxpayers' money
to social services for the disenfranchised black population.[39]

From the start, Reconstruction encountered the resistance of white
southerners, and the issue of taxation was intertwined with the Republicans' plan to transform Southern society. The consequences of
the war only contributed to reinforce their opposition. When General Lee surrendered, the landscape was desolated and many parts of
the South lay in rubble. Southern cities such as Richmond and Atlanta had been totally destroyed. Former vice president of the Confederacy Alexander H. Stephens described the "desolation" of Virginia that was "horrible to behold." The bloody warfare had destroyed
much of the South's tax base, with many citizens living in poor
conditions. The debt held by individual Confederate states was estimated at $66,907,000 in 1865 and the debt of the Confederate States

of America amounted to $1.4 billion. As a consequence, Republican governments decided to increase indirect and direct local taxes (sales, excise, and property) in order to maintain traditional services. In many states, local taxes skyrocketed, and taxpayers' conventions were organized to denounce the Reconstruction government for its extravagance and corruption. Yeomen particularly resented the new Republican tax policy both at the local and federal levels. Carpetbaggers were accused of stealing tax revenue and implementing a wasteful and corrupt policy.[40]

The first federal measures to reconstruct the South drew the fire of Southerners. On March 3, 1865, Congress created the Bureau of Refugees, Freedmen, and Abandoned Lands, known as the Freedmen's Bureau. According to many whites, the stated purpose of the Bureau was to redistribute lands to former slaves. The Bureau controlled over 850,000 acres of abandoned land, and hoped to provide freedmen with forty-acre homesteads. The redistribution process interfered with the issue of confiscated lands to pay for the direct tax. *New York Times*' correspondent Benjamin C. Truman noted in July 1866 that Southerners hated the Direct Tax Commissions as much as the Bureau itself. As a poster of 1866 bluntly put it, the same wasteful and corrupt system was transforming society using white taxpayers' money to provide help to the "idle Negro, and the Bureau for many inhabitants added insult to injury."[41]

During the postwar years, the debate on the issue of confiscated lands continued, and accusations of fraud and misdemeanor went along with it. In South Carolina, complaints were made about the manner in which local commissioners acquitted themselves during the war. In a letter sent to the Florida Direct Tax Commission's office, accusations targeted the clerk of the commission, Adolphe Mot, who sold lands in Fernandina. In order to put an end to these accusations, the treasury secretary issued on August 3, 1866, an order to suspend collection of the tax in the states that had seceded. The federal government eagerly sought a compromise with those whose

Figure 1.2. The Bureau of Refugees, Freedmen and Abandoned was created in March 1865. The poster epitomized the process of tax transfer from hard-working white Southerners to "idle Negro." The message was simple: "Support Congress & you support the Negro." "The Freedman's Bureau and white taxpayers' money," 1866. Courtesy of the Library of Congress.

lands had been sold. However, fears of a Northerner plot to redistribute lands remained strong in the Reconstruction South.[42]

As a consequence, adamant resistance by Southerners gained political clout, and the whisky tax came to embody all the evils of the Radical Reconstruction and the intrusion of Yankees into local matters. As soon as the war ended, Congress divided each former Confederate state into collection districts. Under the supervision of the commissioner of internal revenue, who was a political appointee, collectors headed each district and were helped by assessors. Many

Southerners equated the tax on alcohol with the resented tax-in-kind levied during the civil war. As the correspondent of the *New York Times* in South Carolina put it, taxes on whisky and tobacco were "unknown before the war." A revenue agent from Burke County in North Carolina perfectly captured the novelty of federal taxes when he wrote that "those people had been in the habit of making whisky all of their lives," and believed that "they could do heretofore." In many states, producers of home-made whisky were nicknamed moonshiners, and were supported by local elites. In the Southern highlands, politicians always referred to the revenue laws as "oppressive" and "to the officers enforcing [*sic*] them as oppressors." Moonshiners gained much sympathy among other residents by claiming that liquor manufacturing was an inalienable right and by refusing to pay the federal tax.[43]

Moonshiners were mainly located in Georgia and Tennessee. In the Cumberland Mountains of eastern Kentucky, West Virginia, and western Virginia, they also fiercely campaigned against tax collection. Their activism thrived in tandem with opposition to the alleged radicalism of Reconstruction. Actually, most tax collectors were responsible for enforcing civil rights law and were associated with former Unionists. Lewis Cass Carpenter, a South Carolina collector, was a carpetbagger who arrived in the state in 1867. Another revenue agent, Charles O'Keefe, was a member of the local Union League Club, which was seen as part of the Radical Republicans' plan to transform the South. President Ulysses S. Grant responded to the threats and attacks by sending more federal soldiers, an act that Southerners immediately called "bayonet rule." In 1869 the North Carolina *Asheville News* put it bluntly when it explained that federal taxes were actually collected "at the point of the bayonet." It even equated what it considered to be the tyranny of the federal government with the tyrannical days of King George.[44]

In many counties the Ku Klux Klan, created in Tennessee in 1866, supported moonshiners and helped them attack revenue officers.

Members of the Klan were locally very powerful, and after the election of 1868, Klan dens had spread to all Southern states. Through intimidation and violence, they tried to limit the rules of Reconstruction and to prevent revenue agents from collecting the federal tax. In 1871 collector Pinkney Rollins had no choice but to admit that illicit distillers in Polk, Burke, and other mountain counties were protected by "a kind of protectorship of a secret organization called the Ku Klux Klan." The passage of the Force Act of 1871 gave revenue agents more power to use troops for protection against moonshiners and members of the Klan. The policy, however, only increased the will of moonshines not to pay the tax.[45]

By assuming the same mantle of principles as their fathers, moonshiners staunchly supported the ideal of republican virtue to convince local citizens of the threat posed by federal officers to the daily lives of citizens. The Republican *Raleigh Standard* in North Carolina recalled the glorious fights of the colonists and strongly endorsed the idea of low and local taxes as the only source of revenue. It deplored the disappearance of the Jeffersonian promise and the fact that "taxation without representation" was no longer carried out in good faith.[46]

For many citizens in Southern states, not only for moonshiners, the government's growth during wartime and its expanded tax policy afterward were a natural threat to republicanism and free institutions. Federal taxes came to symbolize the oppressive rules imposed by Northerners, and encouraged moonshiners to hide or escape in the mountainous parts of the region with the help of local communities. Such a radical criticism of the tax helped to delegitimize the internal revenue system shaped during the war years. As more and more Northeastern businessmen disagreed with the bayonet rule imposed in the South, it came as no surprise that they also fiercely questioned postwar taxes, especially the income tax.[47]

With a roster of New York's most influential people on its letterhead, an Anti-Income Tax Association was created in 1871. Henry E. Davies, president of the association, was able to garner the more prominent New Yorkers including Horace Greeley, William Backhouse Astor, Auguste Belmont, Samuel Sloan, and John Pierpont Morgan Sr. Miron Winslow, secretary of the association, stated that their main goal was to put an end to the unfair discrimination of rich people in the nation. During the American Revolution, he asserted, the founders never intended to put the burden of taxation on a minority of citizens. By December 1871, wealthy New Yorkers challenged the constitutionality of the income tax, drawing on long-standing conceptions of uniformity and apportionment. Tensions brewing since the end of the war escalated in 1870 because of the need to reduce the national debt. Under such circumstances, inequalities in tax collection became a matter of contention. The Northeast contributed nearly 75 percent of income tax revenue, and New York, Pennsylvania, and Massachusetts contributed more than 61 percent. The city of New York alone accounted for one-third of total receipts in 1870 but had only one-eleventh of the population. As members of the New York Anti-Income Tax Association asserted during their meetings, the tax was not only "unconstitutional" but also posed a threat to the most industrious citizens.[48]

From January to March 1870 many petitions, signed by members of businessmen's associations, arrived in Congress. Most petitions were channeled through professional organizations. The boards of trade of Buffalo and Cleveland, the California legislature, and the Union League Club of New York City sent petitions to Congress, along with self-described "citizens" from Albany, Syracuse, New York, Pennsylvania, and Connecticut. Most petitions were preprinted and used the same words equating taxation with "inquisition" and "obnoxiousness." Petitions transformed the narrow-base income tax into a universal concern shared by millions of Americans. When congressmen railed against the tax during debates, they drew on the same arguments. New York Republican representative Dennis McCarthy did not mince his words when he defined the tax as "unequal, perjury-provoking, and crime encouraging, because it is at war with the right of a person to keep private and regulate his business affairs and financial matters." The California representative, Aaron Sergent, urged the repeal of the tax, contending that its unpopularity "universally" amounted to "loathing and hate." On July 14, 1870, Congress passed a revenue act that preserved the income tax but lowered the rates on incomes over $2,000. The tax was limited to the years 1870 and 1871, "and no longer."[49]

Appointed commissioner of the revenue on January 3, 1871, Alfred Pleasonton soon appeared as the inside man of rich and powerful businessmen in the federal government. A few days after his appointment, western and Southern congressmen accused him of running a policy for "a class," and not for the country. Otherwise, how could one explain his efforts to abolish the income tax? The son of a hero of the War of 1812, who had saved precious documents including the Constitution and the Declaration of Independence, Pleasonton was a civil war general and a former Internal Revenue collector in New York. He was appointed against the will of Treasury Secretary George Boutwell, who refused to repeal all war taxes. Very soon Pleasanton was seen as overly compliant to the wishes of various big business groups and making no effort to hide it. On January 20, 1871, he sent a communication to the Committee on Ways and Means in which he used traditional antitax rhetoric. He contended that the income tax was "most obnoxious to the genius of our people," "inquisitorial," and exposed "the most private pecuniary affairs of our citizens." Referring to an oft-heard argument in the petitions, he added that it "did not produce great revenue, and should be unconditionally repealed." Pleasanton was contradicted by Treasury Secretary Boutwell, who urged him to be more cautious as it was still necessary to collect revenue to pay the debt.[50]

The following year, the business community reinforced its attacks against the constitutionality of the tax. The continuity of the system, industrialists argued, opened the doors to a policy of discrimination against the wealthiest citizens. In the *New York Times*, an anonymous citizen, who signed himself as "BELLIGERENT," deplored the class tensions and the will to target "the bloated capitalists." On June 19, 1871, prestigious lawyer William M. Evarts took the lead in legal efforts to repeal the tax. In a session of the U.S. Circuit Court of Philadelphia, he defended once again the necessity "to tax wealth" by following the rule of apportionment. Ultimately, these criticisms of federal income taxation eliminated the tax with little difficulty. Republican political leaders acceded to the demands of affected tax-payers, reducing the rate again. Even more significant, legislators agreed that the income tax was near the end of its useful life, and they voted to let it lapse after 1871. Meanwhile, they introduced a variety of refinements to the excise taxes on alcohol and tobacco, and these levies assumed the role—along with customs duties—as the principal sources of federal revenue. On May 20, 1873, in a symbolic action, the records relating to the civil war taxes were shipped to the commissioner of internal revenue in Washington, D.C. The antebellum system of taxation based upon tariff and luxury taxes was restored as Reconstruction drew to an end.[51]

In May 1870 Ohio congressman Robert C. Schenck solemnly asked to put an end to the war experiment in the field of taxation by reducing all internal taxes. Proud of the behavior of the American people, he recalled that the people had done "what was demanded of them in order to keep up the public credit and meet our Government liabilities." Nicknamed "Poker Bob" for his expertise at cards, Schenck contended that federal taxes were a reciprocal and fair deal during the conflict to pay for soldiers and war expenses. As the war came to an end, however, it was time to stop the incremental expansion of federal taxes, especially the inclusion of the progressive provision. Schenck's calls were part of a national desire to close the fiscal experimentation of the civil war, during which Americans encountered for the first time a visible network of tax collectors and revenue agents operating in tax districts throughout the nation. Criticisms grew after the war, increasingly demanding that Congress scale back the federal system, as well as its associated bureaucracy. Resurrecting a military metaphor, one critic even warned in 1865 that Congress must reform the tax structure or "an army of tax-gatherers will swarm through the country, like Lee's disbanded veterans, plundering friend and foe alike." Tapping into constitutional arguments, tax resisters had an easy task criticizing taxes as "un-American, inquisitorial and unconstitutional." Few people shared Ohio representative John Sherman's view when, in 1872, he denounced the injustice in the "fundamental basis of our system" as "wealth accumulates." Sherman was one of the few to understand the impact of industrialization that the war itself propelled forward. In the postbellum years, internal taxes were to remain limited and the tariff became the main source of federal revenue to pay both for the debt and the spending of the federal government. The end of Reconstruction and social tensions in the Gilded Age, however, were soon to revive debates on tax fairness and constitutional rights of taxpayers.[52]

2

Down with Internal Taxes

Under such circumstances, it is a misnomer to
call such an exaction taxation. It is unmasked
confiscation, and a burlesque on taxation.

—*David A. Wells* (1881)

I~N~ 1876 New York governor Samuel J. Tilden was chosen by Democrats to run for president. The well-known millionaire corporate lawyer made political reform and assaults against corruption his two main priorities. In his annual message, echoing arguments against the Radical Reconstruction, he pleaded for the return of the old "foundations of American self-government," that he characterized as "simple, frugal, meddling little with the private concerns of individuals—aiming at fraternity among ourselves and peace abroad— and trusting to the people to work out their own prosperity and happiness." The *New York Times* revealed, however, that Tilden had cheated on the federal government during the civil war. Although he had earned a lot of money from the defense of railroad companies, he forgot to mention it to the Treasury. Actually, he made false returns in 1862 and 1863, and he did not even send in his tax return until 1872 when the wartime income tax expired. According to the estimates, and in spite of his claim that it was pure and simple political persecution, Tilden owed the federal government more than \$131,000. For many years, Tilden's trial ignited passionate arguments about the legitimacy of income tax and its collection method, all the more so as the economic crisis worsened and new proposals in favor of the tax were debated in Congress.[1]

As Reconstruction drew to an end, and the nation moved into the Gilded Age, as Mark Twain wittily described it, the legacy of war taxes was still questioned. The Jeffersonian vision of a nation of small landowners had become a vanished dream. Everywhere in the nation, factories emerged with the help of business leaders and inventors in countless small industries. This stunning industrial growth reinvigorated debates about wealth. Stunned by the rise of economic inequality, reformers and intellectuals promoted a tax reform to shift the burden of taxation onto the shoulders of wealthy businessmen. From the end of Reconstruction to the early 1890s, however, tax resisters refused any form of "class legislation" and hoped to restore the antebellum tax system that had served the early republic.[2]

When the repeal of the income tax in 1872 eliminated hope of a progressive tax system, remnants of the other war taxes became the new target. Not only bankers, who still paid a tax on bank notes, but also small tobacco and alcohol producers agreed that these taxes were "unfair" and should be abolished. In a typical antitax statement, Georgia representative and former vice president of the Confederacy Alexander H. Stephens contended in 1882 that internal taxes were "anti-Republican and anti-Democratic." Evoking the memory of the American Revolution, he added that "they were of British origin, and had always been viewed with British odium." Their abolition was proposed to put an end to the extravagance of federal expenditures by Republicans in power, especially the system of pensions for veterans. The same proposals were heard in the North. The chairman of the Democratic National Committee, Abram Hewitt, added that "there was only one security for the tax-payers [sic] and that was to keep the Treasury poor." Prosperous economic conditions after 1878 made internal taxes an important source of federal revenue and contributed to the budgetary surplus. In his second Annual Address in 1882, President Chester A. Arthur reminded Americans that they brought to the revenue more than $155 million, while customs duties accounted for $220 million. Although Americans disagreed on the tariff issue, many of them agreed that internal taxes should be abolished as they were the Trojan horse of an expansion of federal power and extraction of wealth. The idea of repealing them gained traction, and President Arthur himself called for their abolition.[3]

In 1876, during the gubernatorial campaign in North Carolina, Zebulon Baird Vance did not mince words when he talked about the federal revenue system. He called tax agents "red-legged grasshoppers" and proclaimed that "the time has come when an honest man can't take an honest drink without having a gang of revenue officers after him." Born on May 13, 1830, at the family homestead along Reems Creek in Buncombe County, Vance became famous during the civil war when he was nicknamed the "War Governor of the South" and strongly opposed Jefferson Davies's policy in the name of states' rights. After the four bloody war years, he criticized the new Yankee political regime, and articulated his opposition to the radical rule of Reconstruction with a strong criticism of the federal tax system used by Republicans to finance their policy. If his criticisms focused on the "corrupt centralism which had honeycombed the offices of Federal Government itself with incapacity, waste and fraud," Vance shared the Southerners' views that internal taxes particularly affected the rural Southern economy and wondered why the federal government maintained a tax on alcohol and tobacco that strongly burdened small Southern producers. In the postslavery South, as the Radical Reconstruction faded away, abolition of all internal taxes became an often-heard outcry against the perceived enslavement of citizens by a tyrannical regime.[4]

After the election of 1876, Northern commitment to change Southern society had strongly eroded, and taxation was often at the heart of sectional animosities. White citizens hoped that federal taxes would disappear together with the emancipation of African Americans. "They taxed us," the *Asheville Citizen* in North Carolina still complained in February 1876, "and gave Negro civil rights." The newspaper charged that "corrupt" revenue agents in Buncombe County were "determined to rule the party, and keep all the big offices and all funds in the family." Most Southerners equated taxation with slavery, and still used the same abolitionist rhetoric. For many of them, the end of Reconstruction meant the end of the war tax system.[5]

The will to abolish all internal taxes was increasingly reinforced by the economic depression that started in 1873. The crisis triggered a five-year depression, and unemployment spiked in the South. The lack of cash in circulation increased social difficulties, notably the Southern public debt problem. Many people still pinned the blame on greedy carpetbaggers and accused them of engaging in fraudulent actions. As a consequence, Republican tax policies aroused strong opposition, even more so as after the war, local taxes had been greatly increased in order to maintain traditional services. Many state legislatures increased poll taxes and enacted numerous luxury, sales and occupation taxes that only exacerbated attacks against taxation as a whole. Redeemers took the lead and made tax reduction one of their main priorities both at the local and federal levels.[6]

As Reconstruction drew to an end, scandals revolving around tax collection fueled grievances and matched accusations of the corruption of the federal government. By then, most tax collectors had private contracts and received a percentage of the taxes they collected. In 1873 the procedure came under close scrutiny as the contract signed between federal officials and a tax collector named John D. Sanborn was believed to be illegal. Sanborn was one of the tax agents appointed by Treasury Secretary William A. Richardson to collect internal taxes. Sanborn collected over $400,000 and pocketed a substantive commission of approximately $200,000. The treasury secretary disclaimed responsibility. After investigation, the Committee on Ways and Means condemned the contract procedure, but it did not discover any evidence of criminal intent. One year later, the Whiskey Ring scandal further undermined the credibility of tax collection. It was revealed that revenue officials in patronage positions joined with distillers in major cities across the country to defraud the government of taxes. In 1875 Treasury Secretary Benjamin Bristow investigated and broke up this conspiracy of distillers and internal revenue officials. Orville Babcock, President Ulysses Grant's private secretary, was indicted and the president himself was implicated in the scandal in which more than $3 million in taxes were recovered. Ultimately, 238 people were indicted and 110 convicted. For many Americans, there was no doubt that the purpose of the ring was to funnel money to the Republican Party to enable it to stay in power. Thus, it was seen as another step in the corruption of the government and reinforced the bad reputation that the collection of taxes had given to the central government, especially in Southern states.[7]

Most Southerners still put the blame on the tax on whisky. In his speeches, Zebulon Vance always championed moonshiners as heroes and blamed government officials for the enforcement of such an "odious" internal revenue system. In small communities, tax resistance became increasingly visible, and moonshiners were still strongly defended by local residents. They even posted pickets to give warning of tax collectors' approach. "So complete is the system of signals," complained a revenue officer in 1878, "that no stranger can be seen without instantaneous alarm being given all through the neighborhood." Most of the time, moonshiners were helped by their local neighbors and were seen as heroic soldiers fighting against the tyranny of the federal government. Lewis R. Redmond was probably the most famous resister, and his actions were well known in the small communities. Born in Georgia on April 15, 1854, he moved to North Carolina and carried on illicit distilling. He achieved a reputation by shooting the U.S. deputy marshal, Alfred Duck-worth, in the throat on March 1, 1876, and by escaping to the mountainous areas. Within three years, he earned the nickname "King of the Moonshiners." Books and interviews made Redmond a household name. In July 1878, an interview conducted by C. McKin-ley, a reporter for the *Charleston News and Courier*, was published, in which the moonshiner described himself, with a flamboyance that lived up to his name, as a modern Robin Hood who valiantly fought against the agents of the Bureau of Internal Revenue (BIR). As he resisted the collection of the whisky tax, Redmond appeared as nothing but a Confederate soldier who refused to surrender, and warned his fellow Southerners of the danger caused by federal taxation and Yankee power.[8]

The postwar context made resistance particularly violent, especially as the federal government reinforced the process of tax collection. As Reconstruction rendered federal policy increasingly unpopular, moonshiners flexed their muscles with antistatist fervor. To enforce federal laws, the district tax collector appointed a posse, composed of twelve to twenty volunteers led by a paid deputy tax collector. A deputy marshal, who was the only one with the authority to arrest distillers and to issue warrants, took part in the posse. In a manual for revenue agents published in 1878, the BIR detailed their mission. In Southern states "infested with illicit distilleries" as officials put it, they had to collect information and to help arrest offenders. Only collectors and their deputies could make seizures and only U.S. marshals could arrest tax delinquents. To gather information, tax collectors relied on informers from local communities.[9]

As a consequence, in the mountainous South, the number of resisters grew, and they operated on the assumption that corrupt tax collectors threatened their communities. Attacks of tax collectors became commonplace. As Reconstruction drew to an end, the violence reached its climax. According to estimates by the Bureau of Internal Revenue, more than twenty-five agents were killed by tax resisters between 1876 and 1878. In August 1877 a U.S. marshal named Webster reported having been attacked by an escaped moonshiner, who, with friends and his own posse, bombarded his house one entire night. Two deputies were threatened by "a mob of 100 or more" in Adair County, Kentucky. In Wayne County, Kentucky, a fierce face-to-face conflict occurred between "an armed force of thirty officers" and moonshiners. Distillers had even fortified the distillery and threatened death to all assailants. Tax collectors and their "assistants" were forced to "flee."[10]

Other strategies were sometimes less violent and aimed at frightening revenue agents and their local allies. For instance, collectors were conspicuously followed and their families were threatened. The moonshiners' goal was not to kill revenue agents but rather, to make them leave the region. Although moonshiners were very good hunters, they often aimed too high when they shot at revenue officers. Their goal was only to intimidate and to chase them. Informers became a regular target of moonshiners. These local people, who had revealed the names of illicit distillers to authorities, served as guides during raids, testified against moonshiners, gave directions to stills, and were considered "Judases" by mountain people. In Burke County, North Carolina, an angry distiller knocked down a suspected informer named Ramsey, with a rock, "and then stamped him in the face." Very often, guides and informers were whipped for the help they provided to tax officers.[11]

When the federal government decided to seriously tackle the problem of tax collection, it only reinforced moonshiners' resistance. In 1876 President Ulysses S. Grant appointed a new revenue commissioner, Green B. Raum. A "War Democrat," Raum became a dedicated Republican after the war and promised to enforce federal laws everywhere in the country. In the mountainous South, he estimated in his first report to Congress that moonshiners were operating over 2,000 stills, costing $2,500,000 annually to the federal budget. Lawmakers had no reason to backtrack in face of such violence. Symbolically, Raum made the capture of Redmond the number-one priority of the Bureau. In order to alleviate tensions, however, he proposed amnesty to moonshiners who would pay the tax and stop distilling alcohol on the sly.[12]

From his headquarters in Washington, D.C., and as the debate about civil reform gained political clout in the nation, Raum sought to improve the honesty of tax officials. Eager to improve the process of tax collection, Raum pushed for bureaucratic reforms limiting the arbitrary powers of collectors. In March 1877 he established a system for the inspection of collectors' offices. In August the number of relatives who could be employed in each Internal Revenue district was limited for the first time in order to put an end to accusations of nepotism. The cost of such an enforcement policy raised legitimate concerns. In July 1878 the *New York Times* noted that the amounts of spirits distilled was not large and wondered whether it was necessary to employ so many people to enforce the laws. Raum's strategy helped to ease tensions in small counties, and both the amnesty and the new collection method enabled moonshiners and tax officers to find a common ground.[13]

If many Northern newspapers portrayed moonshiners as backward and violent tax resisters, such dominant stereotypes in the Victorian age failed to mention the rationale behind the defense of their homemade whisky. First and foremost, moonshiners and their numerous allies defended their own of view of republican virtue based on states' rights and local government. As militants intensified their local guerilla warfare against tax officers, Southern politicians criticized the whole internal tax system. Congressman William M. Robbins of North Carolina asked the population to scrutinize the aftermath of such a tax policy. The only remedy, he explained to

Figure 2.1. Thomas Nast, "The Slave of Liberty," *Harper's Weekly*, February 6, 1878.

readers of the *Raleigh News* in July 1877, was to "abolish it." For him, "Down with the internal revenue system" had to become the creed of the New South emerging from the throes of war and the end of slavery. If the ghost of war taxes took the appearance of a tax on whisky in the South, it reappeared in the North in the guise of an income tax.[14]

In 1878 *Harpers Weekly*'s famous cartoonist Thomas Nast captured the centrality of the debate revolving around federal taxation. In a striking image, income tax became a heavy weight around the neck of the female symbol of peace, who was labeled a "slave." The chained woman was surrounded by other symbols of corruption and disasters that plagued the republic only one hundred years after the American Revolution.

Using the same arguments as tax resisters, Nast believed that the income tax was only a temporary wartime measure. Further, he feared that proposals made by southern and western congressmen in December 1877 would cause economic disaster. In the background of the cartoon, the ramshackle American ship appears in disarray; in the sky, vultures symbolize impending death and refer to the economic depression that had started five years earlier. Income tax, Nast insisted, would reinforce the corruption and patronage that already undermined the nation. Behind the enslaved woman is a long list of excessive legislation that favors corruption and nepotism. *Harper's Weekly*'s editor George William Curtis shared Nast's equation of income taxation with slavery and tyranny. Referring to the tradition of "the English-speaking people," he feared the "necessarily inquisitorial" consequence of the bill. He answered those who promoted "class legislation" by underscoring republican virtue and expressing his fear that only the honest would pay, while unscrupulous businessmen would find many ways to circumvent the law.[15]

As the reference to the English-speaking nations made clear, the income tax was then assailed for being a foreign and dangerous ideology. In February 1878 the *New York Times* considered the income tax to be a "communistic tax" and added that "cumulative taxation" was defended by both French and German socialists. Fierce debates in England and France about the income tax had been widely commented on, and revived questions about the fairness of the tax system. By then, many businessmen were seeing strong connections between the growth of social policies in Europe and the labor unrest at home. Laissez-faire intellectuals such as James Laurence Laughlin equated socialism with foreigners such as "Carl [*sic*] Marx."[16]

In the United States the popularity of tax reform resulted from the severe economic crisis and social consequences of the market revolution. In the wake of the panic of 1873, attacks against corporations resurfaced as a result of bitter antagonism between workers and corporations. In the economic slump that followed, managers decided to cut wages and lay off workers. The number of bankruptcies doubled from 5,183 in 1873 to 10,478 in 1878. By 1877, 10 percent wage cuts, distrust of capitalists, and poor working conditions led to a number of railroad strikes that prevented the trains from moving. In many places factory workers went on strike, while corporate leaders enlisted strikebreakers to replace union men. The growth of poverty and pauperism raised strong concerns. In many cities, middle-class associations proposed major tax reforms to equalize the tax burden and to alleviate poverty. The New York Society for the Improvement of the Condition of the Poor even suggested that "salaries be limited to $5,000 a year," and that a tax be imposed on "surplus wealth."[17]

In March 1878, during congressional debates to identify the cause of the nation's troubles, income taxation was proposed by many reformers, even though they had different views of it. The secretary of the National Reform Association, Horatio D. Sheppard, adopted the British model to make the case for the transfer of wealth through taxes. It was necessary in a time of crisis, he added, to impose additional "obligations" on the wealthy. Even the social Darwinist champion and free-trader William Graham Sumner advocated the substitution of an income tax for the tariff as a relief for "non-capitalists," provided that the exemptions were as low as $1,000 and that no graduated tax be adopted. Sumner still considered taxes as a tool of public revenue, not as a tool of solidarity between the rich and the poor. As the federal government needed money to pay the war debt, it seemed to be a better policy to tax income than to regulate the market with customs duties. Such a reciprocal view was defended by Michigan jurist Thomas M. Cooley in a speech entitled "Principles that Should Govern the Framing of Tax Laws," delivered in Cincinnati on April 22, 1878, to the members of the American Social Science Association. The Michigan jurist explained that persons "should be taxed for the support of government in proportion to the revenue they enjoy under its protection." As businessmen benefited from government protection in the event of strikes, it made sense that they were asked to pay their share. Yet, Cooley feared that in practice the income tax would create economic disincentives and social tensions.[18]

The economic crisis that plagued the nation made taxation a contentious political issue. On March 12, 1878, citizens from Humphrey, North Carolina, asked their representatives to share the burden of taxation equally and to vote for a new income tax. Many western and Southern congressmen supported the idea. Ohio representative John A. McMahon alleged that under such circumstances of public distress it was important that "the wealthy of the country" should bear a fair proportion of the tax burdens. The ongoing trial against former presidential candidate Samuel J. Tilden for cheating on his income tax during the civil war invigorated the tax reformers' campaign. However, most representatives cleared a path for the reduction of tariff rates, notably on tobacco, rather than endorse a new sense of social solidarity in the federal tax system by means of a progressive income tax.[19]

The proposed reform revived the mobilization of tax resisters in 1871. Northeastern businessmen bristled at the news of tax reform, and alarm over the bill peaked in the spring of 1878. Industrialists hammered on the income tax by exposing the serious threats it posed to the economy. A petition that circulated among them was published in the New York Times. Although petitioners still used traditional language and constitutional arguments, they added more businesslike statements on economic matters. As the concept of the Lost Cause was being formed in the South, businessmen took a strong and apocalyptic stance against tax collection during the civil war. Most Americans, they argued, had to endure "its odious and inquisitorial character." Contrary to the republican ideal of equality, the income tax caused a double discrimination. First, it created an "unjust" discrimination among citizens as it was not apportioned equally. "Under the old Income Tax," businessmen warned, "the number who paid was not 275,000 and when the exemption was raised to $2000 the taxable [*sic*] were reduced to 116,000 out of a population of forty millions." Second, among taxpayers themselves, it pitched the "unscrupulous" fellow who did not pay his tax against "the honest citizens" who "bear not only their own burdens but those of their neighbors." For all these reasons, industrialists argued, the income tax was unconstitutional, and should be rejected by Congress.[20]

Businessmen staunchly supported the defeat of the bill and campaigned fiercely to preserve a fiscal status quo. The gravity and the danger they perceived in the proposal resembled the crusade they led against local progressive forces. The main threat, the wealthiest argued, would come from the tyranny of a majority that would impose a redistribution of income. There was no need "to be afraid of capital," millionaire Jason "Jay" Gould declared to senators investigating the new aristocracy of wealth. "But what you had to fear," he added, "was large masses of uneducated, ignorant people." In New York, the same businessmen who had petitioned against the income tax sought to limit the right to vote. Putting sectional animosities aside, many Northeastern businessmen articulated their thinking by tapping into the same ideological arguments as Southerners. Ideas such as the "tyranny of a majority," "taxation without representation," and "extravagant spending" propagated themselves in pamphlets, petitions, and newspapers. The Chamber of Commerce of Pittsburgh and the Board of Trade of Burlington, Iowa, endorsed such principles in the petitions they sent to Congress, hoping for a speedy defeat of the bill.[21]

In fact, many congressmen cast doubts about the feasibility of income tax collection and the graduation of tax rates. In April some representatives wondered whether it was possible to have an income tax provision that was not graduated to avoid discrimination among citizens. The tax was fixed at the uniform rate of 2 percent on all sums in excess of $2,000. Eventually, the proposal was rejected due to the coalition of Southern and Northern representatives who opposed the "Western demagogue," as the *New York Times* informed its readers. In the end, Southern elites sided with their Northern counterparts in the hope of a reduction of the tobacco excise tax. The coalition proved central to the defeat of the income tax and the idea of solidarity that it conveyed.[22]

For Thomas Nast, it was a wise decision. In a cartoon published on March 2, 1878, in *Harper's Weekly*, he had already referred to the choice that congressmen had to make by contrasting the internal tax on whisky to the income tax. Was it better to promote idleness for drunken men or the thrift of hard-working citizens? It made no sense that a tax on alcohol was a better choice for the prosperity and the morality of the nation. For tax resisters, there was no choice to be made; most of them contended that it was possible to repeal all remaining internal taxes and to declare the income tax unconstitutional forever.

In 1880 economist and free-trader advocate David Ames Wells deployed the rhetoric of catastrophe to describe the impact of income tax in the republic. Far from taking the moderate stance he had taken when he headed the commission in charge of reviewing the collection of revenue in 1865, Wells assumed the same mantle of principles as tax resisters. His critique stemmed from ideological arguments concerning the origins of the tax, as the title of his article put it bluntly: "The communism of a discriminating income tax." Fearing that a revolution was underfoot, he equated a federal tax on income with pure and simple "class legislation." To bring light into political

Figure 2.2. Thomas Nast, "Will He Dare Do It?" *Harper's Weekly*, March 2, 1878.

darkness, Wells referred to the debates about such a tax in Great Britain, Austria, Germany, and Italy, where it was supported by dangerous idealists and misguided politicians. A tax on income would not only be unconstitutional, but it would also weaken the very foundation of American society. Workers, socialists and feminists had already started to protest against unfair taxation in the name of "un-American" ideals, and an income tax, he claimed, would increase nascent class and ethnic conflicts and the breed of self-promoting women who had plunged into a world of public display and consumption. In a striking conclusion, Wells warned his fellow Americans that "equality and manhood, therefore, demand and require uniformity of burden in whatever is the subject of taxation." Otherwise, it had to be seen for what it was, plain "spoliation and an invasion of the rights of property." Wells's bleak argument was part of the

debate about the constitutionality of the income tax that William
M. Springer had brought to the Supreme Court. Both for Wells
and Springer, the income tax was intrinsically "un-American" and
unconstitutional.[23]

During the civil war, Springer, described by his biographer as
"commanding and dignified," made a name for himself when he refused to pay the income tax. Born in the county of Sullivan, Indiana,
on May 30, 1836, he began his career in 1858 with the publication of
a Democratic newspaper in Lincoln, Illinois, during the famous
Lincoln-Douglass campaign. At the same time, he studied law and
was admitted to the bar in 1861. During the war, when congressmen
accepted the idea of taxing incomes to raise more revenue, the young
attorney decried such a tax as unconstitutional. Upon his failure to
pay his due amount of tax, part of his property in Springfield, Illinois,
was put on sale and purchased by the government in 1867. In 1868,
on account of Mrs. Springer's ill health, he visited Europe with his
family, and had the opportunity to observe the European system of
taxation closely. Foreign systems of taxation convinced him that the
United States was exceptional, and should remain so. Upon his return, he grew increasingly frustrated with the postwar federal system
that maintained a sweeping array of internal taxes. After he was elected
a representative on the Democratic ticket in the County of San-
gamon, Illinois, he defended his view of taxation and contended that
the best system of protection to industry was that which "imposed
the lightest burdens and the fewest restrictions" on the property and
business of the people, and promoted the prosperity of all. A vora-
cious consumer of tax literature, Springer equated the income tax
with "class legislation" and likened government bureaucracy with
corruption.[24]

By refusing to pay his tax on his professional income as an attorney, Springer hoped to demonstrate its unconstitutionality. Contrary
to what Congress during the civil war contended, it was a direct tax,
not apportioned among the states according to the population of each

state. The main problem was that the Constitution did not define clearly what a "direct tax" was. The question was still open in 1881. The only time the Supreme Court had addressed the issue was in 1796 with the *Hylton v. U.S.* decision by holding that a federal carriage tax enacted by the Federalists was not a "direct" tax. As a consequence, it could not be apportioned. The justices added that only capitation and land taxes were examples of direct taxes. The Springer case forced the Supreme Court to clarify the original blurred definition contained in the Constitution.[25]

After examining the contemporaneous writings of James Madison and Alexander Hamilton, the court quoted Hamilton as asserting that direct taxes should be held to be only "capitation or poll taxes, and taxes on lands and buildings, and general assessments, whether on the whole property of individuals or on their whole real or personal estate." The justices concluded that everything else must be considered "of necessity" as indirect taxes. Justice Noah Haynes Swayne, for the unanimous court, concluded that "that direct taxes, within the meaning of the Constitution, are only capitation taxes," and the income tax was within "the category of an excise or duty." Referring to the *Hylton* decision, the court affirmed that Springer had made a false interpretation of the Constitution and should have paid the tax during the civil war. Furthermore, because discussions surfaced in European countries during passionate tax debates, Justice Swayne made it clear that the decision "was one exclusively of American jurisprudence." The underlying assumption beneath the decision was the idea of the legitimate right of the federal government to levy taxes, either direct or indirect, for public purposes.[26]

Even though few citizens paid attention to the technical constitutional debates, the *Springer* decision interfered with Tilden's prosecution, raising the same issues of tax compliance. The two men challenged the assumption that in the case of war it was a civic duty to levy taxes for war expenditures. New circumstances—prosperity and

budget surplus—offered the opportunity for taxpayers to again consider the legitimacy of other internal taxes.[27]

With the end of the severe economic crisis, the federal surplus
became a contentious issue for millions of Americans. By 1885
it amounted to $63 million. Even though the war debt was still
important—$1,593,102,150 in December 1881—tax resisters wondered
whether it was necessary to maintain internal revenue taxes in the
nation. Commenting upon the platforms of both Democrats and
Republicans, David E. Wells was amused by their similar positions
on tax reforms to please voters. On October 5, 1881, the Republican
State Convention contended that the surplus revenue justified the
reduction of taxes "at an early day." At the same time, the Democratic
State Convention of Massachusetts protested that "too much revenue" was raised by the federal government. A former internal revenue
collector during the civil war, Sheridan Shook of the firm Shook &
Everard, replied that it was not a sound policy to pay off our war debt
"too fast" and proposed instead to keep levying "war taxes." Beyond
the issue of debt, tax resisters were confronted and divided around the
tariff issue. Although some, especially Southerners and free traders,
wanted to reduce both internal and external taxes, others still asserted
that tariff revenues were necessary to protect the economy.[28]

The campaign to repeal all internal taxes thrived in the early 1880s.
The surplus gave antitax advocates a strong basis on which to make
their case, and it fused protests into a call for abolition of all internal
taxes. In April 1882 more than three hundred petitioners from Atlanta, Georgia, who defined themselves as businessmen and citizens, echoed an often-heard argument: "That internal taxation was
resorted to by the General Government as a war measure, and should
not be maintained during times of peace." They added that most existing internal taxes were "impediments to commerce," or "petty exactions" that "annoyed and cost the people more than they benefited
the revenue." Wealthy citizens from the county of Otsego, New York,

advocated a reduction of taxes and expenses, complaining that they were paying taxes "largely in excess of all legitimate wants of the government." The surplus provided the opportunity to restore a limited government, relieving citizens of the tax burden. On August 9, 1882, New York cartoonist Bernhard Gillam focused on the poor "taxpayer" forgotten by the plutocracy in Congress that burdened him with indirect and external taxes while trying to repeal all internal taxes.[29]

In the emerging "New South," where many industries flourished, agitation grew stronger and was closely related to the tariff issue. Protests started a few years earlier gained momentum because of the surplus. Most Southerners protested against the high-tariff policy and federal taxes that were "relics of a war" that had "happily been terminated." The cry "Down with the internal revenue system" gained traction among the population. North Carolina representative William Ruffin Cox was not half-hearted in his condemnation of the whole internal revenue business when he favored openly and boldly "the entire abolition of the cumbrous, corrupt, and spying system of internal revenue." Many Democrats denounced "crippling taxes," which were used to redistribute money and jobs by Republicans in power.[30]

As a consequence, it was no coincidence that debates soon revolved around the *internal* impact of customs duties. During a passionate discussion in Congress in 1883, when someone told him that the tariff was "not" a tax, William McKendree Springer vociferously answered, "This is not a tax! I thought the customs duty was a tax that was levied upon articles consumed by the people." Springer worked steadily to prove that the tariff was a hidden tax that functioned as a protection of special interests and was particularly burdensome for workers and poor people. His speeches were imbued with constitutional arguments. He denounced the waste of taxpayers' money and the intrusion of federal officers. Tariffs, he surmised, caused "an immense customhouse force to be employed to inspect articles coming into this country." Furthermore, this collection required "a large number

Figure 2.3. Bernhard Gillam, "Forgotten on Purpose," *Puck*, August 9, 1882. Courtesy of the Library of Congress.

of books to enter those articles coming in from day to day." Referring to Chester Arthur, who became president of the United States after the assassination of James A. Garfield in 1881, Springer drew a parallel between the corruption of tax officers and the tax policy of Republicans in power. As a former tax collector of the great port of New York, Arthur knew a great deal, Springer added, about tariff collection and corruption. Under such circumstances, the repeal of all internal taxes was not only a sound economic decision but first and foremost a virtuous action to restore the republican ideal of limited government.[31]

As the campaign gained political clout, Republicans made proposals to appease the tax resisters, especially as they refused to reduce tariff rates in order to protect American corporations against the unfair competition of foreign corporations. The context of budgetary surplus, however, enabled them to propose the repeal of some internal taxes to divert attention from customs duties. In his annual address, and using the same words as the tax resisters, President Arthur urged Congress to repeal all "unnecessary" internal taxes, and he particularly focused on the tax on bank notes, which he labeled "especially unjust." Adopted in 1866 by Congress, the 10 percent tax on notes was paid by private individuals and state banks. Even though bankers had always opposed it, the Supreme Court upheld the tax in its landmark decision *Veazie Bank v. Fenno* (1869). Tapping into growing protests against internal taxes, Congress decided to abolish it.[32]

On March 3, 1883, all remaining internal taxes, except those on tobacco products, distilled spirits, and fermented liquors, and on the dealers of these products, were repealed. Consequently, the number of internal revenues districts was reduced in the country. In July 1884 Congress decided to limit the number of authorized revenue agents from thirty-five to twenty and limited their compensation to $7 per day. The consolidation of collections' offices resulted in the elimination of ninety-eight separate offices. From a high of 225 collectors' offices in 1873, the Bureau of Internal Revenue had only 127 collectors' offices in 1885. For tax resisters, the disappearance of offices was an important achievement and reflected their conviction that internal taxes had become "unnecessary."[33]

As the national surplus increased, the movement to repeal the so-called luxury taxes grew among small businesses, retailers, and druggists. Most of them asserted that the moral label of "luxury" was not relevant anymore. In 1886 the legislative committee of the Georgia Pharmaceutical Association convened its annual meeting in Savannah. The tiny crowd—around fifty people—made a strong case against such taxes, and detailed eight reasons explaining why they should be repealed:

1. Such taxes have always been unpopular;
2. They are inquisitorial in character.
3. They are special in their nature.
4. They are taxes upon goods produced in our own country.
5. They interfere with freedom of trade among the states.
6. They violate the unwritten law of the land, which is to draw the revenue from the Customs and not from the Excise.
7. The Internal Revenue Taxes are a War Measure and always have been.
8. They were enacted to raise money to meet the wants of the Government in the late civil war, and for no other purpose, with the understanding that these taxes were to be abolished when the exigencies of the government no longer demanded them.

Their far-reaching criticisms were based upon constitutional arguments and the central idea of reciprocity. The druggists considered that war taxes had to disappear in peacetime, and the association urged all of its members to contact their representatives to express their grievances against such a violation of "the unwritten law of the land." Fortified by the existence of the national surplus, the campaign escalated the following year.[34]

Business organizations challenged the public to scrutinize the impact of internal taxes. In January 1887, the New York Board of Trade and Transportation asked Congress to put an end to the "extravagance" of the federal government and reduce taxes. A unanimously adopted resolution refused to continue in time of peace the "excessive taxation that was necessary in time of war." The Leaf Tobacco Board of Trade made similar arguments, and when they were asked to assess the impact of the tax on tobacco producers, members of the board's committee did not mince their words. "The imposition of the internal revenue," they contended, was "repugnant to our system of government and by its very nature odiously oppressive." With its "illegal espionage system," it gave birth to "moral turpitude" among "honest" small businessmen. The argument of unfair discrimination used to debunk the income tax reappeared in the protest against internal taxes.[35]

The most important petition was sponsored in January 1887 by the National Wholesale Druggists' Association. Although druggists had already failed a few years earlier to repeal the tax on alcohol, they nevertheless hoped to convince Congress of the inept and dangerous consequences of federal taxation. Chaired by M. N. Kline of Philadelphia, its committee on legislation issued circulars and petitions to all members for distribution among wholesale and retail druggists. Echoing rhetoric honed by petitioners in 1882, they asserted that taxes were nothing more than "impediments to commerce" and "petty exactions." As spirits were used in medicines, members of the association complained, taxes were "a real burden" upon the people and were not at all "luxury" taxes. The petition was supported by Pennsylvania Democrat Samuel J. Randall who helped create a Revenue Reform Association made up of the representatives of Virginia, North Carolina, South Carolina, and Georgia in order to gather signatures.[36]

From January to February, Congress received more than three hundred petitions signed by 4,850 citizens urging them to repeal "war tax measures." Antistatist and economics arguments were used to explain that the tax on tobacco threatened both agriculture and the industry. The petitioning was far from spontaneous. Some petitions were signed by the same hand that had copied a list of names of retailers and druggists. The Northeast came first in the number of petitions, and some arrived from the South and the West. The repeal of the tax on whisky raised concerns among some petitioners. One petition from Pennsylvania added to the printed plea that this appeal did not ask for "the repeal of the tax on whisky." On January 25, 1887, the Philadelphia Drug Exchange contended that if "it were not possible to bring about a total abolition of the Internal Tax on alcohol," they would favor a reduction for wholesale and retail liquor dealers' licenses as applied to the drug trade.[37]

Such divisions among petitioners explained why the movement failed. The rising Prohibitionist movement in the 1880s rendered impossible a repeal of the tax on alcohol. Founded in 1874, the Woman's Christian Temperance Union strongly denounced the role of alcoholism in health problems and family distress. A repeal of the alcohol tax would have been seen as an incentive to drunkenness. Even in the moonshiners' region, the hero in the rebellion against Reconstruction became the villainous producer of a dangerous beverage and many Prohibitionist laws were voted. Consensus revolving around the repeal of the tax was fragile. Not only did Republicans view it as the only way to divert attention from the tariff, but some businessmen feared the invasion of foreign products in the event of a repeal. Even union-trade organizer Adolph Strasser, president of the Cigar Makers' International Union, opposed abolition of the internal revenue tax and warned his fellow citizens of the invasion of Chinese cigars coming from "the opium dens in Chinatown" if the federal tax disappeared. In Southern states, proposals to abolish all internal taxes were criticized by some citizens and industrialists, who contended that the repeal would increase the burden of the tariff imposed to pay the national debt.[38]

At the end of the 1880s, the Gilded Age tax system resembled the one existing in the antebellum years. Although they failed to close all internal revenue districts, tax resisters instilled in the nation the ideas of limited government and low federal taxes. Under such circumstances, the idea of refunding the money collected during the civil war gained political clout and reinforced the view of federal taxation as a temporary expedient in time of major crisis.

In the 1880s, William Calvin Oates made a name for himself in Congress. Well known in Alabama for his assault with the Fifteenth Regiment against the men of the Twentieth Maine during the Gettysburg battle on July 2, 1863, Oates became an opponent of the expansion of the federal government in the field of education and railroads regulation. In 1888, his new battle revolved around the extravagant proposal made by Republicans: to refund direct taxes collected during the first year of the civil war. In 1888 Congress seriously considered legislation that would have refunded to the individual states the taxes that had been levied upon their citizens. Among Republicans, Thomas Brackett Reed, nicknamed Czar Reed by his opponents, supported the bill to demonstrate the generosity of tariff advocates and to prove that Republicans were not the enemy of the people. Pennsylvania Democrat Samuel J. Randall still supported the measure as a good way to reduce the surplus without reforming the tariff. For Oates and his fellow Southerners, there was no doubt that the proposal was going to reinvigorate sectional animosities, and to provoke passionate debates in the nation.[39]

In 1861, when the direct tax was levied by Treasury Secretary Salmon P. Chase, it raised $20,000,000. Of this amount, $17,359,685.51 was paid or credited and $2,640,314 remained due from southern states. Twenty-three years after the end of the war, the idea arose of refunding the states that had paid it because of the surplus. Such a redistribution of the tax would strongly benefit the northeastern states. The passage of the bill would give New York the sum of

$2,603,918.67 and New Jersey, $450,134. Opponents of the measure argued that such a gift was part of the Republican policy of redistribution of taxpayers' money. Many of them stressed the fact that the money poured into the Treasury came in the 1880s from every part of the nation but would be redistributed to a small section of the national entity.[40]

Furthermore, the "direct tax" reminded Southerners of the odious times of Yankee rule with its cruelty of confiscated lands and delinquent taxpayers, all the more so as the Lost Cause movement gained momentum in the Southern states. After the war, its collection was carried out with great difficulty because of the region's unsettled and impoverished condition. Due to strong resistance, the collection of the direct tax was abandoned in 1869, and all direct tax commissions were dissolved. In 1883 the Treasury secretary was authorized to audit and pay the claims of the original owners of lands that had been sold for nonpayment of direct taxes. It came as no surprise that the proposal was strongly rejected and Southern politicians denounced it as a way to divert attention from other debates on taxation.[41]

In the spring of 1888 the first proposal to refund direct taxes created a congressional deadlock because of Southern opposition. Representative Oates cited Republicans who only tried to "diminish *pro tanto* the force of the otherwise unanswerable argument which that surplus presents in favor of a reduction of tariff duties and other war taxes." Even the conservative *New York Times* took a strong stand against the stated purpose of the bill that proposed to pay money out of the Treasury when there was no strong "requirement of justice, no real demand for it, and no even apparent necessity." Because of Southerners' opposition, Democrats were divided about the bill and proposed to postpone the vote until the next session. Many of them wanted to discuss the tariff before going any further and decided to block the measure by all means available, notably filibustering.[42]

In December, after the victory of Republican candidate Benjamin Harrison, a new proposal was introduced. Southern politicians gave rousing speeches against it. With vociferous arguments, Oates pointed out that it was "unconstitutional, unjust and detrimental" to all Americans. Former captain in the Thirteenth Georgia Regiment, Representative John David Stewart regarded the bill as a piece of "unwise legislation" that would jeopardize the budget and lead to an increase in tariff rates. The proposal gained traction among many Americans. Even though they found the measure particularly "vicious and obnoxious," it was difficult for a large number of congressmen "to resist the demands of their constituents to support it" as the *New York Times* ironically put it. The bill passed in March by a majority of votes in both the Senate and the House. It was vetoed by President Stephen Grover Cleveland as the last act of his second term.[43]

Although he was a strong advocate of tax reduction, Cleveland strongly opposed the refund, suggesting that it would open up a Pandora's box of tax return. He operated on the assumption that there was something more in the payment of taxes, especially in wartime. The sense of reciprocity implied that the direct tax had been levied under the legitimate auspices of the federal government. To pay it back to the states for the relief of current taxpayers would involve no element of equity from one generation to another. "Any other theory," he concluded, "cheapened and in a measure discredited a process, which, more than any other, was a manifestation of sovereign authority." Warning his fellow citizens of the future impact of the decision, Cleveland refused to give the money back to the states as it was paid by individuals during the civil war. For the president, the refund was nothing but a "bald, sheer gratuity."[44]

The presidential veto did not put an end to the debate on the refund of 1861 war taxes. The victory of Benjamin Harrison enabled Republicans in power to make a new proposal. By early 1891, the refunding of the direct tax came back before Congress. Hilary Abner

Herbert, representative from Alabama, denounced what he called "an unmistakable purpose on the part of gentlemen on the other side of this House." The goal of such a tax return, he added, was "to create a deficiency in the Treasury" so that they would have good reason to increase tariff rates to collect revenue. One year earlier, the McKinley Tariff had pushed the tariff to an all-time high, and Southern congressmen feared that the refund would increase it again. Finally, on March 2, 1891, after a bitter congressional debate, the tax refund was signed into law by President Benjamin Harrison. The measure had been passed 172 to 101 votes in the House and overwhelmingly in the Senate. Soon Democrats accused governors of diminishing taxpayers' money when there was a Treasury deficit. In October 1892 the Treasury urged the states to pay back the money to the taxpayers from whom it was collected.[45]

The refund was not only a political strategy of Republicans eager to divert attention from the tariff but also reinforced the idea that direct taxes were temporary war measures that were supposed to end once the benefits ceased for the community. Although, in 1892, the country had the same federal tax system it had possessed during the antebellum years, social and economic conditions had greatly changed. Such a discrepancy sparked debates about the fairness of the federal tax system, and the whole concept of taxation in a democracy was revived by a new generation of intellectuals.

The accumulation of wealth and its distribution into the hands of financiers and manufacturers symbolized the end of the agrarian republic. Thomas G. Sherman, a political economist and founder of the Sherman and Sterling Law Firm in New York City, conducted a study on the topic, which he published in 1889 in *The Forum* under the title "The Owners of the United States of America." Sherman contended that just seventy persons owned a combined wealth of $2.7 billion. Some 50,000 families owned half the nation's wealth, while four-fifths of the people earned less than $500 a year. As tax debates and proposals for income taxes raged in Europe, Sherman became more and more concerned with a major tax reform in the country. Although he represented such prominent American figures as Jay Gould and John D. Rockefeller, Sherman supported a tax reform based upon direct taxation. As he explained, indirect taxes "were maintained for the very purpose of convincing the vast majority that they were *not* taxed." The tax burden, Sherman noted, was disproportionally placed upon the poor, who paid taxes equivalent to 75 to 80 percent of their savings while corporations and the wealthy paid only 8 to 10 percent. Federal taxes had increased sixfold since the civil war, he maintained, while untaxed corporations saw their profits soar tenfold. Even though many economists disagreed with his methodology, Sherman rightly described the inequality of a regressive tax system that served the interests of the few at the expense of the many. Sherman's analysis of inequality led many reformers and scholars to rethink the very goal of taxation and to give to progressive taxation a new legitimacy. Statistician George K. Holmes checked the accuracy of Sherman's analysis, and asserted that actually the top 9 percent (and not 6 percent as Sherman claimed) owned almost 70 percent of the nation's wealth.[46]

At the end of the nineteenth century, Shearman was not alone in fusing protests against inequality into a package of new ideas to redress the flaws of industrialization. Although social Darwinists argued that wealth would flow naturally to those most capable of handling it, economists and middle-class reformers endorsed tax reform and contended that institutions could provide assistance to ordinary people. The most popular reform was proposed by Henry George. In 1879, in his book *Progress and Poverty*, he explained that inequality derived from the profiteering of landowners. With a stridency that lived up to his name, he advocated for a replacement of all taxes with a "single tax" to replace the tariff system. His simple scheme appealed to many Americans, even though economists demonstrated that George's proposal was unsound and conservative.

During a conference held at the American Social Science Association, Edwin R. A. Seligman even called it "repugnant" to our moral sense and "repellant to our logic." What was needed, Seligman contended, was a reform that would implement a progressive system of taxation and put an end to the idea that federal tax was the result of a pure and simple reciprocity system between institutions and individuals.[47]

Influenced by European models and tax reforms in France and in Great Britain, a new vision of tax policy emerged from the debates on inequality and distribution of wealth. Seligman was joined by another economist, Richard Thomas Ely. Both took the lead to promote the adoption of new, more effective, and equitable forms of taxation. Ely's regular target was the "fiction of reciprocity," pretending that each citizen had to gain something from the tax procedure. Industrialization and the market revolution had greatly changed the interaction, and Ely supported a new role for the federal government. By deconstructing the theory of benefits, the academic hoped to propagate the idea that tax reform was necessary, and that it fostered social solidarity and a new sense of fiscal citizenship.[48]

Importantly, Seligman believed that economic and social tensions plagued modern societies, and spoke bluntly in favor of the sacrifice of rich taxpayers and the notion of each citizen paying according to his ability. The income tax was a necessary step to round "out the existing tax system in the direction of greater justice." In his major book published in 1899, *On the Shifting and Incidence of Taxation*, he strongly redefined citizenship in the context of industrialization and income inequality. He also disagreed with the idea of reciprocity and the assumption that people paid taxes because they got "benefits" from the state. Instead, he preferred the notion of social solidarity as the foundation of a modern system of taxation.[49]

Seligman and Ely knew well the criticisms made by tax resisters about the practicability of income tax reform, and the idea that as a tool of public finance it would collect little revenue. Both the Tilden trial and the refund debate had reinforced the conviction that a progressive system of taxation was impracticable. How did you define income? How did you treat equally all sources of income? As the civil war had revealed, such questions needed to be addressed carefully by tax experts. Yet, Seligman and Ely's most difficult task was to explain that progressive taxation was neither a subtle form of socialism, nor an act of confiscation.[50]

To address tax resisters' concerns, Seligman used the marginalist theory of income, proposed by economists Alfred Marshall and John Bates Clark. In his major book *Principles of Economics*, first published in 1890, Marshall detailed his view on marginal utility of rich people's higher income. John Bates Clark worked with Seligman at Columbia and helped him frame his view of taxation. Seligman also drew his inspiration from Thomas Nixon Carver and Francis Ysidro Edgeworth. Particularly interested with the distribution of wealth, Harvard economist Carver proposed a moderate progressive system of taxation. From his office at Oxford, Edgeworth worked on the idea of sacrifice as the intellectual and moral vindication of tax reform, and believed that it was better to tax the richest citizens who have a very low marginal utility of their higher income than to tax poor people who had a very high marginal utility of their low income. Such fresh and innovative studies helped Seligman execute his reform agenda by contending that the wealthy should pay more taxes because they received less utility from their last, or marginal, dollar. The theory rendered possible a tax reform without weakening industrialization and prosperity.[51]

In the early 1890s tax resisters were soon to attack such a foreign view of taxation and had more reasons to contend that progressive taxation was "un-American." The leading intellectual opposing income taxation, David Wells, still opposed such reform on constitutional grounds.[52] Graduated rates of taxation were a form of discrimination, Wells claimed, that was contrary to the notion of "uniformity" contained in the Constitution. The marginal theory was only a tricky way to legitimize "class legislation" and "confiscation." The wealthy businessman Charles Elliott Perkins strongly disagreed with the fact that rich men dissipated their money in extravagant living. He contended that although a small part of their incomes might be wasted "in show or champagne," most of it "was invested in some form of industry which benefited the masses by making something cheaper." Other opponents of income taxation believed that it was necessary to redistribute some of the money through donations and philanthropy. Andrew Carnegie asserted that rich people had a duty to serve in human society. As an answer to the growing inequality in the republic, his "gospel of wealth" pushed him to donate more than $350 million to libraries, schools, and the arts. The debate about progressive taxation of income was only beginning.[53]

In November 1891, during a speech in Iowa, one of the most vocal tax resisters of the Gilded Age, William M. Springer, perfectly summed up the long legacy of the war tax system: "Soon after the war began it became necessary to raise large revenue," and taxes of all kinds were imposed." He added that hopefully "soon after the war was over Congress repealed most of these taxes, especially those bearing heavily upon the wealthy and those most able to pay." During the Gilded Age it was possible to repeal most remaining internal taxes. Even though he failed to convince justices that the income tax was unconstitutional, Springer took the lead to promote their repeal. Springer's crusade was strongly embedded in the idea that internal taxation was "un-American" and betrayed the will of the founding fathers. By refunding the 1861 taxes levied during the civil war, Republicans also reinforced the idea that internal taxes were temporary and should be considered as a war measure once and for all. In the decades following the American Civil War, many Americans shared the same vision of restoring the antebellum system of taxation and kept on debating tariff rates. The only problem was that the country in the 1890s was very different from the one the founding fathers had lived in. Tax resisters were defending and partly idealizing a world that had disappeared. The emergence of colossal fortunes, waves of immigration, and the spread of cities had turned the country into one of rapid modernization. To counterbalance the modernist impulses in American society, some reformers and intellectuals proposed a modernization of the federal tax system. The economic crisis of 1893 would enable them to gain more political clout, and the very supporters of the tariff-only policy would soon turn into fierce resisters against what they considered to be an "odious" tax system.[54]

3

The Odious Income Tax

The present assault upon capital is
but the beginning.
—*Justice Stephen J. Field* (1895)

IN HER POPULAR advice book, *The House in Good Taste* (1913), actress and interior decorator Elsie de Wolfe encouraged wealthy Americans to purchase brighter, simpler, and more refined homes. Even though economist Thorstein Veblen, in his sarcastic analysis *The Theory of the Leisure Class* (1899), satirized such conspicuous and leisurely activities that aimed at flaunting their wealth, de Wolfe was proud to advocate the use of softer wall and woodwork colors and porcelain bowls, flowers, and other knick-knacks to enhance the interiors of the upper class. Although she wanted to distance herself and her rich clients from Victorian taste and refinement, she still believed that good manners defined elites' social status. Houses were expressions of cultural and social superiority. When her book came out, de Wolfe engaged in another battle against the legitimacy of the Sixteenth Amendment (1913) and the new income tax law. For the first time since the civil war, individuals earning more than $3,000 had to pay a federal income tax. De Wolfe decided to test its constitutionality and tried to enroll woman's groups in her crusade. Wasn't

the income tax she had to pay an example of "taxation without representation" for women who did not have the right to vote? British and
French suffragists had already used similar arguments in favor of
women's right to vote.[1]

On December 3, 1913, the energetic decorator filed a lawsuit in
Chicago with the help of her legal and conservative counsel, William Bourke Cockran. A long-time tax resister, Cockran had always
considered that the purpose of the income tax was not to "to raise
revenue, but to gratify vengeance." Cockran and de Wolfe recycled
arguments of apportionment, and alleged that the income tax was
then "imposed upon but 423,000 persons out of a population of some
90,000,000." De Wolfe lost her case and was not able to convince
other women to join her. Most middle-class suffragists asserted that
the wealthiest citizens including the famous actress had a social
responsibility to pay their share. In fact, in the modern nation that
emerged at the dawn of the twentieth century, tax reform became a
major issue, and taxation of both personal and corporate incomes
was seen as a legitimate way to regulate the new industrial order.[2]

As a new white-collar middle-class of urban professionals gained
more political influence, progressive taxation became a popular response to the vast change that had overwhelmed the country. Due to
the economic depression of the mid-1890s, fear gripped millions of
citizens. As a consequence, more and more Americans adopted a
broader view of the government's role in dealing with the social consequences of industrialization. As the tariff system was considered
corrupt, citizens agreed with a reallocation of the fiscal burden and
claimed that they had a legitimate claim upon the profits and earnings capacity of business corporations.[3]

Particularly strong in the South and the West, populists and progressives established their political footing by endorsing the idea of
sacrifice and taxpayers' ability to pay as the foundation of a new federal taxation. In the face of such a profound tax reform, northeastern
businessmen turned into fierce tax resisters. From the first income

tax law since the civil war in 1894 to the ratification campaign of the Sixteenth Amendment in 1913, their opposition had been based on antidemocratic and constitutional grounds. Industrialists, however, found themselves increasingly isolated and eventually lost the support of public opinion.[4]

On June 5, 1894, Simon Sterne, a celebrated corporate lawyer, attended a mass meeting of businessmen and bankers in prestigious Carnegie Hall, New York City. With other members of the upper class, he denounced the new proposal by populists to tax the incomes of rich citizens. Sterne had been involved for years in local and national politics and always subscribed to the power of the ruling elite, fearing that socialism would pervert the ideals defended by the founding fathers. At the end of the nineteenth century, his concern that the country was doomed by demagoguery had grown. In a striking reversal of the revolutionary motto "no taxation without representation," he claimed that there should be no "representation without taxation" and that every citizen had to contribute to the welfare of the nation, regardless of his ability to pay. At a time when rich New Yorkers used the past to reaffirm their identity and their social status, the memory of the American Revolution became a source of legitimacy to oppose federal power. There was no doubt that income tax was the child of "class legislation," warned Sterne, and that progressive taxation was the vanguard of a dangerous socialistic revolution.[5]

At Carnegie Hall, alarm over the bill peaked, and rich citizens refused to pay more than others. The crowd of white men was cemented by a shared belief about the danger posed by democracy. As access to elite status became less restricted by family ties and more open to men of new wealth, New Yorkers found means of closing ranks. Before the civil war, there were few millionaires in town; by 1900, more than four thousand lived uptown. A distinctive culture emerged in a city profoundly transformed by immigration and industrialization. Elites were particularly afraid of the millions who flowed ashore on boats from Europe. As a consequence, they were all the more eager to justify their financial success and the astounding accumulation of wealth due to their superior talent, intelligence, and self-control. In its pamphlet *Who Pays Your Taxes*, published in 1892, the New York Tax Reform Association opposed taxation according to citizens' ability to pay and listed the numerous dangers of the income tax that echoed arguments found in petitions during the Gilded Age:

In its theory (as a mode of encouraging a more equitable
   distribution of wealth), fallacious;
In its discrimination, unjust and impolitic;
In its operation, unequal;
In its practice, inquisitorial and corruptive.[6]

At Carnegie Hall, New York senator David B. Hill fanned the flames of tax resistance by defining the proposal as an "odious" one, advocated by his "fellow-citizens from West and South," who vainly "imagined" that by taxing capital, they relieved themselves of some of the burdens of taxation and threw them upon "our shoulders." Evan Thomas, the president of the New York Produce Exchange, stated bluntly that an income tax was "so un-American and so partial in its injury" that it should not be tolerated among "free people." The enslavement of rich taxpayers was still a powerful argument to derail "class legislation."[7]

During debates in Congress, New York representative William Bourke Cockran became their spokesperson. Born in Ireland, Cockran left his country for the United States when he was seventeen years of age. A prominent lawyer, he was elected to the House of Representatives in 1887 as a Democrat. With his characteristic bluntness and oratorical skills, Cockran tried to convince his fellow Democrats that the inevitable result of making this small number of people contribute to the support of the federal government by means of a direct tax would cause the creation of "class distinction." In other words, it was a plan "vicious in its extreme," and Cockran urged Democrats not to "chase populists," notably their talented leader, William Jennings Bryan.[8]

A passionate advocate of the welfare of the ordinary American, Bryan helped draft the short amendment to the lengthy bill that provided a modest income tax of 2 percent on incomes over $3,000. Born in Salem, Illinois, in 1860, Bryan was then a young politician imbued with both a fierce Protestant faith and a strong sense of social justice. After graduating from Union Law School in 1883, he moved to Nebraska where in 1890 he ran for Congress as a Democrat and was elected. The economic and social plight of midwestern farmers caused him extreme distress. As the panic of 1893 started a full-scale depression with a heavy human toll, Bryan denounced Washington's subordination to financial interests and proposed the first income tax in a peacetime since the war. For Bryan, taxation implied a sense of social justice and solidarity, and was not only a matter of reciprocity.[9]

On January 30, 1894, Bryan delivered a fiercely passionate speech in defense of progressive taxation of incomes. Like many reformers, he found it unbelievable that the burden of taxation fell primarily on the poor through the tariff. To businessmen and lawyers who refused "representation without taxation," he replied that "If taxation is a badge of freedom, let me assure my friend that the poor people of this country are covered all over with the insignia of freemen." With harsh words, he debunked one of the major arguments of tax resisters—that the tax was "inquisitorial and unfair," and vehemently responded to "the gentlemen" who were so fearful of "socialism" when the poor were exempted from an income tax and who viewed "with indifference those methods of taxation which give the rich a substantial exemption." One of his principal targets was the New York Chamber of Commerce, which he accused of "distorting the facts of history" through false statistics and erroneous pamphlets. Bryan's passionate words captured populists' anxiety about corporate power and the necessity of tax reforms to curtail the power of the new greedy octopus whose sprawling tentacles ensnared the American Republic.[10]

At Carnegie Hall, on June 5, 1894, the antagonistic figure of William Jennings Bryan was in everyone's minds. The fear that emerged in the New York business community spread to other parts of the nation. It was reinforced by the corporate consolidation movement that was emerging at the end of the nineteenth century and that enabled businessmen to exert their political influence during debates in Congress.

In the opinion of industrialists, populists were unfairly exploiting the economic downturn and such a demagogic action was denounced in petitions they massively sent to Congress. For many weeks, congressmen's offices were inundated by signed pleas of corporate leaders. Led by the New York Chamber of Commerce, the campaign included the boards of trade of many cities in the Northeast and the chambers of commerce of St. Paul, San Francisco, Pittsburgh, Cleveland, and New York State. Other petitions were signed by "citizens" of Democratic clubs in New York City and other major cities in the nation. Members of the Board of Trade of Waterbury, Connecticut, hammered on the income tax, claiming that it was "inquisitorial, unAmerican, and contrary to the policy of our government under all administrations for more than one hundred years." In addition, several petitions arrived from grocery, import, and wholesale organizations in Providence, Chicago, and Philadelphia. In one petition, the Grocers Importers Exchange of Philadelphia staged protests against a law its members deemed "purely inquisitorial in its nature and unfair to the people of this country."[11]

Petitioners' grievances were filled with references to the antebellum period and the civil war, and helped foster the myth of a republic without taxpayers. In January 1894 the Chamber of Commerce of New York pointed out that "without distinction of party lines," it was a tradition that "the necessary expenses of the Government" were

collected through the customs house with the only exception of wartime. One month later, on February 19, 1894, the Chamber of Commerce of Pittsburgh conveyed similar arguments against the "unwise,
unpolitic and unjust" income tax. Traumatic recent memories of the
civil war were put forward as a reminder of the powerful potential for
resistance among the American people: "Experience during our
late war fully demonstrated that an income tax was inquisitorial and
odious to our people, and only tolerated as a war measure." In spite
of the small number of taxpayers during the war, and the major role
played by the business community in the repeal of the income tax,
it was explained that it had been abrogated by "universal consent" as
soon as the condition of the country had permitted it. All petitioners refused such government interferences in their operations, and
made it a sacred American principle strongly embedded in the nation's past.[12]

Furthermore, in a context of severe economic crisis, petitioners
contended that a tax would pose serious threats. Members of the Manhattan Club pointed out that the business and financial depression
now existing in this country had "already brought much suffering to
the wage-earners" and "unhappiness to all classes of citizens," and
more federal taxation would only worsen the situation. The Philadelphia Board of Trade went even further, asserting that any legislation
that may render such tax necessary would be most "disastrous to the
business, growth and general prosperity of the country." At stake, argued protesters, was the future of American capitalism. Between the
late 1880s and early 1900s, massive corporate conglomerates emerged,
profoundly transforming business operations. The merger movement was supported by bankers and stockholders and won judicial
protection when the Supreme Court ruled in the 1880s and 1890s
that corporations, like individuals, were protected by the Fourteenth
Amendment. The growth of corporations made stock and bond ex-
changes a major activity. In 1886 trading on the New York Stock Exchange exceeded one million shares a day. Facing such a profound

transformation, many businessmen feared the impact of the tax on the reorganization of capitalism.[13]

As a consequence, portions of the bill related to stockholders provoked suspicion. For individuals who owned stocks, it meant that they would pay taxes even if their income was below the exemption amount. If it was above, they would pay twice. Such double taxation reinforced the view of businessmen that direct taxation always created "unfair" discrimination among citizens. New York senator David B. Hill used it as the symbol of the desire "to punish" big corporations. Tapping into the difference in tax treatment between partnerships and corporations, Hill noted that if an individual made "a $3000 profit from a $5000 investment in a partnership," such a profit would not be taxed because the individual was entitled to an exemption, but if he placed that "$5,000 as an investment in a corporation," he would have to pay a federal tax. Such incoherent tax policy would create divisions among citizens. Thus, it constituted a dangerous attack on the founding principles of the American Republic.[14]

It was not a coincidence that most petitioners' arguments revolved around the "un-Americanism" of progressive taxation. Refusing to take the bait of Edwin R. A. Seligman and other academics, Senator Hill gave a rousing speech to denounce the fact that they drew their inspiration from Europe. Such a theory, he explained, was "un-American" and was imported by "European professors" who had decided to promote a "new political economy for universal application." In an apocalyptic tone, he described the collapse of the republic, mixing fears of immigration and warnings against taxation: "From the midst of their armed camps between the Danube and the Rhine, the professors with their books, the Socialists with their schemes, the anarchists with their bombs, are all instructing the people of the United States in the organization of the society, the doctrines of democracy, and the principles of taxation." Fearing the evils of socialism and income distribution, Hill attacked reformers for always invoking the memory of Thomas Jefferson to justify their crusade. In 1888

economist Richard Theodore Ely used Jefferson's philosophy to promote an inheritance tax. The Fontainebleau letter sent by Jefferson
to James Madison in October 1785 became a contentious issue. It
was carefully read by Hill, who disagreed with the reformers' interpretation and contended that "it is actually quoted as helpful authority by men favoring an income tax, in a century, a hemisphere, and a
state where exists not one of all the affecting circumstances that Jefferson's kind heart grieved over." He concluded by asserting and deploring that Jefferson's philosophical mindset was wrongly used by
populists. For Hill and his fellow resisters, both history and memory
proved that idealistic tax reformers were wrong and betrayed the ideals of the founding fathers.[15]

Tax collection methods were still attacked in the name of republican ideals and protection of the household. Philadelphia Representative Robert Adams Jr. even considered that the imposition of
the tax would "corrupt" the people, bringing an undesirable army of
"spies" and "informers." Opponents in the House and Senate argued
that such inquisitorial means would foster tax evasion. New Jersey
senator James Smith Jr. seriously contended that the income tax not
only provided for additional "taxation without representation" but put
"a premium upon dishonesty and evasion of the law." Such extreme
views had an impact on a rising number of Representatives. Ohio
congressman John Sherman even changed his mind about the income tax. After the civil war, he believed it was a necessary tool of
public finance that could help redress some inequalities. Twenty years
later, he spoke bluntly against the income tax, referring to the
Faustian bargain signed by tax reformers. "In a republic like ours,"
he warned citizens, "where all men are equal, this attempt to array
the rich against the poor or the poor against the rich was socialism,
communism, devilism [sic]." Like his new fellow resisters, Sherman
hoped for a speedy defeat of the bill and tended to minimize the
impact of both the economic crisis and the popularity of the measure in the West and the South.[16]

On July 3 the Senate approved the bill, and on August 13 the House followed, approving the version by a substantial margin. The failure of tax resisters' strategy compelled them and their political allies to turn to the Supreme Court. The possibility of filing a lawsuit against the revenue law was investigated by William Dameron Guthrie of the New York law firm of Seward, Guthrie, Morawetz, and Steele at the behest of his clients. The cost of the litigation was supported by New York merchants and businessmen. As a last resort, the Supreme Court would determine the future of the American tax system with the *Pollock* decision in 1895.

In 1887 the country celebrated the centennial of the Constitution, and Justice Stephen Johnson Field, a member of the Supreme Court for almost a quarter of a century, was asked to be the keynote speaker at the New York State Bar Association's centennial celebration. The son of a Congregationalist minister, Field grew up in Stockbridge, Massachusetts, graduated from Williams College in 1837, and practiced law in New York City. In 1863 President Abraham Lincoln appointed him to the newly created tenth seat on the Supreme Court, in part because of his staunch support of the Union. Field soon devoted himself to defending unregulated free enterprise. In a context of industrialization, urbanization, and economic development, he had deep reservations about what he considered "class legislation." Under such circumstances, Americans had to be reminded more than ever that the Constitution guaranteed the protection of property and promised to limit the power of the government. For him, the nascent popular support in favor of an income tax was a major democratic flaw, and had to be fought against by all necessary means.[17]

At the end of the nineteenth century, Field's words depicted a world fragmented by class conflict. Because of immigration and social unrest, "angry menaces against order" found vent in "loud denunciations." With the same firm hand, he exposed the dangers of income tax and became a vocal spokesperson for rich citizens, deliberately

dramatizing the ominous issues at stake. In the volatile debate on
government regulation, Field was a leading advocate of substantive
due process and the freedom of businesses to self-regulate through
contracts, expressing particular opposition to the expansion of income tax, which he claimed represented "usurpation" by Congress.
His attacks drew from long-standing perceptions of the power of
both corporations and the federal government. Since the 1880s, Justice Field had systematically applied his position on the limits of
government power and what he believed to be the vital role of corporations. In the railroad tax cases that involved railroads corporations
that refused to pay new local taxes in California, he praised business
leaders for improving the lives of millions of Americans, arguing that
there was nothing that was "lawful to be done to feed and clothe
people, to beautify and adorn their dwellings, to relieve the sick, to
help the needy, and to enrich and ennoble humanity." In his opinion, the California tax system would represent a dangerous form of
"class legislation" which could only be successfully combated by an
appeal to the Constitution. Thus, he construed the Fourteenth
Amendment as providing "a perpetual shield against all unequal
and partial legislation by the states." For Field, the income tax was
the perfect incarnation of the "envied master of the millions," and
he would soon have the opportunity to quell the irrational fears of
the masses.[18]

At the request of his wealthy New York City clients, attorney William Guthrie filed a lawsuit to test the constitutionality of the income tax. Guthrie's clients belonged to the upper crust of New
Yorkers, "a large body of public-spirited New York merchants and
businessmen" as the New York Sun put it. Guthrie retained as senior
adviser, Joseph Hodges Choate, a lawyer from New England, who
had always taken strong stance against the intrusive power of the
federal government. On December 22, 1894, the first constitutional
challenge to the income tax began in the Superior Court of the District of Columbia to restrain the commissioner of internal revenue

from collecting the tax imposed by the law. Guthrie and Choate widened their attack to include two companies, the Farmers' Loan & Trust Company and the Continental Trust Company, which derived most of their income from property and intangibles. They also located two plaintiffs for the case, Charles Pollock, a resident of Massachusetts and a stockholder in Farmers' Loan, and Louis Hyde, a stockholder in the Continental Trust Company, who lived in New Jersey. The case was dismissed by a lower court but appealed to the Supreme Court, with three constitutional grounds cited as justification and a week of hearings scheduled to begin on March 7, 1895.[19]

Still known for his adamant refusal to pay the income tax during the civil war, William M. Springer attended the hearings and listened carefully to tax resisters' arguments, wondering whether the Supreme Court would change its position on direct taxation. In the *Springer* case, the justices held that an income tax was not a direct tax but an excise tax. When asked for advice, the tax expert Edwin R. A. Seligman reiterated his belief that the constitutional restriction on uniformity applied not to the classification of a tax but to its geographical application. In his article published in the *Forum*, he still pointed out that the new economic conditions warranted a profound change in tax policy. Choate disagreed with Seligman on three principal grounds.

First, he argued that the income tax was a direct tax, but it would not meet the requirement that such measures be apportioned among the states on the basis of population. Second, he contended that the exemption of incomes below $4,000 violated the requirement that taxes be levied uniformly. Thus, he argued, it represented an infringement of state and local government rights by taxing the interest on obligations issued by these bodies. Choate used these points to construct a passionate defense of the company's stockholders, and stressed the views of the nation's founders, among them both "Washington and Franklin." Attorney General Richard Olney drew on similar historical arguments, while maintaining that "taxation" was ultimately "an uncommonly practical affair" that should be adapted to the changing conditions of life, which were "never the same for any two persons, and for any community, however small." Inevitably, within a few days, the Supreme Court debate took an ideological turn, as Choate harangued the court on the grounds that the income tax was "communistic in its purposes and tendencies."[20]

Before the *Pollock* opinion was handed down, Justice Field corresponded with the popular laissez-faire economist David Ames Wells, who was still a fierce opponent of the tax. In an analysis published in the *Forum* in March 1895, and contrary to what Seligman believed, Wells thought it was possible to challenge *Springer* and pointed to the uniformity clause and the Fifth Amendment, both of which prohibit laws that discriminate against particular groups of citizens. Field complimented Wells on his essay, telling him that he intended to share the piece with Justice Melville Fuller. Despite the idea of equality behind the tax scheme, said Field, it amounted to bad public policy because it fell "the heaviest on the most conscientious, and should be reserved as an extraordinary exercise for national emergencies." For Field, to levy an income tax in peacetime was a dangerous mistake that would endanger the republic.[21]

On May 20, 1895, the justices delivered a majority opinion that held that the income tax was not constitutional. While the *New York Post* bitterly complained that "great and rich corporations" had succeeded by "fighting against a petty tax upon superfluity as other men have fought for their liberties and lives," tax resisters had won an important battle. According to Justice Field, the tax law violated the "rule of uniformity, which is prescribed in such cases by the Constitution." The unconstitutionality of the tax law was further aggravated by the exemptions it contained. It was essential that "where property is exempt from taxation, the exemption must be supported by some consideration that the public, and not private, interests will be advanced." Quoting Michigan jurist Thomas M. Cooley, Field attacked the "capricious legislative favor" that produced "favoritism

[that] could make no pretense to equality." The law discriminated between those who received "an income of $4,000 and those who did not," and such discrimination was contrary to the founding principles of the republic.[22]

The four dissenting justices—Justices Henry Billings Brown, John Marshall Harlan, Howell Edmunds Jackson, and Edward Douglass White—disagreed, calling on "future historians" to prove that they were correct in claiming that the income tax was not a direct tax. Although a conservative Republican, Justice Brown counseled greater caution in his dissenting opinion, in which he argued that "even the specter of socialism is conjured up to frighten Congress from laying taxes upon the people in proportion to their ability to pay them." Referring to tax reforms in European countries, he added that it was "certainly a strange commentary" upon the Constitution of the United States and upon a democratic government that Congress had no power to lay a tax, which is one of "the main sources of revenue of nearly every civilized state."[23]

Businessmen around the country admired the wisdom of Supreme Court justices. The editors of the *New York Sun* expressed satisfaction with the decision, proclaiming that the income tax was "dead" and the few were not to be taxed for the benefit of the many." In a typical antitax sentence, it added that "systematic robbery of one part of the country by another" was not to be a feature of our "national system." In an oft-quoted passage, Field had even announced that "it will be but the stepping-stone to others, larger and more sweeping, till [their] political contests will become a war of the poor against the rich—a war growing constantly in intensity and bitterness." For many tax resisters, the assault was over in 1895, even though debate about progressive taxation was revived by the Spanish War three years later.[24]

On February 15, 1898, an explosion ripped the U.S.S. *Maine*, killing 266 of 354 American officers and crew. President William McKinley asked Congress for authorization to use military force and to find new sources of revenue. The *New York Times* was rather confident that Americans would not complain of taxes to provide money "to put an end to the hell on earth in Cuba and punish the destroyers of the *Maine*." People were ready, editors believed, "to put Spain out of Cuba without increasing the National Debt." Although more revenue was needed to finance the war that cost more than $250 million, the *Pollock* decision put important constraints on Congress which had to find out very soon a fair and easy way to collect taxes. Businessmen were still reluctant to levy progressive taxes, especially since many of them feared that the war could jeopardize the slow recovery of the economy. They believed that the war would put their extensive investments at risk in Cuba. The *Bankers' Magazine* stressed the heavy "economic cost" for the business community, and the New York *Journal of Commerce* contended that trade would suffer from a military intervention. Only three years after the *Pollock* decision, federal taxes and their impact became once again contentious issues.[25]

During debates, some congressmen campaigned fiercely to keep taxation as low as possible. Indiana Senator George Wellington contended that "if the war comes, it will open a Pandora's Box of ills," among them, a sweeping array of "federal taxes." To circumvent the *Pollock* decision, members of the Committee on Ways and Means considered excise taxes on the gross receipts of all corporations, as they were not considered a tax on income but "a tax on the occupation of privilege of doing business as a corporation." As a consequence, Thomas Platt, a member of the Senate Finance Committee, urged senators to oppose such a proposal. Although he understood "the sentiment of the present day against corporations," and "the desire on the part of many to get at them through taxation," he drew on the familiar argument that such a tax was "unconstitutional." Congress, he added, should not act in haste. Otherwise, it could "destroy" corporations that were still recovering from the 1893 depression. Eventually, Congress decided to settle on excise taxes that were specifically directed at the sugar and oil trusts. It was perfectly understood that the new tax system targeted the two largest corporations, the Standard Oil Company and the American Sugar Refining Company. In 1897 Standard Oil was the largest corporation in the country with over $256 million in total assets.[26]

In order to find enough revenue, an inheritance tax, called a legacy tax, was also levied. It was a duty on the estate itself, not on its beneficiaries, and tax rates ranged from 0.75 percent to 15 percent. The new tax sharpened political cleavages overnight. Simon Sterne did not mince his words to describe it and feared its impact on the democracy. He deplored that it was "naturally popular among the masses," because it had the appearance of "being a tax on wealth" and contended that once it was enacted, very few politicians would have the courage to repeal it. Even though he was a strong supporter of the U.S. intervention in Cuba, Senator Henry Cabot Lodge of Massachusetts contended that "a minor war" such as the Spanish-American war did not necessitate such a "dangerous measure" as a federal estate tax. Cabot was right on one point: the war was short and would not burden public finance for too long. The Spanish sought an armistice on July 17, and a peace treaty was signed in Paris on July 17. However, until 1902 and the withdrawal of soldiers, the U.S. Army governed Cuba under the command of General Leonard Wood. Such intervention made revenue collection necessary until their departure.[27]

As a consequence, constitutional suits were brought to the Supreme Court. The executors of the estate of the late Edwin F. Knowlton, who lived in Brooklyn, decided to test the constitutionality of the inheritance tax. According to their legal counselor, Charles H. Otis, the law made "a clear discrimination" against the rich and extracted from them "a greater proportional contribution" to the needs of the federal government. Therefore, the tax was not uniformly levied and had to be declared unconstitutional. Justice Edward White, who had energetically dissented in the *Pollock* decision, wrote the majority opinion in *Knowlton v. Moore* (1900). Contrary to what the plaintiff executors surmised, White asserted that the legacies tax was not a direct tax.

Another legal suit was brought by the Spreckels Sugar Company against the excise tax, believing that it was "arbitrary, unjust, and illegal discrimination founded on a pretended difference between the business of manufacturing and of refining sugar." The company asserted that the tax in question was a direct tax and, accordingly, unconstitutional because it had not been apportioned among the states by population. Justice John Marshall Harlan delivered the majority opinion in *Spreckels Sugar Company v. McClain* (1904). In analyzing whether the tax at issue was a direct tax, he noted that Congress had not tried to overreach its taxing authority. He also pointed out that the tax did not reach all gross receipts but only those from the business of refining sugar, and he contended that, in the case in question, it was not a direct tax.[28]

Once the troops were sent home, many members of the business community hoped that all war taxes would soon disappear. In 1900 New York representative Jefferson Monroe Levy urged Congress to "repeal all war taxes levied during the Spanish War" in the name of American ideals. The owner of Thomas Jefferson's house in Monticello could not help but use historical arguments to vindicate his opposition to progressive tax policy, believing that "the people of today" had built "a Nation as the world never dreamed of." If a nation "was laying the foundation for a lasting and wonderful prosperity, which will be the wonder of all countries," was it necessary to levy European-style taxes? Many businessmen agreed with him. Still fearing the socialistic impulse in federal taxation, the Illinois Association of Manufacturers agitated for the repeal of war taxes. Bankers hoped that they were soon to disappear. General Alfred C. Barnes, president of the Astor Place Bank in New York City, agreed to pay, as taxes were levied when "our people, frenzied by the loss of the *Maine*, overran the earth with hollow ships and marching armies." But then, he added, taxpayers' money was used to "pay the piper who furnished the field music for that great Anabasis." In others words, soldiers had become unnecessary, and taxes should be repealed. In 1901 Treasury Secretary Lyman J. Gage shared the same view, especially as the budgetary surplus enabled Congress to relieve pressure on taxpayers. Taxes were nothing more than a nuisance that provided an insignificant source of revenue. Once again, tax resisters contended that progressive taxation had to remain the child of necessity.[29]

As they had promised their northeastern constituency, Republicans repealed all war taxes in 1902, and many businessmen hoped that tax reform would cease in the republic as the justices in the *Pollock* decision had recommended. However, the popularity of tax reform in the country would soon dampen tax resisters' expectations, and progressive taxation would loom large on the horizon of the nation.

At the end of the nineteenth century, the familiar story of Daniel Shays was revisited. During the bitter winter of 1786–87, Shays, a modest farmer and American Revolutionary War veteran, and his compatriot Luke Day had led an unsuccessful armed protest against the state of Massachusetts. Their desperate struggle was fueled by the injustice of a regressive tax system and a conservative state government that seemed no better than British colonial rule. The first historical accounts of Shays's revolt were quite negative. At the end of the nineteenth century, the perspective changed. Shays became a populist hero. "There is nothing new under the sun," proclaimed George B. Rivers in his romanticized portrait, which compared Shays to the end-of-century populists. The popular author of *Looking Backward* (1887), Edward Bellamy, also wrote a romance involving Shays. The book was published posthumously by his brother, Francis Bellamy, who believed that Shays's Rebellion, if not recounted by "the governing classes," could be useful to ongoing debates concerning the adoption of new internal taxes in a context of economic depression and reformist impulse. The new popularity of Shays was part of a democratic trend that pushed for tax reform in the name of social justice. In the nation at large, the idea of progressive taxation gained political clout.[30]

During public meetings, politicians from the South and the West lambasted the Supreme Court for the *Pollock* decision and found that their audiences responded with enthusiasm. Democrats began to introduce constitutional amendments that would permit income taxation, and a more equitable distribution of the tax burden. Support for direct taxation grew steadily over the next fifteen years. In 1906 the American Federation of Labor endorsed the income tax for rich taxpayers. The progressive movement tapped into discontent of monopolistic businesses and corruption. In Wisconsin, Governor Robert La Follette Sr. initiated a multipronged reform program, including a new income tax. Tax reform was for him the best way to curb the power of corporations. In 1897 La Follette opened his gubernatorial campaign with a violent attack against the power of corporations, referring to the Jeffersonian ideal of a nation of small landowners: "The existence of the corporations, as we have today, was never dreamed of by the fathers." He warned his fellow citizens that "the corporation of today has invaded every department of business, and its powerful but invisible hand is felt in almost all the activities of life." Offended by corruption and immorality in business, "Fighting Bob" promoted scientific reform based upon expertise and social sciences. Far from the hasty mechanism of collection that prevailed during the civil war, a scientific system of collection would enable policymakers to implement a fair tax reform.[31]

The corporate merger trend increased such fears. Corruption was disclosed by muckrakers in books such as Frank Norris's *The Octopus* (1901), Lincoln Steffens's *Shame of the Cities* (1904) and Upton Sinclair's *The Jungle* (1906). As progressivism gained political clout, federal regulation became a national priority. In 1904 the Supreme Court ordered the breakup of the Northern Securities Company, the huge railroad combination created by John Pierpont Morgan Sr. The 1907 panic reinforced the desire of citizens to voice concerns about speculation and corporate irresponsibility. In the wake of the initial wave of business collapses, stock market prices plummeted, and depositors made a massive run on the nation's banks. Under these circumstances, tax reform was endorsed by a majority of citizens both at the state and federal levels. It was no surprise that businessmen and lawyers strongly protested proposals to tax both corporate and personal incomes.[32]

Skepticism about the taxation of income faded away in most universities, where battles against legal formalism and laissez-faire policies were won by young scholars to such an extent that in 1910, the dean of the Faculty of Political Science of Columbia, John W. Burgess, seemed to run against the tide. A prestigious scholar, author of books such as *Political Science and Comparative Constitutional Law* (1890) and *The Civil War and the Constitution, 1859–1865* (1901), Burgess perceived a danger in modern American society. Although he barred women from entering Columbia University and he believed that the Spanish War was "disastrous to American political civilization," he also warned Americans not to listen to his colleagues, particularly Edwin R. A. Seligman, who endorsed the idea of taxing incomes in order to protect citizens and to regulate corporations. Burgess feared the impact of such a reallocation of the tax burden in the country. If the income tax became the main vehicle to raise revenue, strong inequalities between sections would reappear and endanger the republic. In other words, would not the tax be levied "upon the northeast" while "the south and the west will be largely exempt?" Burgess feared, as many businessmen did, that the new tax system would weaken the fragile equilibrium between states and the federal government.[33]

In spite of Burgess's warning, such a view of progressive taxation became increasingly popular in the nation as the most effective way to regulate the new corporate power. Tax resisters were soon to bristle at the news of a new corporate income tax that resurfaced in 1909.

On January 29, 1910 the secretary of the Illinois Manufacturers' Association, John Glenn, and Illinois representative James Robert Mann were received at the White House by President Howard Taft. The two men wanted to challenge the new corporate tax law passed a few months earlier in Congress. A salesman, who lauded rugged individualism, Glenn became a combative militant of the small association that he had helped develop. By 1909 its membership had reached 1,100, and most members were afraid of efforts to legislate working hours or to regulate factory conditions. Corporate regulation was a dangerous interference, they believed, with natural economic laws. The new corporate tax was seen as another step in the crusade of progressives who relentlessly attacked corporations. A meeting organized in Chicago two weeks earlier had shown the strong opposition of Chicagoan businessmen to both the corporate tax and the income tax amendment. The president of the Illinois Manufacturers' Association, W. L. Noyes, pointed out the danger of making "these "details" public "for the use and abuse of public curiosity and for competitors' advantage." Glenn himself claimed that public disclosure would jeopardize businesses. To make their grievances heard, Glenn urged industrialists to sign a petition entitled "Repeal of the Corporate Tax Law," and to pay small sums of money for the expenses of the association.[34]

Glenn's campaign capitalized on the momentum caused by tax reform. The progressive movement enabled a new coalition to emerge in Congress, including Democrats and some Republicans who were in favor of reform and were labeled as insurgents. In order to reach an agreement, President Taft pushed Republicans to propose a bill to postpone the income tax in return for a moderate corporate excise tax. In exchange for withdrawing the tax bill, they proposed an income tax amendment that they hoped would be rejected. On August 5, 1909, the Corporation Excise Tax became law. It was described as an "excise on the privilege of doing business" and imposed a tax of 1 percent on net corporate incomes over $5,000. It also included a specific provision that such returns be made public in order to avoid tax evasion. Political cartoonist and editor of *Puck*, Udo J. Keppler, portrayed businessmen's opposition with a well-dressed man labeled "Plutocracy," wearing a top hat, holding a parrot labeled "State Legislature" on his right hand, trying to get it to repeat a phrase after him, "We don't want an Income-Tax Amendment!" and promising it "some nice crackers" in return for correctly learning to repeat the phrase.[35]

Figure 3.1. Udo J. Keppler, "Polly's Chance to Get Some Nice Crackers," *Puck*, August 18, 1909. Courtesy of the Library of Congress.

Protests started during debates in Congress. Senator Nelson W. Aldrich of Rhode Island, a member of the northeastern upper crust and descendant of John Winthrop, became the spokesperson of the business community. Progressive taxation was inept and counterproductive, he explained. Congress "would increase the revenues, instead of reducing them" and the "income tax would be more unnecessary" because they "would have large surplus revenue." The only vindication of the tax, he feared, was "to punish" businessmen. Many industrialists shared his views. In a letter he sent to Aldrich, the owner of American Silk Spinning admitted that he and his peers had to "put ourselves absolutely in your hands, feeling that you will take care of us." The chairman of U.S. Steel Corporation, Elbert H. Gary, hoped that Aldrich could forestall changes to the revenue law. After the disappointing vote, Aldrich encouraged businessmen to petition the government and voice their concerns about the fallout that they expected.[36]

In a series of petitions sent during the winter of 1909–1910, corporate America bitterly opposed the new revenue law on constitutional and antistatist grounds. Most petitions came from northeastern and midwestern states, particularly Illinois and Ohio. All petitioners used the same argument and contended that the federal tax on corporation incomes was "unjust, inequitable, an encroachment upon the rights of the various States, unduly inquisitorial and unnecessary at this time for any purpose." The tax was also characterized as "obnoxious" because of discrimination between corporations and unincorporated businesses that were "exempt." Once again, the issue of stockholders' taxation came under close scrutiny. In February another round of petitions emphasized the danger for shareholders and employees being exposed to the danger of double taxation. Interestingly, the number of employees, the capital invested, and the number of shareholders appeared in the petitions, which were signed by "stockholders" and "employees." Businessmen wanted to warn Americans of the danger caused by such a disincentive to industriousness and work.[37]

Once it became a law, businessmen in particular staged protests against the public disclosure provision. For President Taft and many congressmen, it was seen as a way to protect investors and consumers. Industrialists objected in harsh terms to such a dangerous and intrusive tool of corporate regulation. At that time, many corporations did not publish financial reports, and secrecy of activities was defended by all businessmen, who refrained from divulging business activities. A variety of corporations and trade associations attacked the constitutionality of such a measure, peppering Congress with letters and petitions. In February 1910 corporations in Minneapolis devoted themselves to prove the unconstitutionality of the measure. Small businesses believed that the publication of tax returns would be hazardous since it would divulge trade secrets to competitors. John Don & Co. wrote a petition that assumed that public disclosure would cause a massive loss of competition among American corporations. For tax resisters, it was only the tip of the iceberg, and many of them hoped to renew the victory of 1895 when justices declared federal taxes unconstitutional.[38]

In a couple of months, many legal suits were brought. A few weeks after the law was signed by President Taft, the Title Insurance Company published a pamphlet warning other businesses of constitutional problems. In January, a suit was filed by Fred W. Smith, a stockholder in the Northern Trust Company, to restrain the directors from paying the tax. On March 16 and 17, 1910, a sweeping array of antitax arguments was heard by the Supreme Court. The most prominent lawyers defended corporate interests, and fifteen cases challenged the constitutionality of the tax. Richard V. Lindabury, senior partner in the firm Lindabury, Dupue and Faulks, working for the most important corporations of the time including US Steel, was asked by stockholders of the Coney Island & Brooklyn Railroad Company and the Home Life Insurance Company to demonstrate that the tax was not an "excise tax" upon business or occupation but was a corporate income tax. As a consequence, Lindabury argued that the tax was not constitutional. Charles Howard Williams addressed the court for ten minutes in the case of William F. Fluhrer against the New York Life Insurance Company, while Richard Reid Rogers defended interests of stockholders of the Interborough Rapid Transit Company of New York.[39]

Meanwhile, most corporations seemed to wait for legal decisions before paying the tax. Compliance was discussed in many newspapers, with contradictory percentages quoted. In Chicago it was explained that only 10 percent of local corporations had filed schedules for the new corporation tax. In Buffalo only 300 returns had been received in February out of 5,000 notices sent to corporations. Most lawyers were convinced that it was unlikely that the Supreme Court would hand down a decision before the summer vacation began. They advised big corporations to pay the tax assessments "under protest." The biggest corporations such as US Steel, the American Tobacco Company, and the American Sugar Refining Company announced that they would wait until the last few days of the time allowed by the law to pay the assessments. Some corporations were afraid, however, of becoming tax delinquents. Two weeks before the tax deadline, they began to pay the corporate tax with the proviso that they could reclaim the money in the event the Supreme Court declared the tax unconstitutional. The law firm of Davies, Stone, Auerbach & Cornell reissued a circular in which it reaffirmed its belief that the corporate tax was unconstitutional.[40]

Corporations had to wait longer than they expected as the Supreme Court was unable to decide on the constitutionality of the corporate tax. The fifteen corporate cases filed in March 1910 were consolidated as *Flint v. Stone Tracy Company* and scheduled for argument in January 1911, because the court proved unable to arrive at a decision. The plaintiff was defended by corporate lawyer Maxwell Evarts who resembled his father, the late William Maxwell Evarts, in his hatred of progressive taxation. Born on November 15, 1862, he became one of the best corporate lawyers in the country. His clients were a *Who's Who?* of American corporations including Southern Pacific Railroad Co. and Union Pacific Railroad Co. In January 1911 he defended, in front of the justices, the case of Stella P. Flint. Flint was the general guardian of Samuel N. Stone Jr., a minor and a stockholder in the Stone-Tracy Company of Windsor, Vermont. Stella Flint did not want the corporation to pay the new tax. As his father had many years earlier, Evarts explained that the tax was unconstitutional because it fell upon the corporate franchise of the company. He added that the law interfered with the powers of the state by taxing a franchise. In other words, it was once again "arbitrary and oppressive." As a consequence, it invaded the sovereignty of the state and intruded in the households of ordinary citizens. On March 13, 1911, however, the Supreme Court ruled unanimously that the 1909 corporation tax was constitutional. It reaffirmed that it was not a direct tax but "an excise on the particular privilege of doing business in a corporate capacity" and that the excise was on property measured by the income of the parties subject to the tax.[41]

Although they failed to prove that the law was unconstitutional, businessmen were able to propagate the idea that public disclosure would endanger U.S. corporations. In 1910 Congress repealed the mandatory publicity provision, reverting to the earlier policy of allowing presidential discretion in disclosing tax information. After the court's decision, most businessmen and wealthy individuals were all the more willing to participate in the ratification campaign of the Sixteenth Amendment.[42]

In 1911 Kentucky governor August Everett Wilson took a strong stance against the proposed Sixteenth Amendment. Lamenting the "class legislation" defended by progressives, he instructed readers of the *New York Times* that there was "a fallacy that with a Federal Income tax it will be the Carnegies and Rockfellers and other multimillionaires who will pay for running the government." Instead, Wilson offered an abundance of insight concerning the danger caused by the amendment to democratic values in the nation. He hoped that the ratification campaign would enable Americans to think beyond political lines to the impact of such an amendment on the future of the republic as it was envisioned by the founding fathers at the end of the eighteenth century.[43]

In the first months of the campaign, tax resisters were quite optimistic. In a March 1910 article, the *New York Times* cast serious doubts on the future of the amendment after it was rejected by the Virginia legislature. The newspaper informed its readers that the friends of the measure must now acknowledge that "the tide was turning against them." In Virginia, the speaker of the Virginia House of Delegates, Richard Byrd, revived sectional animosities and considered the tax as part of a northern plot. As a consequence, if Virginians did not react, the conspiracy would take the appearance of "a hand from Washington" that would be stretched out and placed upon a man's business and "the eye of the federal inspector will be in every man's counting house." In other southern states, opponents of the income tax tapped into states' rights arguments to convince citizens. In Louisiana, businessmen defended the interests of the sugar industry, charging that the income tax would destroy the tariff, open the American market to foreign industries, and put thousands of workers out of work. However, in the south, only Virginia voted against the amendment ratification, and Florida did not consider it.[44]

It came as no surprise that tax resisters were particularly active in the Northeast, where prominent bankers and industrialists reviled both class-based legislation and the evils of sectionalism. John G. Milburn, the lead attorney for Standard Oil, helped finance a pamphlet which was distributed in the nation to debunk the fallacy of progressive taxation. Joseph H. Choate, who helped file the *Pollock* case, asked for the support of five attorneys, many of whom had helped him before, to gather arguments. This team of prominent New York

lawyers devoted itself to proving the abuse of power that would follow such an extension of the power of the federal purse. They urged
citizens not to "blind" themselves and to "appreciate the reality of
the danger when we see the total expenditures of the National Government exceeding $1,000,000,000 a year." Should citizens be
abused by "well-informed members of the United States Senate that
at least $300,000,000 is wasted annually in extravagant administra-
tion, and when we hear the clamor for hundreds of millions more to
be spent in irrigation, conservation, National highways, canals?" To
make their case stronger, they added constitutional arguments on
the infringement of federal power on states' rights. As a consequence,
Connecticut and Rhode Island rejected the amendment, and Pennsylvania decided not to even consider it.[45]

Still, most Americans remained unconvinced by antitax arguments. The elections of 1910 and 1912 brought Democrats and reformist Republicans to power in many state legislatures. Elected
president in 1912, Woodrow Wilson advocated progressive taxation of
both individual and corporate incomes, and he won the presidency.
In western states, the amendment was unanimously ratified, with
the sole exception of Utah, where the Mormon Church mobilized
its constituents against the amendment. It came as no surprise that
by February 1913, two-thirds of the states had predictably ratified the
amendment, and in October, the sixty-third Congress instituted a
new tax on individual incomes that was merged with the Corporation Act of 1909. Subdued by the ratification of the Sixteenth Amendment, business leaders and bankers were left only with the power to
lobby Congress in order to limit the impact of the new tax.[46]

By 1914 the National Association of Manufacturers (NAM) had made
the fight against corporate regulation its main priority. Antitrust legislation, campaigns for industrial safety and better working conditions were seen as intolerable. The income tax was viewed as the tip

of the iceberg of a larger movement against businesses. The author of the antisocialist novel, *The Scarlet Empire* (1906), and the former president of NAM, David MacLean Parry, urged manufacturers to demand changes in the name of uniformity of taxation. It was a "vicious" law, he explained during a meeting of the association in Boston, because it created a blatant discrimination between citizens. This feeling of being an oppressed minority of taxpayers ran through many US corporations, which strongly resented both corporate and personal income taxes.[47]

Trust companies and financial organizations made a more concrete protest, which they added to the new 1040 form they had to file. The protest was printed on paper the same size as the tax form so that it could be attached to the filed return. Thirteen unconstitutional elements were listed including the method of collection and the assessment of incomes. The protest explained that the levy of a federal income violated the rights of citizens. The tax was deemed "arbitrary, unequal, not uniform throughout the United States." One of the best experts in the country, however, Joseph Walter Magrath, cast strong doubts on the validity of the protests, and many corporations believed that they would have no impact on Congress.

In order to limit the consequences of the new federal law, business associations sought to revise the mechanics of tax withholding. Members of the Philadelphia Board of Trade declared that collection at the source would be "onerous in their working effect and has entailed a large increase of working force and great expenditures of time." Bankers decried the process of collection and promoted the idea of a "method of information" at the source in lieu of the existing provisions of "collection at the source." In January 1914 the Virginia & Southern Railway, a subsidiary of the Southern Railway, launched the first legal protest against the collection process. Based on estimates made by corporations themselves, the cost would range from a few dollars to $25,000 for the largest banks and corporations in New York City, and hundreds of clerks would be hired to collect the tax.[48]

Figure 3.2. Udo J. Keppler, "Lawyers at Least Have Plenty to Be Thankful For," November 18, 1913. Courtesy of the Library of Congress.

In a cartoon published soon after the adoption of the income tax law, the cartoonist Udo J. Keppler deftly mocked the major role played by lawyers who had plenty of reasons "to be thankful for." Thus, a series of legal arguments were brought by businessmen and stockholders. Two businessmen from Detroit, John F. Dodge and Horace E. Dodge, filed a brief to attack tax on incomes that discriminated unduly in favor of corporations and against individuals and partnerships. With the help of their legal counsel, they explained that the Sixteenth Amendment could only tax "income" and not "personal or real property." As a consequence, they posited, the tax on stockholders was an abuse of federal power.[49]

On May 1914 the first case to test the constitutionality of the federal income tax reached the Supreme Court. A French immigrant, Frank Brushaber, who lived in the borough of Brooklyn, New York, and who claimed to be a citizen of the state of New York but not a U.S. federal citizen, refused to pay taxes for his stock in the Union Pacific Railroad, a corporation chartered in the federal Territory of Utah before it became a state. Mr. Brushaber filed suit in the New York federal district court to prevent the Union Pacific Railroad from paying federal income tax on its profits because he did not want his stock dividends correspondingly reduced as a result of the tax.[50]

The justices disagreed with Brushaber's interpretation and reaffirmed the constitutionality of the tax system. The case raised every point involved in all five income tax cases before the court. Chief Justice White explained that protesters had made a mistake when they argued that the Sixteenth Amendment had empowered the federal government to levy a direct tax without apportionment based on to states' populations. He explained that "the whole purpose of the amendment was to relieve all income taxes from a consideration of the source whence the income was derived." The court also debunked the argument of uniformity. Justice White explained that the uniformity prescribed by the Constitution was only a "geographical uniformity," as Seligman had already put it. With the decision, *Brushaber v. Union Pacific Railroad* (1916), the Supreme Court held that the graduated rate tax structure did not violate the "due process" clause of the Fifth Amendment. In other words, progressive taxation was a mainstay in the United States.[51]

On May 15, 1917, Joseph Hodges Choate died of a heart attack. One of the most prominent lawyers in the nation, he had played a major role over the preceding twenty-five years in the legal battle against the income tax. "Twenty years ago," recalled Oliver Wendell Holmes Jr. to the Harvard Law School Association of New York in February 1913, "a vague terror went over the earth and the word socialism began to be heard. I thought and still think that fear was translated into doctrines that had no proper place in the Constitution." It was terror that had led tax resisters to successfully attack the income tax provision in 1894 in a context of social upheavals and political tensions. In 1895 Congress approved a joint resolution requiring that income tax returns be destroyed following the Supreme Court decision *Pollock v. Farmers' Loan & Trust Company* and *Hyde v. Continental Trust Company* that declared the income tax unconstitutional. The treasury secretary appointed a committee to carry out these congressional orders. All individual tax returns and collectors' lists of income tax paid to the committee on May 5, 1896, were burned. Yet, tax resisters' joy would be short-lived.

Twenty years later, the wealthiest citizens had no choice but to comply with the new progressive taxation. This transformation was the result of the crusade of populists and progressives who advocated for increased government regulation and more progressive taxes. For resisters, this represented a near-total defeat. In 1894 New York Senator David B. Hill had already lamented the betrayal of the ideals of the first Americans with a touch of irony: "The fathers of the Republic so regarded it when they adopted tariff taxation as the best means for securing Federal revenues. They may have been mistaken, and possibly we are wiser than they were." Within the constitutionality debate, however, Hill and his wealthy friends encountered an unexpected outcome: the Sixteenth Amendment was ratified after a long, harsh battle during which tax resisters failed to convince American citizens. The argument for the collapse of the republic and the bankruptcy of corporations failed to persuade a majority of Americans, and by the eve of the First World War, tax resisters had lost their faith in the democratic system and feared that the class-based tax scheme would bring a failure of democracy in its wake.[52]

4

Not for Mothers, Not for Soldiers

The flourishing communities of the United States
do not propose that over-taxation shall endanger
their prosperity.

—Lower Taxes and Better Times (*pamphlet*, 1923)

DURING THE WINTER of 1923, in the cities of North Lima and
Boardman, Ohio, children sang patriotic songs and protested against
new federal expenditures for poor mothers and soldiers coming back
from European battlefields. "Don't pass debts on to us," read one of the
posters made for the occasion. By then, World War I debt amounted
to $22 billion a year, by far the largest single item of federal expendi-
tures. A parade of old wagons—the pioneers' old prairie schooners—
was organized, and many men and women signed petitions opposing the idea of a bonus to veterans. The Reverend L. H. Rohrbaugh
blessed the parade before the first wagon started out. Alvin Victor
Donahey, governor of Ohio, drove wagon number four to Bowling
Green, while members of the local Kiwanis Club coached wagon
number one. This assembly represented the Lower Taxes—Less Legislation League, sponsored by the Ohio State Grange and the Ohio
Farm Bureau Federation. In an area where the Ku Klux Klan was
particularly strong, suspicion of state power was reinforced by fears

of the "mongrelization" of American culture and values. A good many of the lower middle-class people who paraded were no doubt fearful of losing social and economic gains achieved from postwar prosperity, and all agreed with Treasury Secretary Andrew W. Mellon that progressive federal taxes levied during World War I had to be reduced.[1]

To finance the war in Europe, high rates of personal and corporate income taxes had been adopted. Five years after the war ended, Mellon asked citizens to support him in order to convince Congress to limit the expansion of the power of the federal purse. Leaders of the tax resistance movement were mainly elites, old-stock white American men and women who tapped into cultural and social anxieties about the emerging pluralistic and modern society. After some postwar tensions caused by the cost of living and the red scare, the country seemed to be enjoying enormous prosperity, and attacks against progressive taxation resurfaced, fueled by debates about new federal aid for mothers and soldiers. Tax transfer from one category of citizens to another caused the first constitutional challenge to the use of taxpayers' money for a purpose they disliked. Refusing the idea of social solidarity, tax resisters, including many women, boosted their arguments by defending the notion of taxpayer standing, namely, that taxpayers have a legitimate right to contest the allocation of federal taxes. High tax rates and the public disclosure provision defended by progressives and some moderate Republicans embittered opponents. Due to constitutional and political constraints, tax resisters limited themselves to a call to reduce progressive taxes, even though some of them still hoped to repeal them completely.[2]

In 1917 the wealthy financer, Otto Hermann Kahn, asserted the reasons of his strong opposition to the war tax system. To finance war expenditures, new taxes on corporations' profits and personal incomes were levied by the federal government. Such taxes were mocked as "arbitrary" and "unfair" by Kahn, who believed that most businessmen would leave the country and go to Canada to benefit from a better fiscal environment. Like many rich industrialists before him, he recalled the dream of the "framers of our taxation system," who did not intend to tax the richest citizens. Although he took pleasure in giving money to support artists, actors, and musicians, he was more reluctant to pay increased federal taxes. In his crusade against taxes, Kahn was joined by one of his fellow businessman, Pierre du Pont. The president of E. I. du Pont de Nemours and Company became a spokesman for chemical firms, which he believed bore the brunt of the new fiscal system. He wondered why, as part of the war effort, companies manufacturing gun powder and explosives were the only ones to pay a tax on profits. Du Pont used the same words as Otto Kahn had to describe the system: "unjust, inequitable, and discriminatory." However, in spite of a few telegrams emphasizing the large number of people working in the industry, few Americans sided with ammunitions makers and millionaires during World War I, and progressive taxation gained increased political clout.[3]

After Congress declared war on Germany on April 6, 1917, President Woodrow Wilson transformed the country into a Great War machine. The conflict led to unprecedented government economic oversight, and exceptional government financial needs. Commenting upon the Revenue Act of 1917, economist Roy G. Blakey explained that it "was necessary to pay, in a single year, the total of our national debt at the end of the Civil War." Wilson mobilized the nation's resources by establishing a Council of National Defense for the purpose of coordinating several specialized agencies such as the War Industries Board, the War Labor Board, and the Fuel Administration. In all, nearly five thousand government entities supervised home-front activities. To finance war expenses, government spending rose from 3 percent of the gross national product in 1913 to 21 percent in 1917. Wilson and his treasury secretary, William G. McAdoo, pushed for the sale of government war loans, which helped cement national unity. In a few weeks, Americans of all ethnic backgrounds overwhelmingly supported the war effort, sometimes competing with each other to prove their patriotism.[4]

Another means of financing the war was to levy new federal taxes, including taxes on corporate profits. Many progressives feared the extraordinary increase in profits among big corporations. Claude Kitchin, a southern populist and the impassioned chairman of the Committee on Ways and Means, advocated for a broader excess-profit tax on corporations that was far more progressive than the policy of selling liberty bonds, which, he lamented, shifted the financial burden of the war to future generations. In *The New Republic*, prominent Harvard economist Oliver W. Sprague promoted what he called a "conscription of income" to prevent corporations from benefiting from the conscription of men for the European war. Even though some of Wilson's friends in the business community were outraged by such an intrusion of the federal government into the daily management of corporations and investments, the president wanted to make certain that the war's main goal was the promotion of democracy in the world and not the promotion of capital. For the first time since the war in Cuba, an inheritance tax was passed, and the maximum individual income tax rate rose from 7 to 77 percent between 1913 and 1918. The corporate tax rate increased from 1 to 12 percent. Congress also decided to levy a tax on "excess" profits. In 1916 this tax was levied on the munitions industry only; after the United States declared war in April 1917, it was applied to all corporations. After passionate discussions to define rates, Congress targeted all normal profits "over a reasonable return on invested capital," and not merely those attributable to the war. Eight percent was established as the rate of return, and all profits above that level were taxed at graduated rates.[5]

Even if they supported the war effort, many businessmen complained about the impact of such a tax policy on their investment and innovation capacity. Associations such as the National Industrial Conference Board fought against tax proposals and campaigned fiercely to keep tax rates as low as possible. One of the leaders of the Board, James A. Emery, exposed the gravity of the situation and claimed that "those in control of the instrumentalization of government are more interested in chastening than in assisting business." While it urged the federal government to prosecute the war "until Prussianism is utterly destroyed," the U.S. Chamber of Commerce adopted a platform plank including propositions to amend the tax laws. The National Association of Manufacturers (NAM), moreover, believed that federal control and regulation would impair production. As the government pushed for a conservation movement to reduce demand, the National Industrial Conservation Movement, financed by NAM, published a series of posters denouncing both inflationary trends and government intrusion. Citizens were asked to "keep prices down by chasing the flies way from industry," and "unjust taxation" was one of the annoying flies.[6]

Businessmen's fears worsened after Wilson's January 1918 Fourteen Points that detailed his view of the postwar order. On May 27, 1918, the president declared in a very famous address to Congress that "politics" were "adjourned." He also reaffirmed the need for moral fiscal sacrifice and recommended the reinforcement of the excess-profit tax to prevent any forms of profiteering. During hearings of the Committee on Ways and Means, James A. Emery testified in favor of replacing the "obnoxious tax" as soon as possible. Presaging the postwar red scare, the *Journal of Commerce* criticized the "strong flavor of socialism" of Wilson's tax policy because of its "apparent disposition to strike at wealth." The Revenue Act of 1918 granted only some exemptions but remained attached to the philosophy of sacrifice. Soon after his return from the Paris Peace Conference, on May 20, 1919, President Wilson publicly explained that he took it for granted that "the income tax, the excess-profits tax, and the estate tax" would be the "mainstays" of the tax system. In other words, progressivity would be maintained in peacetime.[7]

Once the war was officially over, business leaders vociferously criticized the whole tax system and particularly targeted the excess

DON'T BLAME IT ALL ON THE WAR!

AS A CONSUMER, has it ever occurred to <u>YOU</u> there is a close relationship between your pocketbook (household expenses) and industrial conditions?

<u>YOU</u> complain of high prices but have <u>YOU</u> ever done anything to discourage such price-boosting factors as burdensome laws which impose unnecessary taxes on legitimate American industry and constant waste promoted by destructive agitators?

HELP TO KEEP PRICES DOWN BY CHASING THE FLIES AWAY FROM INDUSTRY

Figure 4.1. "Don't Blame It All on the War!" 1917, pamphlet of the National Industrial Conservation Movement. Courtesy of the Library of Congress.

profit tax. The Investment Bankers Association of America complained that it could no longer be justified in peacetime. A flood of petitions and letters was sent to Congress to protest against the federal war levy. However, as many businessmen soon realized, the very reason that the war tax system was not replaced was the public debt. In 1918 the cost of war represented 58 percent of gross domestic product. General government spending rose from $1 billion in 1916 to $18.5 billion in 1919. As a result, the national debt exploded and reached a peak of $26 billion in 1919. Of these obligations, $7.5 billion were short-term loans due for payment in May 1923. Moreover, the ratification, on January 16, 1919, of the Eighteenth Amendment prohibiting the sale of alcohol caused an important loss of revenue.[8]

In spite of such indebtedness, resisters found reasons to be satisfied with the election of Warren Harding as president in November
1920 and the appointment of Pittsburgh financer Andrew Mellon as
treasury secretary. By then, Mellon was one of the richest men in the
nation, paying more taxes each year than all Americans aside from
John D. Rockefeller Jr., Henry Ford, and Edsel Bryant Ford. As soon
as he became secretary of the Treasury, he sought to revise the general philosophy of the tax system and promoted a scientific approach to public finance. It was wise, he explained to Congress, to
have "diagnosis and cure" rather than "autopsy and verdict." Tax reductions, Mellon argued, were necessary to stimulate economic expansion and restore prosperity. In 1921 he was especially concerned
with the high surtax rates that pushed rich people to drive capital out
of productive enterprise into tax-exempt securities. His plan was to
reduce the top surtax rate from 65 percent to 32 percent and to repeal the excess profits tax. All these measures had the same priority,
which Mellon made very clear in a statement reflecting a popular
attitude in the 1920s that "the government is a business concern and
its revenue can and should be raised in accordance with business
principles."[9]

The business community, however, was divided about tax reform.
Some businessmen promoted a sales tax system to replace all internal taxes, especially the despised excess profits tax, and to pay the
war debt. New Hampshire Republican senator George H. Moses preferred regressive taxation to progressive taxes. The sales tax would
"strike down the vicious principle of graduated taxation" that was
nothing but "a modern legislative adaptation of the Communistic
doctrine of Karl Marx." Members of the Rotary Club in Baltimore
asserted that this turnover tax would be "simple and automatic for
both the Government and the taxpayer." The Chamber of Commerce
of Beloit, Wisconsin claimed it would also avoid tax evasion through
the investment of capital in tax-exempt securities. Yet, other business
organizations such as the Business Men's National Tax Committee,

the U.S. Chamber of Commerce, and the New York Board of Trade opposed the tax, fearing that it would hamper the slow economic recovery.[10]

During debates in Congress, strong opposition of Republicans, led by Wisconsin senator Robert M. La Follette Sr., dashed Mellon's hopes. These insurgent Republicans refused to vote for the repeal of the excess profits tax and wanted to keep the progressive structure of the tax system. They particularly opposed the transfer of greater burdens upon the masses through sales and other excise taxes. Still, Claude Kitchin denounced the fallacy of Mellon's ideas. After long, passionate debates, the new revenue law passed before Thanksgiving on November 23, 1921, repealing the excess-profits tax and slightly reducing the maximum surtax upon individual increases. Mellon and his supporters, however, were not able to significantly lower the surtax rate structure, which remained high at 58 percent in 1921. Under such circumstances, conservative women from Massachusetts decided to attack the constitutionality of progressive redistribution by focusing on public expenditures for poor women and immigrants.[11]

On June 7, 1916, a beautiful sunny day in Boston, Harriet P. Weeks married Randolph Frothingham. In the Frothingham family, politics was a family business. Louis Frothingham, Randolph's brother, had been elected to Congress after World War I, and his wife, Mary, became president of the Massachusetts Association Opposed to the Further Extension of Suffrage to Women. In Mary and Louis's stately home, "Wayside," Harriet met other conservative women and discussed the modernization of the country and the expansion of the federal government. After the emancipation of women in 1920 and postwar social tensions, antistatism and anticommunism became their two main fears. In the reactionary political climate of the decade, Harriet Frothingham founded, with other women, a new organization, the Women's Patriot Corporation, which led a crusade against both women's social ambitions and Washington bureaucrats. Financed by businessmen from New England, women cooperated with other conservative organizations, such as the American Constitutional League, the Massachusetts Public Interests League, the Sentinels of the Republic, and the Women's Constitutional League of Maryland. For Harriet Frothingham, resistance against federal taxes was the best way to limit ever-increasing federal power.[12]

One of their main targets was the Maternity and Infancy Care Act, commonly known as the Sheppard-Towner Act, which provided federal matching funds for health clinics to hire physicians and nurses to educate and care for pregnant women, and mothers and their children. Conservative women deplored the use of their money for this purpose and believed that social policy was not part of the "general welfare" clause included in the Constitution and for which Congress could spend taxpayers' money. Instead, they argued that welfare programs destroyed the traditional values of American democracy based upon the work ethic and a family-centered male breadwinner. Mary Kilbreth, president of the Women's Patriot Corporation, wrote to President Warren Harding to express her concerns about his signing the bill, which was drafted by "childless women politicians," implying that feminists who were not mothers were not capable of coping with maternity issues. Missouri senator James A. Reed used a similar argument during debates when he sarcastically proposed an amendment entitled "A Bill to Authorize a Board of Spinsters to Control Maternity and Teach the Mothers of the United States to Rear Babies." Other conservative organizations supported such a crusade. Louis A. Coolidge, founder of the conservative group Sentinels of the Republic, viewed the bill as a threat to the future of American families. The Sentinels had just been created by members of the Massachusetts' elites to defend states' rights against the infringement of the federal government. According to Coolidge, if Americans did not reverse the past twenty years of "disintegrating tendencies in legislation," it would mean the end of "our form of government" within twenty-five years.[13]

After the bill was passed in April 1921, Congress had the right to appropriate $480,000 for the current fiscal year and $240,000 annually for the subsequent five years to be equally shared among the states. Massachusetts' militants spawned most of the organized effort against the provision of funds for poor mothers. Conservatives, men and women alike, decided to challenge the act's constitutionality on the grounds that revenues legally raised under the taxing power were being used against their will to fund poor people. Such arguments were particularly prevalent in the three states that opposed the bill: Connecticut, Illinois, and Massachusetts. The *Chicago Tribune* contended that the Sheppard-Towner Act promoted the evils of "the centralization of government, the development of bureaucracy, and the weakening influence of paternalism." Another editorial claimed that it was "a trick" to "deceive taxpayers who thought they were receiving a gift from the federal government but who would in reality just pay for it through their taxes."[14]

Fearing that a state was ineligible to file a taxpayer's suit, Harriet Frothingham filed one of her own. When the legislature began considering an enabling act for Sheppard-Towner in 1922, the attorney general—an antisuffragist who had ruled women off the ballot and out of the jury box in Massachusetts—issued an opinion that it would misuse the tax money of Massachusetts. Furthermore, it was unconstitutional because it violated the rights of the states. The state filed suit with the Supreme Court on behalf of its taxpayers to enjoin the law. Once the court dismissed the case and the United States Court of Appeals concurred, Harriet Frothingham appealed to U.S. Solicitor General James Montgomery Beck. Well known among conservatives and strongly attached to a strict reading of the Constitution, the lawyer had just denounced the "new paganism" of the modern times in a speech delivered to the conservative American Bar association. Beck encouraged Massachusetts conservatives to pursue the case even though he cast doubts on its validity. As a member of the administration, Beck knew that these suits seriously threatened the tax collection process and debt payment.[15]

On June 5, 1923, the Supreme Court dismissed the case. Written by Justice Alexander George Sutherland, the *Frothingham v. Mellon* decision allowed the Children's Bureau to use taxpayers' money and to let the states spend matching funds in the fledgling field of social policy. First and foremost, Sutherland dismissed the concept of taxpayers' standing, which had been used by Frothingham and patriotic women. He contended that taxpayers' rights were no different from citizens' rights. Although they could present generalized grievances against the government, they could not identify the specific harm to the plaintiff. As a consequence, Congress not only had the right to tax U.S. citizens, but taxpayers had no specific right to oversee the use of their money. Importantly, Justice Sutherland took the time to define the nature of federal citizenship. "Interest in the moneys of the Treasury," he explained, was "shared with millions of others," and "comparatively minute and indeterminable, and the effect upon future taxation, of any payment out of funds, so remote, fluctuating and uncertain, that no basis was afforded for an appeal to the preventive powers of a court of equity." In other words, even though she disliked the allocation of federal money, Frothingham could not suspend a specific program because some citizens refused to pay for it. Coming from a conservative judge, these words were quite disappointing for Massachusetts' tax resisters as they reaffirmed the constitutionality of progressive taxation.[16]

Because of such constitutional constraints, tax resisters turned to lobbying techniques that spread during the decade to put pressure on Congress. At the request of Treasury Secretary Andrew W. Mellon, they launched a fierce campaign against the bonus claimed by World War I veterans. After needy mothers, soldiers came to symbolize the extravagant expenditures brought by new taxes.[17]

On Christmas Eve of 1923, employees of Mutual Life Insurance Company in New York wrote to their senator, James Wolcott Wadsworth, to complain about soldiers and the American Legion who were urging congressmen to grant them a bonus. They linked their opposition to the more general plan of tax reduction envisioned by Andrew W. Mellon. To convince Americans of the necessity of lowering tax rates, Mellon decided not to focus on constitutional arguments but to propose a simple choice: would you favor tax reduction or government spending? In the letter he sent to the chairman of the Committee on Ways and Means, William Raymond Green, shortly before Armistice Day on November 10, 1923, he laid out a program for tax reduction, showing just how much it would save, in dollars and cents, each of 14,000,000 taxpayers. To convince the largest number of citizens, he added a 25 percent reduction in income tax on earned income and also promised to repeal excise taxes on telephone and telegraph messages and theater admissions. In the context of the red scare and nativist anxiety, Mellon made it clear that "taxation should not be used as a field for socialistic experiment."[18]

The treasury secretary knew that the business community was strongly opposed to the bonus for World War I veterans and the campaign led by the powerful American Legion. The Legion had released many documents and statistics charting the profits made by corporations during the war. As early as 1922, NAM, the National Grange, the American Farm Bureau, and the American Automobile Association opposed the granting of a bonus. NAM president John Emmett Edgerton explained that industrialists were not opposed to "the most generous and liberal care for all those who were disabled, or the dependents of those who were killed or suffered casualties in the war," but he refused to grant soldiers a bonus. In a similar vein, President Warren Harding rejected the proposed 1922 plan, contending that it offered too "niggardly" a gift. Treasury Secretary Mellon surmised that the country could not afford both a bonus and a tax cut. In the fall of 1923 he decided to make tax cuts his main legislative priority. Rapidly, Mellon gained more applause in business circles than actor John Barrymore in his Broadway success of Hamlet, to use *Time*'s own words. In a few weeks there was a rare unanimity

Figure 4.2. New York Republicans (Martin Saxe, Robert W. Bonynge, John A. Dutton, Allen D. Kenyon, Arthur D. Kuhn, Richard W. Lawrence, Herbert Raymond Smith, Mr. Lyons, and Edward Francis Colladay) pledge support to Andrew W. Mellon (center) on December 19, 1923. Courtesy of the Library of Congress.

in the business community, and in New York City all Republicans stood behind Andrew W. Mellon.[19]

With the help of chambers of commerce, boards of trade, men's credit associations, and other business associations, Mellon urged Americans to support his innovative plan in order to convince Congress. Copies of his letter to Chairman Green were sent to businessmen and Republicans across the country. The U.S. Chamber of Commerce urged its branches and its large network of citizens (750,000 organizations and 300,000 individuals) to favor the proposal. From December 1923 to the end of January 1924 Congress received more than 5,000 petitions and letters. The petitions were also sponsored by local chapters of service clubs such as the Rotary, Kiwanis, and Lions clubs. Most were preprinted and circulated throughout the country, urging Congress "to take a persistent and aggressive stand for lower Federal taxes and to support a tax reduction plan." Citizens also wrote letters explaining their support for Andrew Mellon's policy. Stanley Flint, living in Chicago, rejected a bonus in the name of sound economics and asserted that he was "against the much talked of bonus to the ex-soldiers, especially as it means taxes, and taxes do not help the prosperity of this country."[20]

First and foremost, petitioners explained that tax reduction would be a blessing for the American economy and society. On December 19, 1923, during a council luncheon, Lewis E. Pierson, president of the Merchants' Association of New York, delivered a long speech that associated increased "taxation" with "increased government." L. T. Canfield, a resident of Chicago, perceived a fundamental danger in the expansion of government during wartime, and fiercely campaigned to make "commercial enterprise securities" more attractive than "tax exempt bonds." It would be clever, he added, to impose regressive taxes and repeal Prohibition laws to enforce "a $6 per gallon" tax. Accentuating the benefit of the proposed plan, Stewart Browne, president of the United Real Estate Owners Association, went so far as to contend that American workers would take advantage of tax reduction and their earning power would strongly increase.[21]

The campaign took on a life of its own. In January 1924, the conservative *Literary Digest* published a straw poll claiming that 69 percent of the two million people who responded to the poll were in favor of the Mellon plan. In a radio broadcast on January 6, Senator Joseph Robinson, a Democrat from Arkansas, contended that in spite of the "propagandist influences" of the Mellon plan, an overwhelming "public sentiment" was behind the movement for tax reduction. Some specific industries took the lead to propel antitax arguments forward. The American Paper and Pulp Association even organized a referendum in four hundred paper and pulp mills around the country and asserted that "95% responded favorably to the Mellon plan." Known for their adamant refusal to pay federal taxes in highly competitive national and international markets, the lumber and chemical industries assumed the same mantle of principles as rich businessmen and bankers from the Northeast and contended that taxes should be reduced to preserve prosperity.[22]

Petitioners strongly challenged the idea of social solidarity that was being promoted by veterans. John Levy, owner of John Levy Galleries, together with forty "voters," sent a letter to Brooklyn congressman Emanuel Celler to protest against the bonus, pointing out that two of his employees "who were there and in it" did not "fight for pay and would be degraded in accepting it." A payment of compensation ran against petitioners' views of the work ethic and men's duty in a time of war. The president of the Peele Company, a New York company that built fire doors and safety appliances, refused to give money to "able-bodied men." Conservative organizations pushed some veterans to oppose the bonus. Twenty-two veterans from Ohio petitioned to explain why they were in favor of the tax-reduction plan and refused to be paid for serving in the army. An organization called the Ex-Servicemen's Anti-Bonus League, founded in 1922, was very active in sending antibonus letters written by veterans to the national press. Major John F. Ryan became leader of a National Citizens' Committee in Support of the Mellon Tax Reduction Proposals. Between April 6 and 14, the American Bankers' League proposed a "National Tax Reduction Week," and many veterans were asked to explain why they refused the bonus for themselves.[23]

Such petitioning gave rise to fierce political debates. Petitioners were accused of being puppets in Mellon's hands as petitions were too "stereotyped" to be spontaneous. Congressman John Nance Garner characterized the letters as the result of a "huge organized conspiracy" on the part of "the predatory interests constituting special privilege." The American Legion accused some employers of forcing veterans to sign them. Many people attacked Andrew Mellon himself, claiming his fortune made him incapable of understanding the dire straits of veterans. During the dinner speech to the Silk Association of America at the Hotel Astor in Manhattan, New York, Senator Royal S. Copeland changed the terms of the debate by contrasting "the bonus for the soldier" with "the bonus for the rich." For him, there was no doubt that poor soldiers should come first and deserved compensation from the federal government. Still very critical of the wealthiest citizens in the country, William Jennings Bryan described Mellon as the "foremost reactionary in the United States" and a "party dictator." The American Legion, however, insisted that the country could have both the bonus and tax reduction. Yet, Mellon still believed that the bonus would jeopardize the American economy and the debt payment. Many times, he deliberately overestimated the cost of the bonus and even provoked the public protest of Committee on Ways and Means Chairman William Green. To convince citizens, Mellon published a volume of his articles and writings, entitled *Taxation: The People's Business*, to disseminate his scientific approach to tax reduction.[24]

After long negotiations, Congress adopted both the bonus, with payments in the form of bond certificates to be paid in 1945, and the tax cuts, which were less significant than Mellon and his supporters had expected. Facing a growing hostility of insurgent Republicans, President Calvin Coolidge and Mellon were forced to negotiate. On June 2, Coolidge signed the tax bill, even though he was disappointed by the long six months of negotiations and the inadequate tax reductions. For tax resisters, the Revenue Act was a modest achievement, keeping taxes on the rich relatively high while cutting tax rates for upper-middle-class taxpayers. A public disclosure amendment was added in another rebuff to the treasury secretary to fight against "favoritism, arbitrary action, fraud, and collusion." Mellon publicly expressed his disappointment with the "unsatisfactory, uneconomic, and impracticable" Revenue Act. Many businessmen and bankers,

especially in southern and midwestern states, agreed with him, and
started a campaign in favor of a "bold" Mellon plan.[25]

In January 1925, while lobbyist James Arnold was in Richmond, Virginia, he was surprised by the political apathy of local businessmen
and bankers. Persuaded that Mellon had done the best he could to
reduce taxes, they refused to attack the remaining elements of progressivity in the tax system, fearing that it was "unnecessary and might
confuse the situation." With his new organization, the American Taxpayers League, Arnold sought to change their minds and create a
powerful movement in favor of lowering progressive war taxes. Arnold
was born in Illinois in 1869 and began his career as a white-collar
worker, serving as a clerk and a stenographer for railroads throughout
the Midwest. As president of the Texas Business Men's Association,
he opposed progressive taxation at both local and national levels. Arnold's secretary was Ida Darden, a passionate conservative militant,
who protested against women suffrage and prohibition. Darden's
brother, Vance Muse, joined the conservative team, and together
they engaged in a crusade against the federal tax system by promoting the "Mellon plan."[26]

Arnold's followers, mainly located in the rural South and Midwest, were small bankers and businessmen. W. L. Thompson, president of the First National Bank in Portland, Oregon, became president of the new organization, while Arnold served as manager, using
his old connections with bankers, farmers, and businessmen in southern states to further his program. The first tax clubs appeared in the
winter and spring of 1925 in southern states, notably Texas, Virginia,
Alabama, Georgia, and Arkansas. Later on, tax clubs increased in
Iowa—over 1,000 according to some reports.[27]

The election of President Coolidge gave tax resisters a boost. In
his presidential address on March 4, 1925, broadcast for the first time
ever on the radio, Calvin Coolidge urged Americans to accept the
massive reduction of all internal taxes because "both directly and

indirectly" they "injuriously" affected the people. As a consequence, "the collection of any taxes which are not absolutely required, which does not beyond reasonable doubt contributed to the public welfare, is only a species of legalized larceny." He concluded by contending that "under this republic the rewards of industry belong to those who earn them." Coolidge's strong words particularly resonated in the ears of southern businessmen. Many of them complained about the existence of tax-exempt debt as the first grievance that had led them to favor income tax cuts. Businessmen from Houston made it very clear when they complained that "surtax and inheritance tax rates in the higher brackets" were diverting capital "into tax exempt securities and discouraging business activities." Their vision was that tax cuts would ensure prosperity and innovation.[28]

In Iowa, tax clubs run by R. A. Crawford, who lived in Des Moines, Iowa, attacked the very foundation of progressive taxation by hammering on both the income tax and the inheritance tax. In the Hawkeye State, tax resisters hoped to put pressure on William R. Green, chairman of the Committee on Ways and Means and elected in the Ninth Congressional District of Iowa. A fiscal moderate, Green refused to support the first version of the Mellon plan. On September 2, 1925, Crawford organized a meeting in Des Moines. With the help of James Arnold and even the Treasury, the event was heavily publicized and speeches were broadcast on the radio. The American Taxpayers League regretted Mellon's compromise and denounced the tax measure of 1924 as "a partisan measure and disastrous to the taxpayers." Most businessmen still felt that the tax policy was discriminatory. A spokesman for the Iowa clubs deplored the high tax rates and expressed his belief that only the Mellon plan would "invite men who have converted their capital into bonds and gone to California or Florida and are now pitching horseshoes and playing golf, to reconvert those bonds into money and get back into business."[29]

Some southern Democrats joined the crusade at the request of Arnold himself. In March 1925, before the Bankers Club of Richmond,

Senator Carter Glass declared that he "was for out-Melloning Mellon." Four months later, in front of the South Carolina Bankers Association, Glass further contended that the Mellon plan "was the same thing that had been recommended under two democratic secretaries of the Treasury." In Alabama, Senator Oscar W. Underwood, who signed the first income tax bill and was a tax moderate, addressed the Alabama Tax Clubs at Montgomery and in front of four hundred bankers and businessmen urged Congress to "go back to the tax of 1916, where the highest bracket of the surtax was 13%." A strong advocate of states' rights, the senator decried the rising intrusion of the federal government in the daily life of citizens and was particularly concerned with the impact of the war on federal power.[30]

In November 1925 numerous representatives of tax clubs were heard by the Committee on Ways and Means. Among the most interesting witnesses were three tax club delegations from Texas, Iowa, and Georgia. The Iowa delegation came in two special cars, and included the lieutenant governor and several state senators. Arnold paid for all expenses in the hope that the high number of tax activists could influence Congress's decision. They advised the committee to cut surtaxes and derided the inheritance tax for "picking the pockets of the dead." W. R. Orchard, the editor of the *Council Bluffs*, testified that tax clubs were the custodians of working men's interests. He strongly believed that the treasury secretary was right, and that tax benefits for rich men would cascade into the pocketbooks of all citizens.[31]

Tapping into local protests and intense lobbying by bankers and small businessmen, Andrew Mellon was able to pass a "bolder" version of his plan. Both the victory of Republicans and the death of Senator Robert "Fighting Bob" La Follette Sr. on June 18, 1925, facilitated negotiations in Congress. Mellon was very proud of the result. With the new exemption from taxes of every householder's first

Figure 4.3. Kennedy Berryman, "Will the Brakes Hold?" *Washington Star* (1925). Courtesy of the Library of Congress.

$4,000 of income, most Americans, he explained, would not pay taxes anymore. As a matter of fact, the number of taxpayers (2,400,000) was the lowest since 1916. The $400 million surplus was used to reduce domestic debt. Importantly, the public disclosure of income tax returns was also abrogated. With the help of businessmen and bankers, Calvin Coolidge and Andrew W. Mellon put the country on the road to tax reduction, and denunciations of the self-serving maneuvers of a rich man who wanted to make all millionaires even richer faded away even among Democrats. The famous cartoonist of the *Washington Star*, Clifford K. Berryman, perfectly summarized the forces that drove Coolidge and Mellon. In their automobile—and the car was one of the most important status symbols of the period—both enjoyed the freedom to drive farther across a tax-reduced country. The U.S. Chamber of Commerce and the Republicans cheered them on their way.

Some tax resisters hoped to drive the car farther to repeal all remaining postwar taxes, and they targeted the inheritance tax as the symbol of tax progressivity.[32]

In 1926 one editorial writer for the *Saturday Evening Post*, Albert W. Atwood, published *The Mind of the Millionaire*, exposing the daily life of the nation's superrich. Atwood was less critical than turn-of-the-century muckrakers, even though he recognized that Americans were uncomfortable with millionaires and their colossal fortunes. Popular debates on the estate of the infamous industrialist Henry Clay Frick, who passed away in December 1919, had reinvigorated the issue of inheritance and wealth. Although many people contended that wealth jeopardized social mobility in the country, most tax resisters, including Atwood, considered the inheritance tax to be particularly "unfair" as there was no longer any reciprocity for the taxpayer whose money was given to the federal government. Protests also stemmed from states' rights advocates as many business organizations contended that only the states had the right to tax "the pockets of the dead."[33]

In his book, *Taxation: The People's Business* (1924), Mellon made it clear that he disliked the inheritance tax. Evoking the founding fathers to make his claim more legitimate, he contended that "our forefathers wisely abolished primogeniture" in order to prevent the perpetuation of large estates. As a consequence, there was no need to regulate inheritance in the republic. In the *Wall Street Journal* he offered an abundance of insights that equated such a tax with "the methods of the revolutionists in Russia," and added in the *New York Times* that it was nothing but "an economic suicide." The U.S. Chamber of Commerce, the American Bankers Association, the National Industrial Conference Board, and NAM took the lead in lobbying members of Congress in support of tax repeal. In a statement made when he vetoed the Revenue Act of 1924, President Coolidge explained that it was advisable to call a conference of all taxing authorities on the matter in order to ask the best experts to decide. Coolidge referred notably to the conclusions of the National Tax Association that proposed a repeal of the tax during economic growth.[34]

Momentum against the tax escalated in the next few months. Members of the New York Chamber of Commerce attacked it as "a form of socialism." On June 21, 1925, a referendum by the U.S. Chamber of Commerce exposed it as a danger to the economy. In fact, 2,103 members believed that it was unnecessary, and only 106 contended that it was a useful way to collect federal revenue. A report written by its Finance Advisory Committee asserted that to preserve prosperity, the tax "should be abolished." Defending states' rights, thirty-two governors, among them all the southern governors, fiercely campaigned to lower the inheritance tax rates. One of the most famous opponents of the federal government, Governor Albert Cabell Ritchie of Maryland took the lead in the matter and denounced the tax as nothing less than "the robbery of the States." In 1926 Mellon was able to obtain a reduction of the maximum marginal estate tax rate to 20 percent and doubled the estate tax exemption from $50,000 to $100,000.[35]

However, many businessmen contended that it was only a modest achievement, and refused to put an end to their mobilization. Many tax clubs joined the National Council of State Legislatures, recently organized by the American Taxpayers League. Although James Arnold did not pretend to any official connection with the new council, he used his old associates, many of whom testified for the tax clubs in 1925, to found and run the council. A member of the Texas clubs movement, businessman and politician living in the Panhandle, Robert Lee Satterwhite, claimed authority from the Texas legislature to call for a conference in Washington, D.C., to express grievances against the tax. In June 1927 twenty-two states had passed resolutions in both houses asking Congress to repeal the tax. The movement slowly enlarged its constituency. In September 1927, under the leadership of Lewis E.

Pierson, the U.S. Chamber of Commerce launched another campaign and was joined by the American Bankers Association, which contended that such a tax should be limited to "emergencies."[36]

Using money given by some of the nation's leading corporations, such as Westinghouse, Armour, Insull, Kellogg, and the Aluminum Company of America, the American Taxpayers League relentlessly attacked the tax, which was presented in many pamphlets as "the seed and the fruition of socialism." It became the symbol of progressive taxation, and its graduated rates were accused in Coolidgean language of approving "discrimination," to distribute "rewards and penalties," and to visit "exemptions and confiscations upon property and people." As the country was enormously prosperous, the Leaguers stormed the tax for discriminating against the businessmen who had contributed to the welfare of the nation.[37]

However, the repeal of the federal estate tax was defeated in the House by a vote of 191 to 55. According to the League, the largest single influence that contributed to its defeat was a statement made by the chairman of the Committee on Ways and Means, Green, that President Coolidge was against the repeal. Facing the intense lobbying of the American Taxpayers League, Green warned his citizens against the most extraordinary, highly "financed propaganda" that this country had ever known. The conservative press accused Green of misleading the American people with his hostile attitude to what he considered "sinister interests" defended by "an association of rich people." In the end, it was the League's bad reputation and its secret lobbying that brought about its final defeat. The Council of State Legislatures was often accused of being a "paid lobbyist" that, according to the *Arkansas Democrat*, made "hysterical screams." Other newspapers, even the *Council Bluffs*, criticized the level of "high hating" in Washington. Strongly opposed to the repeal, Green decided to retire and was appointed to the prestigious U.S. Court of Claims by President Calvin Coolidge.[38]

Although the business community had failed to repeal the estate tax, it was able to pursue the tax reduction movement in favor of corporations. The U.S. Chamber of Commerce called for another $400 million in tax cuts. The surplus for the fiscal year—$636 million—even pushed Democrats to endorse a cause they had previously derided. The Revenue Act of 1928 increased tax reductions and tax exemptions for corporations so that even Treasury Secretary Mellon became increasingly worried about the budget. For him, following the scientific form of tax resistance he had helped implement, no more tax cuts were possible without jeopardizing the federal budget and the debt payment. More importantly, the Great Depression would put an end to the persistent campaigning by tax resisters.[39]

On December 7, 1929, famous Broadway and radio star Ed Wynn was one of the many Americans concerned with the economic crisis. He was particularly depressed by the payment of federal taxes and explained that he felt "like a piece of carpet" and was "so kept down by taxes." While President Herbert Hoover contended that the economy was sound and prosperous, Wynn believed that heavy federal taxes had caused the Great Depression. On a cold December day, he paraded on Pennsylvania Avenue with actress Mae Murray, opera singer Anna Fitzhugh, and former mayor of New York John Francis Hylan. After the parade, they participated in a public meeting organized on the steps of U.S. Capitol and sponsored by the conservative Hearst Press. On the fringe of the crowd stood a truck bearing the slogan, "Taxes and Surtaxes Can and Should Be Substantially Reduced." In front of the crowd, two men, Reed Owen Smoot and Willis Chatman Hawley, contended that it was necessary to reduce all internal taxes levied by the federal government. A Republican senator from Utah, Smoot had always believed that such taxes were "absurd" and "grotesque." Hawley, the powerful chairman of the Senate Finance Committee, shared his views. In front of them, boxes containing petitions signed by citizens were displayed and used to demonstrate the strong support of mainstream America in favor of tax cuts. Most Americans, argued Smoot and Hawley,

Figure 4.4. On December 7, 1929, a meeting in favor of tax reduction on
the steps of the U.S. Capitol with from left to right: Mae Murray, movie
star; Isaac Gans, Washington business leader; Senator Reed Smoot,
chairman of Senate Finance Committee; Representative Willis
C. Hawley, chairman of House Finance Committee; and Representative
Sol Bloom of New York. Courtesy of the National Archives.

were opposed to the progressive tax system carried out by the federal
government since the adoption of the Sixteenth Amendment in 1913.
Under such difficult circumstances, they argued, it would have been
a mistake to raise more revenue for poor mothers and unemployed
veterans.[40]

On October 24, 1929, stock market prices suddenly plunged, and
stunned crowds gathered outside the frantic New York Stock Exchange. Five days later, prices plummeted again, and President

Hoover assured Americans that "the crisis will be over in sixty days." One month later, businessmen endorsed further tax reductions in order to put an end to the crisis, and both Hoover and Mellon agreed with them. Moreover, they advocated for the protection of the national markets. In April 1930 the Tariff Act, sponsored by Hawley and Smoot, became law. Because of the intense lobbying of industrial and agricultural interests, Franklin Delano Roosevelt dubbed it the "Grundy tariff," after Joseph Ridgway Grundy, a Republican senator from Pennsylvania and president of the Pennsylvania Manufacturers' Association, who had promised that anyone who made campaign contributions was entitled to higher tariffs in return. Even if it was strongly opposed by the major economists and tax experts of the time, tariff protection was defended as both a revenue policy and a barrier against the economic crisis. Contrary to what the president expected, Hoover's policies helped unleash a devastating worldwide depression. From 1929 to 1932, farm prices fell by nearly 60 percent, and the gross national product dropped from $104 billion to $59 billion. Unemployment stood at 25 percent in 1932 with more than 12 million workers out of work.[41]

As the Great Depression deepened, tax resisters feared that policymakers would adopt new progressive taxes. In many cities, social unrest and violence spread, and many people criticized Hoover for doing nothing to fight the economic downturn. In 1931, dreading a budget deficit, the president called for tax increases and, one year later, decided to reinforce the role of the federal government. In 1932 the Reconstruction Finance Corporation provided federal loans to banks, insurance companies, and railroads. Although New York mayor Fiorello La Guardia dubbed the program as "a millionaire's dole," it was a first step toward a more active role for governmental agencies. As a consequence, it forced the president to find new sources of revenue and to envision new social programs. "The soldiers are coming again," complained a bitter James Arnold, "for another bonus, pension or some sort of relief, and there is tremendous influence in

that group." Actually, in the summer of 1932, thousands of unemployed World War I veterans converged on the nation's capital to demand immediate payment of cash "bonuses." When Congress refused, most of the "bonus marchers" went home, but some stayed and
built makeshift shelters on the outskirts of Washington. President
Hoover asked General Douglas MacArthur to intervene. Although
tax resisters were satisfied with Hoover's decision, they feared that,
eventually, he would give satisfaction to voices that called for more
taxes and governmental operation. As a consequence, they devoted
themselves to organizing propaganda in favor of tax reduction, and
giving the appearance of a groundswell of grassroots support.[42]

To make the public aware of the consequences of increased taxation, the American Taxpayers League launched an educational campaign. Largely financed by big corporations and prominent businessmen, including the nephew of Andrew Mellon, the League employed
both the tradition of the American republic and modern ways of lobbying, including radio shows. In 1931 the League proposed a five-year
plan to reduce the burden of local and federal taxes. It marked an
abrupt shift from its previous secret lobbying. Among the program's
nine points was an immediate reduction in the expenses of government, an equalization of the tax burden, and a separation of tax
sources between federal and state governments. The League used
radio to increase taxpayers' awareness and to reach a larger audience.
As chairman of the Radio Committee, former New York senator
James W. Wadsworth introduced the speakers. The selected subjects
included debates on centralization by Wadsworth, the "diminishing
rights of States" by James M. Beck, and economy in expenditures of
government by William R. Wood, a congressman from Indiana.
Eventually, the League published a *Handbook on Taxation* to provide "authentic information regarding the expenditure of funds collected in the form of taxes." A letter to all taxpayers was sent to
members of the association.[43]

This strategy earned the support of small-business owners, especially in the South and the Midwest. W. Hume Logan, manager of the Logan Company in Louisville, Kentucky, advised the league to disseminate the bulletins throughout the United States "for these young men and young women in college today will be out in business soon, and if they are properly taught in the class room, they will not likely go astray afterwards . . ." W. C. Bradley, another manager, agreed with the Leaguers that the government would receive "more tax" if both the "normal and surtax were very much lowered." In spite of the Great Depression, businessmen living in small towns believed that policy makers should always take the road to tax reduction.[44]

Debates on the Revenue Act of 1932 made lobbying more urgent because of the worsening social conditions. On his radio show, Wadsworth urged Congress to adopt a 25 percent reduction in federal tax. In a pamphlet published in March 1932, *Our Government Can Not Last under the Present Tax System*, the League reiterated arguments about debt and the danger of an unbalanced budget as "Each 24 hours, the Government of the United States spends five million dollars more money than it collects." During a meeting held in New York, Wadsworth pointed out that constitutional government was "in danger" and that "confiscatory taxation" was destroying property rights.[45]

Many small taxpayers' associations appeared in connection with protests against local taxes. Based in Chicago, the National Organization to Reduce Public Expenditures, which regrouped 648 organizations in 48 states, mostly local chambers of commerce, urged the government to reduce expenditures in their "respective departments" to a degree commensurate with the "reduced national income." Son of Henry Demarest Lloyd, who protested against accumulation of wealth in the country at the end of the nineteenth century, Demarest Lloyd turned instead to tax resistance and ran the Taxpayers Union that not only pleaded for economy in public expense but also suggested a revision of the whole tax system. In its pamphlet, *Taxpayers Unite!*, the Taxpayers Union denounced the discrimination against the wealthiest citizens, who were "the oppressed minority of this age."[46]

In 1932, during the Republican convention, Lloyd proposed to reform the "present graduated income tax" that had proved inefficient and "discriminatory." The head of NAM, Robert Lund, also intervened and submitted a program calling for tax reduction, resubmission of prohibition, employment stabilization, and modification of the antitrust laws. At the same time, an organization called Defenders of America sent a petition to Congress urging it "to work towards lower taxes, rather than higher ones, by eliminating excessive and overlapping tax-wasting bureaucracies and political subdivisions." It was signed by 4,375 citizens who lived in the famous tax-resisters' Cook County in Chicago. Other petitions were sporadically sent by citizens. In Baltimore, Maryland, more than 1,200 taxpayers fanned the flames of resistance by accusing the government of being "lavish and extravagant in its business methods and in the expenditure of the money paid in the form of taxes." During a radio show sponsored by the American Taxpayers League, Fred W. Sargent, president of the Chicago and North Western Railway, was proud to tell the story of the citizens of Riverton, Wyoming, who petitioned against the $70,000 paid by the federal government to build a post office. All these initiatives, however, were isolated; they never coalesced into a strong and powerful political movement.[47]

During debates in Congress, many businessmen and their political allies preferred regressive taxes to taxes on personal and corporate income. The idea of a sales tax was pushed to prevent Congress from increasing direct taxes. Many congressional Democrats—notably Speaker of the House John Nance Garner—approved the idea, in spite of strong divisions inside the business community. To convince reluctant congressmen, press tycoon William Randolph Hearst sent fifty representatives and four senators on an all-expenses-paid trip to Canada. Southern representatives, however, opposed the new sales tax, fearing its impact on purchasing power. Therefore, the new revenue law created new federal sales taxes (on gasoline, electricity, refrigerators, and telephone messages) and increased revenues mainly by raising personal and corporate income-tax rates. As a consequence, Congress returned exemptions to their 1924 level. The Revenue Act of 1932 put an end to the long decade of tax reduction, and reinvigorated a progressive system of taxation that Mellon had hoped to patiently deconstruct.

In the winter of 1929, trucks containing granite, Indiana limestone, and Tennessee marble began to arrive at a strip between the Capitol and the Potomac that Washingtonians had started to call the Mall. A contract had just been signed to erect a vast $6,000,000 colonnaded building for the BIR. The new building was the pride of Andrew W. Mellon, the "new Hamilton," as his supporters proudly called him. Spurred on by tax resisters, Mellon was able to implement his scientific tax policy, even though he did not go back to the tax rates that had existed before 1913 to pay off the debt. Sixteen years after ratification of the Sixteenth Amendment, whose constitutionality was confirmed by the *Frothingham v. Mellon* decision in 1923, tax reduction epitomized the battle of tax resisters in the country. In the context of prosperity at home and emerging markets abroad, businessmen supported a strong collaboration with the federal government to promote economic growth. The new role of the government thrived with the rolling back of progressive taxes. Social programs for women and soldiers were challenged by opponents. By 1929 the Shepard Towner Act had expired, and soldiers had no choice but demonstrate for immediate payment of their bonuses rather than wait until the bonus payments became due in 1945. More radical calls for complete tax repeal were even heard among small businesses and banks, mainly located in the South and the Midwest. The dynamic lobbyist of the American Taxpayers League, James Arnold, recalled that "the complaint of the colonies and the battle cry of the revolution was 'taxation without representation,'" but he deplored the fact that during the prosperous Roaring Twenties there still existed "representation without taxation in some sections and classes of property and persons." The Great Depression put an end to the movement of tax reduction as the Treasury deficit forced Congress to find new sources of revenue. Businessmen and brokers had overshot their marks. The Revenue Act of 1932, enacted with bipartisan support, imposed the largest peacetime tax increase in the nation's history. The economic crisis had turned the world of tax resisters upside down. As the *New York Post*'s editorial put it in September 1934, Andrew Mellon had become the symbol of "Rich man's government. Twelve years of it. Corrupting high office. Surrendering the nation to a band of plutocrats who steered it into economic disaster." In a book he had just published, *Bankerteering, Bonuseering, Melloneering,* Texas representative and New Deal supporter John William Wright Patman fulminated against what he called "Mellonism" and defended both mothers and soldiers. For the tax resister who was so proud to be the new Hamilton, it was an incredible twist of fate—the seventy-nine-year-old Pittsburgh millionaire was now seen as an "Old Deal devil." A new deal in progressive taxation was on its way.[48]

5

The Bread-and-Circus Democracy

> Under the Sixteenth Amendment, the
> Congress can take the shirt off your back
> if it decides to.
>
> —*Walt Disney* (1939)

IN 1940 Franklin Delano Roosevelt's third election came as no surprise to many tax resisters. The vice president of AT&T, Arthur W. Page, did not mince his words in describing to his closest friends what he considered a gigantic fraud and a triumph of demagogy: "We have, I think, just demonstrated that five billion dollars of bread and circuses is patronage enough to reelect any one over any tradition." Page further charged that the vote of "a preponderance of the least competent will swing elections unless those who make a living all vote one day—and that again makes the class division we so hope to avoid." The exceptional nation was soon to become mainstream by adopting "the European form of Democracy, to wit, a large bureaucracy, a semi-planned economy, a restricted initiative and the heavy taxation necessary to maintain a permanent group of unemployed." As a consequence, social mobility would soon disappear if Americans moved toward a stratified society and away from the "more or less classless society of our past." Five years earlier, Page was forced to defend his company against accusations of fraud under the new Federal Communications Commission's regulations imposed by New Dealers. But what he feared most was the "class legislation" they enabled through their desire to implement a more progressive tax system and to target the richest individuals and corporations. As businessmen had since the Gilded Age, Page defended the minority of rich taxpayers and denounced the double taxation of their incomes through corporate and personal income taxes.[1]

In the first years of the New Deal, President Roosevelt not only increased federal tax rates for the richest citizens but also hoped to combat the "unjust concentration of wealth and economic power." His vision of progressivity included public disclosure of tax forms, high personal tax rates, and taxation of undistributed corporate profits. Taxes were used to finance new social programs that conveyed the sense of national solidarity and of an activist government addressing urgent national problems. As they were the main targets of the new system, businessmen and elites, in particular, intensified their resistance. Strongly opposed to the nascent egalitarian spirit, the American Liberty League dismissed the idea of taxpayers' sacrifice, contending that "the weak should not be artificially maintained in wealth and power." L. O. Broussard, the new president of the American Taxpayers League and a banker in Abbeville, wrote an editorial in the *New York American* warning that Americans were traveling "in the same direction as Russia" and calling for "harvest campaigns" both to restore local self-government and reduce the authority and responsibility of the federal government "to its appointed functions." With the help of their professional and political associations, tax resisters and their lawyers systematically attacked the high-end progressivity agenda of New Dealers but were forced most of the time to negotiate in order to limit the impact of progressive tax policy.[2]

Like many members of the Association against the Prohibition Amendment, Captain William H. Stayton was satisfied with the repeal of Prohibition but soon changed his mind about the new president. Referring to the eighteenth century and "Anglo-American" history, he considered the New Deal a threat to American institutions and traditions, and he joined the recently created American Liberty League. An 1881 graduate of the U.S. Naval Academy, Stayton feared that expanding the power of the president would lead to the dismantling of constitutional safeguards. For him, Roosevelt's tax policy embodied a dangerous transformation of American democracy. Stayton contended that income tax was, as administered in "this age of usurpation, the gravest danger." He further explained that it was the instrument used by "demagogues" to soak the rich and to distribute wealth for the "poor," the "unfortunate," and the "discontented." Two years after Roosevelt's election, for many tax conservatives, New Dealers had revealed their dark side and were increasingly prone to heed the frequent calls of populists such as Huey Long for "sharing the wealth." Tax resisters perceived such a plan as no more than socialism in action.[3]

Between March and June 1933, during the so-called hundred days, Congress enacted a number of major measures to cope with the crisis. Many of them were probusiness, and President Roosevelt included businessmen in his all-American team working for recovery. As a consequence, many corporations began to work with the new administration. Businessmen such as Gerard Swope of General Electric and Walter Teagle of Standard Oil Company cooperated with New Dealers. Even Pierre du Pont had agreed to be one of the five employer representatives of the newly created National Labor Board and to serve on the National Recovery Administration's Industrial Advisory Board. The du Ponts and other industrialists hoped that the new excise tax on whiskey would soon replace all direct taxes. As a matter of fact, it created more than $500 million in revenue and enabled the administration to limit the tax burden. Tax experts in the Treasury were extremely concerned by local tax protests. As they duly noted, such actions began to wane because of their careful fiscal and social policies. The Agricultural Adjustment Act (AAA), passed on May 12, 1933, was supposed to be financed by the profits of the processors of agricultural products, and not by new taxes. The Public Works Administration, led by Harold Ickes, enabled many municipalities to obtain loans after June 1933, and the Home Owners' Loan Corporation provided low-interest mortgage loans that would alleviate taxpayers' concerns.[4]

Progressivity and fairness of federal taxation, however, soon came under public scrutiny. Congressional investigations revealed that many of the richest Americans had paid no or very few taxes during the Great Depression. Ferdinand Pecora, chief counsel of the Senate Banking Committee, led the attack against tax avoiders. Born in Sicily in 1881, Pecora was influenced by William Jennings Bryan's campaign of 1896. Louis Brandeis's *Other People's Money and How the Bankers Use It* (1914) was another source of inspiration. Brandeis's central thesis was that the large banking houses were colluding with businessmen to create trusts in America's major industries. For Pecora, such collusion had led to the severe economic crisis. Using his research, the Senate Banking Committee tried to identify responsibility and started a series of hearings. It was revealed that John Pierpont Morgan Jr. had paid no income tax in 1931 and 1932, without breaking any laws. As the wealthy banker explained, his firms' dramatic losses in the market crash and capital loss deductions had enabled him and his partners to avoid the payment of taxes. Big corporations deftly used the flaws of the tax code to hide the money they earned. The following year, hearings conducted by North Dakota representative Gerald Nye worsened the reputation of businessmen by revealing the huge profits made by munitions makers during World War I. As a consequence, Congress decided to limit the profit margin on major military contracts to 10 or 12 percent. Debates on corporate tax avoidance and excessive profits increased the popularity of share-our-wealth campaigns in the nation.[5]

In 1934, because of the approaching mid-term elections and the nation's financial difficulties, Roosevelt decided to focus on the very rich to find new federal revenues. Challenges from politicians on his left, who resented the moderate nature of the attack on businessmen and the wealthiest Americans, influenced his creation of a more redistributive tax policy. Floyd Olson of Minnesota, Robert La Follette Jr., the son of "Fighting Bob," and Upton Sinclair in California advocated for bolder reforms. Sinclair's End of Poverty League proposed a series of new taxes to eliminate poverty in California. Huey Long proposed a 100 percent tax on all income over $1 million and appropriation of all fortunes over $5 million. In response, Roosevelt announced new measures whose primary purpose was preventing tax avoidance and evasion among the wealthy. Congress was soon to impose new tax rates on personal and corporate incomes.[6]

Fears of more regulation prompted businessmen to mobilize against the new taxes. The American Taxpayers League hammered on the new corporate tax because it must be paid every year whether business was run at "a profit or loss." The League's members decried such "a weapon of discrimination and destruction of wealth." The conservative lawyer James Beck was asked to challenge its constitutionality as a violation of the due process clause of the Fifth Amendment. In July 1934 conservative organizations, including the American Legion, the National Civic Federation, and the Daughters of the American Revolution, met in New York to coordinate their strategies. The American Liberty League, which had replaced the Association against the Prohibition Amendment, took the lead against the New Deal. Comprised of prominent businessmen, bankers, and disaffected conservative Democrats, many of the League's members—among them Jouett Shouse, Irénée du Pont, James Wadsworth, and James M. Beck—charged that there was already an excess of taxation and government regulation.[7]

For resisters, it was necessary to make citizens aware of the dangers of an expanding government that trampled the rights of its citizens. Alfred P. Sloan, the powerful president of General Motors, used its quarterly stockholders' messages to denounce the rapacious political economy of the New Dealers. NAM launched public relations campaigns to expose the tax danger and to explain the basic principles of economy to the public. With advertisements, syndicated columns, and radio shows, the American Taxpayers League hoped to convince the American public that it was in their interest to oppose progressive taxes, and it promoted sales tax as a more efficient and fair levy. A cartoon, published in *The Pittsburgh Sun Telegraph* and drawn by W. J. Pat Enright, urged citizens to avoid a "racket by the Government, with its spying and its oppression of enterprise and of wage and salary earners." As a consequence, they should ask Congress to vote for a general manufacturers' sales tax and "GET RID of the obnoxious income tax." The capital letters indicated the indignation of the tax resisters facing "inept" decisions made by New Dealers. Canada was still presented as a tax haven, a place with no "tax racket." Smiling and well-fed Canadians enjoyed the beauty of a prosperous country, in which "the Canadian Treasury pays its obligations without deficits, the national income is stable instead of fitful, and the taxpayers themselves speak of the revenue measure as the tax nobody feels."[8]

President Roosevelt was not surprised by such reactions, humorously maintaining that the tenets of the American Liberty League seemed to be "love thy God but forget thy neighbor"—"God" meaning "property." In spite of these public cries of alarm, antitax arguments struggled to gain a foothold with the public. Some farmers protested against the AAA and the processing tax, which was not paid by the processors of agricultural products but skimmed from the prices paid to farmers. On the whole, however, tax resisters seemed to be out of touch with the vast majority of Americans, who believed that progressive taxation was necessary. In the first two years, tax protests were isolated and failed to coalesce into a movement. On August 30, 1934, a resident of Los Angeles wrote to President Roosevelt to ex-

Figure 5.1. W. J. Pat Enright, "They Got What They Ordered," *Pittsburgh Sun Telegraph*, January 3, 1934. Courtesy of the University of Texas.

plain that he was at his wits' end with all the taxes he had to pay as the owner of a small business. He described himself as "the consumer that pays and is being taxed to utter desperation to maintain the policies of the New Deal." The mid-term elections confirmed the popularity of New Deal tax programs as the Democrats gained nine seats in the House and nine in the Senate. After this political blow to Republicans, tax resisters found a largely unnoticed provision in the Revenue law that required publication of incomes and taxes and opened up the possibility of a massive campaign against one of the tenets of progressive taxation: public disclosure of tax returns.[9]

In the early months of 1935 Walt Disney was awarded an Oscar for his cartoon *The Tortoise and the Hare* (1934), a retelling of the classic Aesop fable. He wrote a letter to Congress, bristling at the news of a publicity requirement that had been added to his tax form. The amendment sponsored by Senator Robert La Follette Jr., whose father had already endorsed a similar provision in 1924— authorized public access to every taxpayer's name, address, gross income, deductions, credits, and tax payments in order to prevent tax evasion by the wealthy. The proposed law required all taxpayers filing income tax returns to submit an additional form, which was printed on pink paper. For Walt Disney, public disclosure of incomes was profoundly unacceptable. From January to April 1935, thousands of petitioners agreed with him and urged their congressmen to repeal the provision. The pink-slip campaign put moral values at the forefront, and publicity of income was portrayed as an evil that could drag the household into chaos.[10]

Soon after a congressional meeting in January, Representative Robert Low Bacon of Long Island introduced a bill in the House to repeal the income-tax public disclosure clause. Blue-eyed, wealthy, and handsome, Bacon was once chosen by famed anthropologist Ales Hrdlicka as the ideal prototype of the "future American." In the early months of 1935, he was most concerned with the future of democracy and contested the "invitation to snoopery" contained in the revenue law. Conservative organizations such as the Sentinels of the Republic soon followed with attacks on the provision. Raymond Pitcairn, a wealthy lawyer and son of the Pittsburgh Plate Glass Company founder, was appointed to head the Sentinels, providing it with a wider audience and more money to finance its political campaign. In 1935 the Sentinels consisted of 1,500 dues-paying and 10,000 nonpaying members, according to Pitcairn's own and probably inflated estimates. In

February the organization began to pepper Congress with petitions against the "pink slip" and flooded the nation with letters, circulars, advertisements, and radio speeches. It was a politically opportune moment that coincided with taxpayers completing their federal returns.[11]

To stimulate sympathy for the cause, Pitcairn described the provision as a threat to small businessmen and average citizens as well as the wealthy. The core of his argument was the threat of public disclosure itself. Petitioners argued that it would cause "undesirable mendicants, professional and other importunate collectors, and unwelcome salespeople—scrupulous or otherwise—to prey upon citizens . . . and serve the ends of competitors, business enemies, private enemies, and blackmailers of citizens whose private means are thus publicly . . . exposed." Pitcairn drew on the Constitution to mock the New Dealers' attempt to divulge citizens' secrets. "The publicity provision," he contended, "flagrantly invaded the right of privacy to which the citizen is entitled under the Fourth Amendment to the Constitution." Pitcairn advised citizens to include a note with the pink slip that read: "I protest this outrageous invasion of my privacy." Stickers with the slogan "Pink-slip strike" were printed to be displayed everywhere.[12]

Most petitions were signed by small businessmen who felt endangered by the provision. Watson Eastman, president of the Western Cooperage Co., spoke bluntly against the publication of this "*Who's Who?*" of the earnings of citizens. John Fetzen, a businessman from Kalamazoo, Michigan, feared that the pink-slip clause would turn the world of business into a jungle in which only "the large and strong would survive." Harry Cooper, a businessman from Indianapolis and member of the National Association of Insurance Companies, contended that he did not want "to make my incomes available to friend and foe, to highway robbers and kidnappers." The president of the W. M. Glenny Glass Company explained to Robert L. Doughton, the chairman of the Committee on Ways and Means, that disclosing information on the net income of any taxpayer was "exceedingly harmful and decidedly un-American." The Philadelphia

Board of Trade labeled the provision as both "dangerous" and "objectionable."[13]

Income confidentiality became a contentious issue in small towns. H. A. Osborne, a citizen from Brookville, PA, pointed out that everybody in town would know that he earned an income of "$5,818.95," and he warned that many people would "consider this very large." Most petitioners stood resolutely in favor of the secrecy of tax returns. Stuart H. Perry, another small businessman, felt that the disclosure of incomes would provoke "envy and ill-feeling, bad reactions among employees and customers, and various importunities and exactions." Unless petitioners intervened, the American family would face a major danger.[14]

The fear was worsened by the climate of the Great Depression. Many petitioners referred to racketeers and kidnappers to describe the probable abuses of the provision, evoking members of organized crime who would use the public disclosure provision to target victims of their crimes. A small businessman from Dayton, Ohio, feared a state of ensuing "lawlessness" in which the law would be a real menace since "kidnapers, gangsters and racketeers" would have access to financial information about every American family. From January 2 to February 13 the trial of Bruno Hauptmann, who was accused of the Lindbergh kidnapping, gave peculiar resonance to such misgivings. A citizen from California voiced concern about the threat, stating that it was "not illogical to assume that many persons will become the victims of get-rich-quick schemes and other practices engaged in by criminals." In Texas, Webb Hackert highlighted his fears that publication of income tax returns would expose the average individual to solicitation by numerous concerns and individuals "engaged in promotional activities, racketeering, etc." Petitioners challenged the public to scrutinize the impact of public disclosure on the household, and it was no coincidence that the vigor of the movement owed much to women.[15]

Republicans in Congress capitalized on the momentum and put the emphasis on women's concerns. Californian representative Florence Kahn noted that she had received dozens of letters from women "who had their own incomes" and who feared that "their children may be kidnapped" if the fact "was divulged that they would have been capable of paying ransom." Women stepped forward to defend both confidentiality and family values. Mrs. Cutler B. Downer from Winchester, Massachusetts, described the New Deal as a violent attack on the foundation of American values that would open doors "to much offensive publicity and solicitation by unprincipled persons." The Illuminati, a group of women from Brooklyn, used constitutional arguments to decry this opportunity to intrude into the life of citizens. By portraying themselves as custodians of American tradition, Brooklyn women raged over New Dealers' attempts to transform American society.[16]

In many newspapers, the pink slip provision was vehemently criticized and presented as "un-American" and undemocratic. In a harsh editorial entitled "The Fiscal Nudes," the *Chicago Tribune* bluntly informed readers that "the pink slip was adding indignity to the Government's nudity campaign." In the name of social justice, the Roosevelt administration "made the citizen shed his own garments." The *Washington Post* was similarly outspoken in describing the aftermath of the new tax provision by denouncing it as "a picnic for the kidnappers, racketeers, stock salesmen and sucker list boys." On Fred Allen's popular radio show, citizens who tuned into the program were encouraged to give their opinions on the subject. Even though most of them did not pay income tax, many opposed the public disclosure of tax returns.[17]

Soon the number of petitioners began to exert a strong impact on congressmen. A conservative Democrat from Maryland, who was adamantly opposed to government expenditures, Senator Millard E. Tydings became their spokesperson. He tapped into assumptions they made to warn citizens that the pink-slip provision would allow "a neighbor to come in another man's house to see if that man was violating the law . . ." Although very few people paid an income tax, Tydings underscored the aftermath of the provision for the common man "struggling to pay his taxes, to meet his mortgage and insurance payments, and to give his children an education." The battle against the pink-slip provided tax resisters with the opportunity to present themselves as the people's best friends.[18]

On February 28 Congress decided to create a Senate-House survey to gauge sentiment about the provision and eventually decided to repeal it. In a letter he sent to Robert L. Doughton, a small businessman, T. B. Maleon, stated his delight that there was "not the slightest doubt that hundreds of thousands of business men breathed a prayer of thanks when they have learned of the repeal of the pink slip." The political victory was the prelude to a fierce political battle on the constitutional legitimacy of tax progressivity defended by New Dealers.[19]

In 1935 lawyer James M. Beck was increasingly disillusioned with the future of American democracy. Reelected to three consecutive terms as a representative, he finally resigned in 1934, discouraged by the so-called rubber-stamp Congress and his inability to fight Roosevelt's new policies, which he saw as conflicting with his individualism and constitutionalism and with his principles of limited government and laissez-faire. In a 1932 pamphlet entitled *Bureaucracy in Wonderland*, Beck expressed his convictions that federal bureaucracy and progressive taxation were dangerous ideologies coming from European countries. If the founding fathers lived in wonderland, he believed, they would have argued that "tax on tea, and the later stamp tax, should be gladly accepted, in return for the great benefit which the Colonies received from the Mother Empire, which protected them in their infancy by her Army and Navy." The New Deal worsened such fears. As a member of the conservative American Liberty

League, he hoped that a popular upsurge would put an end to hazardous social expenditures and started to mobilize conservative lawyers. On Constitution Day 1935, he advanced the argument that President Roosevelt had launched a program that was deliberately conceived and executed to defy the Constitution. At stake was nothing more than the survival of the American model. Following Beck's example, many businessmen hoped to capitalize on increased resistance to the pink-slip provision in order to stop the New Deal in its tracks.[20]

The relentless attacks against tax evaders and selfish businessmen fanned the flames of tax resistance. Working at the Treasury, lawyer Robert H. Jackson convinced President Roosevelt to make tax evasion a central issue. After closely examining individual tax returns, Jackson came to the conclusion that the fiscal system was morally wrong. The richest families in the country—the Astors, the Rockefellers, the du Ponts and the Morgans—had very low taxable income. The du Pont family had displayed a remarkable ability to avoid the payment of taxes. Even the former treasury secretary, Andrew W. Mellon, used the tax code to pay fewer taxes, and the Roosevelt administration decided to sue him for tax fraud in 1934. In a highly critical article published in *The Nation* on May 15, 1935, Thomas O. Shepard did not mince his words to describe Mellon's behavior and activities both as businessman and treasury secretary. "It is clear," he added, "that Andrew W. Mellon does not understand the significance of the economic order under which he lives." Author of the muckraking book *Mellon's Millions* (1933), Harvey O'Connor explained to the public that "how to make 'Poor Little Rich Men' pay" was "U.S Problem No. 1." More than twenty years after the Sixteenth Amendment, "The rich get richer," Jackson concluded, and the New Deal had to do something about it.[21]

As a consequence, on June 19, 1935, Roosevelt proposed a major reform, focusing on the richest citizens, contending that "wealth in the modern world does not come merely from individual effort; it results from a combination of individual effort and of the manifold uses to which the community put that effort." He urged Congress to adopt a new inheritance tax and steeper corporate and personal income taxes. Such proposals drew fire from businessmen. The industrialist and spokesman of the U.S. Chamber of Commerce, Fred H. Clausen, equated the proposal with pure and simple "confiscation." A member of the Ohio Chamber of Commerce considered that Roosevelt's proposal was not "a redistribution of wealth" but "a redistribution of poverty." The National Association of Manufacturers warned citizens that such a steep taxation of corporations would slow down recovery and jeopardize small businesses.[22]

Facing such an intense challenge, the American Liberty League and the American Taxpayers League tried to make citizens aware of the abuse of power perpetrated by the Roosevelt administration. To accentuate the tone of their already violent campaign, they sought to foster the growth of grassroots taxpayers' clubs. In the Bronx, the American Taxpayers League set up a club that "had for its primary purpose to make the indirect taxpayer 'tax-conscious.'" The Hearst newspapers offered enthusiastic support, and the *New York American* on March 6, 1935, quoted the new tax club's statement of purpose, which alluded to taxpayers' concern about "the reckless and unlimited expenditure of public monies with apparently no thought of the resultant burden upon labor, earnings and savings of the working and productive classes." According to James Arnold, who consistently tended to overestimate the number of militants, more than 10,000 citizens "voluntarily" registered their disapproval of "the redistribution of wealth by taxation," and more than "forty" organizations of the Bronx also joined in the movement, thus bringing its numerical strength to over "50,000" as an initial move.[23]

In June the American Taxpayers League organized a meeting with local groups of tax resisters in Chicago. Their Declaration of Principles, "Stop Spending, Stop Taxing," portrayed the tax policy of the Roosevelt administration as fundamentally "un-American." In a speech delivered in Chicago, Isaac Miller Hamilton, president of the Federal Life Insurance Company and vice president of the American Taxpayers League, equated conditions with the injustices inflicted by the government that finally led American colonists to rebel and to declare independence from the British in 1776. This political tradition was betrayed by New Dealers, who had decided to help "at least 2,000,000 able-bodied men who refuse to work" and "foreigners who came to our shores and quickly qualified for relief." Texas oil businessman Joseph Cullinan agreed to join the League because as an "Anglo-Saxon," he deeply resented "the prominence being accorded to the Jewish race in American governmental affairs."[24]

The American Liberty League publicly charged that the president's fiscal programs were "directed against fundamentals of the American system of government," and that they "further shattered the confidence of business, already weakened by misguided efforts to attain social reform in the guise of schemes for recovery." With the help of fifty persons working in the National Press Building in Washington, D.C., the League published a deluge of pamphlets against New Dealers. At the head of the League's publicity corps, William Murphy was proud to claim that by the end of the year more than 200,000 articles and editorials had been written to promote the League's activities. The League distributed studies of major laws to subject New Dealers to criticism that was centered mainly on legal and constitutional abuse by the administration.[25]

On July 31, 1935, however, President Roosevelt stood firm against rich taxpayers. He held a press conference in which he informed the public that fifty-eight people reporting income over one million dollars in 1932 had paid no federal taxes on 37 percent of their net income, primarily because they held tax-exempt securities. On August 30, the Wealth Tax Act became law, increasing surtax rates on personal income. Congress also increased income tax on corporations and gift and estate taxes. Symbolically, and as an answer to the pink-slip campaign, the Committee on Ways and Means made available to the public a book containing the names of every corporate employee earning $15,000 or more. The book had to be read in the committee room and nobody had the right to remove it from there. Tensions brewing around the high-end progressivity path chosen by the president escalated, and more and more resisters opposed what they perceived to be a soak-the-rich policy.[26]

On January 15, 1936, the American Liberty League sponsored a banquet at Washington's Mayflower Hotel. The keynote speaker was Al Smith, FDR's former close political ally and Democratic presidential candidate in 1928. The ballroom of the Mayflower was sold out, and more than 2,000 people spilled into the hotel lobby. Speeches were broadcasted nationwide over the radio, and Smith seriously contended that "there can only be one capital, Washington or Moscow." He even added the Manichean view that "there can be only the clear, pure, fresh air of free America, or the foul breath of communistic Russia. There can be only one flag, the Stars and Stripes, or the flag of the godless Union of the Soviets. There can be only one national anthem, 'The Star-Spangled Banner' or the 'Internationale.'" Such a radical and apocalyptic tone coming from a former ally was a consequence of the fear that the New Dealers' tax policy instilled among the richest citizens.[27]

The chairman of the National Lawyer's Vigilance Committee of the Liberty League, Raoul Desvernine, organized a team of lawyers to demonstrate that the tax policy was unconstitutional. In his book *Democratic Despotism*, published in 1936, he charged that the New Deal repudiated the "general welfare" clause of the Constitution by creating new social programs that were not envisioned by the founding fathers. In the South, John H. Kirby, with the assistance of Vance Muse and James Arnold, supported that constitutional claim with their new organization, the Southern Committee to Uphold Constitution. To blaze a political path, many tax resisters focused on the Social Security tax. Even though it was paid by only 2 percent of workers, it was easier to gain traction with public opinion by opposing this tax than lamenting the fate of rich men who paid an income tax. Opponents first argued that social insurance and social assistance were subverting the American tradition of individual initiative and self-reliance. Second, they asserted that employees would lose a proportion of their wages to the federal government since there was no guarantee that the money would ever be returned as pension payments. As a consequence, the whole New Deal project would undermine the American family. The American Taxpayers League exposed the dangers it perceived and promised to protect the American family and home, which were "the only base upon which a movement could safely rest." The League added that "the home was a non-profit institution, universal in its interests, sacred in its influence, and the cornerstone of society." By intruding into the household, and by requiring citizens to do the paperwork for the government, the tax system transformed "the housewife" into "a tax collector."[28]

To challenge Roosevelt's policy, many businessmen filed and won suits. On January 6, 1936, the Supreme Court, in *United States v. Butler*, ruled that the AAA and the taxes that it imposed were unconstitutional. In the opinion of Justice Owen J. Roberts, the processing tax was not a genuine revenue measure but a device whereby the federal government sought to exercise control over matters that were previously controlled by the states. Immediately after the Supreme Court decision, Congress passed legislation stating that agricultural processors and producers could file claims and be refunded their share of the processing taxes. On March 12, 1936, farmers in Iowa created the National Farmers' Process Tax Recovery Association to lobby for refunds of the taxes they had paid. Milo Reno, former president of the Iowa Farmers Union, led the campaign. Strongly opposed to New Deal programs, he considered government regulation a threat to farmers' freedom. In a few weeks, farmers' associations filed more than 265 claims with the BIR. However, their claims were

rejected on the grounds that the farmers did not have receipts showing that they had paid the tax.[29]

Such constitutional defeat did not diminish the ambitions of the
Roosevelt administration. Following the advice of Treasury lawyers,
President Roosevelt made taxation of undistributed profits his new
priority. On March 3, 1936, he asked Congress to consider a tax on
the profits that companies kept in their coffers. New Dealers were
convinced that big corporations deliberately retained profits to avoid
being taxed under the individual income tax. Robert H. Jackson and
other advisers convinced Roosevelt that corporate taxes were not sufficient to regulate capitalism and asserted that the new tax would
replace the existing corporate tax. As Adolf A. Berle and Gardiner C.
Means opined in their major book, *The Modern Corporation and
Private Property* (1932), industrialists had been transformed "from a
proprietor to a simple administrator." The two economists challenged
the well-established veneration of individual entrepreneurs, small enterprises, and vigorous competition. The country, they claimed, was
in the "throes of a revolution in our institutions of private property."
The result was that "the individual owner was steadily being lost in
the creation of a series of huge industrial oligarchies." As a consequence, believed New Dealers, it was necessary to invent new taxes
to cope with such a transformation.[30]

The main problem for the BIR was the complex reorganization
process and its impact on corporate taxation. From the early twentieth century to the Great Depression, mergers and acquisitions became commonplace. Large corporations secured control over many
of the nation's largest industries. The reorganization process made
the taxation of corporate revenues very difficult and enabled businessmen to easily avoid taxation. It was in 1918, because of war exigencies, that a reorganization provision was added to the federal tax
code that enabled corporations to avoid the payment of taxes. According to Robert H. Jackson, in 1933, more than 53 percent of cor-

porate property was owned by just 618 companies. In January 1935, the Supreme Court decision, *Gregory v. Helvering,* had limited the use of reorganization to avoid the payment of taxes. The case involved Mrs Evelyn Gregory, the wife of George D. Gregory, private secretary to multimillionaire banker and philanthropist Valentine Everit Macy. By using the reorganization law, she was able to pay fewer taxes. The Treasury commissioner, Guy Helvering, determined that Mrs. Gregory had understated her 1928 income tax by over $10,000, and the justices agreed with him. Based on that outcome, New Dealers proposed to tax undistributed profits in order to limit tax avoidance and to promote economic growth.[31]

Businessmen promptly reacted. G. L. Walters, president of the Illinois Manufacturing Association, tried to tone down the reformist impulse by explaining to Congress that companies needed reserves to make necessary investments. As a consequence, the federal government had no right to intrude into the daily management of companies. In a striking car metaphor, Walters contended that "government would just as well take away from all those who have the responsibility of driving automobiles their control over the brakes, the clutch, the throttle, or the steering wheel." Tax policy, he warned, would create a nation of irresponsible drivers. If the elites were powerless, it would have a tremendous impact on the American people. In the span of a few months, the American Liberty League spent one million dollars criticizing Roosevelt's tax policy and appealing to the "consumer" as "the forgotten man of the administration." They argued that consumers were "paying the costs of misguided experimentation," while also criticizing the efforts of the Roosevelt Administration to "stir up class warfare in the United States." With the help of the Republican Party, tax resisters launched a public relations campaign to oppose both new taxes and social programs. In April the Republican Congressional Committee derided "the tax regimentation" of the American people. Such brainwashing was detrimental to the country as the tax system would "penalize the time-proven policy of saving for a rainy day," and "increase unemployment in times of depression." Therefore, Republican congressmen pointed out, every person "who owns a share of stock," or "who has at heart the welfare of his family and his fellow man" should oppose the decline of American values. In June Alfred P. Sloan Jr. sent a letter to shareholders warning that it would be nothing short of catastrophic if the government were to interfere with "the employment of accumulated profits by aggressive and intelligent management." NAM also organized a letter campaign to shareholders explaining that a desire to avoid the undistributed profits tax, and not the exercise of business judgment, forced the extra dividends. Noel Sargent, the secretary of NAM, argued that the new tax would threaten the prosperity of the economy.[32]

Although resisters' mobilization had a small impact, it managed to limit tax rates imposed by Congress. Tax rates ranged from 7 percent to 27 percent depending on the percentage of profits. As the presidential election drew near, tax resisters hoped to challenge what they perceived as the radical turn of federal taxation, and to convince citizens of its destructive impact on recovery. They decided to focus on corporate taxes, which they pointed out would be passed on to consumers. In other words, they argued, under the false rhetoric of high-end progressivity, "hidden taxes" would burden the average American.[33]

The Republican Party leadership chose a westerner, Alfred M. Landon, to spearhead the presidential ticket in the fall of 1936. Although a traditional western progressive Republican, Landon pledged to repeal progressive taxes imposed by New Dealers. More than once during his speeches, his most vehement words were reserved for the soak-the-rich ideology. His principal target was "taxes" that "were hidden so deeply that they could see them." According to Landon, Roosevelt's tax policy constituted a deception that was at the expense of American citizens: "What it does is protect the big fellow who still has a reserve, and tie a millstone around the neck of the little fellow." With an argument typically deployed by tax resisters, Landon stressed the inflationary aspects of New Deal policies, and attempted to place the blame for the high cost of living on New Dealers and government intervention in the market. "If the major portion of the Government's income," he asserted during a meeting in Buffalo, "is obtained from indirect and hidden taxes—taxes upon such things as food, clothing, gasoline and cigarettes—then the main burden falls upon those of small income." With other tax resisters, he hoped to demonstrate that the New Deal policy aimed at putting the tax burden on the shoulders of all Americans.[34]

Following Landon's lead, Robert Kratky, a St. Louis attorney, was invited to direct a new taxpayer division in the Republican National Committee. In early September, he told journalists that the tax nightmare "begins with the alarm clock, on which there is a luxury tax of ten cents." According to Kratky and the estimates of his tax expert, 1,200 different taxes were imposed on articles for men, while 1,700 "touched his wife and their household." Counting federal, state, and local taxes, Lantsky distributed brochures to depict the tax burden supposedly borne by Americans. One of them was entitled *Soak the Rich Taxes Really Soak the Poor* and told the story of the common man facing an oppressive taxation. "I paid $1.50 for this shirt," reflects an average taxpayer. "Sixty-two taxes took 29% of the price I paid. Sixty-three taxes took $3.53 of this $18 suit. Fifty-three tax collectors took 59¢ of the $3 I paid for this hat. . . ." The pamphlet reversed New Dealers' arguments by inventing the "soak-the-poor" taxes that represented more than $60 out of every $100 being received by the federal government. With a variety of pamphlets, charts, pictures, and displays, the Republican National Committee fully committed itself to rousing the ire of citizens against taxes and to ensuring that President Roosevelt became the focus of their resentment. The conservative magazine, *Tax Facts*, sponsored by the

American Liberty League, helped propagate the extreme view of "hidden taxes" and lamented the effects of the tax system on every American.[35]

One of the brightest ideas to dramatize the Roosevelt New Deal Party's "taxation raids on the family pocketbook" involved the use of blackboards to appeal to women. Robert Kratky decided to order 2,000 blackboards to explain with chalk and erasers the actual causes of high food prices. In Westchester, New York, the Republican Committee distributed buttons and bumper stickers displaying potatoes as symbols of the revolt against high grocery bills caused by new taxes. Contrary to the arguments of the New Dealers, they maintained that the tax system was responsible for a decrease in family budgets, detailing the long list of taxes: "YOU pay: two cents in taxes every time you buy a loaf of bread; six cents in taxes every time you buy a pack of cigarettes; forty cents in taxes out of every dollar you spend for gasoline." Republicans hoped to resuscitate the housewives' meat strikes in protest against high food prices that had been significant a few years earlier. An advertisement titled "Sure, You Pay Taxes!" urged consumers not to blame grocers and butchers, but to blame bureaucrats in Washington. A conservative organization, the Crusaders, sponsored the movie *Don't Blame Your Butcher!*, featuring a butcher and a housewife as the twin victims of an oppressive tax system.[36]

With the help of conservative clubs and associations, women joined the resisters' campaign and added moral arguments concerning the household and the family. "Women hold title to nearly half the homes in America," proudly proclaimed Robert Kratky, and as a consequence, were particularly targeted by New Dealers. In Southern California, Mrs. Rosemary B. Chappel, chairwoman of the Southern California chapter of the Independent Coalition of American Women, distributed pamphlets to persuade housewives and organized a series of demonstrations to protest against the high cost of living. With her organization, Women Investors in America, Catherine Curtis made a name for herself by championing tax resistance. Before being a militant, Curtis had had a brief career as an actress, but much of her financial success had come from investments. In 1934 she began hosting a radio show called *Women and Money*, telling both single and married women that it was important to gain financial knowledge. Her show was canceled the next year when she spoke out against the New Deal, and she went on to found Women Investors in America, which eventually claimed 300,000 members. She strongly opposed the "Wealth Tax," claiming that it would harm widows and their children and that it discriminated against women. During the presidential campaign, Curtis even paid for an ad in the *New York Times*, showing a baby doomed to pay taxes for the rest of his life, already at his tender age a victim of the progressivity of taxation.[37]

During the campaign, Republicans hoped to create a cross-class coalition by convincing workers that the New Deal was a fraud. More than once, they lambasted New Dealers for social programs they deemed dangerous to American families and the economy. The New Deal tax policy was "forcing debts" on American citizens and their children, Republicans claimed, reminding Americans that "we each owe a portion of the Government debt." The head of the Industrial Division of the Republican National Committee, Sterling Morton, even organized the distribution of special pay envelopes to midwestern employers, warning that the new Social Security taxes would cause a loss of wages for employees. Once again, rich businessmen focused on a regressive tax to make their claim against progressive taxes more legitimate by instilling in the nation the idea that such hidden taxes plagued the common man.[38]

Republican strategies were ultimately a failure, however, and Roosevelt retained widespread popularity. His denunciation of "economic royalists" before a mass rally at New York's Madison Square Garden on the Saturday before the election assured him nearly unanimous support. In November, he won by a landslide, winning in all but two states. The liberal *New Republic* applauded and contended that it was "the greatest revolution in political history." It proved the popularity of the "soak-the-rich" policy in the country, and it revealed the yawning gap between tax resisters and the rest of the population.

After the 1936 debacle, many conservative organizations made public relations their highest priority in order to explain the dangerous impact of taxation and the soak-the-rich ideology. In a series of ads carrying the slogan "Prosperity Dwells Where Harmony Reigns," NAM made this plain by contending that "Today many influences are at work to destroy the real value of your citizenship." It accused New Dealers of fanning the flames of "violence as opposed to reason," and of striving to "put class against class." The economic downturn of 1937, dubbed the "Roosevelt Recession," gave tax resisters the opportunity to amplify their attacks against the tax choices the president had made. Indeed, by the end of the year, stock prices had plummeted by more than a third from their peak level the previous August. Industrial production had also fallen by more than 40 percent, while corporate profits had fallen by 78 percent. For many New Dealers, the collapse was more the result of a "capital strike" than their own mistakes. Corporations had deliberately done everything they could to sabotage the recovery so as to undermine New Deal policies. As Harold L. Ickes often complained, big business wanted all or nothing and had clearly refused to negotiate with New Dealers. For Republicans, taxes were the primary cause of the economic downturn. The latest Republican vice presidential candidate, Frank Knox, responded to New Dealers' accusations that political action "had destroyed confidence and dammed up the flow of capital." Tax resisters decided to focus on undistributed profits.[39]

In December 1937, a 108-page pamphlet published by the Brookings Institution in Washington reviewed the state of the American economy, highlighting the danger of its impact on American corporations. The basis of the pamphlet was a questionnaire sent out in the spring by Oregon's Republican senator, Frederick Steiwer, to 3,600 corporations. After the election of the Democrat Roosevelt in 1932, Steiwer devoted considerable effort to lambasting the administration. He served on the finance and judiciary committees and was especially critical of the New Deal and its range of programs. In 1936 he worked strenuously on behalf of Republican presidential contender Alfred Landon, and in the summer of that year he was asked to deliver the keynote speech to the Republican National Convention in Cleveland. His "Three Long Years" speech, broadcasted on national radio, won him many admirers, as well as many enemies. After Alfred Landon's defeat, the impact of tax policy on the U.S. economy became his primary focus. When Steiwer's questionnaire began to bring in the kind of replies he had expected, he shrewdly turned them over to the Brookings Institution, which found them sufficiently informative for a detailed analysis. Prepared by Myron Slade Kendrick, a conservative economist from Cornell University, the Brookings report recorded corporate attitudes toward the new tax. For his pamphlet, Kendrick used the first 1,560 answers to the Steiwer questionnaire. To the question, "Do you believe the imposition of this tax is inconsistent with sound business policy?" 1,212 corporations answered yes, while only thirteen answered no. Corporations found that the worst feature of the tax was its failure to allow the previous year's losses to be applied to the following year's profits before estimating taxable net income. The main conclusion drawn by Kendrick was that the law should at a minimum be amended to correct such failures; at best, it should be repealed.[40]

Following Kendrick's bleak conclusions, tax resisters accused New Dealers of limiting their investment capacity. Many businessmen bitterly lamented the consequences of such a tax. In October the Chamber of Commerce of New York State passed a resolution to protest against a tax that "fell most heavily upon small or weaker corporations." Some disappointed Democrats expressed similar reservations. James Stewart, the owner of a contracting company, James Stewart

& Company, pointed out that during his life, he had been "a regular Democrat, active in the affairs of the Party," but now he was furious against such an "ill-advised and vicious tax system." Most professional organizations, from the Investment Bankers Association of America to the National Association of the Credit Men, wrote letters, pamphlets, and petitions to disparage the tax. Horace Stoneham, president of the New York Giants professional baseball team, even went so far as to blame New Dealers for his team's inability to sign a high-profile star such as Joseph Michael "Ducky" Medwick of the St. Louis Cardinals. According to Stoneham, "If you wanted to spend your surplus on ball players, the government would step in and stop you. That sort of thing was inimical to baseball. . . . But you could not do what you please. You had to distribute a large part of your profits to stockholders." From Wall Street to the Sportman's Park in St. Louis, tax resisters opposed the ominous tax.[41]

These attacks began to exert an influence, as a loosely formed coalition of conservative Democrats joined Republicans and corporate managers in demanding the repeal of the tax. Business leaders, including the president of Chemical Bank, advocated a new tax policy aimed at "restoring confidence among businessmen." The American Institute of Certified Public Accountants issued a report declaring that in order for business "to face the future confidently," Congress must return to "fixed principles of . . . taxation" and abandon the failed undistributed profits tax. Debates in Congress for the next revenue bill were expected to restore confidence and prosperity and to help tax resisters convince the American people to repeal the villainous tax.[42]

It came as no surprise that tax resisters focused on the undistributed profits tax and its effects on corporations. The U.S. Chamber of Commerce recommended the repeal of the "thoroughly discredited tax," while NAM filed a report contending that "the psychological effect of this tax has been even more serious." Most businessmen explained that the repeal would improve revenues and worker purchasing power. Headed by Congressman Fred Moore Vinson, the Committee on Ways and Means was all the more inclined to listen to the complaints of tax resisters because of the recession. On April 26, 1938, a coalition of Republicans and conservative Democrats passed the Revenue Act of 1938, giving tax resisters what they hoped for. Progressive senator Robert La Follette Jr. accused tax resisters of launching one of the most widely organized and most successful propaganda campaigns "in the history of tax legislation." Their arguments had an influence on the Treasury's policy. Even Treasury Secretary Henry Morgenthau Jr. believed that the tax actually produced little revenue. Although Roosevelt still hoped the undistributed profits tax principle could be maintained beyond its scheduled expiration, he was left with very few allies. On May 28, 1938, the Revenue Act of 1938 became law without his signature. Roosevelt expressed strong disapproval of the large tax break that it provided for corporations. In a West Virginia high school, he reminded the audience that "for a great many years, the Nation as a whole has accepted the principle that taxes ought to be paid by individuals and families in accordance with their capacity to pay." For the first time since Andrew W. Mellon, progressive taxation had been rolled back, and tax resisters had good reason to believe that federal expansion would be even more limited since the Republicans had added eight seats in the Senate and eighty in the House in the mid-term elections.[43]

After the defeat, however, Roosevelt felt that it was necessary to find a common ground with the business community. The appointment of John W. Hanes as a new undersecretary of the Treasury was a sign of appeasement sent to businessmen. A former governor of the New York Stock Exchange, Hanes was very sensitive to business concerns, and his appointment announced reconciliation between businessmen and the federal government. Even a staunch opponent such as economist Henry Simon toned down his opposition to New Deal taxation. Although he still believed that the main direction of New Deal policies was "toward authoritarian collectivism," he nevertheless urged businessmen to consider the role of taxes to support the economy. In his book *Personal Income Taxation* (1938), he endorsed a limited form of progressivity to promote economic growth, even though he still hated "the pseudoscientific arguments of the case against inequality." Although some businessmen and intellectuals started to accommodate themselves to New Dealers, others still strongly resented progressive taxation of personal and corporate incomes.[44]

In 1939 Samuel Pettengill wrote *Jefferson, the Forgotten Man* to show the extent to which the principles of Jefferson had been abandoned by New Dealers. Mr. Pettengill, a Jeffersonian Democrat, after being reelected three times in Indiana, terminated his congressional career in 1939. Although his election was generally considered certain, he chose to return to his law practice in South Bend because of his disagreement with President Roosevelt's policies. Referring to Thomas Jefferson and the American political tradition, Pettengill defended the rights of the working man and emphasized the danger of tax increases, warning that "the tax collector has become the greatest middleman in history," and that tax collection held "producer and consumer far apart." For Pettengill, as for many tax resisters, reducing taxes was not enough to save the principles of the American Republic; it was time to attack the constitutional basis of the new fiscal order: the income tax and the Sixteenth Amendment.[45]

The idea of a constitutional amendment to limit federal tax rates was proposed by Robert Dresser, a Rhode Island lawyer. Dresser was involved in most tax resisters' organizations of the 1930s, among them NAM, the American Taxpayers Association, which replaced the American Taxpayers League, and the National Committee to Uphold Constitutional Government. The latter was created by the newspaper publisher Frank Gannett in 1937 to denounce the infringement of New Dealers upon citizens' rights. With conservative politicians who backed conservative senator William Borah for the Republican presidential nomination, Gannett hoped to utilize the organization to help make citizens tax conscious. Hired by the committee to search for a constitutional path to constrain federal expansion, Dresser wrote the amendment to vilify the power to tax "that had been misused to siphon revenues into Washington until local self-governments faced the danger of becoming 'bankrupt and powerless pawns' of the federal bureaucracy." James Arnold sought to popularize the idea of tax limitation with a book entitled *The Desire to Own.* With the same title as many pamphlets of the American Taxpayers League, it portrayed income taxes levied on the rich as a threat to every citizen's property rights, arguing that "titles to homes, deeds, stocks and bonds are scraps of paper if their income is taken by government." Arnold's new organization, the American Taxpayers Association, persuaded Representative Emanuel Celler of New York to introduce an amendment in 1938 and 1939, but the proposal never made it out of committee. The association then decided on a new strategy to force Congress into action by calling a constitutional convention under Article V of the Constitution, which mandates that such a convention be ratified by the state legislatures by a two-thirds margin.[46]

By then some business organizations hammered on the high tax rates. Still very committed to battling the New Deal, NAM decided to focus on the double taxation of stockholders as a new line of attack. Noel Sargent wondered aloud, in testimony to the Committee on Ways and Means in 1939, why dividends were taxed twice, first when they were "earned by a corporation, and then again when received by the individual." The U.S. Chamber of Commerce financed a campaign to explain the alleged links between tax policy and unemployment with the slogan "Less Taxes, More Jobs." 25,000 posters were put up all over the nation as part of a drive for reduction in taxes. The new president of the Chamber of Commerce, George H. Davis himself, plastered the billboard with the poster.[47]

Meanwhile, the American Taxpayers Association increased its calls for repeal of all taxes. "Taxation methods that destroy the taxable

Figure 5.2. On January 18, 1939, George H. Davis, president of the U.S. Chamber of Commerce, plastered the billboard with the poster "Less Taxes— More Jobs." Courtesy of the Library of Congress.

income are suicidal," the first bulletin of the association asserted, adding that "they would kill the goose that lays the golden tax egg." With the upcoming presidential election in mind, it focused on two important groups: workers and women. The association further pointed out that "workers pays 60% of all taxes collected by the tax spenders in this country today." Women were also characterized as victims of the federal tax racket: "The American housewife has the reputation of being a bargain hunter. In the matter of taxes, she has fallen far short of her reputed ability." Once again, lamented tax resisters, the tax system undermined the foundation of the American household and economy. Still strongly opposed to federal taxes, Walt Disney's criticisms were quoted in the association's bulletin. A bitter

Disney turned into a historian when he explained that "this started when the States very erroneously committed the grievous error of adopting the Sixteenth Amendment without any ceiling on what Congress could do on taxation of income." At the end of the decade, the most radical tax resisters joined the No Third Term movement run by Samuel Pettengill, who replaced Gannett as the head of the Committee for Constitutional Government. Using constitutional arguments, they sought to prevent Roosevelt from running for a third term. His reelection came as a major disappointment for tax resisters, confirming the popularity of the president.[48]

In the play *You Can't Take It With You* (1936) by Moss Hart and George S. Kaufman, known for their lighthearted comedies, one character describes to an old man the virtues of taxation and the duty of the citizen: "And let me tell you something else! You'll go to jail if you don't pay, do you hear that? That's the law, and if you think you're bigger than the law, you've got another thing coming. You're no better than anybody else, and the sooner you get that through your head, the better." While the comedy elicited laughs among Americans in 1936, few tax resisters saw humor in the administration's progressive tax policies, and guests at John Pierpont Morgan Jr.'s dinner parties were forbidden from mentioning the "R" word. The Roosevelt administration's fiscal policy explained why not only owners of small firms but large companies were engaged in a fierce battle against high-end progressivity. In 1935, while he opposed the pink-slip provision, the president of the Sentinels of the Republic, Raymond Pitcairn, put it bluntly: "We are living in America, not Russia. Not even a Mussolini or a Hitler imposed such indignity upon taxpayers." The following year, Pierre du Pont asked whether his efforts to end Prohibition would not have been better directed at repealing the Sixteenth Amendment. Tax resisters, however, had difficulty in convincing citizens that their crusade involved more than just the defense of interest groups. Roosevelt had studiously targeted the rich to avoid the formation of such a coalition. Some of the New Dealers' inconsistencies in terms of fiscal policy provided an opportunity for businessmen to align themselves against Washington bureaucrats in order to limit the expansion of the fiscal state. But because they failed to organize the "harvest campaigns" envisioned by L. O. Broussard in 1933, they had no choice but to negotiate in order to limit high-end progressivity. Tensions in Europe and imperialism in Japan would soon revive debates on progressive taxation.[49]

6

From the Kitchen
to the Capital?

There seems to be no restraint in this
lust for taxes.

—*General Douglas MacArthur (1958)*

O<small>N</small> M<small>ARCH</small> 5, 1959, white middle-class women from Ritzville, Washington, joyfully marched down the streets to the governor's office in Olympia. Wearing long white coats and hats with velveteen bows, flowers, and greenery, two housewives from Seattle, Mrs. Harry A. Trimble and Mrs. Joseph G. Sebren, led the small parade and brought to Governor Albert Dean Rosselini a large bucket containing petitions signed by angry taxpayers who championed economic freedom and attacked both local and federal taxes. With the optimistic slogan, "From the kitchen to the Capitol in one week," they hoped to spark a massive movement of resistance against the postwar liberal leviathan and the "acute spendicitis" of policymakers in the nation. Among them was Governor Rosselini, elected in 1957, who angered conservatives by expanding the budget with his liberal policy. In the Evergreen State, where McCarthyism had been particularly intense a few years earlier, tax protest was initiated by organizations such as

Figure 6.1. Conservative women on the steps of the Capitol in Olympia, Washington on March 5, 1959. On the right, Governor Albert Rosselini, the first Italian American elected governor west of the Mississippi. Courtesy of the University of Oregon Libraries.

the Lions Club. A petition entitled, "A New Declaration of Independence," circulated from agricultural Adams County to Spokane and other nearby parts of the state. Crossing the Cascade Mountains, it even found an echo in the Seattle area, where Mrs. Trimble and Sebren, aided by enthusiastic volunteers, obtained 30,000 signatures in one week. As mothers who cared about their households, they pointed out that "it is not fair to leave payment for the wild orgy of irresponsible spending, state and federal, to our children and their children." The massive expansion of progressive taxes during World War II, adopted by what they considered to be "irresponsible" policymakers, threatened future generation of Americans.[1]

In the booming economy of the postwar years, tax resistance was defended by successful middle-class men and women with modern lifestyles and bright futures. Often depicted as the paranoid actions of eccentric mavericks, such protests appeared at a time when the federal government and many of the country's elites were working toward a new social contract. From the Japanese attack on Pearl Harbor to the onset of the Vietnam War, both the Cold War and the Keynesian consensus had transformed tax resistance. As many big corporations and a majority of Americans accommodated themselves to the progressive tax structure and the postwar economy at home and abroad, few people were left to attack progressive taxation in postwar America.[2]

Resistance did, however, reach a middle-class constituency, forging a grassroots identity against the Washington elites and bureaucrats. The feminization of the movement had an impact on both the tax resisters' strategy and rhetoric. Interestingly, women tended to portray tax resistance as a life-or-death crusade against the evils of liberalism and the permissiveness of modern society. As the civil rights movement gained momentum in the nation, opposition was also fueled by white activists who opposed the intrusion of the federal power. Eventually, the crusade of suburban housewives and small business owners, from the kitchen to the capital, led up to the Barry Goldwater campaign in 1964, which carried out the hopes and limits of tax protests. Like the women in Ritzville who had failed to convince the majority of citizens in the state of Washington to follow their antitax crusade, white middle-class resisters also found themselves isolated in the new taxpayers' nation.[3]

A few months after the end of World War II, the sixteen million personnel in the army received an educational manual, prepared by the Armed Forces Institute, which strongly irritated the American Taxpayers Association. Among many elements, the manual endorsed the Revenue Act of 1942 that implemented a mass-based income tax paid by more than forty million Americans by the end of the war. It was explained that tax reforms, especially the income tax, were necessary and part of the New Deal project "to promote equality not only by relieving the rich of their surpluses, but by bestowing upon the poor revenues collected in this way." For many resisters, the indoctrination of soldiers revealed the true brainwashing nature of the New Deal. But to their dismay, the Roosevelt administration had effectively managed the transition to a mass-based and progressive tax regime. Although the use of propaganda and a generalized sense of sacrifice among the population played an important role, taxpayer compliance was ultimately ensured through a range of deductions and a large tax cut that was intended to convince citizens and businessmen.[4]

As the war broke out in Europe in September 1939, and after Germany scored its first victories in Western Europe in the spring of 1940, President Franklin Delano Roosevelt hoped that the United States would become the "arsenal for democracy." With the help of their organization, America First Committee, isolationists urged Congress not to send any American boys abroad and their meetings gathered thousands of citizens, especially in the Midwest. Tax resisters, many of whom attended such events, chatted about Roosevelt's new crusade against "war millionaires" and "profiteers" and the idea that taxes, notably the excess-profit tax, should be implemented to avoid war profiteers. After he left Congress, former representative Samuel B. Pettengill wrote a semiweekly column as "The Gentleman from Indiana," which was syndicated to over 100 newspapers all over the country, to denounce the dangers of President Roosevelt's third term and the close links between taxation and socialism. His book, *Smoke Screen*, which was published in 1940 and claimed that the increasing federal control over every facet of American business had its counterpart in developments in Germany and Italy, became a bestseller. The American Taxpayers Association used the smokescreen metaphor to denounce tax increases and contended that there was "only one safe way to avoid turning the national defense effort into a national tragedy." Intervention in Europe was nothing but a smokescreen to legitimize the expansion of the federal government and "the people of the United States, the businessmen of America, must shut their ears to these magicians who see the defense program as an opportunity to try, on a grander scale than ever before, their hocus-pocus formula of borrowing and spending." As most tax resisters feared, the war would allow New Dealers to enact a major tax reform.[5]

After the Japanese attack on Pearl Harbor on December 7, 1941, the Roosevelt administration had no choice but to find new revenues to finance military expenditures. Once the war broke out, most Americans supported the war effort and accepted the financial burden that it entailed. War bond purchases illuminated the depth and character of the average American's involvement. Within a few years, citizens bought a staggering total of eighty-five million bonds, virtually one for every American adult. Small investors purchased $40 billion in E bonds, and wealthy individuals and corporations invested nearly twice that amount. However, bond sales raised almost half of the money needed to finance the war, which amounted to $320 billion. Once again in time of war, the federal government had to levy new taxes. During debates in Congress, it appeared clear that businessmen and bankers still opposed them, advocating a sales tax as the best way to stimulate growth without limiting the purchasing power. While President Roosevelt remained a strong opponent of such an unfair tax, he had to face growing opposition to the idea of taxing corporations' profits, not only among industrialists and financial leaders but also among Democrats. Under the leadership of Georgia senator Walter F. George, who had become chairman of the Senate Finance Committee in 1941, many congressmen rallied to the idea of not weakening corporations in wartime, instead using personal income tax as the main provision of the Revenue Act. To support the war effort, the number of individual taxpayers grew from 3.9 million to

42.6 million in 1945. At the end of the war period, income taxes accounted for nearly 40 percent of federal revenues. In contrast, corporations were able to negotiate fairly business-friendly provisions, which lowered the corporate tax rate far below the rate the Treasury expected. The mass-based income tax system meant that citizens, not corporations, were asked to finance the war.[6]

As many businessmen were satisfied with the tax system and benefited from important government contracts, tax resistance was limited to conservative organizations and small-business owners. The American Taxpayers Association immediately equated the Revenue Act of 1942 with a subtle form of brainwashing, and explained that millions of "sleeping Americans" were unaware of the tyrannical world they lived in. The association decided to reinvigorate the campaign in favor of an amendment to limit federal taxation, an idea proposed earlier by Robert Dresser. The Committee for Constitutional Government joined the crusade. In April 1941, three States—Iowa, Massachusetts, and Maine—had already passed a resolution; one year later, thanks to the field work of the two conservative organizations, seven more state legislatures called for a constitutional convention.[7]

Such criticism and the mobilization of resisters were expected by the Roosevelt administration, which was more concerned with the reaction of ordinary citizens. A Treasury survey conducted by a young economist named Milton Friedman described the way ordinary Americans viewed the new tax system and the collection of taxes via withholding. Tax resisters represented only 10 percent of the sample. According to Friedman, they could be "classed as rugged individualists" and "are typified by such comments as 'I don't like to have my pay check touched' and 'I prefer to manage my own affairs.'" Only four people objected to the compulsory nature of the plan, arguing that it represented a form of regimentation and was the first step toward dictatorship. Six respondents expressed their concerns about further burdens on their already precarious situation. As one person put it, "Pretty soon there won't be anything left in the pay envelope." As Friedman noted, the attitude toward taxation varied according to the taxpayers' occupation and gender. While only two-fifths of the people interviewed were white-collar workers, three-quarters of the unfavorable answers came from this group. Women also tended to react less favorably than men. Other taxpayers contended that they preferred the withholding system to direct assessment and collection by the federal government. The new mechanism, it was felt, would mean considerably less hardship. "You will hardly miss a little at a time," or "it would be a lot easier than paying it out in a lump sum," were arguments put forth by some of those interviewed. However, Milton Friedman urged policymakers to be cautious and concluded that "while only very few people opposed the plan on the ground that it was a form of regimentation, it was conceivable that this argument could assume larger proportions." Citizens who were aware that the withholding system would mean double payments in 1943 seemed anxious about their ability to save enough money.[8]

In May 1943 the popular magazine *Life* published a stunning editorial that criticized the tax "mess," citing in particular the tax payment envisioned by the Treasury. "Collecting two years in one is old Chinese custom," mocked the editorial, referring to the government's intention of asking citizens to pay for two years of taxes in 1943. Why did the government not accept the idea of tax forgiveness for all citizens, the op-ed continued? The chairman of the New York Federal Reserve Bank and treasurer of R. H. Macy and Company, Beardsley Ruml, made a name for himself by objecting in harsh terms to the Treasury's plan. A former professor of education, Ruml became an expert and a prolific writer in the field of taxation. As debates centered on the tax system, he accepted the withholding mechanism but proposed a forgiveness of 1942 taxes to ease the pinch in 1943. Treasury Secretary Henry Morgenthau Jr. and President Roosevelt

Figure 6.2. Beardsley Ruml as the "forgotten man"
(1943) defending his own plan for the taxpayers against
the will of Treasury Secretary Henry Morgenthau,
Chairman of the Committee on Ways and Means
Robert Doughton, and tax expert Randolph Paul. On
the left, the average taxpayer hoped not to pay two years
of income tax in 1943. Clifford Kennedy Berryman,
"Beardsley Ruml as the 'Forgotten Man,'" *The Evening
Star*, April 1, 1943. Courtesy of the Library of Congress.

were reluctant to propose such a tax relief for the richest taxpayers in
time of war.[9]

The Chamber of Commerce of New York and many associations
endorsed Ruml's ideas. Its president, Frederick E. Hasler, believed
that it was a good idea to advance the tax clock. Mary H. Donlon, a
member of the National Federation of Women's Republican Clubs,
explained at a public meeting that the Ruml plan was the "only
sound method." Within a couple of months, congressmen received

petitions and letters endorsing the proposal. Most petitioners accepted to pay federal taxes but asked Congress to relieve them of their tax liability for the year 1942. In March, 421 workers from Newport News in Virginia explained that withholding seemed a fair approach since they very much doubted "the possibility of collecting taxes from the great number of people who spend all they earn and will be without funds when taxes are due." If the plan was not adopted, they were of the opinion that "many who should pay will not do so." Meanwhile, 168 taxpayers and residents of Dutchess County in New York State alerted Congress to the economic dangers of a double payment.[10]

Business organizations staunchly supported Ruml. In January 1943, the Buffalo Fur Merchants Association presented a motion adopted during one of its meetings. Although fur merchants agreed to comply with the war tax system, they asked for something in return. At the same time, the Board of Commerce of Parkersburg, West Virginia, petitioned for taxpayers' "relief" in time of war. On March 15, 1943, the Jefferson Chamber of Commerce in Missouri lauded the virtues of the plan, and the Home Loan & Finance Company of Flora, Illinois, also petitioned its local congressman. On June 9, 1943, as President Roosevelt signed the new revenue law, he gave citizens what they wanted: current payment of all individual income tax liabilities and the cancellation of 75 percent of one year's existing taxes. If the specter of heavy taxation disappeared for citizens, it became one of the main targets of small-business owners.[11]

As the war years went by, small businesses increasingly resented the new system of taxation, contending that they did not have the administrative and financial capacities of big corporations. Furthermore, they did not benefit from the same large-scale procurement contracts and could not lower their tax burden by taking advantage of the depreciation on industrial plants and machinery. In 1942, the Senate Small Business Committee indicated that 75 percent of all contracts had been awarded to only fifty-six large companies. Two years later, in January 1944, a small airplane company president, William S. Jack, purchased a half-page newspaper ad in New York City and Cleveland, criticizing the burden of taxes which would leave the company $2,826 in the red for the year. Exposing the danger of federal intervention, he warned reporters that the "Roosevelt administration was flirting with revolution," predicting that soldiers would come home to "the worst mess in the nation's history" if industry was not left with enough funds to provide postwar jobs.[12]

By then, when invited to speak at the Women's Chamber of Commerce in Kansas, businesswoman Vivien Kellems called for a new "Tea Party" and announced that she had not paid her December 1943 installment of the income tax. She accused the government of placing the burden of the tax reform on small businesses and refused to become a tax collector, arguing that industrialists "have paid for every bit of engineering, every bit of travel expense, every telephone call, every wage to our workers, every machine and tool in our shop." If she paid, she told the Kansas crowd, she would "be forced to mortgage her home, cash her war bonds, use the operating capital for the business and then go into bankruptcy." She made outlandish demands, including the repeal of the Sixteenth Amendment, the abolition of "at least 2,000,000 Federal employees," and the elimination of "every world-wide boondoggling project which has no connection with winning the war." For years to come, Kellems would be one of the most vocal tax resisters in the country.[13]

Born on June 7, 1896, in Des Moines, Iowa, Kellems was the daughter of David Clinton and Louisa Flint Kellems. Attending the University of Oregon, she was the only woman on the debate team, completing a bachelor's degree in 1918 and a master's degree in economics shortly thereafter. Following graduation, she moved east to New York to pursue a doctorate at Columbia University with expert on progressive taxation Edwin R. A. Seligman. While she was in New York, her older brother, Edgar, improved an existing cable grip that was patented in the late 1920s. Using his patent as a cornerstone, Ms. Kellems made a name for herself when she founded Kellems Cable Grips, Inc. in 1927, eventually relocating the plant to Stonington, Connecticut. She successfully ran the company as president, and the company's devices were used most notably during the construction of the Chrysler Building and the George Washington Bridge. During World War II, Seligman's former student hoped to launch a movement against progressive taxation.[14]

In January 1944 her public denunciation of the income tax attracted national attention. Treasury Secretary Morgenthau publicly stated that "to advise citizens not to pay taxes—particularly in time of war—smacked of disloyalty." As a consequence, the BIR followed standard procedure when it decided to impose legal penalties on Kellems for not honoring her tax obligations. Other politicians were more outraged than Morgenthau, even accusing Kellems of treason. In the House, Representative George E. Outland from California, referring to the waves of strikes, publicly asserted that "if there is anything worse than a strike, it is this refusal to pay taxes by someone making profits out of the war." Representative John M. Coffee from Washington, warning that Kellems's denunciation would harm the war effort and discourage the purchase of war bonds, called on the U.S. Department of Justice for summary action. Kellems defended herself, proclaiming that she was "not only proud but eager to pay taxes to win the war," but deplored the tax burden for small businesses. Refusing to engage in a long constitutional debate, Secretary Morgenthau confirmed that the BIR would proceed with legal penalties.[15]

As the war years went by, the campaign for constitutional limitation on taxation gained political clout. In March 1944 the American Taxpayers Association proudly announced that New Jersey and Kentucky had "joined the parade." Their success started to draw an angry response from New Dealers who were concerned about the danger posed by a tax limitation in time of war. The Committee for Constitutional Government was accused of being "the most sinister lobby in America" by Texas congressman John William Wright Patman. In an attempt to offset the public backlash against them, the two conservative organizations sought to demonstrate their loyalty to the war effort by adding an emergency clause that would allow Congress to exceed the constitutional limit of 25 percent in wartime. As a consequence, eighteen states adopted the Joint Resolution in 1945. The Allied victory in Germany and Japan, however, put an end to criticisms of the war tax system.[16]

Although after 1945 most Americans paid their income and corporation taxes by the deadline, at the request of the Treasury (as alluded to in the song by Irving Berlin: "I Paid my Income Tax Today"), they found room for negotiations with the BIR and the Treasury. Throughout the war, Roosevelt and his tax advisers were reluctant to impose a highly coercive system of assessment and collection either for ordinary citizens or businessmen. The new collection system based upon withholding gave businessmen—not BIR agents—the task of implementing the new tax code. Designed to allay taxpayers' fears, the system made it more difficult to criticize taxes that citizens paid each month out of their paychecks. Economist Milton Friedman contended that it was "enthusiastically favored by a large majority of people," as it would be a "sound business procedure, insuring maximum collection." For tax resisters, it rendered tax collection less visible.[17]

Through this clever system, the Roosevelt administration gained the support of middle-class taxpayers and big corporations. During those years, hundreds of American companies enjoyed massive tax refunds that had the effect of erasing most of their reconversion losses. According to Carl Shoup, a Columbia University economics professor and leading tax expert, the 1945 law gave "corporations all, if not more than they could have hoped for in a quick tax reduction bill." Beardsley Ruml could then urge the government to "give up the corporation tax," defined as "evil" for both the corporation and the public welfare. In a world dominated by the United States, and with the promise of economic growth, Ruml considered federal tax reve-

nue as "obsolete" and hoped that Americans would put an end to the
war tax system, as they had after the American Civil War and World
War I. Conservative women in the South and the West took the lead
against progressive taxation in the nation.[18]

In 1945, as the war came to an end, Ida M. Darden was a fifty-nine-
year-old southern lady, still very active in the field of politics. The
former secretary to James Arnold hated the postwar world order. In
1949, in her overtly racist and antistatist review, *The Southern Conservative*, she spoke bluntly against the postwar United Nations, the
"devil's workshop" in her own words, and was strongly repulsed by
the nascent civil rights movement. But most of all, she denounced
the tyranny of the liberal state and particularly attacked the federal
power to tax, which she labeled "larceny by taxation." She added
that there "was nothing wrong in this country" that "could not be
corrected by taking from Washington politicians the power of the
purse." Darden was particularly hostile to President Harry Truman's
Fair Deal that reinvigorated Roosevelt's vision of social reforms. In
1948 the surprising election of Truman proved that New Deal liberalism still appealed to a majority of Americans. Even modern Republicans, as President Dwight D. Eisenhower labeled them, endorsed
the statist agenda and Cold War spending. In 1950 the country spent
more than \$16 billion on military and international commitments,
and most politicians supported war taxes. Many big corporations
worked with federal agencies and General Motors CEO Charles E.
Wilson, chosen as defense secretary by Eisenhower after his presidential victory in 1952, was proud to explain that "what was good for
our country was good for General Motors, and vice versa." Such a
consensus pushed Darden and her fellow tax resisters to the isolationist and conservative fringes of American politics.[19]

During the postwar years, tax resistance spread to the world of
suburban housewives and small-business owners, where it became
an important feature of the conservative culture. In the new suburbs

that flourished in the 1940s, men and women criticized the liberal leviathan and the waste of taxpayers' money. Many of them despised the alleged permissiveness apparently encouraged by the liberal state and its elites. In the anticommunist atmosphere of the time, investigations of the BIR confirmed the suspicions of the bureaucrats in Washington. After the war, accusations made against high-level employees of the Treasury, such as Nathan Gregory Silvermaster or Harry Dexter White, reinforced the idea of a communist infiltration of the government. In December 1947, freshman senator John J. Williams, a conservative Republican from Delaware, attacked the BIR. For more than five years, congressional investigations into alleged fraud by tax agents raged. By the end of that time, several hundreds of BIR employees had left the agency, either voluntarily or under indictment for offenses against the tax laws. Such scandals provided tax resisters with a strong sense of legitimacy. During the postwar years, conservative women were at the forefront of the battle and expressed their views in a series of publicized attacks.[20]

On February 13, 1948, the *Cedar Rapids Gazette* ran the headline, "Woman Quits Withholding," to describe Vivien Kellems's new spectacular action. In a speech to the Los Angeles Rotary Club, she announced that she "deliberately would stop withholding Federal income taxes from [her] employees' wages." Protesting against the fiscal policy of President Truman, whom she nicknamed "High Tax Harry," she once again lamented the financial burden of withholding for small businesses. "I am not a tax collector and if an American can be fined and thrown into prison for not collecting taxes from his workers, then let's know about it now." Kellems decided to pay her employees in full, forcing them to pay the collector of internal revenue directly. Once again, she invited Treasury Secretary John W. Snyder to indict her. To support her cause, she called for women, who, she argued, were naturally inclined to make balanced budgets because of their traditional role in the household, to mobilize and solve the man-made problem of debt and taxation: "Women, women of America, let us band together!"[21]

Kellems attracted more supporters when she was interviewed on the *Meet the Press* program on May 21, 1948. She received many letters from women and small-business owners. On May 25, Mrs. Pearl Bussey Phinney wrote to *Meet the Press* and Kellems to congratulate them, offering her opinion in capital letters that "with programs such as this based on unconstitutional happenings, such as have been the case during the last twelve years, it is indeed heartening to think AT LAST the PEOPLE will know the truth." One year after the Marshall plan was proposed to European countries, Miss Catherine A. Maue feared that "the United States Government was trying to raise the standard of living of the peasants of Europe to that of the American citizen and at our expense, or else they intended to lower our standard of living to that of the peasants of Europe." Small businesses also supported Kellems's attack. The owner of Broadway Knitting Mills, Walter Marquart, claimed that he agreed to stop "this so-called SLAVERY of Withholding Tax." From his home in Montebello, California, Joseph T. Craig equated fiscal policy with "Gestapo tactics," and a similar argument appeared in a letter written by Chauncey H. Whitcher, who found the "whole procedure . . . highly coercive, forcing a wage-earner to sign a withholding statement (contract), in most instances, against his or her will, and the collection thereof making you an unwilling party to the conspiracy." The president of Kelly Brothers, Inc., F. M. Kelly, used antistatist arguments, contending that he had paid clerks for this work, and wondered whether there was "not some clause in the Constitution or some precedent on the law books that a good American lawyer can find to uphold such a business expense?" Reactions to Kellems revealed the emerging discontent among conservatives living in the new, postwar, American suburbs.[22]

In southern states, a series of local protests emerged as a reaction to the expansion of New Deal programs, and tax resistance was particularly strong in Texas. After World War II, the Lone Star State was riddled with political tensions, and conservatives strongly opposed New Deal liberalism. In Houston, local civic organizations mobilized against schools and the use of subversive textbooks by progressive instructors and administrators. In the liberal nest of Austin, conservatives attacked the left-wing-oriented curriculum of the university. But it was in the city of Marshall that opposition to federal taxes grew stronger. In this city, located in East Texas, less than thirty miles from the Louisiana border, women filed a complaint against the federal government to protest against Social Security taxes and argued that the federal government had no authority "to force American housewives to become tax collectors."

In 1950 the city of Marshall was prone to racial and political tensions. After Wisconsin senator Joseph McCarthy's famous speech before a Republican women's club in Wheeling, West Virginia, white citizens who belonged to the Marshall Board of Censors banned Elia Kazan's movie *Pinky* (1949) because it portrayed an interracial couple. When in February, W. L. Gelling, the manager of the Paramount Theatre, decided to screen *Pinky* anyway, he was arrested. Racial tensions stemmed from the importance and vitality of the local African American community. In the city, two black colleges, Bishop College and Wiley College, were thriving intellectual centers for young African Americans, including the young activist and cofounder of the Congress of Racial Equality, James L. Farmer. For white middle-class women, the spark that ignited the fight was the 1950 amendment to the Social Security Act which covered domestic employees, a category excluded in the 1935 Social Security law to satisfy southern congressmen. Under the new amendment, domestic staff and gardeners owed 1 percent of their salaries to Social Security, and their employers owed a matching amount. As a majority of domestic employees were black, the tax reform challenged racial boundaries in the Jim Crow city of Marshall.[23]

In January 1951, two housewives from Marshall, Winifred Furth and Dorothy Whelan, wrote a petition called "Storm Signals" to protest against payment of the tax. Soon they were joined by fourteen other women. Most were young mothers. Only five worked outside the home, all of them for their husbands, with the exception of Mrs. Carolyn Abney who owned a bookstore called "Carolyn's Corner." On March 14, their action became public, and their petition was signed by 300 people in town. The Marshall housewives described the household as a nurturing place that had come under attack by Washington bureaucrats. It was their duty to defend both the family and the community against such intrusion. Their protest was supported by Millard Cope, the publisher of the *Marshall News Messenger*, whose wife was one of the signatories. A sixteen-year-old journalist named Bill Moyers, who worked at the daily, wrote his first article on these women who thought that "requiring us to collect the tax was no different from requiring us to collect the garbage." When they filed their tax form, they wrote "none" on the blank "Taxes Due" line. Conservative columnist Westbrook Pegler, advised women to sue the government. A close friend of Vivien Kellems, Pegler knew about her legal battle and invited her to speak at the city auditorium on April 20.[24]

In order to explain their action, the housewives wrote a letter to Treasury Secretary Snyder to signify that, if "they had wished to become tax collectors instead of housewives," they "would have gone to the Internal Revenue Department and applied for a job." They signed it with their given names to show that the crusade was theirs, not their husbands'. By using Lost Cause arguments, Texan newspapers made it clear that the case involved more than a question of money and regressive taxes. It implied first and foremost a sense of social and racial solidarity, which they opposed. On May 4, 1951, the *Dallas Morning News* put it bluntly: "Back under slavery, of course, every slave holder provided Social Security for his retired slaves . . . Under the welfare state, Uncle Sam moves in to compel the colored help of East Texas to take out Social Security . . . by attempting to compel the housewives to compel the Negro workers to take it out." As it did for Kellems, the BIR notified the housewives that they had to pay; otherwise, local tax agents would enforce the law.[25]

The Marshall affair unfolded on a national stage the battles against New Deal liberalism. The women decided to hire the services of a famous lawyer and politician—Martin Dies, an ex-congressman well known for his work as head of the House Committee on Un-American Activities in the 1930s and 1940s. A passionate advocate of Americanism and a strong anticommunist, Dies also believed that the expansion of the federal government had to be stopped. To consolidate their legal stand, only one housewife, Mrs. Carolyn Abney, sued the government. The wife of the local attorney, Mrs. Abney asked that the $12.57 the government took from her bank account to pay Social Security for domestic servants be returned. Soon after, Dies handed the case to Austin attorney Dean Moorhead who brought it to the Dallas Division of the U.S. District Court, arguing that the tax "was erroneously and illegally seized from them because the Federal Insurance contributions cannot be applied to them." The housewives themselves claimed they were being forced into slavery because "the withholding provision violates the 13th Amendment . . . by imposing involuntary servitude upon domestic employers." Carlton Fox, the government attorney, qualified the housewives' arguments and explained that, on the contrary, their defense was "inconceivable." Although he contended that "these Texas women" were "good women," he urged them to "search their conscience" and consider how servants too old to work had "to face the haunting fears of poverty and old age." As it had with Vivien Kellems, the federal government moved against the women's bank accounts and found that several women had withdrawn their money. Two BIR agents reached Marshall National Bank with federal seizure warrants, and ordered that the accounts be made available for inspection.[26]

The case became a *cause célèbre* for many conservatives. Texan oil magnate Haroldson Lafayette Hunt used his new radio program

Facts Forum to support the housewives. The angered women gave speeches at various locations, benefiting from the network of the Texas Federation of Women's Clubs. Other conservative women joined the movement. One St. Louis housewife told the *Wall St. Journal* that she would not pay "until someone yelled." A Pittsburgh woman pointed out that she had "never given it any thought" and that she did not "suppose [her] cleaning girl had either." In Louisiana, Mrs. Mary D. Cain, editor of the weekly *Summit Sun*, wrote an open letter to Treasury Secretary Snyder and denounced Social Security as both "immoral and illegal." Mrs. Cain refused to pay the new self-employment tax because she had had "enough of the New Deal" and was "sick of the whole Truman administration." However, the Texas women lost their first case in 1952. U.S. District Court judge William H. Atwell, who himself resented paying taxes for his domestic servants and called the tax "a nuisance," was sympathetic but unmoved by the group's legal arguments. He made it clear that collection of the tax by the employers of domestic workers was constitutional.[27]

In spite of the legal defeat, the feminist impulse fanned the flames of tax resistance. Vivien Kellems created the Liberty Belles, a grassroots organization, in September 1951. Like the Minute Women of the U.S.A., founded in 1949 by Suzanne Silvercruys Stevenson, the Belles were meant precisely to provide Kellems with a "hard core of resistance" to support her political endeavors, though the group quickly grew beyond her personal ambitions. The first national rally held in Los Angeles the next month was attended by six thousand people. The organization, whose California chapter proved to be particularly active, functioned as an interest group, stating that it would sponsor candidates "following the basic American principles outlined in the LIBERTY BELLE pledge." Between 20,000 and 35,000 joined the group in 1952, the overwhelming majority being middle-class married women, primarily from California but also the Great Lakes region and New England.[28]

As a group committed to repealing the income tax, the Liberty Belles threatened to outflank other right-wing organizations such as the Committee for Constitutional Government and the American Taxpayers Association. These two groups, both overwhelmingly male, advocated a constitutional limitation on the income tax, whereas Kellems demanded its outright repeal on moral grounds. The Belles employed a constitutional language that entailed a new moral absolutism. "Trying to have a 'little' income tax is like trying to have a 'little' pregnancy," Kellems argued. "Neither will stay little; both rapidly swell to amazing proportions."[29]

In the context of McCarthyism and women's mobilization, the Committee for Constitutional Government had free rein to compare New Deal programs to socialism. In a pamphlet distributed around the country, Robert Dresser presented the dream of Karl Marx and his plan to tax all incomes and estates. In the 1930s his dream came true in the United States, where, according to Dresser, the country lived under a socialistic system of taxation. In 1949 the Committee for Constitutional Government spent $750,000 to promote the antitax cause. In November 1950 the American Taxpayers Association celebrated Louisiana as it became the twentieth state to adopt the resolution in favor of tax limitation. In 1951 eight more states passed the amendment. Two Illinois congressmen, Representative Chauncey Reed and Senator Everett Dirksen, introduced a version of the amendment in the House and Senate for a constitutional convention. Reed was a long-time advocate for small-business tax relief and had recently introduced amendments to revise tax legislation for small-business owners. Criticizing his endorsement of Andrew Mellon's views, his detractors called him the "Neanderthal Man" or "Syngman Reed" in reference to the troublesome president of South Korea, Syngman Rhee. The failure of the amendment did not put an end to his will to greatly reduce federal taxation.[30]

All these conservative associations, however, faded away with the end of McCarthyism. The Liberty Belles were torn apart by factional strife between moderate members and the more conservative California state chapter. By late 1953, the group was in disarray. In November, the Marshall housewives appealed to the Supreme Court and explained to the commissioner of internal revenue, Thomas Coleman Andrews, that "it is a sad day in the history of the American people when Communists and subversives hide behind the Fifth Amendment, yet We American Housewives, [*sic*] legally testing a law widely believed to be unconstitutional are not permitted to invoke the Fifth Amendment to prevent arbitrary and discriminatory unreasonable seizure." The court refused to hear the case. Ironically, the housewives' rebellion became a political cause championed by the leading newspaper of the Texas area, the *Houston Post*, whose publisher, Oveta Culp Hobby, became Eisenhower's secretary of Health, Education, and Welfare in 1953 and was in charge of administering the Social Security Act. Once again, middle-class tax resisters met middle-of-the-road Republicans who endorsed Keynesian principles. As the crusading against domestic subversion lost its appeal, foreign policy and the threat of internationalism drew tax resisters' scrutiny.[31]

In 1955, Utah governor Joseph Bracken Lee announced his intention of withholding a portion of his federal income tax that was not already collected or withheld from salary in order to contest the government's right to spend taxpayers' money on foreign aid. "I am refusing," Lee wrote to the BIR, then renamed Internal Revenue Service after the scandals, "to pay that portion of my tax which was not withheld in order to instigate a court test of the constitutional right of the U.S. government to appropriate taxpayers' funds for foreign aid." With particularly harsh words, Lee demonized "internationalism" as the handmaiden to taxation. He also forced the issue in his political capacity, filing a Supreme Court suit on behalf of the state of Utah, making the same argument. The Utah governor hoped to use the conservative mobilization against the Bricker amendment that would put a limit on the president's ability to sign international treaties. The main target of conservative organizations such as the National Federation of Women's Republican Clubs or the Vigilant Women for the Bricker Amendment was the United Nations. Because of Eisenhower's opposition, the amendment failed, and sparked rancor among conservatives against the president. A strong isolationist, Lee pushed for a tax limitation on foreign aid and hoped to organize a successful grassroots movement.[32]

Among tax resisters, Lee was a familiar face. He was born in Price, Utah, on January 7, 1899, and his family soon moved to Fruita, Colorado, where he attended school, completing eighth grade before the family returned to Price. While later managing an insurance business, Lee became a registered Republican and was by 1931 so involved in politics that he ran for mayor of Price, losing by a huge margin. He ran again in 1935, won by two slim votes and served five consecutive terms, a total of twelve years in office. After World War II, he became a staunch opponent of the expansion of federal government. According to *Time* magazine, one of his favorite statements was: "I sometimes think that I am more afraid of the spenders in Washington than I am of the Russians." Many Americans first heard of him in 1952 in a series of articles in national periodicals as journalists were intrigued by his novel budgetary policies in Utah. On April 28, 1952, he gave a speech at the National Convention of the U.S. Chamber of Commerce in Washington, D.C. After presenting his own philosophy of government in an extended introduction, he vehemently decried the transformation of the country's income tax system during World War II, arguing that "it is also time to get more and more of the eyes of more and more of our citizens out from under the wool that has been pulled over them." Referring to the brainwashing argument used during the war, he deplored "the cleverly devised scheme facetiously called the withholding tax—the government being the withholder of course." The whole tax system, Bracken regretted, was invented to trap the American people, and the withholding scheme was a particularly clever mechanism to extract money.[33]

As the campaign against the Bricker amendment put foreign policy at the forefront of the political debate, the governor focused on the use of taxpayers' money to finance the Cold War. In 1954, before the Governors' Conference, he lobbied his fellow governors and urged them to join him in his antitax crusade. He contended that the states possessed exclusive rights to levy income taxes and that the federal government should present them with an annual tax bill. In turn, they should levy within their boundaries and remit to Washington. Lee's argument attracted more and more attention. He received many letters suggesting that he run for president. J. S. Kimmel, president of the Chamber of Commerce in Davenport, Louisiana, compared him to "a lighthouse" because of his "valiant efforts in behalf of the American way of life." Aided by these new supporters, Lee went a step further in October 1955 by announcing his refusal to pay his income tax on constitutional grounds.[34]

In a couple of days, hundreds of letters and telegrams to congratulate him arrived in his mailbox. A postcard from Monroe, Louisiana, bore a small song endorsing Lee's antitax crusade:

> Two, four, six, hut—
> We want a tax cut—
> Seven, eight, nine, ten—
> We want to know when—
> We don't want no hem or haw—
> We're for the governor of Utah.

One congratulatory message came from Vivien Kellems, others from small business owners. Democrats reacted as they did when Kellems declined to pay her taxes, accusing Lee of breaking federal law and calling on him to resign. The press echoed these accusations. An editorial in the *Washington Post* mocked him for being an "international tax dodger" and recalled the intentions of the founders. More sarcastically, the *Milwaukee Journal* called Lee a "Neanderthal politician," while locally he was criticized for being irresponsible.

Signs were painted on the front steps of the governor's mansion that said "Pay up, Brack" and "Grow up, Gov." Treasury Secretary George Humphrey reminded Lee of his obligations, while Roland V. Wise, director of the Utah IRS office, informed him that the constitutionality of the income tax had been tested many times, notably in the *Frothingham v. Mellon* (1923) decision. As usual, the Treasury tried to avoid publicity, but the agency did announce its intention to sue him, and Humphrey announced that the IRS would collect the money from his bank accounts. In response, Lee's attorneys filed an original action in the U.S. Supreme Court to restrain the treasury secretary from making new foreign aid payments. The court, however, declined to hear the case.[35]

Even if they failed to challenge the Keynesian and Cold War consensus, such battles cemented a common worldview, and a grassroots subculture of tax resistance emerged behind the scenes of the nascent conservative movement.

In the mid-1950s few Americans knew about the academic and voluminous books written by conservative intellectuals Friedrich von Hayek and Milton Friedman such as *The Road to Serfdom* (1944). In the conservative network of bookstores, tax resisters read small magazines and books that were unknown to the general public. All these publications helped them reformulate their opposition to progressive taxation in a moralistic way. The literature that circulated fostered a language of urgency and action to confront the conspiracy that was underway in Washington, D.C. Couched in plain, accessible language, many books won widespread popular by deriding the perils of the leviathan state.[36]

Although the *Reader's Digest*, edited by the anticommunist Eugene Lyons, was quite popular, many books were written by other famous antitax figures. Published in May 1952, Vivien Kellems's book *Toil, Taxes and Trouble* was one of them. With a preface written by anticommunist historian Rupert Hughes, her book captured a nationwide conservative audience. Most copies were sold by direct mail, especially in California and the Midwest. Sales figures were but one side of the story, as excerpts were also reproduced in leading conservative newsletters such as *Spotlight*, edited by the Committee for Constitutional Government, whose circulation of about 60,000 ensured a much broader distribution. Furthermore, in conservative women's reading groups, a single copy of the book was likely to be read by several different people. Kellems's book explored the "brain-washing" of taxpayers. The income tax, she wrote, was a way for the government to deliberately "hide" from employees the payment of their taxes and thus to prevent them from becoming "tax-conscious." Throughout the book, she identified the foes against which she was struggling with a vivid, and at times colloquial, vocabulary: they were the "tax grabbers and tax planners . . . yellow cowards, mangy little bureaucrats in Washington," all supposedly striving to "destroy the capitalist system" in the name of a projected communist dicta-torship. To cure this "evil," she suggested several remedies that were traditional among tax resisters: restoring a proper understanding of the Constitution, appealing to God, and using the average Ameri-can's "good common sense."[37]

Another book, *Taxation with Representation or Your Tax Money Went That A'way* (1962), written by Corinne Griffith, was displayed on the shelves of conservatives bookstores. A regular customer of the bookstore Poor Richard's, run by Florence and Frank Ranuzzi in Los Angeles, Griffith was a former actress who turned activist after meeting Vivien Kellems. Born in Hill County, Texas, in 1895, the blue-eyed brunette, who was tagged "The Orchid of the Screen" in her early movie career because of her beauty, became very rich after her marriage to George Marshall, the owner of the Washington Redskins. In the early 1950s, she began campaigning for abolition of the income tax, giving more than 480 speeches across the country. In 1956, when the Senate Judiciary Committee held hear-ings on tax limitation, Griffith clearly explained that her crusade aimed at "repealing the income tax" and "reverting it to our original Constitution."[38]

Other intellectuals made a name for themselves by criticizing the income tax. Frank Chodorov, a libertarian intellectual, published *The Income Tax: Root of All Evil* in 1954. The sixty-year-old man denounced the evils of the Sixteenth Amendment that "put no limit on government confiscation," a message that found an eager readership in conservative circles. Chodorov, who had founded the Intercollegiate Society of Individualists one year earlier and had recently been appointed editor of *The Freeman*, a publication of the Foundation for Economic Education, was known for his uncompromisingly libertarian and antistatist politics. Similarly, John T. Flynn, a former New Dealer who had turned conservative and isolationist during World War II, published many articles to denounce the taxing power of the purse. Flynn's columns were quite popular among tax resisters.[39]

Many speeches by antitax figures circulated in conservative circles, such as Myron C. Fagan's *J. Bracken Lee Unmasks the Income Tax Law* published in 1957. Small newsletters helped promote the antitax cause. In California retired executives and small businessmen financed the publication of *American Progress*, devoted to the cause of tax resistance. Businessmen from New Orleans also gave money to an antitax organization, Tax Foundation, Inc. Its monthly publication, *Tax Features*, popularized an imaginary white-collar worker named Charlie Green. Charlie was a married man, burdened by taxation. The white-collar worker had a twelve-year-old daughter in elementary school and a fourteen-year-old son in junior high. He earned $10,000 a year but had to pay more and more taxes. All these publications spread the idea of a tax conspiracy fomented by liberal policymakers against the American people.[40]

At patriotic rallies and local civic clubs, prominent resisters gave talks to promote their cause. Kellems was one of the stars of the speaking circuit, attracting numerous supporters in California. At mass meetings and luncheon clubs, she derided "the rapacious, grasping, greedy, unscrupulous, thieving gangsters and scoundrels in Washington." In Los Angeles, more than 5,000 people—mostly women—attended her meeting. Radio programs conveyed antitax arguments as well. Financed by oil billionaire Haroldson Lafayette "H. L." Hunt, the show *Facts Forum*, with former FBI agent Dan Smoot as its commentator, railed against fiscal irresponsibility and welfare statism and constantly blasted the income tax.[41]

Another famous star of the conservative tour was the former revenue commissioner, Thomas Coleman Andrews, whom Marshall housewives met to protest against Social Security tax. Born in Richmond, Virginia, in 1899, Andrews became an accountant in the 1930s before joining the BIR in 1953. The new revenue commissioner contemplated, from within, the process of tax collection. After his resignation in 1955, he turned into a strident opponent of the federal government and used his intimate knowledge of the agency to denounce its inquisitorial methods. The income tax was bad, he warned his fellow-citizens, "because it was conceived as class hatred, an instrument of vengeance," that played "right into the hands of the Communists."[42]

For tax resisters, however, the main problem remained the lack of national organization as the Republican Party was strongly opposed to any radical changes on tax issues. As a consequence, the movement was still composed of small organizations and clubs led by retired businessmen and housewives. These clubs operated separately from one another. In southern California, businessmen reinvigorated the Californian Taxpayers' Association. At the head of it, Arthur Kemp, professor of economics at Claremont Men's College, feared the rising of taxes, both at the local and national levels. Founded in 1958 by candy manufacturer Robert H. W. Welch, the John Birch Society became a revered place for tax resisters. A fierce anticommunist, Welch believed in free enterprise and denounced the dictatorial

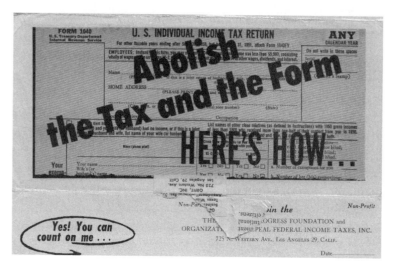

Figure 6.3. Pamphlet of the American Progress Foundation and Organization to Repeal Federal Income Taxes, Inc. (1957). Courtesy of the University of Iowa Libraries.

power of the federal government. From his office in Belmont, he carefully organized fundraising and membership drives for his organization. The Organization to Repeal Federal Income Taxes, with actress Corinne Griffith as honorary president, was also created and focused on the abolition of the income tax.[43]

A retired chemical manufacturer named Paul K. Morganthaler Jr. vigorously directed the organization from Los Angeles, hoping to put an end to "the competition our own government is thrusting upon the tax paying American business man." Among the well-known names associated with this movement were Joseph Bracken Lee and Vivien Kellems. Their goal was to forbid federal income taxes and privatize almost all federal assets. General William H. Wilbur criticized "the expensive government activities in competition with private business" that "served to stifle the free enterprise system which was the backbone of America's strength."[44]

Equipped with such a proposal, tax resisters began to organize lo-cal chapters that would pressure state legislators with petitions and demonstrations to call for a constitutional convention. In 1957 a well-known conservative representative from Michigan, Clare Eugene Hoffman, introduced a joint resolution for the repeal of the Sixteenth Amendment. On his weekly radio program, the *Manion Forum Show*, Clarence Manion popularized the crusade. In one show, the *Forum* lambasted the "murderously oppressive Marxist Federal Income Tax; gigantic and unnecessary subsidies of tax money for fantastic highway and housing projects; Federal aid to education which would inevitably be followed by Federal Socialist control." A former execu-tive at Morton Salt, and member of the Republican Party, Sterling Morton gave $500 for the "repeal or limitation" of the Sixteenth Amendment. General Douglas MacArthur even joined the parade, calling taxation "the hidden tyrant" and informing his fellow citizens that in 1958 "they will pay for government this year more than they will spend in food, clothing, medical care, and religious activities."[45]

The popularity of tax resistance increased because of growing con-cerns about bankruptcies due to the recession of 1957. The rise of unemployment and the high number of business failures—the high-est rate since 1940—pushed more and more small businessmen to complain about the burden of federal taxation. Furthermore, in south-ern states, the civil rights movement increased the number of white tax resisters. With the *Brown v. Board of Education of Topeka* (1954) decision, many seized the opportunity to tap into southern antistatism to promote the issue of taxes. Vivien Kellems hoped that the *Brown* decision would shed new light on the dictatorial goal of the federal government. The founder of the John Birch Society, Robert W. Welch, made it clear in his *Letter to the South on Segregation* (1958) that communism asserted itself in the decision. In many places, small-business owners and middle-class professionals created White Citi-zens' Councils for the purpose of resisting the school desegregation order. Segregationists repeatedly identified whites as virtually the only meaningful group of taxpayers. A grocer in Memphis claimed that African Americans would not have made such progress "had it not been for the whites," and contended that the black population in his area accounted for "37%" but supported "much less than 20% of the taxes and responsibility of the city or Federal government." Segregationists sent reams of letters to the Supreme Court protesting *Brown*, arguing that their constitutional rights were being violated. A citizen named Tulio Vasquez contended that "95% of taxpayers within the United States" were white people, and that segregation could not be abolished without their direct consent because the "money of white taxpayers" should not be used against the "general welfare."[46]

Uneasy with mainstream Republicanism, most tax resisters admired Arizona senator Barry Goldwater. This charming man, who often posed in cowboy boots and Stetsons, epitomized the individualistic and tax-free world militants dreamed of. Goldwater bolstered his reputation by criticizing Eisenhower's overly moderate policy with straightforward language that appealed to them. By the summer of 1960, many groups called "Goldwater for President" had emerged, and were supported by antitax militants. As the conservative movement gained political clout, the IRS's surveillance increased. In the fall of 1961, after the election of John Fitzgerald Kennedy, the federal agency launched the Ideological Organizations Project, a secret structure whose mission was to investigate the financial organization of right-wing groups and to scrutinize their tax-exempt status. A study of the Life Line Foundation, financed by oil magnate "H. L." Hunt in Texas, was used to demonstrate the relentless attack against the power of the federal purse, as illustrated by the following quotation from a *Life Line* publication: "The Sixteenth Amendment to the U.S. Constitution has done more to promote the growth and expansion of government than any other single factor . . . the income tax has drained from the American people the money necessary to finance governmental growth on a terrifying scale." Even though they were under close scrutiny by the Kennedy administration, grassroots organizations would soon have the opportunity to have their arguments heard on a national scale with the presidential campaign of Barry Goldwater in 1964.[47]

In 1962 Mr. Walter Knott was a seventy-three-year-old, distinguished, grey-haired man. A successful entrepreneur who founded Knott's Berry Farm and Ghost Town, one of southern California's most popular amusement parks, he was retired but remained very active in the field of politics, defending both Americanism and free enterprise. A typical militant of Orange County, and a passionate reader of books on American history, he was dismayed by cultural and social changes in postwar America. A decade earlier, he had supported Fred Schwarz's Christian Anti-Communist Crusade. In September 1962 he attended a three-day meeting of the California Tax Parties at the Wilsbire Ebell Theatre to promote the Liberty Amendment which would repeal the Sixteenth Amendment. The meeting was sponsored by a new organization, Operation America, whose specific purpose was to expand public understanding of the attack on progressive taxation.[48]

Under the guidance of Willis E. Stone, the Liberty Amendment campaign had been launched a few years earlier. Stone, who was born in Denver, Colorado, on July 20, 1899, was an industrial engineer who had attended local schools and graduated from the University of Denver. As a young adult, he had been, at various times, a newspaper reporter, an advertising executive, and a realtor. In 1930 he became an industrial engineer. During World War II he was shocked by the brutal arrest of businessman Sewell Lee Avery, and the event awakened him to the tyranny of federal power. A rich entrepreneur, Avery repeatedly opposed President Roosevelt's National War Labor Board. When he refused to settle a strike in 1944, endangering the delivery of essential goods, Roosevelt's administration used emergency measures to remove him from office and temporarily seize his company. On June 2, 1944, Stone wrote an article for the local newspaper *Sherman Oaks Citizen Tribune*, advocating for both constitutional tax limitations and retrenchment of federal intervention.

After retiring in 1958, he devoted his energy to the ratification of the Twenty-Third Amendment to the U.S. Constitution. The amendment, which called for the elimination of the federal income tax, was introduced in Congress in 1959 by James Boyd Utt, a Californian senator elected in Orange County.

To make citizens aware of the financial consequences of the federal government's taxation policies, Stone founded the National Committee for Economic Freedom in 1959 to assist state groups that supported the Liberty Amendment. Stone started the formation of affiliated committees in each state, and was chairman of the organization, renamed The Liberty Amendment of the USA in 1963 in order to better identify its sole purpose. By then there were active state committees in forty-seven states, and prospects were bright for the formation of active units in the remaining three states within the next few months. Locally, militants used the conservative network to defend their ideas. In South Carolina, the radio station WOKE broadcasted special programs on the issue. In Southern California, many small business owners in Los Angeles and Orange counties, "freedom-loving companies" as *American Progress* called them, publicly supported the amendment. All freedom lovers chose Arizona senator Barry Goldwater, hoping that a radical policy change was soon to come.[49]

As the election drew close, Goldwater and his supporters started to focus on welfare and the waste of taxpayers' money. For Willis E. Stone, the year 1964 promised to be a very "exciting" one as Americans would have to make a choice. "On the one hand," he contended, "was a $40 billion-a-year federal bureaucracy which had no intention of taking its hand out of our pockets," and on the other hand, "there was the American side, driving to restore the Constitution and revitalize the glories of human freedom." Some long-time resisters financed the campaign. The du Pont family gave more than $25,000, and Walt Disney himself no longer hid his admiration for the conservative senator. On September 14, 1964, when he received the

Medal of Freedom, the highest civilian honor in the country, from President Lyndon B. Johnson, he wore a Barry Goldwater campaign button. Hundreds of small businessmen claimed their admiration for Goldwater. The Liberty Belles convinced many Republicans to vote for him in the decisive California primary in June, 1964. In her own state of Connecticut, Vivien Kellems raised funds to finance meetings and travels. The National Association of Republican Women took a strong stance in favor of the conservative candidate and used its local network to promote his nomination.[50]

Supporters of Goldwater, however, were divided about the best political strategy. Tax resisters refused to compromise their conservative principles in order to win the presidency. As a consequence, many of them found themselves unwelcome in the Goldwater team. Kellems was accused of bringing bad publicity. In a speech on Social Security, she contended that "it was not an ordinary political campaign," and explained that the country was "locked in a life-and-death struggle for our freedom." These passionate groups of activists alienated modern Republicans as well as many journalists. Prestigious magazines such as *Life* and *The Reporter* spoke of "a tide of zealotry" and the "conquest" of the Grand Old Party (GOP) by fanatics. Goldwater militants, at times, played into their opponent's hands by making rambunctious remarks to reporters. Vivien Kellems was asked by Republicans in her home state of California to remain publicly silent until the end of the campaign. Democrats portrayed Goldwater and his supporters as schizophrenic and dangerous individuals. It came as no surprise that Lyndon Johnson won a landslide victory, with 43 million votes to Goldwater's 27 million. The GOP lost thirty-eight House and two Senate seats. Goldwater's defeat ultimately put a limit on the conservative tax resisters' campaigning. Following the debacle of 1964, moderates within the party sought to regain control and move it toward the political center. It meant purging Goldwater supporters from high-level positions within the party hierarchy, and most tax resisters lost credibility and political clout.[51]

The defeat of Goldwater, claimed tax resisters, was due to the American people's lack of information on the real issues. In 1965 Californian tax organizations decided to organize demonstrations in front of IRS buildings to explain the burden of taxes "for it was every American citizen's right to know that there was available a means by which constitutional government could be restored to his nation." At the end of the 1960s, tax resisters still toiled in the wilderness and were often very isolated. In Missouri, Merle Parker published an overtly racist pamphlet *Taxpayers' Power!* and drove his Liberty Van alone to denounce both the high level of taxation and the civil rights movement. By 1967, Willis Stone was forced to acknowledge that his political project had failed. As the decade drew to an end, the "freedom-lovers" militants were in disarray.[52]

From World War II to the end of the sixties, tax resisters displayed the ideological intensity of the grassroots conservatives as they fiercely waged war against New Deal liberalism at home and abroad. Through their fight against taxes, they defended what they believed were the founding virtues of the American republic: the principle of limited government, the rule of law, and unalienable individual rights. The high representation of women militants at the grassroots level and within organizations gave new life to tax resistance. In a political world overwhelmingly dominated by men, they defended their rights as housewives and mothers by contending that federal taxation was a threat to the American household. After winning the primary in East St. Louis, conservative militant Phyllis Schlafly declared that "as a housewife" she was "greatly concerned about the fact that we have the highest prices and highest taxes in our country's history— caused by wasteful government spending, graft, and a policy of betraying our friends and arming our enemies." Ms. Carolyn Abney, one of the Marshall housewives, went even further, contending that "you couldn't legislate women." Eventually, from the Japanese attack on Pearl Harbor to Barry Goldwater's campaign in 1964, the tax resistance movement took a western and southern turn. In spite of their grassroots base, however, tax resisters remained a marginal force. Goldwater's defeat reflected the prevalence of the tax consensus in postwar years among the majority of Americans. The close alliance between big corporations and modern Republicans epitomized by the Eisenhower administration increased the limit of tax resistance. As Ronald Reagan prepared for his successful 1966 California gubernatorial election, he published a memoir, *Where's the Rest of Me?* in which he discussed his motion picture career and his political transformation from New Deal Democrat to conservative Republican. Reagan explained the financial difficulties in which he found himself in the late 1940s: "True, I'd been making handsome money ever since World War II, but the handsome money lost a lot of its beauty and substance going through the 91 percent bracket of the income tax. The tragic fact of life in this evil day of progressive taxation is that, once behind, it is well-nigh impossible to earn your way out." Soon, Reagan's view would be shared by millions of Americans. While tax resisters would come out of the wilderness, women would cede the limelight to men.[53]

7

The Tyranny of the "Infernal Revenue Service"

> If even bigger government, more spending, and
> higher taxes were the answer, Great Britain and
> New York City would be the two most prosperous
> areas in the world. They are the opposite.
>
> —*Jack Kemp* (1977)

O N T H E D E S K of New York representative Jack Kemp stood a statuette of Don Quixote. In the mid-1970s, Miguel de Cervantes's famous hero came to symbolize Kemp's attempt to revive tax resistance in order to challenge the Keynesian hegemony. A Republican congressman from upstate New York, Kemp was born in California to Christian Scientist parents. After working on the loading docks of his father's trucking company as a boy before majoring in physical education at Occidental College, he became a successful quarterback for the Buffalo Bills. An admirer of Barry Goldwater and a careful reader of Ayn Rand, the football star wanted to become a conservative JFK, whose initials he shared. Elected in the suburban Buffalo region in 1971, the new congressman chose tax cuts as his distinctive brand and the *New York Times* explained to its readers that "Old No.

15" (Kemp's Buffalo Bills jersey number) could become "Taxpayers' No. 1." With the help of *Wall Street Journal* editor Jude Wanniski and economist Arthur Laffer, Kemp decided to promote an innovative tax policy based on income tax cuts. If such proposals were still anathema to many businessmen and politicians, Kemp was able to bank on middle-class discontent, which grew stronger in the 1970s. His slogan was simple and universal: "We don't need tax reductions for upper incomes or lower incomes. We need reduction for *all* taxpayers." The simplicity of the proposal struck a chord among the sixty million taxpayers as they grappled with the problems of stagflation—a painful combination of inflation and recession—and political crisis in a country torn apart by debates revolving around the Vietnam War and moral values.[1]

As the ideals of the sixties and Lyndon Johnson's hopes for a Great Society came to an end, Kemp tapped into a new militancy that included middle-class activists, neoliberal intellectuals and politicians who contended, for the first time since World War II, that massive tax cuts were the only way to promote economic growth and national prosperity. With the loss of industrial jobs, Americans found little reason for optimism. Conservative intellectual Irving Kristol explained in the *Wall Street Journal* that the Keynesian orthodoxy was showing "some signs of sclerosis, even senility" both in Europe and in United States. As the Watergate scandal widened the gap between the citizens and the elites in Washington, D.C., distrust of the legitimacy of the IRS grew stronger. In the context of economic crisis and intense competition in foreign markets, some big corporations decided to rejoin the antitax parade, even though it was a difficult decision to make. As a consequence, the founding principles of taxpayers' sacrifice and graduated rates came under public scrutiny. During the 1970s, tax resistance, as conservative organizer Richard Viguerie put it, "kicked the sleeping dog" in western and southern states and enabled white middle-class tax resisters to come out of the wilderness. Their attacks against the tyranny of the federal government reverberated in the country, and their resistance brought light into what they considered a political darkness.[2]

To celebrate the Bicentennial anniversary of the Boston Tea Party in 1973, the Tax Rebellion Committee of Los Angeles organized parades. Robert Lyon, the committee organizer, held such an event in Sacramento, and asked his fellow rebels to serve tea packages. Wearing an Uncle Sam costume, Lyon denounced the burden of both national and local taxes. Timed to coincide with Tax Day on April 15, the "Tax Protest Tea Dumping" was followed by a series of tax seminars organized in many cities. As Lyon explained, "the objective is to start all state legislatures with Boston Tea Parties which so united the colonists." He added that "the tea party gave people hope" and his organization "hoped to make people realize their need for liberty." Lyon, an outspoken antitax militant, strongly involved in the Liberty Amendment campaign, used a more powerful argument to convince citizens: the IRS was the root of all evils. In the early 1970s tax resisters found an easily identifiable target in the federal agency that embodied their heightened fears of an invisible enemy whose aim was to pollute the minds of American citizens. California was at the forefront of this reinvigorated tax resistance movement.[3]

After World War II, the Golden State was significantly transformed by economic growth and the defense boom during the Cold War era. From 1943 to 1954 Republican governor Earl Warren poured resources into the state, building highways, schools, hospitals, prisons, and parks to accommodate the rapidly expanding population. His successor, Governor Edmund Gerald "Pat" Brown, reinforced this liberal policy, hoping to make California the symbol of the Great Society and social justice in the nation. In the southern part of the state, however, conservatives were very much concerned by the tax-and-spend policy. For many of them, the postwar embodiment of the American Dream—a heterosexual nuclear family with a working father and a stay-at-home mother living in an upwardly mobile suburban neighborhood—appeared on the verge of collapse. Social movements such as feminism and gay rights simultaneously challenged the boundaries of the traditional domestic ideology, heralding, for some, society's moral collapse. Middle-class tax resisters expounded in newsletters and pamphlets their belief that the leviathan state had increased both permissiveness among citizens and the waste of taxpayers' money because they resented federally funded social programs, such as community action programs, which were financed with their money. Martin A. Larson, author of an essay published in 1968 and entitled *The Great Tax Fraud: How the Federal Government Favors the Rich and Exploits the Masses,* explained to the readers of *Tax Strike News* "that the federal bureaucracy has among its principal objectives the destruction of the family, the elimination of the middle-class, and the creation of a vast mass of people who can be completely controlled." Such a disaster, he warned, "must be obvious to anyone who contemplates this monster at all carefully." Liberals in power, he asserted, had blurred the nation's sense of right and wrong and forced tax resisters to assume a more active posture.[4]

Taxpayers feared that liberal policymakers were usurping their authority as parents. The gravity and danger they perceived led them to take matters into their own hands and join the number of small antitax organizations that already existed. In San Francisco, the organization Parents and Taxpayers established a place for itself by attacking welfare policy as an agent of moral decay. Many parents felt guilty that their own money was used to finance permissive and immoral social policies. The association's bulletin devoted many articles to the multiple causes of evil, including busing, the Black Panthers, and welfare programs. "The Conspiracy within the United States will continue to use [our] children and [our] money as it wishes." The *Roe v. Wade* (1973) decision was compared to the *Dred Scott* (1857) decision, prophesying a similar civil war to come. Tax resisters believed that their households and their communities were under siege.[5]

For the Parents and Taxpayers' association, a moral revolution was underfoot and middle-class people were the victims of an inquisitorial state. Newsletters were filled with stories of "martyrs" of the IRS. Such was the case for Mr. and Mrs. John Marthaler, a typical middle-class couple living in Sonoma, California. Their car was unsuccessfully "seized by agents of the U.S. IRS for non-payment of [their] 1967–1968 income taxes." Their prosecution was a perfect example, the association claimed, of the vicious tactics of a federal department whose agents considered citizens as enemies. In a special issue that celebrated the "not guilty" verdict rendered by a federal court jury, the Parents and Taxpayers' bulletin quoted IRS special agent Toral O. Solberg, who wrote in a report to his supervisor that "If the Court makes an example out of MARTHALER, it might deter others from similar efforts to frustrate the operations of the IRS."[6]

Another story about a woman named Barbara Hutchinson fueled the perception that the country was particularly attuned to the dangers of subversion. A tax expert and tax law professor at the University of San Diego, Hutchinson was sent to jail after announcing that she would no longer pay her taxes. Founder and executive director of the Association of Concerned Taxpayers, she became famous nationwide when she equated the IRS with the Gestapo. Hutchinson was seen by conservative militants as a "mini-martyr," as one *San Francisco Examiner* journalist described her. She blamed authorities for treating her like a criminal, and described her jail experience with an acute sense of despair. "I was taken in handcuffs from the Federal Court House in San Diego to the San Diego County Jail—I arrived at the jail, escorted by eight Federal Marshalls, at 2:30 p.m. I was made to strip," she told readers of the newsletter of Parents and Taxpayers. She added that she "was put in what is called a holding tank," where "the most de-humanizing thing was open toilets and showers." The goal of the IRS, she claimed, was to make tax resisters look insane as the agency refused to recognize them as political dissenters. Such stories reinforced tax resisters' siege mentality.[7]

According to the head of the Los Angeles Tax Rebellion Commit-tee, Jim Scott, a federal conspiracy started when, "on December 23, 1913, two days before Christmas and without a duly assembled quo-rum, the sixteenth amendment to the U.S. Constitution and Federal Reserve Act became so-called law." Doors were then open for "inter-national bankers, opportunists, and selfish interests to drain our re-sources and wealth." In another pamphlet published by the same Tax Rebellion Committee, it was argued that income taxes should not be paid because the Federal Reserve notes were not redeemable in specie and were therefore not legitimate currency. In this pam-phlet it was explained that "the Constitution prohibited Americans from authorizing their government to 'Rob Peter to pay Paul.'" Most of their arguments revolved around the Sixteenth Amendment. Some contended that it was not lawfully ratified, because different states had slight differences in the punctuation; others contended that it was not lawfully ratified, because Ohio was not legally a state at the time it ratified the amendment. All these arguments framed progres-sive taxation as an illegal exercise of federal power that gave tax re-sisters a legitimate right to rebel.[8]

Facing what he perceived to be tyrannical government, Scott saw himself in the midst of a revolt. An outspoken militant in his mid-fifties, he considered the "Internal Revenue Bureau [*sic*]" as a "conspir-acy," a "gang of real criminals," and he compared "dead wrong" bu-reaucrats to "vipers of the Federal Mafia." Still equating federal taxation with slavery, he urged "millions of irate tax slaves" to help him "restore our lost freedoms and re-enthrone that precious document, the U.S. Constitution." In the context of expansion of federal power, he felt obliged to reaffirm his constitutional rights. Contesting the testimo-nies of IRS agents who sued him, he explained that he did file his form for the years 1969, 1970 and the filings were made "under protest and in blank with no information and no money." He saw it as "an act of civil disobedience since the Internal Revenue Code of 1954 was blatantly unconstitutional," and violated his "constitutional rights guaranteed to [him] under the 4th and 5th amendments of the U.S. Constitution." Other militants from the Tax Rebellion Committee underscored the impact of the landmark *Miranda v. Arizona* (1966) decision, which forced police officers to ensure that suspects were informed of their rights. In the face of tax agents, they argued, the decision "spells out CONSTITUTIONAL DEFENSES for tax rebels against income tax strategy" and therefore should be used against the IRS. It was important, tax resisters insisted, to master the tax code in order to trump the expertise of tax bureaucrats.[9]

In California, face-to-face encounters with revenue agents increased. In July 1971 Scott confronted two "inquisitors" of the IRS for refusing to file a 1040 form. To welcome the two agents, Scott asked six "witnesses" to be present, and installed "two tape recorders, a camera and a sawed 12 gauge shotgun leaning against the wall." As the two agents departed, Scott proudly concluded that "all good citizens who wanted to avoid entrapment by the con-men of the bureau, the masters of extortion, harassment and intimidation be counseled to use witnesses, tape recorders, camera and a visible weapon." With his organization, he even set a list of good rules to follow against the "awesome powers of tyrannical government:

1. Produce no records, books or papers . . . 4th amendment.
2. Make no statements . . . cooperate in no way, as per 5th amendment on self-incrimination.
3. Sign nothing.
4. Never have an interview without one or more favorable witnesses."[10]

As the number of small antitax organizations grew, the flurry of newsletters exhibited a very pessimistic view of the perceived oppressive power surrounding honest citizens. As a consequence, tax resisters felt they had to reaffirm their values and redeem a spiritual core that the country had lost.

At a time when religious revival was gaining ground, religious motives fuelled the discontent of middle-class conservatives. Members of the Tax Rebellion Committee of Los Angeles promulgated the view that "this confiscation by our government was not only 'illegal,' but 'un-Christian.'" They even contended that "Jesus was not a Socialist" but "believed in the profit motive." Criticizing the secularization of society, tax resisters saw the world as riddled with anxieties and fears. They lived in an atmosphere of general crisis in which citizens seemed to be losing their grip and considered resistance as an antidote against what they perceived to be a moral crisis and as a rejuvenation of the people's ability to defend their own rights.[11]

On March 17, 1973, the Tax Rebellion Committee of Fresno and other antitax organizations transformed St. Patrick's Day into St. Patrick Henry's Day in honor of "the great American patriot who led our early nation's fight against unjust taxation and stifling tyranny." They handed out a declaration to be sent to local organizations: "Yes I am tired of seeing IRS decorated with my 'green' on St Patrick's Day or any other day! I want to learn how others have successfully avoided unjust taxation." History and the memory of the American Revolution shaped the view of antitax militants and reinforced their belief in the nation's decline since the days of the founders.[12]

Although these small organizations had no significant political impact, they helped to give conservatives a sense of purpose. Taxation became the monolithic evil that conflated the collapse of moral values with the growth of the federal power. Yet, Californian militants still failed to achieve national attention in the early 1970s. They accused Republican politicians of betraying their cause by endorsing Keynesian principles. Only two were admired—a local hero, Ronald Reagan, and the southern rising star, Jesse Helms. It was in the 1950s that Ronald Reagan, the former president of the Screen Actors Guild in Hollywood, became a corporate spokesman and a staunch conservative. In 1964, during the presidential campaign, Barry Goldwater put him at the forefront of the audience and Reagan foreshadowed a "time for choosing" between free enterprise and big government. As governor of California, he pledged, as he was sworn into office on January 5, 1967, to "cut and squeeze and trim" the state budget. Tax resisters knew him well as he attended many tax seminars organized by the Taxpayers Committee of Los Angeles and shared their antitax rhetoric and denunciation of the federal government. In the mid-1970s, Reagan started to endorse Jack Kemp's proposal as the only way to restore economic growth.[13]

Another promising politician was Jesse Helms, after his successful senatorial campaign of 1972. The son of a police chief in a small North Carolina town, Helms started out as a journalist and entered the conservative ranks after a career in the Democratic Party. He began offering regular opinions on the air in the early 1960s, and the body of his thought was familiar to many tax resisters. Jesse Helms's loyalty to the Democratic Party wavered at the time of Barry Goldwater's campaign. One year later, he switched his registration. His antistatist editorials circulated in the tax resisters' literature. Using the same apocalyptic tone as resisters did, Helms frequently explained that Americans were "being required to finance their own destruction." The idea of solidarity and sacrifice had perverted the values of the American way of life, complained the bitter militant: "It was the lure of something-for-nothing that did America in. We were looking for the easy way out, the fast buck. We believed—we really did—that there was such a thing as 'federal aid' and 'free money' from Washington. So we elected the men who promised the most." For Helms and for Reagan, the bread-and-circus democracy had dispossessed Americans of their right to choose.[14]

In the early 1970s, however, such assumptions remained in the shadow of traditional politics and mainstream values. The first militant to come under the spotlight was long-time tax resister, Vivien

Kellems, who gave her antitax crusade a middle-class constituency that marked the revival of interest in national tax protests.

When Women's Lib and Girl Power was holding sway in the nation, the motto "Uncle Sam is penalizing us girls!" could have been expressed by a young and energetic feminist in her twenties. Instead, these words came from the mouth of the seventy-year-old Vivien Kellems. With her typical vibrant rhetoric, she explained that she was "perfectly willing to pay taxes but at the same rate as anybody else" and added that Uncle Sam was "penalizing us girls just because we couldn't get husbands." While spending the winter of 1968 in Scotland to complete a PhD dissertation she had started in the 1920s with Edwin R. A. Seligman, Kellems realized "the vulnerability" of the income-tax disparities between single and married taxpayers. For her, it was the symbol of the false progressivity of the tax system, and she wondered why single men and women's sacrifices were more important than those of married couples.[15]

Since 1948 and the adoption of the income-splitting joint return to substitute for individual returns, a couples' total income had been divided in two, with the tax computed on one half doubled to produce the couple's tax. A deliberate side-effect of the law was that it created what came to be known as the "singles penalty." In other words, singles paid more taxes than couples with the same total income. In some cases, the additional tax burden could be as high as 42 percent more. Kellems realized this was a way for legislators to protect and strengthen their traditional ideal of American society as dominated by the male-breadwinner family, and she dove back into politics after the severe Goldwater debacle. Kellems perfectly captured the antiauthority mood of the sixties. In an open letter published in the *Washington Post* and using the same rhetoric as the Students for a Democratic Society's militant Mario Savio, Kellems compared the federal government to "A MACHINE," and directly attacked the "cogs" of the MACHINE. "If you pressed the IRS

button," she added, "the wheels whirred, the ponderous, creaky MA-
CHINE moved into action, exactly as it was programmed." Using a
language of discrimination and taxpayers' rights, she created an awk-
ward coalition with left-wing politicians who also blamed the unfair-
ness of the tax code for singles, even though they still supported the
progressivity of the tax system.[16]

On April 15, 1969—the deadline for filing income tax returns—
Kellems announced to the press that she had sent a blank income
tax return form for the past year. She had written a letter to Treasury
Secretary David S. Kennedy to inform him that she would not pay
further taxes until the government refunded her $73,409.03, which
she claimed had been "illegally taken" from her since 1948 because
she "had no husband." She argued that she would not pay "another
penny in taxes until single persons were taxed at the same rate as
married persons filing jointly." For the first time, she was not a loner,
and her views found an echo on Capitol Hill. A few months after her
breaking announcement, she announced that she would support a
bill by Senator Eugene McCarthy to abolish the singles penalty. That
her cause was appealing to liberal Democrats such as McCarthy was
not surprising: by assuming the defense of the rights of a specific
constituency group, she was echoing a fundamental leftward shift in
the liberals' agenda. Kellems, however, remained a staunch conservative. The idea was not to justify an illegitimate and out-of-wedlock
lifestyle. She confessed she had been "sickened by the spectacle of
'welfare moms,'" who stormed the governor's office in Massachusetts, demanding, with the help of the National Welfare Rights Organization, $50 for each of their children for Christmas.[17]

Using her personal mailing list, she wrote to her supporters and
asked them to put pressure on Congress in various ways: calling in to
radio shows, writing letters to newspapers, circulating petitions, get-
ting in touch with local clubs, and "MOST IMPORTANT—Bombard
your two Senators and your Congressman with letters. . . . Talk, talk,
talk, write, write, write, write." She also prompted them to send the

overpayment refund form to the IRS to complain against the penalty. Her intense personal involvement yielded only limited results. Although the landmark Tax Reform Act enacted that year lowered the maximum tax surcharge of single persons from 42 to 20 percent more than married persons in the same tax bracket, McCarthy's bill—which would have abolished the penalty instead of merely reducing it—was soundly defeated in the Senate by 66 to 25 votes. Kellems was utterly displeased with this partial reform, which she labeled "a fraud and a cheat." At the same time, she considered Mc-Carthy's bill a "moral victory" for the attention it generated, and pledged to continue her militancy. She had the feeling that the number of Americans concerned with the issue of federal taxation had greatly increased.[18]

Immediately after her declaration in April 1969, she received numerous phone calls and invitations to attend radio and television shows throughout the country, and hundreds of letters. Possibly a little over 20,000 letters poured in from every state in the Union, written by single people, widows and widowers, young and old, men and women, Republicans and Democrats alike, an enthusiastic reaction that took her largely by surprise. A fan club sprang up in Denver, Colorado, with volunteers who helped her compile her mailing list and distribute her periodic letters and information releases. Attacks against the IRS expanded the tax resistance movement into new realms of legitimacy. In January 1971, Representative Edward I. Koch from New York sponsored a bill and Senator Abraham A. Ribicoff introduced another one. To support the bills, Kellems called upon her supporters to reenact the Boston Tea Party and prompted them to send letters to Congress enclosing either tea bags "or used coffee grounds."[19]

New advocacy groups emerged to support the movement. The Committee of Single Taxpayers (CO$T) was founded in July 1971 by Washington bachelor businessman Robert Keith Gray. A staunch Republican and former vice president of the D.C. office of Hill &

Knowlton—a conservative firm which was very innovative in the field of public relations—Gray decided to stage protests against discrimination of America's estimated 30 million single, divorced, and widowed men and women. He explained that "he got very tired every April 15 of paying much higher taxes than [his] married counterparts." According to Mae Rapport, employed by CO$T, the organization had "members in all 50 States," and the most important committees were in California and in New York.[20]

In Minnesota, the Single Persons for Tax Equality Association was founded in 1968 in the Twin Cities with Dr. Shirley Corrigan, a clinical psychologist, as president. The membership fee ($5) was very low. The organization recruited its members in local communities. Many middle-class professionals joined the movement—doctors, teachers, social workers, nurses, secretaries and psychologists. Mrs. Vernon Klenk, a widow living in St. Paul who had recently retired from a government job contended that "my feeling is that as an individual maintaining a household, I have the same bills as a married person." Layne Wilson, a St. Paul laboratory technician and a vocal supporter of the organization, was able to compare the differences between each tax regimen: "I was single, then married, now I'm divorced. I've felt the tax burden of three groups, and it's mighty difficult to support two separate households while paying taxes at a penalized rate."[21]

In response to the pressure for tax reform on this issue, the House Committee on Ways and Means held hearings in the spring of 1972 and 1973. Witnesses reflected the wide appeal of singles' rights across political as well as geographical lines, and the extent to which the discussion had ceased to be reserved to some elites and experts in Washington, D.C. Not only did eight congressmen (four Democrats and four Republicans) testify against the singles penalty, but also professionals, including the vice president of the Air Line Pilots Association's Steward and Stewardess Division and a U.S. Coast Guard chief officer who also deplored the impact of the tax. Senators Eugene McCarthy (who had left office in January 1971) and George L. Murphy (a Republican from California) accepted to cochair the CO$T organization. Despite all this attention and the fact that CO$T claimed to have rallied 275 congressmen by early 1974, the Committee on Ways and Means never reported the bills favorably.[22]

There were several reasons for this failure. The chairman of the Committee on Ways and Means, Wilbur Mills, reacted to the constraints of a changing political and fiscal environment as the Vietnam War weighed heavily on the national budget. The dire economic situation was certainly detrimental to Kellems's efforts. A tax break awarded to single people, which essentially meant a loss in tax revenue for the federal government, was deemed unaffordable. Besides, advocates of the abolition of the singles penalty found it hard to claim the moral high ground, for they appeared to be undermining what was considered by many as a cornerstone of American society. Several legislators and experts were indeed concerned that the singles penalty was warranted on the grounds that it safeguarded the "institution" of marriage against companionship or cohabitation. In a context where "family values" were taking center stage in the national public debate, this was a very salient public concern and many conservatives did not support this crusade against tax discrimination. The campaign, however, shed new light on the public perception of tax resistance.[23]

Contrary to the press's negative comments during the Goldwater campaign, many editors sided with Kellems and her fellow tax resisters. The traditional image of the "crackpot old lady" changed and no longer provoked laughter. "The petite, 74-year-old Miss Kellems, neat in a grey suit and with her grey hair well-coiffed as usual, showed up at mid-morning at the Federal Building where the IRS is located," Bill Ryan enthusiastically wrote in the *Hartford Times*. Famous television commentator Harry Reasoner likened her to Gandhi and Martin Luther King Jr. Columnist John Chamberlain wrote that "only an occasional Vivien Kellems has the fortitude and the nerve to fight things out with the IRS." Many newspapers sensationalized her actions. In the *Los Angeles Times*, Gwen Gibson equated Kellems with "a rebel in the truest sense of the word," all the more since "she believes in fighting the system through studied, legalistic and nonviolent means." In January 1974, in its Lonely Causes series, the *Wall Street Journal* devoted a long article to Vivien Kellems. Her "Tea Party revisited," as the journalist put it, was a good example to follow both in terms of networking and legal strategy.[24]

Although the movement did not revisit the action of Bostonians who had dumped tea two hundred years earlier, it gained political clout because of growing concerns about the federal government's policies and brought much attention to the tax code. Americans who chided tax resisters for propagating conspiracy theories came to use the same words against the IRS as a series of scandals incited fears of tax agents' actions across the country.

At the end of the sixties, the *Reader's Digest* was still one of the most widely read magazines in the United States. From suburban houses to waiting rooms across the country, it was possible to read the *Digest*'s stories about the future of the nation. By then, many articles dealt with the methods of tax collection. With the help of information from readers, lawyers, accountants, and even IRS employees, the associate editor of the *Reader's Digest*, John Daniel Barron, recounted the tragic case of John J. Hafer. In October 1958 this businessman from Cumberland, Maryland, was notified by an IRS agent that his books and records should be made available for a routine tax audit. According to Barron, the audit turned into a nightmare. "The IRS tactics ultimately had their effect. Hafer had long been known as a community leader, an "honest, free speaking" man. "One thing about John, he was never afraid to stand up and be counted," recalled County Commissioner Lucile Roeder. But belief spread that Hafer had "to be guilty of *something*," explained Barron. As a consequence, in the small town, Hafer's customers, even friends, shied away from him, and his business dwindled. "Eight years spent fighting the IRS to prove his innocence," concluded Barron, "consumed his life." A few days after having been cleared by the IRS, John J. Hafer died. Such a story revealed the discrepancy between claims of social justice by advocates of progressive taxation and the harsh reality of tax collection. The narrative of tax martyr spread into mainstream media.[25]

Most importantly, this story found a strong echo in the country as it matched the "far-ranging, fast-spreading revolt of the little man against the Establishment," as *Newsweek* put it in 1969. Distrust of the IRS became one of the defining characteristics of the 1970s. John Barron contended that the periodical had "received hundreds of specific complaints about the IRS—from ministers, lawyers, janitors, doctors, housewives, policemen, accountants, truck drivers, businessmen— even from soldiers in Vietnam." To demonstrate the popularity of antitax feelings, Barron quoted Olin Earl Teague, a Democratic representative from Texas who "seldom goes to [his] district" and "doesn't receive complaints about IRS." At the same time, the popular *Time* magazine quoted France's controller general of finance under King Louis the Fourteenth, Jean-Baptiste Colbert, who contended that "the art of taxation consists in so plucking the goose as to obtain the largest amount of feathers with the least amount of hissing." Three centuries after Colbert's cynical appraisal, *Time* explained to its readers, the contemporary American taxpayer felt "thoroughly plucked." In a spontaneous outpouring of popular indignation, citizens by the thousands deluged Washington, D.C., with complaints about the fairness of taxation. Even Treasury Secretary Joseph W. Barr was forced to admit that in 1967 there were 155 individuals with incomes of more than $200,000 "who paid the U.S. government not one cent of taxes." Twenty-one of them earned over $1 million, and in 1967, according to the U.S. Treasury, they paid no federal tax at all by using the law's countless loopholes. As the tax loopholes were given much attention in the media, middle-class Americans realized that the tax percentage the federal government collected from corporations had dropped from 20 percent of federal revenues in 1955 to 12 percent in 1970. The principle of citizens' ability to pay seemed to be fading away, and the IRS seemed more concerned with honest citizens than with big corporations.[26]

The reputation of the IRS plummeted. When Donald Crichton Alexander was sworn in as commissioner in mid-1973, he inherited an agency whose prestige was rapidly sinking. The new revenue commissioner had to face growing criticism and acknowledged that maintaining public confidence in the agency was his "No. 1" task. Revelations about the IRS's Special Services staff then appeared in the national press. In August 1973, *Time* learned that an IRS Special Services Group, set up in 1969 at the White House's request, had collected files on 3,000 organizations and 8,000 individuals—not all of them radical, though clearly left-wing. While many of the persons and groups listed had tax violations on record, others had nothing substantial lodged against them. A top-level memo indicated that "a great deal of material had not been evaluated." The functions of the Special Services Group were described in a January 12 memo written by John J. Flynn, the North Atlantic regional commissioner, to the directors serving under him. Noting that the group worked closely with other federal investigative agencies, Flynn called it a "central intelligence-gathering facility within the IRS." The purpose of the group was to "receive and analyze all available information on organizations and individuals promoting extremist "views or philosophies"—whether right- or left-leaning. Suspects were included "without regard to the philosophy or political posture involved." *ABC News* aired an hour-long documentary on national TV accusing the IRS of being too willing to share confidential tax returns with other government agencies and of occasionally using heavy-handed tactics to collect money.[27]

Newspapers were also filled with reports of Operation Leprechaun, a typical Nixon-era scandal involving alleged recruitment by IRS tax sleuths of a sex spy to collect information on prominent people living in Florida. Commissioner Alexander responded to these attacks with aplomb, proclaiming that he was not "a PR man" and would "finish last in a popularity contest." He promised to only reform the Special Services Group's activities, not to abolish it. The Watergate scandal, however, made things worse for the IRS. Investigations by the Watergate Special Prosecution Force proved that IRS officials had been asked to investigate people who appeared on Nixon's enemies list. Congressional inquiries put IRS activities in a bad light and eroded taxpayers' trust. Senator Sam J. Ervin warned Commissioner Alexander that the greatest threat to the IRS was that it might be used "as a governmental weapon to be employed against the political beliefs and expressions of American citizens." Texas senator Lloyd Bentsen proposed a widely supported legislation to increase the confidentiality of tax returns. Under the guidance of Congresswoman Bella Abzug, the Joint Committee on Internal Revenue Taxation launched an investigation into IRS methods. Its findings only served to increase the bad reputation of the agency.[28]

In the fall of 1974, the powerful chairman of the Committee on Ways and Means, Wilbur Mills, was arrested with Mrs. Annabelle Battistella, a frequent companion of Mills over the preceding year. When tax resisters learned that the thirty-eight-year-old Battistella worked under the name of Fanne Fox as a striptease dancer at a Washington nightclub, they scoffed at the collapse of the architect of the country's postwar taxation. As Americans started to prepare for the bicentennial anniversary of the American Revolution, the new scandal increased evidence of the betrayal of democratic ideals by a clique of bureaucrats and politicians. In its July 1976 issue, the Parents and Taxpayers' bulletin put it bluntly when it called for "bringing back Uncle Sam:" "Would our real Uncle Sam favor taxation that impedes our personal progress, our free enterprise and voluntary charity?" In California, the newly formed association, United States Taxpayers Union, took a strong stance against the IRS and hoped that "members of the silent majority" would soon become a "vocal minority."

Interestingly, Republican president Gerald Ford made a similar argument when he explained that "the people are fed up with the petty tyranny of the faceless federal bureaucrats today as they were with their faraway rulers in London in 1776." Even southern Democrat and White House candidate Jimmy Carter called the tax code a "national disgrace" during the 1976 presidential campaign. If criticisms against the tax system were scattered and widespread, they would soon be captured by conservative tax resisters who would fuse them into a coherent intellectual framework.[29]

On a hill overlooking the Pacific, conservative economist Arthur Laffer and his family relished the beauty of the Californian landscape. Laffer especially enjoyed working by the pool on his iconoclastic tax-cut articles in the company of an impressive menagerie of pets. Born in Youngstown, Ohio, in 1940, the economist received a BA in economics from Yale University in 1962 and graduated from Stanford University with a PhD in economics in 1971. From his new office at the University of Southern California, after leaving the University of Chicago in the mid-1970s, he had the opportunity to watch first-hand the growing tax resistance movement and he gave militants a broader view of the benefits of tax cuts for the American economy. In 1974, during a dinner with two young politicians, Richard Cheney and Donald Rumsfeld, he sketched the outline of his theory on a napkin: "If you tax something, you get less of it. If you subsidize something, you get more of it. We tax work, growth, investment, savings, and productivity, while subsidizing non-work, consumption, and debt." At a time of economic crisis, Laffer's iconoclastic views reframed the tax resisters' arguments in a neoliberal language. Although few economists and businessmen took his ideas seriously— George Stigler of the University of Chicago even publicly stated that "he was no longer a very serious scholar"—Laffer offered welcome and practicable solutions at a time of severe crisis.[30]

By then Laffer was not alone in seeking alternatives to the Keynesian way of thinking. The University of Chicago's economics department had popularized monetarist policies among policymakers and elites. One of the stars of the Chicago school, Milton Friedman, had already published a famous book, *Capitalism and Freedom* (1962) that disseminated a vision equating government intervention with tyranny. This way of thinking opened doors to an abrupt shift in tax policy. Although most conservative intellectuals assumed the same mantle of principles, they disagreed on the most efficient way to dismantle progressive taxation. Friedman opted increasingly for slashing all federal expenditures and reinvigorating incentives to work and investments. Other intellectuals split on the extent of tax cuts and whether individuals or corporations should come first.[31]

In the context of inflationist pressure, businessmen cast doubts on Keynesian tax policy and the role of the federal government in creating inflation. In the mid-1970s, more aggressive competition in foreign markets made a serious dent in the American economy. New business organizations were set up to ponder fiscal and economic policies, among them, the Business Roundtable, whose members included the chief executive officers of most of the large corporations in the country. Under the leadership of Richard Lesher, the U.S. Chamber of Commerce entered a new phase and decided to mobilize its constituents around tax reforms. In 1975 the Carlton Group, named for the Sheraton Carlton Hotel, established a name for itself by gathering intellectuals and economists to analyze the severe economic crisis.[32]

These new organizations financed more research on taxation and monetary policies. As early as 1971, Norman Ture, a brilliant economist working at the National Bureau of Economic Research, was hired by the National Association of Manufacturers to explain the stagflation and to find solutions. Misguided Keynesian policies, he argued, cost the nation as much as half a billion dollars each year in lost growth. His answer was soon to appear in a series of papers read in business circles: federal taxes and public spending were responsible as they created disincentives to invest. Harvard economist, Martin Feldstein, who worked at the conservative think tank American Enterprise Institute, believed that it was necessary to lower tax rates and promote a reduction in the capital gains tax. The Business Roundtable stressed the problem of "capital formation" for American companies that only tax cuts could solve. The National Federation of Independent Business, the National Association of Manufacturers, and the U.S. Chamber of Commerce supported such tax cuts for themselves.[33]

Another group promoted tax cuts for individuals as the best way to raise revenue. Among them were Jack Kemp and his two intellectual allies, Arthur Laffer and Jude Wanniski. From his office at the *Wall Street Journal*, Wanniski started to promote the idea of tax cuts in 1974, after reading Robert A. Mundell's work on the impact of Keynesian policy. One year later, in the conservative journal *Human Events*, Kemp proposed a bold plan to "slash corporate taxes," but he soon turned to a tax cut for all taxpayers. As it was difficult to convince Congress, Kemp used the simplistic message of the "Laffer curve," which suggested that, beyond a certain point, raising taxes would actually force government revenues to decline because taxes sapped the willingness to invest and the will of individuals to work. Jude Wanniski's op-ed in the *Wall Street Journal* and his book *The Way the World Works* (1978) helped popularize Laffer's iconoclastic views on taxation. With the help of the head of the editorial page of the *Wall Street Journal*, Robert L. Bartley, Wanniski and Kemp stressed that the Kennedy tax cuts had been "successful gambles." In other words, an ambitious policy should give priority to investment and innovation and should propose tax cuts for both individuals and corporations. To reassure businessmen, Kemp explained that these two measures would restore incentive in the United States and would bring the necessary political support to win elections.[34]

This intellectual revision of Keynesian dogma gave middle-class tax resisters a boost. In the mid-1970s, local resistance mobilizations would put these ideas at the heart of public debates and transform tax resistance into a national concern. As she traveled the country to denounce the danger of the Equal Rights Amendment (ERA), Phyllis Schlafly supported Kemp's proposals: "When the government hires more employees, every paycheck must come out of the pockets of taxpayers." If the American people did not listen to the wise advice about tax cuts, she added, the liberals in power "will take us down the Socialist-Keynesian road Great Britain traveled." As the conservative upsurge put an end to the ERA ratification campaign, it was no surprise that tax protests gained political clout in both western and southern states.[35]

In 1978 Howard Jarvis's smiling face appeared on the cover of *Time* and *Newsweek*. The septuagenarian militant was a well-known figure among tax resisters in California. A long-time opponent of the New Deal, Jarvis was born in Utah, before moving to conservative Orange County, California. In the 1950s he had served on the national board of the Liberty Amendment Committee to promote the repeal of the federal income tax. In 1962 he retired from business after earning more than $1 million from a number of successful industrial ventures and, like many tax resisters, became more involved in politics. In 1964, during the presidential campaign, he helped organize Businessmen for Goldwater and strongly supported the Arizona senator. After the electoral debacle, he decided to turn to local politics and became the first head of the newly founded United Organizations of Taxpayers. In the context of inflation and new methods of property tax assessment, property taxes became a major contentious issue in California and in many other states. A savvy political organizer, Jarvis devoted his energy to replicating at the local level strategies used by tax resisters for so many years.[36]

Thus, Jarvis' new organization mirrored organizational techniques that had already been practiced. Militants met regularly at the home of one woman, Leona Magidson, to protest against property taxes. The women who participated in the meetings were asked to recruit more volunteers and circulate petitions against the property tax. Jarvis's wife, Estelle, organized a crew of women to gather signatures. To promote his cause, Jarvis himself traveled all around the state, became a frequent guest on talk radio, and wrote a newspaper column entitled "The People Must Know." Local chambers of commerce, real estate brokers associations and apartment owners associations offered their organizational help with the campaign. The idea of tax limitation was derived from the campaigns launched in the 1940s and 1950s to limit federal taxes. Strategically, in order to further his movement's aims, Jarvis turned complex debates on taxation and assessment into simple and anecdotal stories of "hardship" caused by the tax burden. Like tax resisters in the early 1970s, he tirelessly told stories of tax martyrs, including the demise of a friend of his, hounded to death by insensitive tax collectors.[37]

Jarvis and his supporters started an initiative in 1968 to gather signatures to place tax limitation on the ballot. In 1968, 1971, and 1976, however, they failed to obtain the required valid signatures. Runaway inflation changed the situation and increased the number of angry taxpayers. Jarvis, realizing the necessity to better coordinate efforts by militants and to professionalize the antitax crusade, forged an alliance with Paul Gann, a former car and real estate salesman residing in Carmichael, a suburb of Sacramento. Gann's organization, the People's Advocate, would help Jarvis gather enough signatures to place the property tax limitation on the ballot. In December 1977, Jarvis and Gann submitted more than one million signatures.[38]

Once the campaign started, the United Organization of Taxpayers attracted the attention of many citizens and was able to provide important financial support. Jarvis claimed that more than 120,000 were dues-paying members, each paying the $5 membership fee. Jarvis even hired a fund-raising organization, Romagen Corporation, to promote his cause. Launched on February 7, 1978, the "Yes on 13 Committee" aimed at raising money in California to pass Proposition 13 that aimed at reducing local property taxes. The public relations side of the campaign was led by Roland Vincent who ran Governor George Wallace's 1976 presidential bid in California. To promote the issue, Jarvis enlisted UCLA economist Neil Jacoby and Nobel-prize winning economist Milton Friedman, who taught at Stanford. Friedman made TV commercials free of charge to back Proposition 13 and claimed that "if we continue the growth of government and its involvement in our lives, it will destroy us."[39]

On June 6, 1978, Proposition 13 easily passed with a two-thirds majority of the public vote. Jarvis trumpeted the passage at a victory party over the strains of the song "Happy Days Are Here Again." A retired schoolteacher, Fannie Cain, justified her vote by arguing that "we feed foreigners and welfare bums with our tax money and my neighbors, 100 percent American, lost their land. Does that make any sense?" Referring to the founding fathers, Jarvis himself explained that "the people who wrote the Constitution said the people of the United States [should] be protected in their life, liberty, and property." They didn't say, he added, "life, liberty and welfare or life, liberty and food stamps."[40]

Howard Jarvis celebrated his California victory by anchoring the movement in national affairs. In order to centralize antitax activities, he created the American Tax Reduction Movement. Echoing the siege mentality of middle-class resisters, he explained that "the moment was clearly with us, the taxpayers, but the battle was far from over." On a similar note, Friedman considered that the country was on the verge of a "new American Revolution," and championed capitalism as a fountainhead of freedom, contending that progressive taxation was a hidden form of slavery and brainwashing. As a consequence, he promoted the adoption of a tax-limitation amendment to scale back the expenditures of the federal government. He interpreted the Proposition 13 victory as a sign that the American public had become tax conscious: "The populace is coming to recognize that throwing government money at problems has a way of making them worse, not better."[41]

As the mid-term elections drew near, tax resisters focused on the idea of tax limitation at the national level. Tax resisters' associations thrived and assumed the nuts-and-bolts field work. The National Taxpayers Union, founded in 1969 by James Dale Davidson, a libertarian student activist and publisher of *The Individualist*, issued press releases, held press conferences, and developed a mailing list. After the success of Proposition 13, the Union hoped to conflate local and national concerns, contending that the American taxpayer was simply "fed up." On July 29 antitax activists converged on St. Louis for a National Tax Limitation Conference to discuss how they might replicate Proposition 13's success in other states and at the federal level. In many states, debates centered on the progressivity of federal taxes and the waste of taxpayers' money. Arguments against the power of government were raised by numerous state and local taxpayers' organizations that cooperated with the National Taxpayers Union. In New York, five hundred leaders of eighty local groups rallied to the cry of "More for the people, less for the state" and formed a coalition, the United Taxpayers of New York State, affiliated with the National Taxpayers Union. In Oregon, Ray Phillips founded the Oregon Taxpayers United, which eventually attracted some 35,000 supporters.[42]

Brewing in the West and the Northeast, the fledgling movement of angry taxpayers cascaded into southern states, where the IRS sparked a major controversy by reversing the traditional policy of tax exemption for private schools in order to favor racial solidarity. By fanning the flames of tax resistance, events in the South would enable the conservative movement to find a common ground.

During the summer of 1978, the American Conservative Union (ACU) became particularly active against federal taxation and found for the first time since its creation in 1965 a receptive audience for its relentless stance against federal bureaucracy and the "new" federal "despotism." The forces that propelled such attacks were new federal guidelines published in August by the IRS that tried to regulate the tax-exempt status of private schools in the nation. In order to enforce desegregation in southern states, the IRS enacted strict conditions for educational institutions to benefit from tax exemption. Repulsed by the new guidelines, ACU's members vigorously reacted and claimed that the new regulations were part of a plot to limit the freedom of American citizens. The ACU helped generate the overwhelming number of letters sent to the IRS through one of its "legislative alerts," which bore the title "IRS Says: Guilty until Proven Innocent." In a few weeks, more than 100,000 letters poured into the IRS; another 400,000 protest letters were sent to members of Congress. By staging protests, southerners assailed the very idea of solidarity and contended that federal taxes should not be used for social and racial justice.[43]

Tax resistance in the southern states was part of a broader movement against the school desegregation process. White resistance to the *Brown* decision cascaded into the 1960s and early 1970s. By then, less than 20 percent of white primary- and secondary-school students were enrolled in private academies. The white flight from desegregated public schools slowly increased the number of private-school students and was facilitated by the tax-exempt status of some of these private schools, which were called Christian schools. As institutions of religious instruction, they could claim tax exemptions.[44]

Importantly, the new IRS regulations marked an abrupt shift. Conservatives vividly reacted to what they perceived as another bureaucratic attempt to undermine parental authority. Jerome Kurtz, an IRS commissioner, tried to defend the nondiscriminatory policy of his agency. After detailing the list of measures adopted by the agency since the *Brown* decision in 1954, Kurtz indicated the necessity to strengthen IRS policy in terms of racial discrimination since a number

Figure 7.1. ACU
pamphlet, "IRS Guilty!
Unless You Can Prove
Your Innocence" (1978).
Courtesy of the National
Archives.

of private schools continued to enjoy tax exemptions even though
they had been held by the court to be "racially discriminatory." Under
the 1978 guideline, schools not only had to enroll minority students,
but also needed a "significant" number of them to justify tax exemption. According to the IRS estimates, no less than 20 percent was
necessary to match with the new guidelines. In many southern states,
many schools were considered as "unreviewable," and their tax-
exemption status would soon be removed.[45]

In Mississippi, taxpayers dismissed the set of recommendations and
were furious about the denial of their rights to enroll their sons and
daughters wherever they wanted. It was no coincidence that the fierc-
est resistance occurred in the Magnolia State—the birthplace of the
White Citizens' Council. During the civil rights movement, Missis-
sippians were responsible for some of the high-profile acts against

African Americans, including the murder of Emmett Till in 1955. White people strongly opposed the new IRS guidelines, which they felt to limited their rights as taxpayers and which they associated with both racial and social decline. Resistance soon gained political clout, and more than 120,000 letters were sent to the IRS, most of them arguing that the federal government had no right to interfere with parents' decisions about their children. "Clearly, the bill [was] not only a bureaucratic nightmare, but a direct attack on America's religious community," wrote the *National Religious Broadcasters* in a letter sent to church authorities across the country.[46]

To boost their arguments, conservative militants anchored their crusade in constitutional and religious arguments. For many church supporters, the IRS had overstepped its constitutional prerogatives. The new regulations were seen as a violation of the First Amendment. Arno Q. Weniger Jr., the vice president of the American Association of Christian Schools, invoked the memory of his Baptist forefathers in Virginia who had "languished in jail until the establishment of that first amendment." By denying tax exemptions, the IRS had set a dangerous precedent in which the federal government could use the power of the purse to discourage all manner of political behavior. For many southerners, taxes became the number-one problem they had to face, and they strongly challenged the idea of taxpayers' sacrifice that permeated the IRS's' regulation Thus, from the West Coast to the southern states, tax resistance became an important local political force before turning into a national movement as mobilization in California and Mississippi soon cascaded into other states.[47]

In 1979 new Republican rising star Jack Kemp believed that an "American Renaissance" was on its way. Referring to the fallacy of the Soviet model, he was very proud to live in a country "where there is more democracy than in the rest of the world." A few months before, the mid-term elections had been a success for tax resisters. Kemp himself had been supported by the National Taxpayers Union, which labeled him "a real friend of the taxpayers." With William V. Roth, a Harvard Business School graduate and a long-time opponent of tax increases, Kemp wrote a proposal to cut taxes for individuals. Using the same words that Arthur Laffer wrote on his napkin, Kemp told his fellow congressmen that the nation was suffering under a "tax code that rewards consumption, leisure, debt and borrowing, and punishes savings, investment, work and production." He convinced the Republican National Committee to endorse his tax cuts for individuals with a clear-cut argument: "We are the party of lower taxes." As the decade drew to an end, tax resistance turned into a national movement, even though resisters disagreed on political priorities.[48]

Tapping into local discontent, tax resisters stepped forward and claimed authority to speak on behalf of all Americans. In 1979 Jarvis's American Tax Reduction Movement published a poster entitled "Death and Taxes are Inevitable! Being Taxed to Death is not," referring to Benjamin Franklin's famous assertion. Jarvis's aim was to defend a massive tax reduction at the federal level. Lamenting the burdens of taxation and "hidden taxes," his poster depicted a powerless middle-class family crushed by heavy taxation. Deliberately conflating local and national taxes, Jarvis explained to citizens particularly concerned with the price of gas that 50 percent of the price of "an $8,000 automobile consists of taxes."[49]

Ranks of activists grew slowly and were backed by strong financial support. By 1979, the National Taxpayers Union had more than 130,000 members and was spending two million dollars a year. Its publication *Dollars and Sense* contained many articles arguing that taxes harmed businesses and should be reduced. *Dollars and Sense* also frequently deplored the fact that politicians were unresponsive to citizens and that the government wielded excessive power that jeopardized individual freedoms. On the eve of the 1980 presidential election, the Union launched a "People Power Plan for the 1980s," an ambitious proposal for grassroots organization. A fund-raising letter sadly pro-

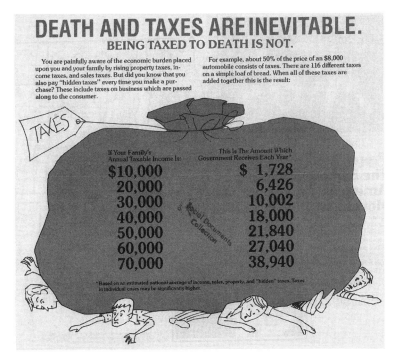

DEATH AND TAXES ARE INEVITABLE.
BEING TAXED TO DEATH IS NOT.

You are painfully aware of the economic burden placed upon you and your family by rising property taxes, income taxes, and sales taxes. But did you know that you also pay "hidden taxes" every time you make a purchase? These include taxes on business which are passed along to the consumer.

For example, about 50% of the price of an $8,000 automobile consists of taxes. There are 116 different taxes on a simple loaf of bread. When all of these taxes are added together this is the result:

TAXES

If Your Family's Annual Taxable Income Is:	This Is The Amount Which Government Receives Each Year*
$10,000	$ 1,728
20,000	6,426
30,000	10,002
40,000	18,000
50,000	21,840
60,000	27,040
70,000	38,940

*Based on an estimated national average of income, sales, property, and "hidden" taxes. Taxes in individual cases may be significantly higher.

Figure 7.2. "Being Taxed to Death Is Not Inevitable," American Tax Reduction Movement (1979). Courtesy of the University of Iowa Libraries.

claimed, "The truth is we got a government of, by, and for the politicians and government employees," and it insisted that things had to change in the next decade.[50]

Another powerful organization created after the adoption of Proposition 13 was the National Tax Limitation Committee, founded by Lewis K. Uhler, who worked with Ronald Reagan when he was governor of California. The committee's main goal was to organize a campaign in favor of a national-budget amendment that proposed to limit future federal expenditures to a given increase in gross national product. To widen its audience, the committee began convening meetings of local taxpayer groups from around the country and distributed a manual of campaign advice, titled A *Taxpayer's Guide to Survival*. Uhler attempted to distill lessons for would-be tax resisters and to decipher the complexity of the federal tax code. The committee's *Taxpayer's Survival Guide* informed local taxpayer groups around the country that putting limits on the growth of government budgets was necessary because the progressive income tax, if left unchecked, could ultimately lead to a policy of confiscation.[51]

All these networks coalesced in 1980 to choose Ronald Reagan as their antitax champion. During the campaign, Reagan supported tax cuts for both businesses and individuals, and promised to reduce the size of the federal government to avoid excessively large deficits. He told conservative crowds that it was the only way to curb the unemployment rate, which had reached 7.8 percent in May 1980. Jack Kemp played a major role to promote the antitax message, "hoping that people weren't smothered in government regulations and taxes." In September the candidate announced the details of his plan, which *Newsweek* dubbed Reaganomics. Many business groups still opposed tax cuts for individuals. During a meeting in June with Reagan, Edwin Van Wyck Zschau, a computer industry CEO, complained that an individual tax cut "would decrease revenues and contribute to inflation." The U.S. Chamber of Commerce dubbed the Kemp-Roth proposal "irresponsible and demagogic." Instead, it appealed for a $27 billion tax reduction for corporations only, including faster depreciation and a two-point drop in corporate taxes. Such measures, said the Chamber's chief economist, Richard W. Rahn, "should greatly increase the supply of savings, and that was a very positive program." In June President Jimmy Carter explained that the tax cut was nothing but an "election-year gimmick born of political desperation."[52]

However, Reagan remained committed to tax cuts for both individuals and corporations. In June he proposed a "$36 billion tax cut" with a 10 percent reduction in income taxes for individuals. At the heart of Reagan's program in September there was, as before, a 30

percent slash in personal income tax rates and 10 percent in each of
the next three years. Beginning in the fourth year, tax rates would be
tied to inflation rates so that only a rise in income greater than the
rise in prices would push a taxpayer into a higher bracket. Furthermore, with the help of Trent Lott and Jesse Helms, Reagan promised
tax resisters in Mississippi he would help them in their battle against
the IRS. In January 1980 the candidate gave a speech before a cheering crowd of over 6,000 students and faculty at Bob Jones University.
At the 1980 Republican National Convention, Lott helped draft the
plank in the Republican platform that denounced the IRS. In a landslide election, sixteen years after the Goldwater defeat, an avowed tax
resister stepped into the White House. From Mississippi to the southern California counties, resisters cheered the election of their tax
champion who was all the more eager to reverse the progressive system of taxation.[53]

In 1973 Terry Oakes, a vice president of the Los Angeles County Tax
Rebellion Committee said he did not want "the government on his
back" anymore and he wished the IRS would be "put out of business." In the years following the defeat of Barry Goldwater, tax resisters targeted tax agents, throwing a new light on federal taxes. The
IRS came to symbolize all the evils of the federal government. In the
mid-1970s, with the help of neoliberal intellectuals, opposition to progressive taxation was reframed, enabling conservatives to coalesce
around one single issue. As the United States tried to peacefully celebrate its bicentennial, tax resisters were proud to use historical
metaphors and references to the Tea Party rebellion in 1773. If religious and moral values played a role in the mobilization of conservatives, it was the very opposition to federal taxes that proved to be at
the core of the movement from California to Mississippi. In an essay
written in 1967, Harvard Professor James Q. Wilson presciently warned
his colleagues to take "Reagan country" seriously. Thirteen years
later, Reaganism was no longer an oddity in the political landscape

but a powerful political and social movement. Such a victory gave optimistic intellectual Jude Wanniski high hopes for the American people. An ambitious reform would put an end to such problems as "crime, poverty, pornography, divorce, suicide, mental illness, alcoholism, abortion, and child-and-wife abuse." He even added that "Instead of a society smothered, crushed by disincentives, with all of its tensions, there would be light, air and hope, we would once again feel confident about ourselves as a nation, and the Russians would view us in a different light." In other words, in Reagan country, the main tenets of progressive taxations would soon disappear.[54]

8

Tea Parties All Over Again?

Death and taxes may be inevitable,
but unjust taxes are not.

—*Ronald Reagan* (1986)

I N   T H E   O L D colonial neighborhood of Williamsburg, Virginia, in early June 1985, President Ronald Reagan electrified the crowd by attacking the federal tax system. Standing in front of the Capitol, he told a very familiar story to the cheering and friendly crowd of 4,000 citizens: "The members who spoke in this Capitol said no to taxes because they loved freedom. They argued, 'Why should the fruits of our labors go to the Crown across the sea?' In the same sense, we ask today, 'Why should the fruits of our labors go to the capital across the river?'" With great oratorical skill, Reagan continued, contending that "the tax system has earned a rebellion—and it is time we rebelled." With his tendency to oversimplify both history and political issues, Reagan embraced the conservative movement's fiscal agenda, evoking a somewhat mythical era when American life seemed simpler and traditional values prevailed in a tax-free world. A few days later, in Oshkosh, Wisconsin, the president asserted his claim that tax reforms would be good for Main Street America, not just for Wall Street, as his opponents argued. Speaking to more than 10,000 enthusiastic, mostly middle-class listeners, Reagan proudly declared that his plan would reduce "the tax burden on working Americans and their families," and happily accepted the gift of a pair of Oshkosh overalls emblazoned with the words, "TAX CUTTER-IN-CHIEF." In contrast to historical symbolism and conservative gimmicks, Reagan's election ushered in an important period of resistance from within the federal government that would impose its mark upon the progressive tax system.[1]

At a time when corporate globalization was accelerating deindustrialization, conservatives in power focused on nonproductive citizens, high taxes, and deficit spending to legitimize their policy. Deregulation, heightened competition, and corporate downsizing profoundly altered the domestic market, and economic globalization fueled both prosperity and inequality. The economic boom produced an amazing accumulation of wealth for many, much like what happened during the Gilded Age. In a time when more and more municipalities and citizens looked to private businesses to replace the basic functions of government, federal taxes became anathema in public discourse, and most politicians adopted a "no-more tax" creed. Under such circumstances, tax resisters aimed their fire at two tenets of progressive taxation: graduated rates and the sense of sacrifice. First and foremost, they debunked the idea of redistribution of income through taxation. Attacks against "welfare queens" who "used 80 names, 30 addresses" and "12 Social Security numbers" in Reagan's own words, undermined the credibility of welfare in the nation and questioned the very idea of public solidarity. Furthermore, arguments about the magical incentives for investment that would be created by tax cuts helped shape a tax policy focusing on capital gains and tax cuts for both individuals and businesses. One of the most popular books of the period, George Gilder's *Wealth and Poverty* (1981), celebrated the triumph of a new class of entrepreneurs that would emerge in a mythical tax-free world.[2]

However, in the context of deep national indebtedness and military spending to finance the Cold War and the War on Terror, tax resisters were forced to continue to look for alternatives to progressive income taxes. As a consequence, regressive taxes such as a flat tax or a sales tax were proposed as the best way to "kill" the income tax. The failure to radically transform the tax system provoked the paradox of the New Gilded Age: a hegemonic defense of a tax-free world enmeshed in a progressive tax scheme. Such a paradox fueled discontent that was sometimes irrational, and made tax resistance an everlasting crusade even during a period of tax reduction.

On September 15, 1981, Nancy and Ronald Reagan organized a thank-you reception at the White House for businessmen who helped them pass the Economic Recovery Act that the president dubbed the "largest tax and budget cuts in our history." "After decades of big government spending" and "an adversary relationship between government and its own business community," Reagan told the friendly crowd in his speech on the South Lawn, he was as "committed today as on the first day I took office to balancing the budget, freeing the people from punitive taxation, and making America once again strong enough to safeguard our freedom." Although the president had specifically courted businessmen once he was elected, he claimed the authority to speak on behalf of all taxpayers in his desire to address the progressive taxation that had increased since the 1930s. Following in the path of his political hero, Calvin Coolidge, he explained that Coolidge's tax cuts ended up achieving "more revenues," because of the almost "instant stimulus" they afforded the economy. With his staffers, Reagan sought to reduce graduated rates for both individuals and corporations and highlighted the failure of income distribution, putting the blame on the "welfare mess" that had plagued the country for so many years then.[3]

In tandem with Jack Kemp and advocates for capital gains tax reductions, Reagan consistently favored tax cuts as a goal in itself and refused to choose between individuals and businesses. His plan boiled down to the belief that the free-enterprise system, if relieved of heavy taxes and regulations, would achieve wonders of productivity. It drew in large part on the belief that progressivity was an obstacle to economic growth. At the heart of the dispute simmered the idea of the marginal utility of money for rich people, a concept that had legitimized graduated rates of taxation at the end of the nineteenth century. Instead, Reagan proposed a 30 percent cut in federal income taxes over three years, operating on the assumption that the wealthiest citizens and businesses would reinvest their money for the welfare of the nation. Yet, his economic advisers, Alan Greenspan and Charls Walker, advised him to give priority to businesses. Many industrialists still feared that ballooning deficits would be a factor in inflation and higher interest rates. Reagan stood firm and defended tax cuts as a sacrosanct priority and one of the hallmarks of his presidency. In his first televised speech, he made it clear that he refused to follow "those who told us that taxes couldn't be cut until spending was reduced." Such a policy was like lecturing "our children about extravagance until we run out of voice and breath." To his cautious advisers, he added that he had not come "to balance the budget" but to reduce government intrusion in the economy. With the help of David Stockman, head of the Office of Management and Budget, his administration proposed a five-year plan to balance the federal budget through economic growth, tax cuts, and reductions in social programs.[4]

At the heart of Reagan's policy was an impassioned aversion to the progressive idea of sacrifice. For many years, Reagan had vilified welfare recipients and accused the Aid to Families with Dependent Children (AFDC) program of wasting taxpayers' money. The "welfare queens" epitomized the scandalous aftermath of tax transfer, which had allowed "unwed" women to live lavishly on public support. To boost his arguments, he advocated that the power of the purse be limited to "legitimate" government purposes. Taxes must not be used, he added, "to regulate the economy or bring about social change." The redistribution of income through progressive taxa-

tion was a fundamental mistake because overly generous social policies, Reagan believed, did not encourage poor Americans but, rather,
promoted "illegitimate" behaviors. The federal government should
encourage the development of private institutions to control the power
of regulation. It was important to stop income transfer and enact important cuts in welfare programs such as Food Stamps and Aid to
Families with Dependent Children programs. Echoing the moralistic arguments of middle-class tax resisters, he went so far as to argue
that progressive taxation had "threatened the character of our people."
For poor and homeless people, the only option was private sector programs in lieu of public institutions.[5]

The two-pronged agenda—tax cuts and limitation of income
transfer—was supported by the antitax lobby. The National Tax Limitation Committee devoted itself to sending postcards to Congress.
The Business Roundtable and the Carlton Group provided statistics
and charts to demonstrate the tremendous impact of Reagan's ambitious agenda. The National Taxpayers Union took to the field to explain the necessity of tax reduction. Donald J. Kroes, manager of the
U.S. Chamber of Commerce's lobbying effort, contended that it was
crucial to keep a united front within the business community. Kroes
feared that small-business owners, who preferred immediate tax deductions for capital expenditures, would oppose big corporations. Less
popular, after the victory in 1980 that reduced the militancy, but better organized as a lobby inside the Washington beltway, antitax associations brought all the support they could to the president.[6]

The Economic Recovery Tax Act, which became law in August
1981, was the first signal sent by Reagan to tax resisters. Opposition
leaders such as Dan Rostenkowski, chairman of the Committee on
Ways and Means, derided the law as a "windfall to the rich" and explained to reporters that people in the upper income brackets would
profit the most. Opponents explained why congressmen only voted
for a 25 percent cut: 5 percent in 1981, and 10 percent in 1982 and
1983. Although Congress's expectations of the new president were

diminished, the legislation enacted the promised tax cuts for both individual taxpayers and corporations by cutting the top marginal rate of personal income tax from 70 to 50 percent, and introducing deep rate cuts and exemptions for corporations. It also included a provision that indexed personal income tax brackets to inflation. The law was accompanied by the Omnibus Budget Reconciliation Act that promised to slash federal budget expenditures for people on welfare by $130 billion over the next three years.[7]

As part of his attempt to revive the pre-Keynesian mode of thinking, President Ronald Reagan was eager to put an end to the fiscal controversy in southern states. He gave credit to the reciprocal view of taxation held by southerners. In a statement to senators, the new commissioner of internal revenue, Roscoe L. Egger Jr., sided with tax resisters in Mississippi, pointing out that "there was a huge outcry" and many people were strongly opposed to the IRS's methods. As a consequence, he promised to stop the "unauthorized, aggressive, 'guilty until proven innocent' intrusion by his service into educational and racial policies. A few months after Inauguration Day, however, many conservatives felt that President Reagan had not kept his promise. In April, Mississippi representative Trent Lott flooded the U.S. Department of Justice with letters. In December, Strom Thurmond and other southern congressmen summoned Egger for not doing enough to defend the "First Amendment issues" raised by the Jimmy Carter's policy.[8]

On January 8, 1982, the Treasury decided to act, announcing that it was unable to support the IRS enforcement of public policy denying tax exemption to racially discriminatory private schools. The president himself challenged the public to see for themselves that there was no "basis in the law" for denying such a tax exemption. Many conservative tax resisters applauded Reagan's decision. Bob Jones III, grandson of the founder and president of the Bob Jones University, was so happy that he felt "numb from what had happened" and called conservatives not to forget that "God in his own way has allowed this to happen and he gets all the glory for it." The decision allowed 111 private schools to reopen, 37 of which were in Mississippi.[9]

However, Reagan's decision sparked immediate and often furious reactions that went well beyond what the administration had expected. As Deputy Attorney General Edward C. Schmults contended, it was perceived by many as a dramatic retreat from the administration's commitment to pursue "an active and vigorous enforcement of civil rights policy in the area of civil rights." Inside the administration, more than 100 of the 175 lawyers in the Civil Rights Division of the Department of Justice signed a petition to stage protests against such a clear violation of the law and called for a sense of racial solidarity. The Americans for Democratic Action labeled Reagan's decision "obscene." Jerome Kurtz, former commissioner of the IRS in the Carter administration, denounced it as "outrageous and clearly contrary to the law." Senator Daniel Patrick Moynihan, a member of the Senate Finance Committee, urged Congress to reimpose as soon as possible the tax exemption ban. Most newspapers shared their sense of indignation with readers. The *Seattle Times* called it "another official blow to American minorities." The *Los Angeles Times* accused the administration of subsidizing "discrimination," and the *Washington Post*, in a harsh editorial, alluded to the infamous Jim Crow laws and called the president "Ronald Crow." Reagan's measure was equated with tyrannical action, and on January 14, 1982, the *Detroit News* portrayed Reagan as a despotic king who listened to the segregationist anthems of southerners.[10]

The National Association for the Advancement of Colored People (NAACP) announced on January 12 that it would ask the Supreme Court to allow it to replace the Department of Justice in prosecuting two private schools that practiced discrimination and were seeking tax-exempt status. Calling Reagan's decision a slap in the face of black people, the head of the South Carolina NAACP vowed to "wage a storm" over it. The Reverend Jesse Jackson, who was born in

Figure 8.1. "King Ronald Reagan and IRS Rules," *Detroit News*, January 14, 1982. Courtesy of the National Archives.

Greenville, South Carolina, and was very familiar with southern segregation, equated the decision with "a payoff to the religious right" and "racists like Bob Jones." Benjamin Hooks, executive director of the NAACP, accused Reagan of "pandering to the worst racist attitudes in this nation." John E. Jacob, president of the National Urban League, criticized the decision which had "begun to dismantle the desegregation process in America." In the *New York Times*, Anthony Lewis argued that he had never heard anything as "preposterous, lame, cynical or outrageous." The strong reaction in favor of racial solidarity through taxation forced the Reagan administration to step back.[11]

On January 12 public uproar led President Reagan to request federal legislation that would outlaw tax exemptions in cases similar to the ones that his January 8 announcement had approved. Trying to justify such a fast change of policy, he announced that he regretted "the misunderstanding of the purpose of the decision." His only intention in changing the tax regulations, he explained, was to remove from the IRS the power to determine "public policy," and he vociferously refused to be labeled a "racist." Two days earlier, he sent a bill to Congress denying tax exemptions to racially discriminating private schools. Such a reversal infuriated Bob Jones III, who encouraged his 6,300 students to write letters to their representatives in Congress, with copies to President Reagan, to protest proposals that would deny school tax exemptions. He hoped that the campaign would send a million letters to Washington within a month. On ABC's *Good Morning America*, Bob Jones once again defended his position and accused the IRS of infringing on "first Amendment rights." His segregationist policies, he claimed, were grounded in his interpretation of the Bible, and the IRS had no right to interfere with parents' rights to send their children to such schools.[12]

The political fiasco drove the administration to concentrate its efforts on the judicial crusade led by private universities. On October 12, 1982, the Supreme Court heard oral arguments in cases involving parents and taxpayers, drawing a very large crowd. Most arguments denounced the intrusion of the IRS into private matters and deplored the southern white taxpayers' loss of freedom to send their sons and daughters to whichever schools they wanted. On May 24, 1983, the Supreme Court issued its decision in the consolidated cases of *Bob Jones University v. U.S.* and *Goldsboro Christian Schools Inc. v. U.S.* in which it ruled that educational institutions practicing racial discrimination based on religious beliefs were not charitable organizations in the common-law sense and were therefore not entitled to federal income-tax exemption. Bob Jones III expressed his disappointment to the president and his counsel, Fred F. Fielding, stated that he was sorry that "once again" the White House had shown itself totally "insensitive" to the interests of conservative tax resisters. As a result, their confidence in the ability of the Reagan administration to change the tax system eroded, leading to violent forms of dissent.[13]

On June 2, 1983, Mayor Billy Davis of Smithville, Arkansas, a small town of 113 inhabitants, experienced the violence of radical tax resisters. The town was suddenly invaded by half a dozen police cars late in the afternoon. The officials, including four state troopers, a dozen federal marshals and FBI agents, the sheriff, and three deputies, headed four miles north of town and set up roadblocks. Then, they drove a mile down a dirt road to an isolated house that resembled a bunker. They were looking for Gordon Wendell Kahl, aged sixty-three, a retired farmer and conservative militant. Their search came to a fiery and bloody end. During the previous few weeks, Kahl had become the symbol of tax resistance in the country. The violence of his confrontation with tax collectors and police officers coincided with the emergence of a new radicalism in the rural lower middle class, and it was also part of a growing individualism and distrust of the federal tax system.[14]

Gordon Wendell Kahl belonged to the libertarian world of tax resisters that thrived in the 1960s and 1970s in the South and the West. Born in 1920 in Heaton, North Dakota, he graduated from high school in 1938 and served in World War II as a turret gunner for the U.S. Army Air Corps. He worked on and off as a mechanic, during which time his grudge against the IRS grew. His opinions of the government were closely related to his religious values. Kahl had been raised in the Congregationalist Church and, according to his daughter Lorna, believed that paying taxes would send him to hell. In 1977 he was sentenced to two years in prison and five years' probation for not filing his federal income taxes for the years 1973 and 1974. He served only eight months and, after his release, again failed to file his taxes. He also lived briefly in Texas with his wife and became more involved with the Posse Comitatus, a local organization whose members believed that the power of the county superseded that of the

Constitution. In an interview with the *Harvey Herald* in North Dakota, Kahl proudly expressed his fears of progressive taxation, asserting that the income tax was one of the "ten planks of the Communist Manifesto" and calling it "the ten commandments of Satan." In a context of growing radicalism, he promoted the legitimacy of violence against tax agents and the federal government. Because tax evasion and moving across state lines without authorization constituted a violation of his probation, the IRS decided to seize his property. When four carloads of agents came to arrest him, he engaged in a desperate holdout, killing and wounding agents.[15]

Elsewhere in the country, illegal forms of resistance appeared. More and more tax resisters called for cheating on the IRS. Two years after the election of Ronald Reagan, Ron Saranow, chief of the region's IRS Criminal Investigations Division, complained that "Many forms of tax evasion seem to start in California and spread elsewhere." The local figure who most irritated Californian tax authorities was Armen Condo, a self-styled "maverick minister," who headed an organization called Your Heritage Protection Association, based in Orange County, where conservatives found very fertile ground. Condo used traditional tax resistance arguments to contend that federal taxes were not constitutional. Eventually, he was charged with tax and mail fraud and sentenced to eight years in prison with a $92,000 fine. He was freed on appeal, but the IRS, which estimated that he and his followers had cost it $100 million in tax losses, was glad to report that the several hundred people who used to attend Condo's weekly meetings had shrunk to four in the week after his sentencing.[16]

Although such radical actions remained few in number, the fear of contagion was prevalent in the Reagan administration. "The mindset of America has changed since World War II," warned Roscoe Egger Jr. In an interview with *Time* magazine, the IRS commissioner voiced his conviction that tax resistance was on the rise, and that it was not as antisocial as it was to evade taxes. The American Institute of Certified Public Accountants helped propagate the idea that more and more taxpayers were "not paying their full tax." According to the figures given by the Treasury, the number of citizens claiming that they were not liable for income taxes had increased dramatically over the previous several decades. In 1982 Congress responded to this increase by enacting provisions, including Number 6702, imposing a $500 civil penalty on frivolous income tax returns, and Number 6673 permitting courts to punish taxpayers who filed frivolous complaints.[17]

Popular distrust of taxation was reinforced by Reagan's growing unpopularity due to his inability to cope with the economic crisis. Since the spring of 1982, more and more Americans were concerned about balancing the budget and questioned the solutions defended by "supply-siders." The problem was that the tax cuts adopted the previous year, coupled with significant defense spending, had dramatically increased the deficit. As a consequence, Reagan's approval rating had plummeted to 35 percent. Although the president attributed the economic downturn to psychological factors that played "a great deal" in economics, many cast doubts on his ability to cope with the crisis.[18]

Even in conservative circles, Reagan's tax policy raised concerns. In the July 1982 issue of *Conservative Digest*, widely read in conservative suburbs, Richard Viguerie published a strong criticism of Reagan's tax policy and accused him of being willing to increase federal taxes. Viguerie feared that the president would renounce his tax-cut agenda as many Republicans had before him. Paul Weyrich, the director of the Committee for the Survival of a Free Congress, also attacked the president, asking him whether he still had the political will to pursue his ambitious fiscal program. An angry Reagan responded to the editor, drawing his attention to the large tax cuts still in place under the 1981 legislation and pointing out that the 1982 tax increases were narrowly targeted tax hikes. The controversy revealed the difficulties faced by the administration as it tried to reduce federal taxation at a time when military spending was increasing.[19]

As the Cold War was the administration's main priority, Reagan's advisers told him that he was compelled to increase taxes. A number of supply-side advocates had already, symbolically, left the Treasury to protest against such a policy reversal. Refusing to abandon his tax-cut agenda, Reagan focused on tax loopholes, an easy expedient to avoid tax increases. The business community immediately urged him not to roll back previous tax cuts. The National Association of Manufacturers staged a protest against the retrenchment policy and the abandonment of the goals of growth and capital formation. In August 1982, after many debates with his allies, Reagan had no choice but to sign the new tax act, which limited the depreciation relief that had previously been enacted. To raise more revenue, he added new regressive taxes on airports, communications, and tobacco. The administration had to exert immense pressure on Jesse Helms and other conservative congressmen to support this $99 billion tax increase. Naturally, this reversal greatly disappointed many tax resisters, provoking increased tax resentment.[20]

In March 1983 the cover story of *Time* was devoted to tax evasion. The magazine feared that it could become a national disease. The antitax rhetoric increased distrust of government entities and sapped the very legitimacy of taxation. The president felt obliged to modify the tax code to accommodate the antitax impulse that he had helped to foster. He promised to carry this out in his second term. In November 1984 nearly 60 percent of the electorate and every state but Minnesota and D.C. voted for him. After his victory, he proclaimed that it was "morning in America," and announced the end of the darkness in tax policy through a major reform of progressive taxation.[21]

In a forceful television address, the reelected president portrayed his tax reform proposal as nothing less than "a second American Revolution."

If enacted by Congress, he predicted grandiosely, it would produce a "great new era of progress, the age of the entrepreneur." Reform was needed, he told his fellow citizens, because the existing tax system was "complicated, unfair, and littered with gobbledygook and loopholes." Drawing a stark comparison between the existing tax law and his proclaimed simpler and fairer plan, he implied that the taxpayers' choices would be easy. After Reagan's reelection, the administration faced a daunting task: rewrite the progressive tax code by accommodating it to the tax resisters' vision. In the many cities he traveled to in order to defend his plan, the president attacked the idea of sacrifice, the graduated rates, and the transfer of income. Developments proved transformative enough to give a central place to reciprocity as the cornerstone of the new tax system.[22]

Because of budgetary constraints, the president refused to opt for a radical alternative to the income tax. By then, old-time tax resister Jack Kemp was one of the few to promote an idea that revived from within progressive taxation: a flat tax. According to Kemp's ever-optimistic expectations, it would "create up to 10 million new jobs." Such a FAST plan (acronym of Fair and Simple Tax Act) was based on the idea that "the free enterprise economy," not the "Congressional finance committees," should determine the allocation of resources and investment in our economy. Instead, Reagan proposed to reform the tax code for the purpose of "fairness, simplicity, and incentives for growth" and lower progressive tax rates. On November 27, 1984, Treasury Secretary Donald Regan announced a three-tiered tax-rate schedule of 15, 25, and 35 percent. The president himself confined his reform to reasonable boundaries and, with strong antistatist rhetoric, mapped his proposal to put the individual and the family at the heart of his grand design.[23]

Tapping into traditional antitax rhetoric, he derided the inept federal system, provoking easy laughs from his audience during the numerous meetings he held in 1985. In early June, during meetings in Virginia, Wisconsin, and Pennsylvania, he assailed a tax code that ran "roughshod" over Main Street America, calling for an end to "un-productive tax shelters, so that no one will be able to hide in the ha-vens privilege builds." He derided the complexity of the existing tax code by frequently reeling off the incomprehensible last sentence of Section 509(a): "For purposes of paragraph (3), an organization de-scribed in paragraph (2) shall be deemed to include an organization described in section 501(c) (4), (5), or (6), which would be described in paragraph (2) if it were an organization described in section 501(c) (3)." By repeating such strikingly memorable examples of the technicality of the tax code, he undermined the expertise of tax agents, as had tax resisters a decade earlier.[24]

To reassure his conservative constituency that he still rejected the idea of social solidarity that had fueled the philosophy of progressive taxation, Reagan promised to make tax reform a family issue to en-sure that "the vitality" of the family would become a "central focus" of American tax and economic policies. Gerald P. Regier, president of the Family Research Council, congratulated the Reagan adminis-tration for this "Family-First Bill" and for using tax policy as a tool of social policy that would "continue to stimulate the strong consider-ation of families and children of America in the final formulation of tax policy." By focusing on middle-class families, President Reagan made it certain that federal taxation would be allied with moral val-ues and economic incentives.[25]

In order to promote the tax reform, the administration helped cre-ate the privately funded organization, Americans for Tax Reform, which would "seek to educate and persuade the voting public in key States." Grover Glenn Norquist, a young Harvard graduate and a former executive of the National Taxpayers Union, agreed to run the organization in order to convince citizens of the benefits of Reagan's tax plan. Both his parents were Republicans, though more moderate than their son. At an age when other children were still watching cartoons, he claimed to have read the entire works of Herbert Hoover at the local library. In 1968 he took a train from his home in Weston,

Massachusetts, to work in Richard Nixon's campaign office in Boston. At the end of the 1970s, after his graduation from Harvard University, he became the executive director of the National Taxpayers Union before taking the reins, in 1985, of the White House-sponsored Americans for Tax Reform.[26]

The Tax Reform Action Coalition was another organization that played a major role in influencing the political process. The organization was an offspring of the Coalition to Reduce High Effective Tax Rates, founded in 1982. It first met on June 11, 1985, and in a few months enlisted 175 major companies including trade organizations and businesses such as NAM, General Motors, IBM Corporation, PepsiCo, and Philip Morris. Charls Walker's American Council for Capital Formation also lobbied Congress to foster capital-intensive investment. The National Tax Limitation Committee helped the president to promote his family-centered tax reform by sending more than 16,000 petitions to Congress.[27]

Conceived as a way to reassure tax resisters of Reagan's resolve to put an end to taxation as "Americans knew it," the Tax Reform Act of 1986 reduced individual tax rates, lowered the marginal rate on the highest incomes from 50 to 28 percent, and increased personal exemptions and deductions, taking six million poorer Americans off the tax rolls. On October 22, on the White House lawn, President Reagan signed the act and proudly contended that he had created "the most modern tax code." Jack Kemp celebrated "the most sweeping revision of the tax code since 1923 [sic]" and explained that it "will be good for American families, good for American investors, and good for the small-business men and women of America." Even though it retained its progressive framework, the federal tax system now seemed to be tailor-made for tax resisters.[28]

In spite of the optimistic forecasts of national prosperity, the attack on progressive taxation and the rejection of social solidarity had a major impact on inequality in the nation. Between 1977 and 1989, the wealthiest 1 percent of American families reaped most of the

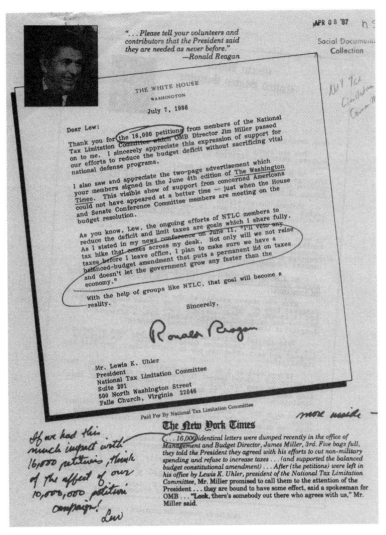

"...Please tell your volunteers and contributors that the President said they are needed as never before."
—Ronald Reagan

THE WHITE HOUSE
WASHINGTON

July 7, 1986

Dear Lew:

Thank you for the 16,000 petitions from members of the National Tax Limitation Committee which OMB Director Jim Miller passed on to me. I sincerely appreciate this expression of support for our efforts to reduce the budget deficit without sacrificing vital national defense programs.

I also saw and appreciate the two-page advertisement which your members signed in the June 4th edition of The Washington Times. This visible show of support from concerned Americans could not have appeared at a better time -- just when the House and Senate Conference Committee members are meeting on the budget resolution.

As you know, Lew, the ongoing efforts of NTLC members to reduce the deficit and limit taxes are goals which I share fully. As I stated in my news conference on June 11, "I'll veto any tax hike that comes across my desk. Not only will we not raise taxes before I leave office, I plan to make sure we have a balanced-budget amendment that puts a permanent lid on taxes and doesn't let the government grow any faster than the economy."

With the help of groups like NTLC, that goal will become a reality.

Sincerely,

Ronald Reagan

Mr. Lewis K. Uhler
President
National Tax Limitation Committee
Suite 201
500 North Washington Street
Falls Church, Virginia 22046

Paid For By National Tax Limitation Committee

The New York Times

... 16,000 identical letters were dumped recently in the office of Management and Budget Director, James Miller, 3rd. Five bags full, they told the President they agreed with his efforts to cut non-military spending and refuse to increase taxes ... (and supported the balanced budget constitutional amendment) ... After (the petitions) were left in his office by Lewis K. Uhler, president of the National Tax Limitation Committee, Mr. Miller promised to call them to the attention of the President ... they are bound to have some effect, said a spokesman for OMB ... "Look, there's somebody out there who agrees with us," Mr. Miller said.

If we had this much impact with 16,000 petitions, think of the effect of our 10,000,000 petition campaign!
Lew

Figure 8.2. Letter from Ronald Reagan to the National Tax Limitation Committee (1985). Courtesy of the University of Iowa.

gains from economic growth and tax cuts. Poverty in the country increased along racial and gender lines. During the tax-reduction era, the number of African Americans and women living in poverty rose, along with the number of homeless people. The Reagan administration continued to promote the expansion of private and religious institutions to help the poor. Taxpayers' money would no longer be used to finance the transfer of wealth but to pay for the national security state. The remaining progressive taxes soon came under attack, especially the income tax and the inheritance tax. Tax resisters were all the more eager to eliminate the entire progressive architecture of federal taxation.[29]

In 1995 William Reynolds Archer Jr., the new chairman of the Committee on Ways and Means, decided to put on display in Congress the original nineteen-page law establishing the income tax. "This small 19-page baby," explained Archer "was the original document that grew up to become today's monster." After the Republican victory of 1994, this lawyer from Texas, elected for the first time as a representative in 1971, targeted the income tax as a major obstacle to economic growth. During the mid-term elections of 1994, he explained that he wanted "to tear the income tax" out by its roots and throw it overboard. Archer found many receptive ears among the middle class and the wealthy, major beneficiaries of the prosperity of the 1990s, which was fueled by the dizzying rise of the stock market.[30]

The cornerstone of the progressive tax came under fire in the 1990s with a new generation of politicians who took the lead to revive the Reagan's crusade. In 1994 Georgia congressman Newton Leroy Gingrich promoted his Contract with America that was soon to epitomize the desire to end big government. Most of the twenty-one items included in the contract would turn into amendments to the Internal Revenue Code and welfare reforms. Gingrich promised to go back to the roots of the Reagan Revolution and the spirit that animated his followers in the 1970s. It came as no surprise that conservatives focused on welfare reforms as their main priority. After passionate debates, the Personal Responsibility Act was signed into law by President William Clinton on August 22, 1996. The reform undermined the idea of social solidarity, and endorsed the notion of limited reciprocity as the cornerstone of welfare assistance in the country.[31]

By then, violent antitax rhetoric had become a mainstay of American politics. During meetings he held in 1995, Gingrich made a name for himself by urging citizens to express their grievances against the IRS and the tax system. In January 1995, in his suburban Atlanta district, a woman identifying herself as a tax lawyer, attacked the income tax and proposed to "eliminate the current tax law." She added that her "most cherished dream" was the suppression of the IRS because she simply "hated it." Presidential candidate Steve Forbes went even further when he announced that the tax code was "a monstrosity" and that there was only one thing to do with it: "Scrap it, kill it, drive a stake through its heart, bury it and hope it never rises again to terrorize the American people." For many Republicans, it was high time to consider radical alternatives to change the system. Gingrich and Senate Majority Leader Bob Dole jointly announced the appointment of Jack Kemp to lead a task force to hold hearings and to recommend legislation to fuse protests into a radical transformation of the progressive tax system.[32]

During debates in Congress and due to budgetary constraints, many conservatives proposed to enact regressive taxes in lieu of the income tax. House Majority Leader Dick Armey and presidential candidate Senator Arlen Specter of Pennsylvania both sponsored a proposal for a flat income tax. The idea came from Robert Hall and Alvin Rabushka, two economists from the conservative Hoover Institution. In a 1981 article in the *Wall Street Journal*, Hall and Rabushka had offered many hints of the virtue of a flat tax for both businesses and individuals at a 19 percent rate. All income would be taxed at source, and the simplicity of collection would enable the federal government to save taxpayers' money. To convince Americans, Armey used the same argument as Archer, contending that the tax return would fit on a postcard and could be completed in only fifteen minutes. He added that the effect would be "tremendous" for taxpayers. A married couple filing jointly, for example, would reduce their taxable income through a $26,200 personal exemption and subtract an additional $5,300 for each dependent child. A family of four with an income below $36,800 would owe no income tax under the Armey plan, as opposed to the $3,100, or 8.4 percent, that such families paid on average. Referring to the rule of uniformity and tapping into the conservative ideology of common sense, Armey explained that the flat tax "was based on the idea of fairness we learned in grade school: *Everyone should be treated the same.*" The Treasury, however, announced that such a flat tax would cost $244 billion in lost revenue annually, and it would be necessary to find out other sources of revenue.[33]

Another hopeful presidential candidate, Senator Richard Lugar of Indiana, announced his will "to abolish" both the income tax and the IRS in favor of a national sales tax to be collected by the states. Under his system, Lugar promised that taxpayers would not longer need to "account, report or hide" their money from the IRS. Referring to the traditional criticism among tax resisters, he added that they would not be "guilty" until they proved their "innocence to the IRS." Lugar brought the simplicity of tax resisters' plans on a national level: first, abolish the income tax and the IRS; second, levy at the states' level a single rate of 16 percent on sales on everything except food and medical services. A Republican representative from Pennsylvania, Jon Fox, added that it would "get the IRS and government off the backs of individual and corporate taxpayers," and would "allow all of us to redirect our energies to more productive pursuits." Joel Slemrod, a Michigan University economist, calculated that to raise as much revenue as the current income tax did, Lugar's sales tax would need to be 25 percent. But such proposals stirred opposition on several fronts. As many opponents contended, it was regressive, falling most heavily on the poor, who spent the highest share of their income on consumption.[34]

Capitalizing on the support of tax resisters in the country, conservatives in Congress crafted a bill entitled the Tax Code Termination Act, which was voted in the House in June 1998 but failed in the Senate. The main problem was that congressmen did not propose a way to replace the $1 trillion of revenue raised annually under the income tax. Disappointed by the tax deadlock, tax resisters turned to the estate tax that had to be "exterminated," in Trent Lott's own words.[35]

In 1999 Congresswoman Jennifer Dunn responded to President William Clinton's State of the Union speech. At that time, the Monica Lewinsky scandal was attracting much of the nation's attention, but Dunn was more interested in the issue of taxation and explained that it was high time to "repeal the death tax" so that families did not have to sell their businesses and farms "when mom and dad died." Dunn characterized the repeal as a lifeline for grieving families who were taxed unfairly when "loved ones died" and were forced to sell their business to pay Uncle Sam. With tears in her eyes, she expressed the concerns of "parents who worked hard" during their lives, and concluded that the "death tax" was "their enemy." Four years earlier, as a member of the Committee on Ways and Means, she had introduced the first piece of legislation since the 1926 efforts of tax resisters to repeal what they were already calling a "death" tax. Jennifer Dunn was born in Seattle on July 29, 1941. After graduating from college, she secured a job as an IBM systems engineer. She became involved in politics as the Washington State coordinator for Ronald Reagan's unsuccessful 1976 presidential campaign. Despite this early disappointment, she became even more engaged in Republican politics, becoming the state's first woman to be chair of the Washington State Republican Party from 1980 to 1992, in addition to serving as vice chair of the Republican National Committee's executive board from 1988 to 1991. Over the years Dunn became an expert on tax policy. "Too often, we assumed that women were going to be liberals," she contended. Yet women, she asserted, were particularly qualified to "solve our problems with non-governmental, non-invasive solutions." Although the repeal of the death tax was not included in Newt Gingrich's Contract with America, Dunn would make its repeal one of her highest political priorities.[36]

In order to do so, she worked closely with conservative organizations that were calling for the repeal of the tax. In 1995 the first "death tax summit" was organized in Washington by tax resisters who formed the Family Business Estate Tax Coalition. At that time, only the wealthiest 2 percent of Americans were subject to the tax, which applied to money transferred to heirs at rates ranging from 37 percent to 55 percent. For individuals, the tax kicked in only on estates valued at $675,000 or higher; for married couples that figure doubled. Numerous loopholes such as trust funds, charitable foundations, and gifts to relatives permitted most people, even the wealthiest, to avoid it entirely. Capitalizing on the conservative momentum after the midterm elections of 1994, James L. Martin, the president of 60 Plus, a Virginian small association, helped promulgate the idea that it was necessary to rename the inheritance tax in order to avoid its equation with the very rich. In 1995 Frank Luntz, a political science professor at the University of Pennsylvania, was asked to find a better name for it. "Death tax" was found more appropriate than other alternatives such as the "exit tax" or "the departure tax." The new name enabled tax resisters to attack what they considered to be the worst aspect of the tax: its complete lack of reciprocity. Dead taxpayers had no opportunity to benefit from the income transfers they had contributed to. Another slogan used by resisters, "taxation without respiration," captured the alleged absurdity of the tax.[37]

Thriving on the national prosperity and tapping into the strong conservative network, the coalition grew, and the number of militant organizations escalated, most of them similar to the small antitax associations of the 1970s. Patricia Soldano, an estate planner from Orange County, California, founded two organizations to support the campaign—the Policy and Taxation Group, and the Center for the Study of Taxation. Conservative think tanks, including the Heritage Foundation and the libertarian National Center for Policy Analysis, wrote reports and memorandums criticizing the estate tax, and made the requisite op-eds and TV appearances as well. The antigovernment group Citizens for a Sound Economy encouraged its members to lobby their senators and representatives against the tax. Other groups involved in the anti-estate tax crusade included private campaign organizations such as the Club for Growth, the libertarian Cato Institute, and the American Conservative Union. With abundant financial backing, the activities of resisters mirrored the organizational and lobbying techniques of previous campaigns. First and foremost, they claimed that the tax paid by the few was a disaster for the many.[38]

Importantly, the strategy reflected a very pessimistic view of the alleged impact of the tax. The symbol of tax excess became Chester Thigpen, an elderly black farmer from Mississippi who, tax resisters claimed, would be unable to pass his property to his heirs because of the dreaded tax. An analysis of the conservative National Center for Public Policy Research warned all Americans that they could be victims of the tax at any time. "What Chester Thigpen spent a lifetime working for," lamented the center, "the federal government wanted to tax away in nine months—in most cases, the required time period to pay the tax—after he and his wife died." The reason for this, it was added, was the philosophy of progressivity, and the desire "to make the rich man pay his fair share." During debates in Congress, small-business owners were asked to testify against the burden of the death tax. In 1997, without giving detailed statistics for his claim, Senator Robert Torricelli contended that for small business the estate tax "was devastating." He added that "the family-owned pizza parlor, dry cleaning store, grocery and family farm are unable to provide the kind of intergenerational continuity that national policy should be encouraging." Putting the emphasis on the lack of reciprocity, Bill Archer focused on "double taxation," contending that it was morally wrong to tax people on the income they "made while they were alive" and "to double-tax them when they die." Such blatant injustice, Archer asserted, had a strong impact on their family. By receiving "the undertaker and the taxman on the same day," in Senator Trent Lott's own words, the death tax set out to undermine the work ethic and the family values upon which the nation had been built. In 2000, conservative congressmen organized a symbolic event similar to the ones organized by tax resisters in 1923 with their Prairie schooners: a Montana rancher driving a red tractor delivered to the White House the Death Tax Elimination Act. For tax resisters, mainstream America had to take the lead in the crusade for the repeal of the death tax.[39]

Thanks to strong support in the Committee on Ways and Means and in the Senate, the Death Tax Elimination Act passed in 2000 but was vetoed by President Bill Clinton. The election of George W. Bush Jr. gave tax resisters the hope that the two tenets of progressive taxation—the death tax and the income tax—could be "eliminated," to quote the new violent rhetoric used by the resisters.

"Not over my dead body will they raise your taxes," George W. Bush Jr. told a national audience a few weeks after the terrorist attacks against the Pentagon and the World Trade Center on September 11, 2001. As soon as the Supreme Court confirmed his election, President George W. Bush challenged Ronald Reagan's title of "Tax Cutter in Chief" by using the same life-or-death arguments against taxation. In 2000, during the Republican primaries, he announced the most important tax-cut program since Reagan, and overbid other candidates on tax issues. During a January speech in Durham, New Hampshire, Bush contended that his plan was "not only no new taxes," but, as he solemnly put it, "This is tax cuts, so help me God." He promised to reduce tax rates for individuals in most tax brackets. To convince middle-class citizens, he included a reduction in the tax rate paid by a married couple with relatively equal taxable incomes. He also announced the complete elimination of the death tax. Other Republican candidates made similar promises. Steve Forbes stated that it was necessary to tear down the "Berlin Walls" of big government, especially the wall of taxes. For many tax resisters, the election of George W. Bush Jr. marked a renewed period of tax cuts, in spite of growing military spending.[40]

Once he was elected, the new president moved quickly to enact his tax-cut plan, warning Congress not to alter it. Even Federal Reserve Chairman Alan Greenspan endorsed the idea of a significant tax reduction. In February 2001 President Bush proposed $1.6 trillion in income-tax cuts over a ten-year period with the largest reductions going to wealthy taxpayers. Tax resisters were given free rein to advocate a more ambitious plan. For instance, Jack Kemp contended that it "would not be unreasonable for Mr. Bush to seek tax rate reductions twice the size of what he has proposed." Conservative congressmen, led by Dick Armey and Tom DeLay, proposed to increase the tax reductions to $2.2 trillion over ten years. The Economic Growth and Tax Relief Reconciliation Act of 2001 enacted the promises Bush made when he was candidate. After the passage of the tax cuts, Bush hoped to press forward with additional reductions for rich taxpayers including cuts in capital-gains taxation and the provision of corporate tax breaks. Treasury Secretary Paul O'Neill repeatedly presented the tax code as "an abomination," and claimed that it "hurt our competitiveness" and that the nation "deserved a better tax code." In November 2002 the *Wall Street Journal* stressed the fact that the wealthiest Americans accounted for a huge share of income tax revenues. As the editorial contended, in 2000 the richest 5 percent of taxpayers accounted for 56 percent of income tax collections. The death tax became once again a major issue for conservative tax resisters.[41]

By 2001 death tax summits were being organized and included the major businessmen's organizations, notably the U.S. Chamber of Commerce, NAM, and the National Association of Women Business Owners. The call for the repeal of the so-called death tax gained political clout. When William Gates Sr. defended the tax, in which he was supported by some fellow billionaires, his argument for social solidarity was mocked by conservatives. He was accused of being a "billionaire against real families," to quote the president of the National Federation of Independent Businesses. Instead, tax resisters stressed once again the plight of minorities and small farmers. Senator Connie Mack III of Florida referred to the sad story of small farmers, whose children had to come up "with the cash to pay the estate tax" when "the parents died." Tax resisters objected in harsher terms to the tax. Jack Kemp quoted Robert Johnson, the founder of Black Entertainment Television and the first African American billionaire, who criticized Gates Sr.'s call for retaining the estate tax as a misunderstanding of U.S. basic principles. On her popular television show, Oprah Winfrey publicly explained her irritation by speaking bluntly of the "double taxation" of her income once she died. On his television show, conservative host Bill O'Reilly always referred to the estate tax as "unconstitutional double taxation." In 2001 the National Taxpayers Union asked Milton Friedman to explain the benefits of tax repeal. In a public statement, cosigned by 278 other economists, the Nobel Prize winner explained that if you "spent your money on riotous living—no tax; left your money to your children—the tax collector got paid first." That was the message sent by the estate tax, concluded Friedman, who deplored the fact that individuals were not encouraged to "live frugally" and "to accumulate wealth." Moral arguments denouncing the tax abounded, and contributed to the emerging view of the estate tax as a national burden, even though few citizens actually paid it.[42]

Therefore, in early January 2003, Bush asked Congress to make the repeal of the estate tax permanent, as well as to repeal all taxes on investment income and taxation, and to allow individuals to exclude dividends from taxation. Economist Milton Friedman applauded the plan, contending that "there is one and only one way of cutting government down to size—the way parents control spendthrift children, cutting their allowance." Conservative women strongly endorsed George W. Bush's tax cuts. The association Concerned Women for America contended that if politicians wanted to do something for children, they should simply "cut taxes." The Jobs and Growth Tax Relief Reconciliation Act, passed in 2003, included substantial cuts in the taxation of dividends and capital gains, and bonus depreciation allowances for corporations. In an article published in the *New York Times*, journalist David Rosenbaum perfectly captured the rationale behind the conservative "tax cut without end" that became the distinguishing characteristic of the administration. The ongoing program of tax reduction occurred during military interventions in Afghanistan and Iraq, the latter costing American taxpayers around $800 billion. It led editorialist Roger Cohen to regret in the *New York Times* that "while America's young men and women fought, other Americans enriched themselves." Yet, tax cuts remained limited, and the repeal of the estate tax was not permanent. By promising a mythical tax-free world and maintaining a progressive system of taxation to pay war expenditures, conservatives fueled resentment "without end" among middle-class citizens, which exploded after the economic crisis of 2007 and the election of the first African American as president.[43]

In September 2010 former President Jimmy Carter was one of the few people to see a parallel between Tea Partiers and 1970s tax resisters when he explained that "a number of readers of my new book have noted parallels between today's frustrated and even angry mood and a similar mood in the mid-1970s." Recalling his successful campaign, he added that "in some ways my successful campaign for the presidency in 1976 resembled the Tea Party movement of today." He depicted the same "dissatisfaction with the policies and practices of government officials, especially those who served in Washington." If Carter was right to show the similarity between the two periods, he forgot to mention the strength of the conservative movement during the 1970s and its legacy many years later. Since 2009 tax resisters had expressed their distrust of the tax code and the tax regime in a similar way to that of antitax militants forty years previously. Although some Tea Partiers were already very active in the 1960s and 1970s, during the Goldwater campaign for instance, most were newcomers who staunchly supported the endless crusade against tax cuts and feared that the economic crisis would reinvigorate the idea of social solidarity and increase progressive taxes.[44]

During the spring and summer of 2009 the world was amazed to see conservative Americans across the country hold "tea parties" in protest of the use of their tax dollars for liberal social programs such as a new health insurance program. Evoking the American Revolution and the famous act of 1773, the word Tea in Tea Party was an acronym for "Taxed Enough Already." Throughout the country, conservatives vented their frustration against the federal government. On April 15, 2009, to protest Barack Obama's stimulus plan, more than 750 Tax Day tea parties were held in cities across the nation, including Boston, Washington, East Hampton, New York, and Yakima, Washington. Fox News covered the events all day with on-the-scene hosts and reporters; Sean Hannity broadcasted his show live from the Atlanta protest. New York Times journalist Liz Robbins was impressed by those thousands of demonstrators who "offered a modern take on a 1773 demonstration." Yet speaker of the House of Representatives Nancy Pelosi labeled the movement "astroturf by some of the wealthiest people in America to keep the focus on tax cuts for the rich instead of for the great middle class."[45]

For many Democrats, the money that poured into the Tea Party movement came from wealthy billionaires to support Dick Armey's FreedomWorks, Jenny Beth Martin's Tea Party Patriots, and Lloyd

Marcus's Tea Party Express. The support of the strong conservative network and the wealth of some billionaires helped to coalesce and popularize the movement. David and Charles Koch, sons of Fred Koch, one of the founding members of the John Birch Society, were among the most generous of the movement's donors. Advocates of a libertarian revolution, the Koch brothers were strong opponents of Barack Obama, whom they labeled a socialist. Other conservative organizations, from the Heritage Foundation to the antitax Club for Growth, came out in support of the movement. FreedomWorks received money from large companies, notably in the oil, gas, and financial industries. Armey became a lobbyist and seized the opportunity to promote his deregulation agenda with Tea Partiers. Another organization, Americans for Prosperity, did the same and used the fledgling mobilization as an opportunity to increase its contact lists and its local networks.[46]

However, although big conservative networks played a major role in the mobilization, it was first and foremost a reinvigoration of the crusade of middle-class tax resisters that started after World War II. From 2009 to 2011, more than 1,000 groups spread across all fifty states, and energized the Republican Party from within. Tea Partiers belonged to the same social and political spheres as the militants of the 1970s. The 18 percent of Americans who identified themselves as Tea Party supporters tended to be Republican, white, male, married, and older than 45, according to a *New York Times/CBS News* poll released in April 2010. According to polls and interviews, Tea Partiers were wealthier and better educated than the general public. Many worked in professional occupations such as medicine and engineering, and were small-business owners. Women still played a major role in the local organization of the Tea Party movement. In Virginia, the Tea Party Patriots Federation had been launched by Jamie Radtke, a middle-aged woman, who organized meetings in Richmond. In other states, they also played a major role.[47]

When asked what they were angry about, Tea Party supporters stated three main issues that all revolved around the expansion of progressive ideas: the recent health-care overhaul, government spending, and a feeling that their opinions were not represented in Washington. In spite of the traditional divide between social conservatives and libertarians, a sense of unity still prevailed. As one Tea Partier from Virginia explained, "The conservatism that unites us is governmental and fiscal, not social." A dynamic and eloquent taxpayer, sixty-six-year-old Elwin Thrasher expressed the traditional fear of strong government: "The only way they will stop the spending is to have a revolt on their hands" Trasher lamented that she was "sick and tired of them wasting money and doing what our founders never intended to be done with the federal government." The election of President Barack Obama was seen as a major threat to their taxpayers' rights. Most of them hated him and equated his values with un-Americanism. They also believed that the Obama administration was racially biased and tended to favor blacks over whites. "Obammunism is communism," complained a militant in the Washington, D.C., streets, on August 28, 2010.[48]

The Constitution still occupied a revered place. The popularity of a book published in 1981 by Willard Cleon Skousen, *The Five Thousand Year Leap*, which became one of Glenn Beck's favorites, revealed to what extent originalist theories prevailed in the Tea Party movement. Sousken was a Mormon and former Salt Lake City police chief with ideas similar to those of the John Birchers and who spent the 1960s writing and crusading against communist plots in the United States. The book took an originalist view of the Constitution, and Skousen argued that the Constitution had been inspired by religion. Furthermore, he posited that the founding fathers had never intended to implement a government that would levy taxes to finance social programs and had rejected collectivist "European" philosophies. Tapping into the central role played by constitutional debates among conservatives, Skousen had founded the National Center for

Constitutional Studies in Utah to promote such views. During the 1990s the center typically offered no more than a dozen seminars a year; in 2009 it organized over 200 of them for Tea Party groups across the country. During Tea Party meetings, Michael Johns of the Heritage Foundation did not mince words when he told President Obama that "every historical document signed in Philadelphia, every founding document in this nation, had cited our Creator."[49]

For many Tea Partiers, Obama epitomized the arrogance of elites and their misreading of the Constitution. In a chapter entitled "The Opposite of Constitution Is Prostitution," Joseph Farah explained that Barack Obama reads the Constitution as he reads the Bible, by not taking "either too literally." There was still a strong sense of anxiety among Tea Partiers about the moral and cultural decay of American democracy. "We have lost respect in the world. We are going broke. The American dream is dying and our social and cultural fabric is unraveling," said Mike Pence, a Republican from Indiana, who spoke at the Washington Tea Party rally. He added that people were scared that "all that once was good and great about this country could someday be gone." A nurse from Worcester, who rallied the Tea Party movement, complained vehemently about Obama's recovery plan: "I don't want the government giving money to people who don't want work. Government is for the post office, and to defend our country, and maybe for the road. That's all." What they feared the most was to pay higher taxes and they anticipated such tax increases as a political response by the Obama administration to the economic downturn.[50]

Tea Partiers employed similar symbols and metaphorical images that tax resisters had used in the 1970s. The same historical references were displayed during meetings, and many demonstrators were dressed in the same colonial garb. On her blog, Keli Carender, a Tea Party protester in Seattle, called herself a Liberty Belle. "Could you imagine if the British said not only do you have to pay a tax on the tea, but you have to buy the tea and have to buy for your neighbor?"

asked another Tea Party militant. The same constitutionalist legitimacy was also stressed by militants during demonstrations. "I'm not
a Republican anymore. I'm a Constitutionalist," proclaimed sixty-
three-year-old Susan Chilberg. Ryan Hecker, a twenty-nine-year-
old organizer of the Houston Tea Party Society, created the Contract
from America, which urged Congress "to identify the specific provision of the Constitution that gives Congress the power to do what
the bill does." A provision in the Contract from America would scrap
the tax code and replace it with one no longer than 4,543 words—
namely, the length of the original, unamended Constitution.[51]

From the Reagan election to the Tea Party movement, tax resistance
became the only game in town in the country, forcing every politician and citizen to address the issue. In 1995, as Congress debated
the benefits of a flat tax, John Richard Kasich, the budget committee
chairman in the House of Representatives and Ohio governor, perfectly explained the goal of the political maneuvers of tax resisters
since the election of Ronald Reagan in 1980. The "end game," he asserted, was "to strip the government of the financial means for butt-
ing into the lives of Americans, and thus, returning power and responsibility to families and localities." In other words, it was necessary
to cut federal taxes to satisfy both middle-class and businessmen's
claims. Attacks on graduated rates and income transfers challenged
the progressive tax system. In a world where privatizations of services
held center stage, tax resisters were able to limit the impact of most
progressive taxes, even though they were not able to repeal them.
The ideologies of tax reduction and individualism were so enmeshed
that they sparked overnight a resistance movement that labeled itself
Tea Party after the election of Barack Obama, because they feared
that the first African American president would ramp up the high-
end progressivity scheme that had been implemented by New Dealers in the 1930s. Importantly, their persistent campaigning undermined public confidence in the tax system and helped to delegitimize

federal taxation. Yet, as military expenditures soared, the public debt reached approximately $11.959 trillion or about 75 percent of GDP in 2013. Facing indebtedness of such immense proportions, some wealthy businessmen questioned the legitimacy of tax resistance. In an op-ed piece for the *New York Times*, billionaire Warren Buffet wondered whether it was possible to go back to a more progressive system targeted to rich people. Mark A. Bloomfield, the president of the American Council for Capital Formation disagreed with the "Buffet rule" and feared that it "could exacerbate a weak economy, will generate very little revenue to offset the large American debt crisis and will undermine the American dream." Tax resistance remains a mainstay of conservative view of both U.S. economy and the founding principles of the nation.[52]

Epilogue

I feel like we just played the World Series of
tax reform. And the American people won.

—*Ronald Reagan* (1986)

Wɪᴛʜ ʜɪs ꜰᴏʀᴄᴇꜰᴜʟ optimism and his Manichean sense of
history, President Ronald Reagan had always given tax resisters a revered place in American memory. Embracing the founding fathers
and some famous tax rebels, including his favorite one, Daniel Shays,
he participated in the formation of a powerful political and cultural
construction. The country was born out of a tax revolt, Reagan believed, and tax resistance was an essential and sacred character of the
American identity. It did not matter for him that Thomas Jefferson,
like many founding fathers, was an advocate of progressive taxation,
and that he abandoned that principle only when he was confronted
with the harsh reality of power in 1800. It also did not matter that tax
grievances had not caused the War of Independence except in very
indirect ways. Likewise, it did not matter that, for many years, tax
rebels were considered outlaws by conservatives who contended that
such revolts threatened the right to property and the very foundation
of the American Republic. During the centennial celebration of the
Tea Party in 1873, Robert C. Winthrop, the direct descendant of the

Puritan leader and Massachusetts governor, John Winthrop, evoked the prestigious figures of Benjamin Edes and Paul Revere but regretted the "destruction of the tea." He added that members of Boston's upper crust were "not here today to glory over a mere act of violence, or a merely successful destruction of property." What mattered for Reagan at the end of the twentieth century was that American national identity had long hinged on the rejection of progressive taxation and that fact made the country exceptional. Echoing rhetoric honed by tax resisters for many years, such imprints on the historical imagination still loomed large in the nation as angry Tea Partiers gathered on the streets of many cities in 2009 and 2010 to defend a mythical tax-free world and no longer disavowed the destruction of the tea. In their relentless attacks, conservatives have equated progressive taxation with tyranny, unconstitutionality and "un-Americanism."[1]

From the American Civil War to the present, tax resistance has challenged progressive taxation, an intellectual and political construction that has been part of the nation's fabric since the American Revolution. An optimistic intellectual and Reaganite, Jude Thaddeus Wanniski, has perfectly described these two different worldviews with his famous Santa Claus metaphor. In his conservative Christmas carol published in the *National Review* in 1976, he told the story of two Santa Claus—one Santa spends everything, while the other promotes tax reduction. For Wanniski, the spending Santa resembled President Franklin Delano Roosevelt whose famous prescription was "tax and tax, spend and spend, elect and elect." This Santa Claus preferred the dangerous idea of "income redistribution to growth," and his goal "was to tax money away from the well-to-do, because they were not spending it fast enough, and spend it for them."

To bring light into what he perceived to be political darkness, Wanniski supported reduction of progressive taxation. The other Santa resembled Treasury Secretary Andrew W. Mellon. Wanniski extolled Mellon's espousal of free market and individualism as an example for all generations of Americans. "Any man of energy and initiative in this country," Wanniski declared, could get what he wanted if his "initiative" was not "crippled by legislation or by a tax system." By the time Wanniski died in early September 2005, the tale of the two Santas had been enlivening American politics for twenty years. That year, after Hurricane Katrina hit the city, events in New Orleans sparked a debate on the same ideas of solidarity and progressivity that Wanniski had assailed his entire life.[2]

For historians, the story of tax resistance is more nuanced and less Manichean. Opposition to the progressivity of tax emerged during the American Civil War. Those four bloody years of warfare revealed the deep economic and social transformations that had taken place in the country since the early republic. The market revolution and its sectional impact made the rules of apportionment and uniformity contained in the Constitution obsolete. Furthermore, social inequalities exacerbated by industrialization led intellectuals and reformers to rethink the very goals of federal taxation. It was neither a tool for market protection through tariffs nor a limited form of reciprocity of exchange in major crises, especially wartime. First and foremost, it became a system of solidarity in peacetime that aimed at redressing inequalities and regulating corporate power. Intellectual and tax expert Richard Thomas Ely perfectly captured the essence of progressive taxation when he contended at the end of the nineteenth century that there was no such thing as "wealth" without "a society." As a consequence, he defended progressive taxation as a fair system based on graduated tax rates, a sense of sacrifice and income distribution. At the dawn of the twentieth century, the idea of progressive taxation gained political traction and led to the adoption of the Sixteenth Amendment in 1913. Since then, tax resisters have challenged the main tenets of progressivity.[3]

Progressive taxation has conveyed the idea of a federal government that redistributes wealth to redress social and economic inequalities. When conservative president George W. Bush Jr. argued that money in the Treasury did not "belong" to the government but to the people, he was debunking the main foundation of progressive taxation: the sense of sacrifice that enabled policymakers to redistribute money. The long-time claim for taxpayer standing is embodied in the conservative view that citizens should have the right to refuse the allotment of their taxes if they disapproved the use to which that taxation was put. Their criticism has always contained a strong sense of exceptionalism based upon the idea that progressive taxation was un-American. Since the American Civil War, progressive taxation has been decried as a Pandora's box of foreign ideologies promoted by idealistic professors and politicians. As a consequence, tax resisters have characterized their enemies as cosmopolitan elitists or naïve citizens who want to dupe honest Americans, and they have always believed they were uniquely positioned to defend individuals and the market against the intrusion of the federal government. Margaret Thatcher's famous motto, "There is no such thing as 'a society,'" perfectly aligns with their own assumptions, and captures their response to the philosophy of progressivity.

By focusing on the social, racial, and gender composition of tax resisters, this book hopes to offer greater insight into the evolution of American conservatism. The continuity of the movement and the similarity of arguments complicate the traditional assumptions that made conservatism the child of Keynesian policy in the 1930s. This account of U.S. taxation history brings back money and taxes to a literature dominated by moral and religious values. Because of their centrality in American life, taxes have contributed to the emerging protest of taxpayers, particularly conservatives. By defending their households and their values from the invasion of the federal government, they have promulgated a vision of a minority of "oppressed" taxpayers who have had no choice but to defend a beleaguered people. More than anything else, pocketbook politics gave cohesion to the diversity of the conservative movement.[4]

By looking at the practices of tax resisters—mainly petitions, meetings, and lobbying—this study uncovers the singularity of militancy among conservatives. The vigor of tax resistance owes much to the fieldwork of older, white, upper middle class Americans. Because they were retired or worked at home, these militants had the time to write newsletters, decipher the tax code, and organize meetings. Thus, citizens who were most advantaged socially and economically were least able to redress their grievances politically and helped move federal taxes to the center of the political stage. The high number of small conservative organizations of taxpayers gave them more local power than they were able to obtain nationally, which explains their siege mentality and their use of irrational explanations, tapping into fears of conspiracy and the illegitimate intrusion of the federal government into their households.

By expanding the scope of this study from grassroots Texas, Illinois, Massachusetts, California, Iowa, and Oregon's associations to top-down organizations in Washington, D.C., we have seen how the diversity of the movement and the division between local and national elites came together during the twentieth century. Among tax resisters, radical small-business owners often opposed big corporations and their internationalist, more state-centered agenda, especially after World War II. Tax resisters have never formed a monolithic block but, rather, a more nuanced and segmented movement.

In the end, their struggle has had a long-lasting impact on the architecture of federal taxation in the United States. Public disclosure of tax returns disappeared in the 1930s, and it comes as no surprise that secrecy and tax evasion have come to the fore since the 1980s. Graduated tax rates have been reduced from their peak after World War II, and the impact of income transfer from one class to another has been limited. Although tax resisters failed to "exterminate," as they put it in the 1990s, the progressive structure of federal taxation—the federal income tax still generated more than 55 percent of annual receipts—they had been able to undermine the very notion of social solidarity. From attacks against "welfare queens" to fascination with private goods and ownership, the neoliberal ideology instilled its vision not only in the United States but also in the rest of the world.[5]

Beyond their radical antitax and antistatist rhetoric, conservatives have always, and paradoxically, offered a clear-cut view of both statism and taxation. Even though there have been differences and tensions among them, they have always preferred to finance temporary crises with regressive taxation paid by all citizens than with progressive taxes paid by the richest. When many politicians and citizens made fun of Tea Partiers who denounced the federal government and yet endorsed Social Security, they failed to understand the ambiguous relationship between conservatives and centralized power. If the government were to offer reciprocal benefits, federal taxation could be accepted along with many other relationships with institutions such as foundations, corporations, and local philanthropic associations.[6]

By anchoring taxation analysis in the social world, this book invites historians to consider taxation as a serious field of study and to pursue their approach to research on the basis of how citizens saw tax mechanisms. Historians need to uncover the complex relationships between individuals and their institutions to understand the strength and legitimacy of the American federal government. In his famous article, entitled "War Making and State Making as Organized Crime," Charles Tilly rightly reminds us that "war making, state making, protection, and extraction" plays a major role in, and depends upon, "the state's tendency to monopolize the concentrated means of coercion." Such an account, based upon political centralization and a powerful bureaucracy, masks the importance of individuals and their ability to resist or negotiate with the state. By looking at resisters, we can indirectly put the emphasis, instead, on the millions of individuals who agree to pay their taxes.[7]

An insightful social history of taxation will be able to capture the concrete functioning of the fiscal state that has emerged in the context of the new industrialized society. The emphasis of this study on the American resistance to federal taxes highlights the need for taxation to be analyzed more thoroughly on individual and local levels if we are to understand the relationship between local discontent or consent and national resistance. During the Reconstruction period, the 1920s, and the 1970s, protests thrived both at the local and federal levels, but to articulate the complex relationship between the local and the national, more local studies are necessary.[8]

As debts and taxes hold center stage in the Western World in the early twenty-first century, and shutdown of the federal government loomed large in the horizon of the United States, a historical presentation of the ebb and flow of tax resistance could be useful in the debate. Everywhere, difficulties have arisen from the discrepancy between the progressive scheme of taxation, still based upon income tax, and the crisis of social solidarity. During the War of 1812, when Americans had no choice but to levy new direct taxes, President James Madison promised to implement a "well digested system of internal revenue." That is precisely what this book is all about: the creation of a "well-digested" tax system in the name of equality and social justice.[9]

ABBREVIATIONS

NOTES

ACKNOWLEDGMENTS

INDEX

ABBREVIATIONS

Manuscript Collections

ALP	Alexander Lincoln Papers, AESL
APP	Arthur Page Papers, WHS
CAF	Carl Anderson Files, RRPL
CGMP	Christopher Gustavus Memminger Papers, UNC
CWP	Charles Walker Papers, HIA
DWP	David A. Wells Paper, LOC
FSP	Frederick Steiwer Papers, UOSP
GHGH	Gordon Hall and Grace Hoag Collection of Dissenting and Extremist Printed Propaganda, 1926–1996, BU
IDP	Ida Darden Papers, HPL
JBF	Jack Burgess Files, RRPL
JCSP	John S. Cullinan Papers, UH
JDH	J. Douglas Holladay Files, RRPL
JKP	John Henry Kirby Papers, UH
JkP	Jack Kemp Papers, LOC
JLB	J. Lee Bracken Papers, USA
JRP	John Raskob Papers, HL
JSC	Jouett Shouse Collection, UKSC
LCF	Linda Chavez Files, RRPL
NAP	Nelson Aldrich Papers, LOC
NLP	Nicholas Longworth Papers, LOC
OKP	Otto Kahn Papers, PUL
RWC	Right-Wing Collection, UI
RG 56	Record Group 56, Department of the Treasury, NARA-II
RG 58	Record Group 58, Internal Revenue Service, NARA-II
RG 233	Record Group 233, Petitions and Memorials, NARA
RJF	Robert Johns Files, RRPL
RJP	Robert H. Jackson Papers, LOC
RMP	Richard Memminger Papers, UNCL
SCP	Salmon Chase Papers, LOC
SPP	Samuel B. Pettengill Papers, UOSP
WBF	William L. Barr Files, RRPL
WBP	William Borah Papers, LOC
WEP	William Evarts Papers, LOC
WESP	Willis E. Stone Papers, UOSP

NOTES

PROLOGUE

1. Nicolas Delalande, *Les batailles de l'impôt: Consentement et résistance de 1789 à nos jours* (Paris: Le Seuil, 2011); Charles Tilly, *Coercion, Capital, and European States, 990–1992* (Cambridge, MA: Blackwell, 1992); Martin Daunton, *Trusting Leviathan: The Politics of Taxation in Britain 1799–1914* (Cambridge: Cambridge University Press, 2001); Michael Kwass, *Privilege and the Politics of Taxation in Eighteenth-Century France* (Cambridge: Cambridge University Press, 2000); Carolyn Webber and Aaron B. Wildavsky, *A History of Taxation and Expenditures in the Western World* (New York: Simon & Schuster, 1986); Walter J. Blum and Harry Kalven, *The Uneasy Case for Progressive Taxation* (Chicago: University of Chicago Press, 1974).

2. Letter from Thomas Jefferson to James Madison, October 28, 1785, in *Our Sacred Honor: Words of Advice from the Founders in Stories, Letters, Poems, and Speeches*, ed. William J. Bennett (New York: Simon and Schuster, 1997), 226–227; Bruce Ackerman, "Taxation and the Constitution," *Columbia Law Review*, vol. 99 (1999): 1–58.

3. Max Edling, *A Revolution in Favor of Government: Origins of the U.S. Constitution and the Making of the American State* (New York: Oxford University Press, 2003); Roger H. Brown, *Redeeming the Republic: Federalists, Taxation, and the Origins of the Constitution* (Baltimore, Johns Hopkins University Press, 1993); James Madison, *Notes of Debates in the Federal Convention of 1787* (New York: W. W. Norton, 1987).

4. Paul Douglas Newman, *Fries's Rebellion: The Enduring Struggle for the American Revolution* (Philadelphia: University of Pennsylvania Press, 2004); Thomas P. Slaughter, *The Whiskey Rebellion: Frontier Epilogue to the American Revolution* (New York: Oxford University Press, 1986);

Richard H. Kohn, "The Washington Administration's Decision to Crush the Whiskey Rebellion," *Journal of American History* 59, no. 3 (1972): 567–584.

5. "Second Inaugural Address," in *A Compilation of the Messages and Papers of the Presidents, 1789–1908*, vol. 1 (Washington, D.C., 1908), 379.

6. Thomas M. Cooley, *A Treatise on the Law of Taxation* (Chicago: Callaghan, 1876); Robin Einhorn, *American Taxation, American Slavery* (Chicago: University of Chicago Press, 2008); William J. Novak, *People's Welfare: Law and Regulation in Nineteenth-Century America* (Chapel Hill: University of North Carolina Press, 1996).

7. Edwin R. A. Seligman, "The Income Tax Amendment," *Political Science Quarterly* 25, no. 2 (1910): 214; Edwin R. A. Seligman, *Progressive Taxation in Theory and Practice* (New York: American Economic Association, 1914); Ajay K. Mehrotra, *Making the Modern American Fiscal State: Law, Politics, and the Rise of Progressive Taxation, 1877–1929* (New York: Cambridge University Press, 2013).

8. Eric Homberger, *Mrs. Astor's New York: Money and Social Power in a Gilded Age* (New Haven: Yale University Press, 2002), 271–272.

9. Marjorie E. Kornhauser, "Corporate Regulation and the Origins of the Corporate Income Tax," *Indiana Law Journal* 66, no. 1 (1990): 53–136.

10. Letter from Mason Hammond to Robert Doughton, Feb. 15, 1835, Folder Revenue Revision (February 1935), Box 454, RG 233.

11. David A. Wells, "The Communism of a Discriminating Income Tax," *The North American Review* 130, no. 280 (1880): 236–246.

12. Liam Murphy and Thomas Nagel, *The Myth of Ownership: Taxes and Justice* (New York: Oxford University Press, 2002).

13. Joel Slemrod, *Why People Pay Taxes: Tax Compliance and Enforcement* (Ann Arbor: University of Michigan Press, 1992); John Scholz and Mark Lubell, "Trust and Taxpaying: Testing the Heuristic Approach to Collective Action," *American Journal of Political Science* 42, no. 2 (1998): 398–417; Isaac W. Martin, Ajay K. Mehrotra, and Monica Prasad, eds., *The New Fiscal Sociology: Taxation in Comparative and Historical Perspective* (New York: Cambridge University Press, 2009), 1–27; Margaret Levi, *Of Rule and Revenue* (Berkeley: University of California Press, 1988); Marcelo Bergman, "Tax Reforms and Tax

Compliance: The Divergent Paths of Chile and Argentina," *Journal of Latin American Studies* 35 (2003): 593–624; Clarence Y. H. Lo, *Small Property versus Big Government: Social Origins of the Property Tax Revolt* (Berkeley, CA: University of California Press, 1990); William Isaac Martin, *The Permanent Tax Revolt: How the Property Tax Transformed American Politics* (Palo Alto, CA: Stanford University Press, 2008).

14. Sidney Tarrow and Charles Tilly, *Contentious Politics* (New York: Oxford University Press, 2006); Nicolas Delalande and Romain Huret, "Tax Resistance: A Global History?" *Journal of Policy History* 25, no. 3 (2013): 1–7.

15. Lila Abu-Lughod, "The Romance of Resistance: Tracing Transformations of Power through Bedouin Women," *American Ethnologist* 17, no. 1 (1990): 41–55; Jocelyn A. Hollander and Rachel L. Einwohner, "Conceptualizing Resistance," *Sociological Forum* 19, no. 4 (2004): 533–554; James C. Scott, *Weapons of the Weak: Everyday Forms of Peasant Resistance* (New Haven: Yale University Press, 1985); Gary Gerstle and Steve Fraser, eds., *Ruling America: A History of Wealth and Power in America* (Cambridge, MA: Harvard University Press, 2005).

16. Sidney Ratner, *Taxation and Democracy in America* (New York: Wiley, 1967); David Zaret, "Petitions and the 'Invention' of Public Opinion in the English Revolution," *American Journal of Sociology* 101, no. 6 (1996): 1497–1555; David Zaret, *Origins of Democratic Culture: Printing, Petitions, and the Public Sphere in Early-Modern England* (Princeton: Princeton University Press, 1999); Stephen Higginson, "A Short History of the Right to Petition Government for the Redress of Grievances," *The Yale Law Journal* 96, no. 1 (1986): 142–166; Lex Heerma van Voss, *Petitions in Social History*, Special Issue, *International Review of Social History*, Supplement 9 (Cambridge: Cambridge University Press, 2001); Daniel Carpenter, "The Petition as a Recruitment Device: Evidence from the Abolitionists' Congressional Campaign," November 2003, Unpublished Paper (in author's hands).

17. Brian Balogh, *A Government Out of Sight: The Mystery of National Authority in Nineteenth-Century America* (Cambridge: Cambridge

University Press, 2008); Meg Jacobs, William J. Novak, and Julian E. Zelizer, eds., *The Democratic Experiment: New Directions in American Political History* (Princeton: Princeton University Press, 2003).

18. Sidney Ratner, *American Taxation: Its History as a Social Force in Democracy* (New York: W. W. Norton, 1942); Randolph E. Paul, *Taxation in the United States* (Boston: Little Brown, 1954); John F. Witte, *The Politics and Development of the Federal Income Tax* (Madison: University of Wisconsin Press, 1985); Sven Steinmo, *Taxation and Democracy: Swedish, British, and American Approaches to Financing the Modern State* (New Haven: Yale University Press, 1993); Joel Slemrod and John M. Bakija, *Taxing Ourselves: A Citizen's Guide to Debate over Taxes* (Cambridge, MA: MIT Press, 2008); Kevin Philipps, *Wealth and Democracy: A Political History of the American Rich* (New York: Broadway Books, 2002); Joseph J. Thorndike, *Their Fair Share: Taxing the Rich in the Age of FDR* (Washington D.C.: Urban Institute Press, 2013); Isaac W. Martin, *Rich People's Movement: Grassroots Campaign to Untax the One Percent* (New York: Oxford University Press, 2013).

1. Unconstitutional War Taxes

1. *Congressional Globe*, 41st Congress, 2nd Session, June 22, 1870, 4715; "The Income Tax," *New York Times*, June 20, 1871; Axel Madsen, *John Jacob Astor: America's First Multimillionaire* (New York: Wiley, 2001), 262.

2. Richard Franklin Bensel, *Yankee Leviathan: The Origins of Central State Authority in America, 1859–1877* (Cambridge: Cambridge University Press, 1990); Heather Cox Richardson, *The Greatest Nation on Earth: Republican Economic Policies during the Civil War* (Cambridge: Harvard University Press, 1997); Mark R. Wilson, *The Business of Civil War: Military Mobilization and the State, 1861–1865* (Baltimore: Johns Hopkins University Press, 2006); Jane Flaherty, *The Revenue Imperative: The Union's Financial Policies during the American Civil War* (London: Pickering & Chatto, 2009); Irwin Unger, *The Greenback Era: A Social and Political History of American Finance, 1865–1879* (Princeton: Princeton University Press, 1964).

3. Petition sent on March 5, 1862, Folder "Taxation—December 4, 1861 to January 22, 1863," Tray HR 37A-G20.8, RG 233; "The Tax Bill," *Saturday Evening Post*, March 22, 1862, 7; *Congressional Globe*, 37th Congress, 2nd Session, 1225.

4. Frederik J. Blue, *Salmon P. Chase* (Kent, OH: Kent State University Press, 1987); John Niven, *Salmon P. Chase: A Biography* (New York: Oxford University Press, 1996); Laura Smith Porter, "The Last, Best Hope of Earth: Abraham Lincoln's Perception of the Mission of America 1834–1854," *Illinois Historical Journal* 78 (1985): 207–216; W. Elliot Brownlee, *Federal Taxation in America: A Short History* (New York: Cambridge University Press, 1996), 32–36.

5. Joseph A. Hill, "The Civil War Income Tax," *Quarterly Journal of Economics* 8, no. 4 (1894): 417; Rafael A. Bayley, *History of the National Loans of the United States from July 4, 1776, to June 30, 1880* (Washington, D.C.: Government Printing Office, 1884); Ellis Paxson Oberholtzer, *Jay Cooke: Financier in the Civil War* (Philadelphia: George W. Jacobs & Co., 1907), 1:312–325; Melinda Lawson, *Patriot Fires: Forging a New American Nationalism in the Civil War North* (Lawrence: Kansas University Press, 2002), 55–57.

6. *Congressional Globe*, 37th Congress, 1st Session, July 24, 1861, 271.

7. Ibid., 248–249, 282, 306–307.

8. Ibid., 254, 326; Hill, "The Civil War Income Tax," 416–452.

9. Quotation in Elmer Ellis, "Public Opinion and the Income Tax 1860–1900," *Mississippi Valley Historical Review* 27, no. 2 (1940): 226; Report of the Secretary of the Treasury on the State of the Finances for the Year Ending June 30, 1861, Vol. 90, Entry 372, RG 56.

10. Edward J. Balleinsen, *Navigating Failure: Bankruptcy and Commercial Society in Antebellum America* (Chapel Hill: University of North Carolina Press, 2001); Christopher Clark, *Social Change in America: From the Revolution to the Civil War* (Chicago: Ivan R. Dee, 2006).

11. Petition, March 18, 1862; Petition, January 1, 1862; Petition, March, 19, 1862; March, 24, 1862; March, 24, 1862, Folder "Domestic Tapes—Dec. 4, 1861, to Mar. 24, 1862," Tray HR 37A-G20.8, RG 233; *Congressional Record*, 37th Congress, 2nd Session, 1222; Steven A. Bank, *From Sword*

to Shield: The Transformation of the Corporate Income Tax 1861 to Present* (New York: Oxford University Press, 2010), 12–23.

12. Mary Ryan, *Cradle of the Middle Class: The Family in Oneida County, New York 1790–1865* (Cambridge: Cambridge University Press, 1996).

13. "Income Tax," *The Crisis*, September 10, 1862; Petitions, Folder "Domestic Taxes—Jan. 26, 1863, to Feb. 10, 1863," HR 37 A-G20.8 (Jan. 26, 1863–Mar. 11, 1863, and undated), RG 233.

14. "Instance of Triple and Quadruple Taxation," *New York Times*, June 28, 1862, 2; E. B. Ward, "Manufacturers Opposition to the Income Tax," *Merchants Magazine and Commercial Review* 49, no. 2 (1863): 150–154; "The Manufacturers and the Income Tax," *New York Times*, May 28, 1863.

15. Lawson, *Patriot Fires*, 41–44; Hugh McCulloch, *Men and Measures of Half a Century* (New York: Charles Scribner' Sons, 1889), 459–462.

16. Quotation in McPherson, *Battle Cry of Freedom: The Civil War Era* (New York: Oxford University Press, 1988), 592; Frank L. Klement, *The Limits of Dissent: Clement L. Vallandigham and the Civil War* (Lexington: Kentucky University Press, 1970).

17. Jennifer Weber, *Copperheads: The Rise and Fall of Lincoln's Opponents in the North* (New York: Cambridge University Press, 2006); Wilson, *The Business of Civil War*, 149–150.

18. Harris Proschansky, "The Origins of the National Association of Life Underwriters," *Business History Review* 29, no. 3 (1955): 238–262; Petition, December 8, 1862; Petition, March 16, 1863, Folder HR 37 A-G20.8 (Jan. 26, 1863–Mar. 11, 1863, and undated), Tray HR 37A-G20.8, RG 233; Robin Einhorn, *American Taxation American Slavery* (Chicago: Chicago University Press, 2006), 201–250.

19. McPherson, *Battle Cry*, 591–625; Mark E. Neely Jr., *The Union Divided: Party Conflict in the Civil War North* (Cambridge, MA: Harvard University Press, 2002); Quotation in Leslie M. Harris, *In the Shadow of Slavery: African Americans in New York City, 1626–1863* (Chicago: University of Chicago Press, 2002), 126.

20. Quotation in Robert Stanley, *Dimensions of Law in the Service of Order: Origins of the Federal Income Tax 1861–1913* (New York: Oxford University Press, 1993), 33; Richard R. John, *Network Nation: Inventing*

American Telecommunications (Cambridge, MA: Harvard University Press, 2010), 133–134; Brownlee, *Federal Taxation*, 34; Franklin Noll, "Repudiation! The Crisis of United States Civil War Debt 1865–1870," Paper presentation at the Graduate Institute of International and Development Studies, Geneva, Government Debt Crises: Politics, Economics, and History, December 14–15, 2013 (in author's hands).

21. "Our Internal Revenue: The Sixth Collection District in Full," *New York Times*, July 8, 1865; Marjorie Kornhauser, "Shaping Public Opinion and the Law: How a 'Common Man' Law Ended a Rich Man's Law," *Law and Contemporary Problems* 73 (2009): 123–130; "Publication of Income Tax Lists," *New York Times*, January 20, 1865.

22. Philip J. Roberts, *A Penny for the Governor, a Dollar for Uncle Sam: Income Taxation in Washington* (University of Washington Press, 2002), 29; "Women's Income Tax," *New York Times*, January 28, 1865; Letter written by George Boutwell, commissioner of internal revenue, August 2, 1862, to Dessle Little, Esq., assessor of taxes, Great Salt Lake City, Utah, vol. 1A of two vols., from Aug. 1, 1862, to Sept. 19, 1862, RG 58.

23. Inspectors' Book, June 1, 1864, to May 17, 1865; Letter from R. S. Corvin, Esq. to special agent, Easton, PA; Letter sent from D. L. Whitman, Esq. to James A. Briss, revenue agent, New York; Letter from Commissioner Joseph Lewis to Capt. Harrison, revenue inspector, Ohio; Records for the Civil War Period, Letters sent to Revenue Agents and Inspectors, 1864–1865, RG 58.

24. Charles B. Dew, *Apostles of Disunion: Southern Secession Commissioners and the Causes of the Civil War* (Charlottesville: University of Virginia Press, 2001); Stephanie McCurry, *Confederate Reckoning: Power and Politics in the Civil War South* (Cambridge, MA: Harvard University Press, 2010); "Jefferson Davis' Message: The External and Internal Condition of the Southern Confederacy," *New York Times*, December 12, 1863.

25. Lacy K. Ford, "Republican Ideology in a Slave Society," *Journal of Southern History* 54, no. 3 (1998): 405–424; William W. Freehling, *Prelude to the Civil War* (New York: Harper & Row, 1966).

26. Anonymous, *A Plan of the Provisional Government for the Southern Confederacy* (Charleston: Evans and Cogswell, 1861); Eugene M. Lerner,

"The Monetary and Fiscal Programs of the Confederate Government 1861–1865," *Journal of Political Economy* 62 (1954): 506–522; Christopher Memminger, Report of May 10, 1861, Folder 1, CGP; Jonathan Daniel Wells, *The Origins of the Southern Middle Class, 1800–1861* (Chapel Hill: University of North Carolina Press, 2004).

27. Lerner, "The Monetary and Fiscal Programs," 506–509; Sidney Ratner, *Taxation and Democracy in America* (London: Octagon Books, 1980), 102–13; Seligman, *The Income Tax*, 482–483.

28. Stephen V. Ash, "Poor Whites in the Occupied South, 1861–1865," *Journal of Southern History* 57, no. 1 (1991): 39–62; Peter Wallenstein, "Rich Man's War, Rich Man's Fight: Civil War and the Transformation of Public Finance in Georgia," *Journal of Southern History* 50, no. 1 (1984): 15–42; Randolph E. Paul, *Taxation in the United States* (Boston: Little Brown, 1954), 19–21; Joseph H. Parks, "State Rights in a Crisis: Governor Joseph E. Brown versus President Jefferson Davis," *Journal of Southern History* 31, no. 1 (1966): 3–24.

29. The two Southern articles appeared in "The New Rebel Tax Law," *New York Times*, May 16, 1863 and "Affairs in Richmond," *New York Times*, April 26, 1863; McCurry, *Confederate Reckoning*, 155–156; Mark W. Geiger, *Financial Fraud and Guerilla Violence in Missouri's Civil War, 1861–1865* (New Haven: Yale University Press, 2010).

30. Ovid L. Futch, "Salmon P. Chase and Civil War Politics in Florida," *Florida Historical Quarterly* 32 (1954): 163–188; Daniel W. Hamilton, *Property Confiscation in the Union and the Confederacy during the Civil War* (Chicago: University of Chicago Press, 2007); Letter from William Henry Brisbane to Secretary Chase, November 18, 1963, Reel 22, SPCP; Letter from Harrison Reed to S. P. Chase, May 20, 1864, Folder "Direct Tax Commissions in Southern States, Florida," Box 1, Entry 77; Report on the Matter of the Florida Tax Commission of the Florida Tax Commission by Austin Smith to Secretary Chase, July 30, 1864, Folder "Direct Tax Commissions in Southern Florida, 1864–1867," Box 1, Entry 76, RG 58.

31. Douglas B. Ball, *Financial Failure and Confederate Defeat* (Urbana: University of Illinois Press, 1991), 236; Bensel, *Yankee Leviathan*, 170–172.

32. Gabor S. Boritt, ed., *Why the Confederacy Lost* (New York: Oxford University Press, 1992); David Donald, ed., *Why the North Won the Civil War* (Baton Rouge: Louisiana University Press, 1960).

33. Letter from Joseph Lewis to D. C. Whitman, December 9, 1865, Inspector's Book, June 1, 1864, to May 17, 1865, Records for the Civil War Period, Letters Sent to Revenue Agents and Inspectors, 1864–1865, RG 58; *Congressional Globe*, 39th Congress, 1st Session, 2438.

34. Brian Balogh, *A Government Out of Sight: The Mystery of National Authority in Nineteenth-Century America* (New York: Cambridge University Press, 2009), 289; Morton Keller, *Affairs of State: Public Life in Late 19th Century America* (Cambridge, MA: Harvard University Press, 1977); Petition, January 25, 1868, Trail HR 40A-H 19.18 (Mar. 12, 1867–Jan. 9, 1868), 40th Congress, RG 233.

35. Memorial, December 18, 1867, Trail HR 40 A-H 19.18 (January 13, 1868–February, 26, 1868), 40th Congress, Committee on Ways and Means, HR 40A-H19.18, "Tax Reduction, January 13, 1868, to February 4, 1868"; Petition, February 1868, Trail (February 24, 1868–Feb. 26, 1868), RG 233.

36. Petition, October 4, 1868, Trail HR 201–H19.18, February 27, 1968 to February 1, 1869 and undated, 40th Congress, Committee on Ways and Means, HR40 A–H19.18, Tax reduction, July 8, 1868 to February, 1869 and undated; Petition, January 17, 1868; Petition, January 17, 1868, Trail HR 40 A-H 19.18 (January 13, 1868–February 26, 1868), 40th Congress, Committee on Ways and Means, HR 40A-H19.18, "Tax Reduction, January 13, 1868, to February 4, 1868," RG 233.

37. J. S. Gibbons, *The Public Debt of the United States* (New York: Charles Scribner & Co., 1867), 1; Eric Foner, *Reconstruction: America's Unfinished Revolution, 1863–1877* (New York: Harper & Collins, 2002), 22; Revenue System of the United States, 39th Congress, 1st Session, House Ex., Doc. 34, January 29, 1863, 36–37; David A. Wells, *Our Burden and Our Strength, or, A Comprehensive and Popular Examination of the Debt and Resources of Our Country, Present and Prospective* (Boston: Gould & Lincoln, 1864); Stanley, *Dimensions of Law in the Service of Order*, 44–45; *Congressional Globe*, 39th Congress, 1st Session, 1866; "Taxes on Manufacturers," *New York Times*, August 27, 1865.

38. Quotation in Christopher Michael Shepart, *The Civil War Income Tax and the Republican Party* (New York: Algora Publishing, 2010), 89; *Congressional Globe*, 39th Congress, 1st Session, 3496.

39. Quotation in Ball, *Financial Failure*, 221; Bruce E. Stewart, *Moonshiners and Prohibitionists: The Battle over Alcohol in Southern Appalachia* (Lexington: University of Kentucky Press, 2011), 91.

40. Foner, *Reconstruction*, 415–416; James L. Sellers, "An Interpretation of Civil War Finance," *American Historical Review*, 30, no. 2 (1925): 286, 289; John C. Schwab, *The Confederate States of America, 1861–1865* (New York: Charles Scribner's Sons, 1901), 76.

41. Ben C. Truman, "The Workings of the Direct Tax Commission—Remarkable Developments of Fraud and Corruption," *New York Times*, July 23, 1866; Williamjames Hull Hoffer, *To Enlarge the Machinery of Government: Congressional Debates and the Growth of the American State, 1858–1891* (Baltimore: Johns Hopkins University Press, 1991), 63–88; Mark Wahlgren Summers, *A Dangerous Stir. Fear, Paranoia, and the Making of Reconstruction* (Chapel Hill, University of North Carolina Press, 2009).

42. Letter sent to the secretary of the Treasury, December 4, 1866, Direct Tax Commissions in Florida, Correspondence of the Commission, Box 1, RG 58.

43. Bruce E. Stewart, ed., *King of the Moonshiner: Lewis R. Redmond in Fact and Fiction* (Knoxville: University of Tennessee Press, 2008).

44. Ibid., 78–79, 195.

45. Bruce E. Stewart, "When Darkness Reigns then is the Hour to Strike: Moonshining, Federal Liquor Taxation, and Klan Violence in Western North Carolina," *North Carolina Historical Review* 80 (2003): 453–474; Stewart, *Moonshiners and Prohibitionists*, 102–105; Miller, *Revenuers and Moonshiners*, 43–44, 53–54; Allen W. Trelease, *White Terror: The Ku Klux Klan Conspiracy and Southern Reconstruction* (New York: Harper & Row, 1971).

46. Edward L. Ayers, *Vengeance and Justice: Crime and Punishment in the Nineteenth Century American South* (New York: Oxford University Press, 1982), 262; Quotations in Stewart, *King of the Moonshiners*, 143, xviii.

47. Foner, *Reconstruction*, 460–511.

48. Sven Beckert, *The Monied Metropolis: New York City and the Consolidation of the American Bourgeoisie, 1850–1896* (Cambridge, Cambridge University Press, 2001), 228–229; "Down with the Taxes," *New York Times*, March 30, 1871.

49. Petitions located in Tray HR 37A-G20.8 (Dec. 4, 1861–Jan. 22, 1863); HR 37A-G20.8 (Jan. 26, 1863–Mar. 11, 1863, and undated); 40th Congress, Committee on Ways and Means, HR 40 A-H19-11, Folder "Income Tax," RG 233; *Congressional Globe*, 41st Congress, 2nd Session, 3496, 4030; Annual Report of the Commissioner of Internal Revenue on the Operations of the Internal Revenue System for the Year 1872 (Washington, D.C., November 30, 1872), RG 56; *Congressional Globe*, 41st Congress, 2nd session, June 23, 1870, 4760.

50. "Complications—Pleasonton's Appointments," *Chicago Tribune*, December 21, 1870; "Nominations," *Chicago Tribune*, February 8, 1871, 8; "Letters from Commissioner Pleasanton on the Income Tax," *Chicago Tribune*, January 27, 1871.

51. "The Income Tax," *New York Times*, June 20, 1871; "The Income Tax Doomed," *New York Times*, January 20, 1871; "Note from the People," *New York Times*, February 18, 1871; *Congressional Globe*, 41st Congress, 2nd Session, June 2, 1879, 4023.

52. W. Elliot Brownlee, *Federal Taxation in America: A Short History* (New York: Cambridge University Press, 1996), 36–39; *Congressional Globe*, 42nd Congress, 2nd Session, March 18, 1872, 1708.

2 . Down with Internal Taxes

1. Quotation in Samuel Rezneck, "Distress, Relief, and Discontent in the United States during the Depression of 1873–1878," *Journal of Political Economy* 58, no. 6 (December 1950): 494–512; John Bigelow, *The Life of Samuel J. Tilden* (New York: Harpers Publishers, 1895), 224–260; Mark D. Hirsch, "Samuel J. Tilden: The Story of a Lost Opportunity," *American Historical Review* 56, no. 4 (1951): 788–802; A. B. Nettleton, *Governor Tilden's Income Tax: His Defence Reviewed* (Philadelphia, PA: 1876); "Mr. Tilden's Income Tax," *New York Times*, March 27, 1878.

2. Mark Twain and Charles Dudley Warner, *The Gilded Age. A Tale of Today* (New York: American Publishing Company, 1873); Olivier Zunz, *Making America Corporate, 1870–1920* (Chicago: University of Chicago Press, 1990); Philipp Scranton, *Endless Novelty: Speciality Production and American Industrialization, 1865–1925* (Princeton: Princeton University Press, 1997);

3. "The Reduction of Taxes," *New York Times*, June 24, 1882.

4. Gordon McKinney, *Zeb Vance: North Carolina's Civil War Governor and Gilded Age Political Leader* (Chapel Hill: University of North Carolina Press, 2004); quotation in Bruce Stewart, *Moonshiners and Prohibitionists: The Battle Over Alcohol in Southern Appalachia* (Lexington: University of Kentucky Press, 2011), 88; Roberta Sue Alexander, *North Carolina Faces the Freedmen: Race Relations During Presidential Election 1865–1867* (Durham: Duke University Press, 1985); Eric Foner, *Reconstruction: America's Unfinished Revolution 1863–1877* (New York: Harper & Row, 1988); Dan T. Carter, *When the War Was Over: The Failure of Self-Reconstruction in the South, 1865–1867* (Baton Rouge: Louisiana State University Press, 1985); Heather Cox Richardson, *West from Appomattox: The Reconstruction of America after the Civil War* (New Haven: Yale University Press, 2007), 175.

5. Quotation in Stewart, *Moonshiners and Prohibitionists*, 145.

6. Steven R. Hyman, "Taxation, Public Policy, and Political Dissent: Yeoman Dissatisfaction in the Post-Reconstruction Lower South," *Journal of Southern History* 55, no. 1 (1989): 49–76; "The People of South Carolina," *New York Times*, January 12, 1878; Steven Hahn, *The Roots of Southern Populism: Yeoman Farmers and the Transformation of the Georgia Upcountry, 1850–1890* (New York: Oxford University Press, 1983); Michael Perman, *The Road to Redemption: Southern Politics, 1869–1879* (Chapel Hill: University of North Carolina Press, 1984); "From Various Quarters," *New York Times*, July 6, 1877.

7. *Sanborn and other Contracts, Letter from the Secretary of the Treasury in Answer to a Resolution of the House of February* 13, February 17, 1874, House of Representatives, 43rd Congress, 1st Session, (Washington, D.C., 1874); *Discovery and Collection of Monies Withheld from the Government*, May 4, 1874, House of Representatives, 43rd Congress, 1st

Session (Washington, D.C., 1874); Mark W. Summers, *The Era of Good Stealings* (New York: Oxford University Press, 1993), 89–90, 184–185; Wilbur Miller, *Revenuers & Moonshiners: Enforcing Federal Liquor Law in the Mountain South 1865–1900* (Chapel Hill: University of North Carolina Press, 1991), 64–65.

8. Quotation in Stewart, *Moonshiners and Prohibitionists*, 146; Miller, *Revenuers and Moonshiners*, 47–50; Bruce E. Stewart, ed., *King of the Moonshiners: Lewis R. Redmond in Fact and Fiction* (Knoxville: University of Tennessee Press, 2008), xiv–xv, 1–29 (interview); W. Scott Poole, *Never Surrender: Confederate Memory and Conservatism in the South Carolina Upcountry* (Athens: University of Georgia Press, 2004), 106–108.

9. Lawrence F. Schmeckbier and Francis X. Eble, *The Bureau of Internal Revenue: Its History, Activities and Organization* (Baltimore: Johns Hopkins University Press, 1923).

10. "Kentucky Moonshiners," *Chicago Tribune*, August 22, 1877; "A Whisky War," *Chicago Tribune*, January 17, 1878; "Miscellaneous," *Chicago Tribune*, February 10, 1878.

11. Stewart, *Moonshiners and Prohibitionists*, 97–111; Letter from J. A. George to Green B. Raum, April 28, 1877; Letters Received by the commissioner, Records of the Internal Revenue Service, RG 58; Report of G. W. Atkinson to Green B. Raum, May 18, 1877, Box 895, RG 58.

12. Miller, *Revenuers and Moonshiners*, 97–100; Quotation in "The Government Disposed to Be Lenient to Repentant Moonshiners," *Chicago Tribune*, August 3, 1878.

13. "The 'Moonshiners Plea,'" *New York Times*, July 19, 1878; "Illicit Distillation South," *New York Times*, July 21, 1878; "Raum's View of It," *Washington Post*, July 12, 1879.

14. George Wesley Atkinson, *After the Moonshiners, by One of the Raiders* (Wheeling, West Virginia, 1888).

15. Fiona Dans Halloran, *Thomas Nast: The Father of Modern Political Cartoons: A Biography* (Chapel Hill: University of North Carolina Press, 2012); "Retrenchment or Taxation," *New York Times*, February 16, 1878; Kenneth T. Jackson, "Curtis, George William," in *The Encyclopedia of New York City* (New Haven, CT: Yale University Press, 1995), 305–306.

16. Martin Daunton, *Trusting Leviathan: The Politics of Taxation in Britain, 1799–1914* (Cambridge: Cambridge University Press, 2001); Robert Stanley, *Dimensions of Law in the Service of Order: Origins of the Federal Income* (New York: Oxford University Press, 1993), 76.

17. Rezneck, "Distress, Relief and Discontent," 500; Joanne Reitano, *The Tariff Question in the Gilded Age* (University Park: Pennsylvania State University Press, 1994), 137–140; Scott Reynolds Nelson, *A Nation of Deadbeats: An Uncommon History of America's Financial Disasters* (New York: Alfred A. Knopf, 2012), 157–170.

18. Stanley, *Dimension of Law*, 83; Petition, Folder "Committee on Ways and Means, Income Tax," HR 46A, RG 233; "The Great Social Problem," *New York Times*, August 6, 1878; Gaines M. Foster, *Moral Reconstruction: Christian Lobbyists and the Federal Legislation of Morality, 1865–1920* (Chapel Hill: University of North Carolina Press, 2002); Quotation in Jeffrey Sklansky, *The Soul's Economy: Market Society and Selfhood in American Thought, 1820–1920* (Chapel Hill: University of North Carolina Press, 2002), 110; Bruce Curtis, "William Graham Sumner On the Concentration of Wealth," *Journal of American History* 55, no. 4 (1969): 823–832; "House of Representatives," *New York Times*, February 5, 1878.

19. Stanley, *Dimension of Law*, 83; Petition, Folder "Committee on Ways and Means, Income Tax," HR 46A, RG 233; "The Great Social Problem," *New York Times*, August 6, 1878; "House of Representatives," *New York Times*, February 5, 1878; "Mr. Tilden Done For," *New York Times*, April 5, 1878; "Sam Tilden's Income Tax," *Chicago Tribune*, April 1, 1878.

20. Stanley, *Dimensions of Law*, 63–64; Petition, Folder "Committee on Ways and Means, Income Tax," HR 45 A–H25.17 (March 12, 1878–March 19, 1878, 10F3), Trail HR 45 A–H25.17 (March 12, 1878–June 4 1878), RG 233; "The President, Mr. Evarts, and the Revival of the Income Tax," *New York Times*, January 23, 1878; "The Income Tax," *New York Times*, March 2, 1878.

21. Stanley, *Dimensions of Law*, 71; Quotation in David Nasaw, "Gilded Age Gospels," in Steve Fraser and Gary Gerstle, eds., *Ruling America. A History of Wealth and Power in a Democracy* (Cambridge: Harvard

University Press, 2005), 133; Stanley Coben, "Northeastern Business and Radical Reconstruction: A Re-examination," *The Mississippi Valley Historical Review*, 46, no. 1 (1959): 67–90; Sven Beckert, *The Monied Metropolis: New York City and the Consolidation of the American Bourgeoisie, 1850–1896* (Cambridge, Cambridge University Press, 2001).

22. "Discussing the Ways and Means," *New York Times*, April 4, 1878; "Internal Revenue Bill," *New York Times*, April 21, 1878; Stanley, *Dimensions of Law*, 62–66.

23. David A. Wells, "The Communism of a Discriminating Income-Tax," 280; Tom E. Terrill, "David A. Wells, the Democracy, and Tariff Reduction, 1877–1894," *Journal of American History* 56, no. 3 (1969): 540–555; Michael Les Benedict, "Laissez-Faire and Liberty: A Re-Evaluation of the Meaning and Origins of Laissez-Faire," *Law and History Review* 3, no. 2 (1985): 293–331; Carolyn Jones, "Dollars and Selves: Women's Tax Criticism and Resistance in the 1870s," *University of Illinois Law Review* (1994): 265–310; "The Communism of an Income Tax," *Chicago Tribune*, March 19, 1880; "Concerning the Income Tax," *Chicago Tribune*, May, 20, 1879.

24. William M. Springer, *Tariff Reform: The Paramount Issue: Speeches and Writings on the Questions Involved in the Presidential Contest of 1892* (New York: Charles L. Webster & Company, 1892), 9–18.

25. *Springer v. United States*, 102 U.S. 586 (1880); Bruce Ackerman, "Taxation and the Constitution," *Columbia Law Review*, vol. 99 (1999): 1–58.

26. Robin L. Einhorn, *American Taxation, American Slavery* (Chicago: University of Chicago Press, 2006), 160.

27. Editorial, *New York Times*, January 26, 1881, 4; Editorial, *Washington Post*, January 27, 1881, 2; "No parallel Between It and the Springer Case," *New York Times*, January 28, 1881, 1; "The Income Tax Constitutional," *New York Times*, January 26, 1881; "The Tilden Income Tax Suit," *Chicago Tribune*, January 31, 1881, 3.

28. Reitano, *The Tariff Question*, 2–3; David A. Wells, "Reform in Federal Taxation," *The North American Review* 133, no. 301 (1881): 611–628.

29. Petition undersigned by merchants and citizens of Atlanta in the state of Georgia, April, 21, 1882; Petition signed on June 29, 1882, Folder

"Internal Revenue, Taxation," HR 47A-H22.10–H22.20, Committee on Ways and Means (Glass-Matches), RG 233.

30. Springer, *Tariff Reform*, 83; Richard Bensel, *The Political Economy of American Industrialization 1877–1900* (Cambridge: Cambridge University Press, 2000), 468–472.

31. Springer, *Tariff Reform*, 65.

32. "Abolishing Internal Revenue," *New York Times*, December 21, 1881; "Income Tax: Sheridan Shook Explains Why It Should Be Abolished," *New York Times*, December 10, 1882; Gregory J. Dehler, *Chester Alan Arthur: The Life of a Gilded Age Politician and President* (New York: Nova Publishers, 2006), 134; "The Bankers' Convention," *New York Times*, September 15, 1877; "Taxes to Be Taken Off," *New York Times*, March 23, 1882; "Lighter Internal Taxes," *New York Times*, March 22, 1882; "The Abolition of the Bank Tax," *New York Times*, March 23, 1883; Richard Franklin Bensel, *Yankee Leviathan: The Origins of Central State Authority, 1859–1877* (New York: Cambridge University Press, 1990), 316–317.

33. "The Perfumery Tax," *New York Times*, June 14, 1882; "Tobacco-Growers' Association," *New York Times*, December 27, 1882; "Efforts to Repeal the Tobacco Tax," *New York Times*, May 18, 1884; "Relief from Internal Taxes," *New York Times*, July 17, 1883; "Speakership Candidates," *New York Times*, November 16, 1883.

34. Robert Cumming Wilson, *Drug and Pharmacy in the Life of Georgia, 1733–1959* (Atlanta: University of Georgia Press, 1959), 342; Edward L. Ayers, *The Promise of the New South: Life after Reconstruction* (New York: Oxford University Press, 1992), 13–14.

35. "Against Internal Revenue," *New York Times*, January 13, 1887; "A Tobacco Dealer's Grievances," *New York Times*, January 6, 1887; "Want the Taxes Reduced," *New York Times*, October 21, 1887.

36. National Wholesale Druggists Association, *A History of the National Wholesale Druggists Association from Its Organization to Nineteen-Twenty Four* (New York: 1924).

37. Petitions sent to the Committee on Ways and Means, January–February 1887; Letter From the secretary of the Philadelphia Drug Exchange sent to the Hon. Charles O'Neill, January 25, 1887, Folder "Repeal of Internal Taxes," Box 178, RG 233.

38. "Why He Wants Tax Retained," *New York Times*, February 25, 1888; "Is this Republicanism?," *New York Times*, January 11, 1888; "Internal Revenue Taxes," *New York Times*, January 27, 1884; "Sherman and the Surplus," *New York Times*, January 5, 1888; William A. Link, *The Paradox of Southern Progressivism, 1880–1930* (Chapel Hill: University of North Carolina Press, 1992); Stewart, *Moonshiners and Prohibitionists*, 171–188.

39. Glenn W. LaFantasie, *Gettysburg Requiem The Life and Lost Causes of Confederate Colonel William C. Oates* (New York: Oxford University Press, 2006); Joanne Reitano, *The Tariff Question in the Gilded Age: The Great Debate of 1888* (Philadelphia: University of Pennsylvania Press, 1994); Rebecca Edwards, *Angels in the Machiney: Gender in America Party Politics from the Civil War to the Progressive Era* (New York: Oxford University Press, 1997), 75–90; Nina Silber, *The Romance of Reunion: Northerners and the South 1865–1900* (Chapel Hill: University of North Carolina Press, 1993). 93–123; Gaines M. Foster, *Ghosts of the Confederacy: Defeat, the Lost Cause, and the Emergence of the New South 1865 to 1913* (New York: Oxford University Press, 1987).

40. Charles F. Dunbar, "The Direct Tax of 1861," *The Quarterly Journal of Economics* 3, no. 4 (1889): 436–461.

41. Ben C. Truman, "The Workings of the Direct Tax Commission—Remarkable Developments of Fraud and Corruption," *New York Times*, July 23, 1866.

42. "To Break the Dead-Lock," *New York Times*, April 12, 1888; Quotation in "Last Wednesday's Session," *New York Times*, April 10, 1888; "The Deadlock in the House," *New York Times*, April 9, 1888.

43. "The Tariff Bill in Hand," *New York Times*, December 6, 1888; "Triumph of the Minority," *New York Times*, April 13, 1888; "Extra Session Problem," *New York Times*, December 2, 1888; "Four New Sister States," *New York Times*, February 21, 1889.

44. Reitano, *The Tariff Question*, 48; "The Direct Tax Bill," *New York Times*, December 14, 1888; "Cleveland's Last Veto," *New York Times*, March 4, 1889; "Vetoed by the President," *New York Times*, March 3, 1889; *Congressional Record*, 51st Congress, 2nd Session, 3215; Allan Nevins, *Grover*

Cleveland: A Study in Courage (New York: Dodd, Mead, & Company, 1933), 393; "A Sheer, Bald Gratuity," *New York Times*, February 27, 1891.

45. *Congressional Record*, 51st Congress, 2nd Session 3216; "Direct Tax Bill Passed," *New York Times*, February 25, 1891; "Serves Them Right," *New York Times*, October 3, 1891; "Direct-Tax Refund," *New York Times*, October 3, 1892.

46. Jeffrey Sklansky, *The Soul's Economy: Market Society and Selfhood in American Thought, 1820–1920* (Chapel Hill: University of North Carolina Press, 2002); Thomas G. Sherman, "The Owners of Wealth," *Forum* (1889): 262–273; Thomas G. Sherman, *Natural Taxation: An Inquiry into the Practicability, Justice and Effects of a Scientific Method of Taxation* (New York: Doubleday & McClure Co., 1898), 38; "Thomas G. Sherman Dead," *New York Times*, September 30, 1900; Ajay K. Mehrotra, *Making the Modern American Fiscal State: Law, Politics, and the Rise of Progressive Taxation, 1877–1929* (New York: Cambridge University Press, 2013), 91–96; George K. Holmes, "The Concentration of Wealth," *Political Science Quarterly*, no. 8, 4 (1893): 589–600.

47. Dorothy Ross, *The Origins of American Social Science* (Cambridge: Cambridge University Press, 1991); Barbara H. Fried, *The Progressive Assault on Laissez Faire: Robert Hale and the First Law and Economics Movement* (Cambridge, MA: Harvard University Press, 1998); Edwin R. A. Seligman, "Single Tax Debate," *Journal of Social Science* 27 (1890); John L. Thomas, *Alternative America: Henry George, Edward Bellamy, Henry Demarest Lloyd and the Adversary Tradition* (Cambridge, MA: Harvard University Press, 1983).

48. Ajay K. Mehrotra, "From Berlin to Baltimore: German Historicism and the American Income Tax, 1877–1913," in *Taxation, State, and Civil Society in Germany and the United States from the 18th to the 20th Century*, ed. Alexander Nützenadel and Christoph Strupp (Baden-Baden: Nomos, 2007): 167–184; Daniel T. Rodgers, *Atlantic Crossings. Social Politics in A Progressive Age* (Cambridge, MA: Harvard University Press, 1998); Henry Carter Adams, *Taxation in the United States, 1789–1816* (Baltimore: Johns Hopkins University Studies, 1884); Leon Fink, *Progressive Intellectuals and the Dilemmas of Democratic Commitment* (Cambridge, MA: Har-

vard University Press, 1997); William J. Novak, *People's Welfare: Law and Regulation in Nineteenth Century America* (Chapel Hill: University of North Carolina Press, 1996); Richard T. Ely, *Taxation in American States and Cities* (New York: T. Y. Crowell, 1888), 13–14.

49. Edwin R. A. Seligman, "The Income Tax," *Political Science Quarterly* 9 (1894): 610; Edwin R. A. Seligman, *Essays in Taxation* (New York: Macmillan & Co, 1895), 70, 72.

50. Seligman, "The *Income Tax*," 16.

51. Ross, *American Social Science*, 103–109; Daunton, *Trusting Leviathan*, 143–146; T. N. Carver, "The Ethical Basis of Taxation and Its Application to Taxation," *Annals of the American Academy of Political and Social Science* 6 (1895): 97–99; F. Y. Edgeworth, "The Pure Theory of Taxation," *Economics Journal* 7 (1897): 550.

52. Seligman, "The Theory of Progressive Taxation," *Political Science Quarterly* 8 (1893): 220, 222.

53. Quotation in Edward Chase Kirkland, *Dream and Thought in the Business Community, 1860–1900* (Chicago: Ivan R. Dee, 1956), 48; Andrew Carnegie, "Wealth," *North American Review* 148, no. 391 (1889): 653–665.

54. Springer, *Tariff Reform*, 269.

3. The Odious Income Tax

1. Thorstein Veblen, *The Theory of the Leisure Class: An Economic Study in the Evolution of Institutions* (New York: The Macmillan Company, 1899); Elsie De Wolfe, *The House in Good Taste* (New York: The Century Co., 1913).

2. "Elsie de Wolfe Fights Income Tax," *New York Times*, December 3, 1913; "Should Women Resist Income Tax?" *New York Tribune*, January 4, 1914.

3. Ajay Mehrotra, "The Public Control of Corporate Power: Revisiting the 1909 U.S. Corporate Tax from a Comparative Perspective," *Theoretical Inquiries in Law* 11 (2010): 491–532; W. Elliot Brownlee, *Federal Taxation in America: A Short History* (New York: Cambridge University Press, 2004), 41–57.

4. Lawrence Goodwyn, *The Populist Moment: A Short History of the Agrarian Revolt in America* (New York: Oxford University Press, 1978); Charles Postel, *The Populist Vision* (New York: Oxford University Press, 2007); Steven J. Diner, *A Very Different Age: Americans of the Progressive Era* (New York: Hill & Wang, 1998); Michael McGerr, *A Fierce Discontent: The Rise and Fall of the Progressive Movement in America 1870–1920* (New York: Free Press, 2003).

5. "Death of Simon Sterne," *New York Times*, September 23, 1901; John Ford, *Simon Sterne, 1839–1901* (New York: Macmillan, 1903); David C. Hammack, *Power and Society: Greater New York at the Turn of the Century* (New York: Columbia University Press, 1982); "Against an Income Tax—Mass Meeting of Business Men Last Evening," *New York Times*, June 6, 1894; Quotation in Sven Beckert, "Democracy in the Age of Capital: Contesting Suffrage Rights in Gilded Age New York," in *The Democratic Experiment: New Directions in American Political History*, ed. Meg Jacobs, William Novak, and Julian Zelizer (Princeton: Princeton University Press, 2003), 158; Clifton Hood, "An Unusable Past: Urban Elites, New York City's Evacuation Day, and the Transformations of Memory Culture," *Journal of Social History* 37, no. 4 (2004): 883–913.

6. Eric Homberger, *Mrs. Astor's New York: Money and Social Power in a Gilded Age* (New Haven: Yale University Press, 2002), 181; Frederic Cople Jaher, *The Urban Establishment: Upper Strata in Boston, New York, Charleston, Chicago, and Los Angeles* (Chicago: University of Illinois Press, 1982); Sven Beckert, *The Monied Metropolis: New York City and the Consolidation of the American Bourgeoisie, 1850–1896* (Cambridge: Cambridge University Press, 2001); Bolton Hall, ed., *Who Pays Your Taxes? A Consideration on the Question of Taxation* (New York: G. P. Putnam's Sons, 1892), 146.

7. David Nasaw, "Gilded Age Gospels," in *Ruling America: A History of Wealth and Power in a Democracy*, ed. Steve Fraser and Gary Gerstle (Cambridge, MA: Harvard University Press, 2005), 123–148; Richard Franklin Bensel, *The Political Economy of American Industrialization 1877–1900* (New York: Cambridge University Press, 2000).

8. James McGurrin and Bourke Cockran, *A Free Lance in American Politics* (New York: Charles Scribner's Sons, 1948); "Against an Income Tax," *New York Times*, November 18, 1893; "Would Fight an Income Tax," *New York Times*, November 28, 1893.

9. Richard Joseph, *The Origins of the American Income tax: The Revenue Act of 1894 and Its Aftermath* (Syracuse: Syracuse University Press, 2004); Charles F. Dunbar, "The New Income Tax," *Quarterly Journal of Economics* 9 (1894): 26–42; Scott Reynolds Nelson, *A Nation of Deadbeats: An Uncommon History of America's Financial Disasters* (New York: Alfred A. Knopf, 2012), 198–199, 209–210.

10. Quotation in *Congressional Record*, 53rd Congress, 2nd Session, 1894, 1655; Goodwyn, *The Populist Moment*; Quotation in Sidney Ratner, *American Taxation: Its History as a Social Force in Democracy* (New York: W. W. Norton, 1942), 173; William L. Wilson, "The Income Tax on Corporations," *North American Law Review* 1 (1894): 158.

11. Petitions, Folder "Tax on Incomes, Sept. 8, 1893–Apr. 30. 1894," Box 180, RG 233.

12. "At the same old stand," *New York Times*, January, 20, 1893; "May Tax the Corporations," *New York Times*, December 3, 1893, 1; Charles W. McCurdy, "Justice Field and the Jurisprudence of Government-Business Relations: Some Parameters of Laissez-Faire Constitutionalism, 1863–1897," *Journal of American History* 61, 4 (1975): 970–1005.

13. Petition, Folder "Tax on Incomes, Sept. 8, 1893–Apr. 30. 1894", Box 180, RG 233; Quotation culled from *Speech of Hon. David B. Hill of New York in the Senate of the United States against the Income Tax Features of the Wilson Tariff Bill, Monday April 9, 1894* (Washington, D.C., 1894), 67.

14. Glenn Porter, *The Rise of Big Business 1860–1910* (New York: Cromwell, 1973); Naomi Lamoureaux, *The Merger Movement in the United States* (New York: Cambridge University Press, 1985); Alfred D. Chandler, *The Visible Hand: The Managerial Revolution in American Business 1977* (Cambridge, MA: Harvard University Press, 1977); Steven A. Bank, *From Sword to Shield: The Transformation of the Corporate Income Tax, 1861 to Present* (New York: Oxford University Press, 2010),

50–55; Joseph, *Origins*, 76–88; Julia C. Ott, *When Wall Street Met Main Street: The Quest for an Investors' Democracy* (Cambridge, MA: Harvard University Press, 2011), 11–34.

15. Herbert J. Bass, *"I Am A Democrat": The Political Career of David Bennett Hill* (Syracuse: Syracuse University Press, 1961); Letter from Thomas Jefferson to James Madison, October 28, 1785, in *Our Sacred Honor: Words of Advice from the Founders in Stories, Letters, Poems, and Speeches*, ed. William J. Bennett (New York: Simon and Schuster, 1997); *Speech of Hon. David B. Hill*; Michael Kazin, *A Godly Hero. The Life of William Jennings Bryan* (New York: Random House, 2006), xiii–xxi.

16. *Congressional Record*, 53rd Congress, 2nd Session, 1894, 1655; Quotation in Edwin R. A. Seligman, *The Income Tax: A Study of the History, Theory and Practice of Income Taxation at Home and Abroad* (New York: Macmillan, 1911), 504.

17. Paul Kens, *Justice Stephen Field: Shaping Liberty from the Gold Rush to the Gilded Age* (Lawrence: Kansas University Press, 1997); Robert A. Burt, *The Constitution in Conflict* (Cambridge, MA: Harvard University Press, 1992).

18. Kens, *Justice Stephen Field*, 241, 243.

19. Theron G. Strong, *Joseph H. Choate: New Englander, New Yorker, Lawyer, Ambassador* (New York: Dodd, Mead and Company, 1917).

20. Edwin Seligman, "Is the Income Tax Constitutional and Just?," *Forum* 19 (1895): 48; Francis R. Jones, "Pollock v. Farmers' Loan and Trust Company," *Harvard Law Review* 9, no. 3 (1895): 198–211; "Arguing the Income Tax," *New York Times*, March 13, 1895; Gerald G. Eggert, "Richard Olney and the Income Tax Cases," *The Mississippi Valley Historical Review* 48, no. 1 (1961): 31; 157 US at 532.

21. David A. Wells, "An Income Tax: Is It Desirable?," *Forum*, (1894): 10, 12–13; David Ames Wells, "The Income Tax: A Popular View of the Case," *New York Tribune*, May 9, 1895, 3.

22. Quoted in Robert Stanley, *Dimensions of Law in the Service of Order: Origins of the Federal Income Tax 1861–1913* (New York: Oxford University Press, 1993), 166.

23. Ibid., 166; 158 US 601, 695 (1895) (Brown, J., dissenting).

24. Joseph, *The Origins of the American Income Tax*, 106; David Nasaw, "Gilded Age Gospels," in Fraser and Gerstle, *Ruling America*, 123–148; Charles V. Stewart, "The Federal Income Tax and the Realignment of the 1890s," in *Realignment in American Politics: Toward a Theory*, ed. Bruce A. Campbell and Richard J. Trilling (Austin: University of Texas Press, 1980), 263–287.

25. "Let us Pay as We Go," *New York Times*, April 27, 1898; Quotation from Piero Gleijeses, "1898: The Opposition to the Spanish-American War," *Journal of Latin American Studies* 35, no. 4 (2003): 681–719.

26. Gleijeses, "1898: The Opposition to the Spanish-American War," 692.

27. "Federal Inheritance Tax," *New York Times*, June 12, 1898.

28. "The Federal Inheritance Tax," *New York Times*, December 13, 1899; "Supreme Court Says Tax Legacy Is Valid," *New York Times*, May 15, 1900; Ajay K. Mehrotra, *Making the Modern American Fiscal State: Law, Politics, and the Rise of Progressive Taxation, 1877–1929* (New York: Cambridge University Press, 2013), 252.

29. "To Repeal the War Taxes Law," *New York Times*, April 20, 1900; "Bankers' Meeting Closes," *New York Times*, October 5, 1900.

30. Leonard L. Richards, *Shays's Rebellion: The American Revolution's Final Battle* (Philadelphia: University of Pennsylvania Press, 2002); Richard Peet, "A Sign Taken for History: Daniel Shays' Memorial in Petersham, Massachusetts," *Annals of the Association of American Geographers* 86, no. 1 (1996): 21–43; George B. Rivers, *Capitain Shays: A Populist of 1786* (Boston: Little, Brown and Co., 1897); Edward Bellamy, *The Duke of Stockbridge: A Romance of Shays' Rebellion* (New York, 1900).

31. Ajay Mehrotra, "More Mighty Than the Waves of the Sea: Toilers, Tariffs, and the Income Tax Movement, 1880–1913," *Labor History* 45, no. 2 (2004): 165–198; Elmer Ellis, "Public Opinion and the Income Tax," *Mississippi Valley Historical Review* 27 (1940): 237; David Thelen, *The New Citizenship: Origins of the Progressivism, 1885–1900* (Columbia: Missouri University Press, 1972); Morton Keller, *Regulating a New Economy: Public Policy and Economic Change in America, 1900–1933*

(Cambridge, MA: Harvard University Press 1990), 208–215; W. Elliot Brownlee, *Progressivism and Economic Growth: The Wisconsin Income Tax, 1911–1929* (Port Washington, NY: Kennikat Press, 1974).

32. Robert F. Bruner and Sean D. Carr, *The Panic of 1907: Lessons Learned from the Market's Perfect Storm* (Hoboken, NJ: John Wiley & Sons, 2007).

33. Ajay Mehrotra, "Envisioning the Modern American Fiscal State: Progressive-Era Economists and the Intellectual Foundations of the US Income Tax," *UCLA Law Review* 52 (2005): 1793–1866; Daniel Rodgers, *Atlantic Crossings: Social Policy in a Progressive Age* (Cambridge, MA: Harvard University Press, 1998): "Income Tax Wrong, Says Dean Burgess," *New York Times*, June 11, 1911; Edwin R. A. Seligman, "The Income Tax," *Political Science Quarterly* (1894): 610; Wilfred M. McClay, "John W. Burgess and the Search for Cohesion in American Political Thought," *Polity* 26, no. 1 (1993): 67.

34. Alfred H. Kelly, *A History of the Illinois Manufacturers' Association* (PhD, University of Chicago, 1938); "Corporation Tax Changes," *New York Times*, January 30, 1910.

35. Stanley D. Solvick, "William Howard Taft and the Payne-Aldrich Bill Tariff," *Mississippi Valley Historical Review* (1935); Bank, *Frow Sword to Shield*, 57–81.

36. Nathaniel W. Stephenson, *Nelson W. Aldrich: A Leader in American Politics* (New York: C. Scribners' Son, 1930); Quotation in Philipp Magness, "From Tariffs to Income Tax: Tariff Protection and Revenue in the United States Taxation System (unpublished PhD dissertation, George Mason University, 2009), 214; Letter from the American Silk Spinning Company to Nelson Aldrich, May 1, 1909; Letter from Elbert H. Gary to Nelson W. Aldrich, April 20, 1909; Letter from Nelson Aldrich to W. H. Bowker, April 25, 1909, microfilm, Reel 9, NWAP; "Income Tax is the Real Issue," *Boston Globe*, April 21, 1909; "Schiff's Tax Plan Would Hit Trusts," *New York Times*, February, 20, 1909.

37. "Protests in Minneapolis," *New York Times*, February 17, 1910; Bank, *From Sword to Shield*, 62–83; "Strange Reason for Favoring the In-

come Tax," *The American Economist*, September 3, 1909; "From Widows and Orphans," *The American Economist*, September 24, 1909; Petitions, Folder Jan. 27, 1910, to Feb. 11, 1910, Box 810, RG 233; Marjorie Kornhauser, "Corporate Regulations and the Origins of the Corporate Income Tax," *Indiana Law Journal* 66, no. 1 (1990): 126–127.

38. "Fight on Corporation Tax," *New York Times*, March 10, 1910.

39. "Final Fight Begun on Corporation Tax," *New York Times*, March 18, 1910; "Richard V. Lindabury," in *Biographical Dictionary of American Business Leaders*, ed. John N. Ingham (New York: Greenwood Press, 1923), 801–802.

40. "Corporations Slow in Paying Tax," *New York Times*, May 20, 1910; "Few Reports in Buffalo," *New York Times*, February 17, 1910; "Corporations Paying Up," *New York Times*, May 16, 1910.

41. "A Burden on Franchises," *New York Times*, January 18, 1911; Chester Leonard Barrows, *William M. Evarts, Lawyer, Diplomat, Statesman* (Chapel Hill: University of North Carolina Press, 1941); Petition, Folder Feb. 17, 1910, to Feb. 23, 1910, RG 233; Marjorie Kornhauser, "Corporate Regulation and the Origins of the Corporate Income Tax," *Indiana Law Journal* 66, no. 53 (1990): 99–100, 115–118; Editorial, "Mr. Taft's Tax Bill," *New York Times*, June 24, 1909, 6; "Corporations Must Pay Federal Tax," *New York Times*, March 14, 1911.

42. "Realty Companies and Corporate Tax," *New York Times*, August 22, 1909; "To Test Corporation Tax," *New York Times*, January 16, 1910; "Popularity of the Corporate Tax," *New York Times*, February 27, 1910; "Denounces Corporation Tax," *New York Times*, October 19, 1909; "Oppose Publicity Clause," *New York Times*, January 15, 1910.

43. "Gov. A. E. Wilson on the Income Tax Amendment," *New York Times*, February 26, 1911.

44. "Virginia's Blow at Income Tax," *New York Times*, March 9, 1910; "The Income Tax," *New York Times*, November 16, 1910.

45. Quoted in John D. Buenker, *The Income Tax and the Progressive Era* (New York: Garland, 1985); Joseph Choate et al., *The Proposed Sixteenth Articles of Amendment to the Constitution of the United States*

(Albany, NY, 1910); Roy Blakey and Gladys Blakey, *The Federal Income Tax* (New York: Longmans, Green & Co., 1940), 68–69; Steven R. Weisman, *The Great Tax Wars: Lincoln-Teddy Roosevelt-Wilson: How the Income Tax Transformed America* (New York: Simon & Schuster, 2002), 263–264. "Attack Income Tax in the Legislature," *New York Times*, April 14, 1910.

46. Karen Schnietz, "Democrats' 1916 Tariff Commission: Responding to Dumping Fears and Illustrating the Consumer Costs of Protectionism," *Business History Review* 72, no. 1 (1998): 1–45; Joseph A. Hill, "The Income Tax of 1913," *The Quarterly Journal of Economics* 28, no. 1 (1913): 46–68.

47. "Opposes $4,000 Tax Limit," *New York Times*, May 18, 1913; "Form of Protest on Income Tax," *New York Times*, February 5, 1914; "Answers Protest of the Income Tax," *New York Times*, February 8, 1914; Albert Steigerwalt, *The National Association of Manufacturers, 1865–1914: A Study in Business Leadership* (Ann Arbor, MI: Dean Hicks Company, 1964).

48. "Attack Income Tax Source Collection," *New York Times*, January 25, 1914.

49. "Income Tax Test," *New York Times*, March 17, 1914; "Fight Surtax on Incomes," *New York Times*, June 27, 1915.

50. "Testing the Income Tax," *New York Times*, May 8, 1914.

51. "Income Tax Upheld in Broad Decision," *New York Times*, January 25, 1916.

52. "Joseph Hodges Choate Dies Suddenly," *New York Times*, May 15, 1917; Oliver Wendell Holmes, Jr., "Law and the Courts," Speech at the Harvard Law School Association of New York, reprinted in *The Mind and Faith of Justice Holmes: His Speeches, Essays, Letters, and Judicial Opinions*, ed. Max Lerner (Boston: Little Brown, 1943), 390; Joseph, *The Origins of the American Income Tax*, 105–117; Cynthia G. Fox, "Income Tax Records of the Civil War Years," *Prologue* 18, no. 4 (1986); *Speech of Hon. David B. Hill*, 16.

4. Not for Mothers, Not for Soldiers

1. The event is undated in the archives. It occurred between November 23 (Mellon letter) and mid-December when the petition process started, Folder "Tax Reduction," Box 386, RG 233; Roy G. Blakey, "Shifting the War Burden on the Future," *Annals of the American Academy of Political and Social Science* 75 (1918): 90–104; William D. Jenkins, *Steel Valley Klan: The Ku Klux Klan in Ohio's Mahoning Valley* (Kent, OH: Kent State University Press, 1990); Louis Galambos, *The Public Image of Big Business in America, 1880–1940* (Baltimore: Johns Hopkins University Press, 1975).

2. Theda Skocpol, *Protecting Soldiers and Mothers: The Political Origins of Social Policy in the United States* (Cambridge: Harvard University Press, 1992); Lynn Dumenil, "The Insatiable Maw of Bureaucracy": Antistatism and Education Reform in the 1920s," *The Journal of American History* 77, no. 2 (1990): 499–524; Kevin Boyle, *Arc of Justice: A Saga of Race, Civil Rights, and Murder in the Jazz Age* (New York: Henry Holt Company, 2004); "Tax Reduction and Politics," *Washington Post*, January 6, 1924, 4.

3. Otto Kahn, *War Taxation: Some Comments and Letters*, Box 294, Folder 14, "Government Ownership of Rail Roads," OKP; "Otto Kahn Attacks War Tax System," *New York Times*, September 2, 1919, 16; Theresa Collins, *Otto Kahn: Art, Money and Modern Time* (Chapel Hill: University of North Carolina Press, 2002); Robert F. Burk, *The Corporate State and the Broker State: The Du Ponts and American National Politics, 1925–1940* (Cambridge: Harvard University Press, 1995); Kim Phillips-Fein, *Invisible Hands: The Making of the Conservative Movement from the New Deal to Reagan* (New York: W. W. Norton, 2009), 3–25; W. Elliott Brownlee, "Wilson and Financing the Modern State: The Revenue Act of 1916," *Proceedings of the American Philosophical Society*, 129 (1985): 173–210; "Powder Makers Oppose Tax on Munitions," *Wall Street Journal*, July 20, 1916, 6; Steven A. Bank, *From Sword to Shield: The Transformation of the Corporate Income Tax 1861 to Present* (New York: Oxford University Press, 2010), 90, 91; Colin Gordon, *New Deals: Business, Labor, and Politics in America, 1920–1935* (New

York: Cambridge University Press, 1994), 70; Letter from David A. Cetner to John H. Parr, July 24, 1916; Telegram sent by employees of Hercules Powder Company, July 23, 1916, Folder "Munitions," Box 480, RG 233.

4. Joseph McCartin, *Labor's Great War: The Struggle for Industrial Democracy and the Origins of Modern American Labor Relations 1912–1921* (Chapel Hill: University of North Carolina Press, 1998); Gary Gerstle, *American Crucible. Race and Nation in the Twentieth Century* (Princeton: Princeton University Press, 2001); Christopher Capozzola, *Uncle Sam Wants You: World War One and the Making of the Modern American Citizen* (New York: Oxford University Press, 2008); Julia C. Ott, *When Wall Street met Main Street: The Quest for an Investors' Democracy* (Cambridge, MA: Harvard University Press, 2011), 75–100; quotation in Roy G. Blakey, "The War Revenue Act of 1917," *American Economic Review* 7, no. 4 (1917): 791–815.

5. Ajay Mehrotra, "The Story of the Corporate Reorganization Provisions: From 'Purely Paper' to Corporate Welfare," in Steven A. Bank and Kirk J. Stark, *Business Tax Stories* (2005), 41; "Business Men Are Stirred," *New York Times*, October 5, 1917; Oliver M. W. Sprague, "The Conscription of Income," *The New Republic*, February 24, 1917, 93; Charles F. Speare, "Uncle Sam's Revenue," *American Review* 56 (September 1917): 293; Bank, *From Sword to Shield*, 89–98; "Daniel Tells of U-Boats," *New York Times*, July 5, 1918, 8.

6. "Attack 8-Hour Law in War Industries," *New York Times*, May 16, 1917; Richard S. Tedlow, "The National Association of Manufacturers and Public Relations during the New Deal," *Business History Review* 50, no. 1 (1976): 25–45; Meg Jacobs, *Pocketbook Politics: Economic Citizenship in Twentieth-Century America* (Princeton: Princeton University Press, 2005), 53–66.

7. Quotation in Steven A. Bank, Kirk J. Stark, and Joseph J. Thorndike, eds., *War and Taxes* (Washington, DC: Urban Institute, 2008), 75, 79.

8. Naomi R. Lamoreaux, *The Great Merger in American Business, 1895–1904* (New York: Cambridge University Press, 1985); Bank, *From Sword to Shield*, 103–106: "Excess Profits Taxes Inequitable and Unjust," *Wall*

Street Journal, December 18, 1918, 9; "Sees Inequalities in Income Tax Bill," *New York Times,* January 4, 1919, 14; "Otto Kahn Says Tax Revision Is First Necessity," *New York Times,* September 23, 1920; Sheldon D. Pollack, *Refinancing America: The Republican Antitax Agenda* (Albany: State University of New York Press, 2003), 33.

9. David Cannadine, *Mellon: An American Life* (New York; Vintage Books, 2006), 266–274; Thomas Ferguson, "Industrial Conflict and the Coming of the New Deal: The Triumph of Multinational Liberalism in America," in *The Rise and Fall of the New Deal Order 1930–1980,* ed. Gary Gerstle and Steve Fraser, (Princeton: Princeton University Press, 1989): 1–31; Andrew W. Mellon, *Taxation: The People's Business* (New York: Macmillan, 1924); Susan Murnane, "Selling Scientific Taxation: The Treasury Department's Campaign for Tax Reform in the 1920s," *Law and Social Inquiry* 29, no. 4 (2004): 826–829.

10. Resolutions adopted by the Rotary Club of Baltimore, February 4, 1921, Folder "Internal Revenue," Box 874, RG 233; Quotation in *Commercial and Financial Chronicle,* October 22, 1921, 1728; Platform for Federal Taxation Legislation, December 13, 1920, Folder "Internal Revenue," Box 874, RG 233.

11. Roy G. Blakey, "The Revenue Act of 1921," *American Economic Review* 12, no. 1 (1922): 75–108.

12. "Randolph Frothingham Marries," *New York Times,* June 8, 1916; Hazel L. Varella, *Wayside: The Home of Mr and Mrs Louis Frothingham* (Easton Historical Society: undated); Yen-Chuan Yu, "Women Patriots: The 'Antifeminists' in the United States in the 1920s," *American Studies* 19, no. 1 (March 1989): 53–89; Susan Marshall, *Splintered Sisterhood: Gender and Class in the Campaign against Woman Suffrage* (Madison: Wisconsin University Press, 1997); Richard M. Abrams, *Conservatives in a Progressive Era: Massachusetts Politics, 1900–1912* (Cambridge, MA: Harvard University Press, 1964); *The Woman Patriot* 7, no. 6 (March 1923): 2–6; Kim E. Nielsen, *Un-American Womanhood* (Columbia: Ohio State University Press, 2001), 87–88; Kirsten Marie Delegard, *Battling Miss Bolsheviki: The Origins of Female Conservatism in the United States* (Philadelphia: University of Pennsylvania Press, 2012), 72–75.

13. Linda Gordon, *Pitied but Not Entitled: Single Mothers and the History of Welfare* (Cambridge: Harvard University Press, 1994), 93–96; Rebecca Ann Rix, "Gender and Reconstitution: The Individual and Family Basis of Republican Government Contested, 1868–1925" (PhD dissertation, Yale University, 2008); "Childless Women Politicians," *The Woman Patriot* 4 no. 9 (February 1920): 5; Quotation in Lemons, *The Woman Citizen*, 160; Sheldon M. Stern, "The Evolution of a Reactionary: Louis Arthur Coolidge, 1900–1925," *Mid-America* 5, no. 2 (1975), 89–105; "History of the Sentinels of the Republic," Folder "Sentinels," Box 1, ALP; "Collect Fund to Make Campaign on States Rights," *Chicago Daily Tribune*, July 5, 1925, 4.

14. "Illinois Needs No Federal Nurse," *Chicago Daily Tribune*, April 25, 1923; "Illinois Needs No Federal Nurse," *Chicago Daily Tribune*, April 22, 1923.

15. Morton Keller, *In Defense of Yesterday: James M. Beck and the Politics of Conservatism 1861–1936* (New York: Coward McCann, 1958), 153; "Fights Maternity Bill Suit," *Washington Post*, February 9, 1923, 4; "Dismisses Suit against Maternity Act," *New York Times*, February 17, 1923.

16. Samuel R. Olken, "Justice Sutherland Reconsidered," *Vanderbilt Law Review* 62 (2009): 639–93; Rix, "Gender and Reconstitution," 356–361; Nancy C. Staudt, "Taxation without Representation," *Tax Law Review* 55 (2002): 555–600; *Frothingham v. Mellon*, 262 US, 489.

17. Lynn Dumenil, *The Modern Temper: American Culture and Society in the 1920s* (New York: Hill & Wang, 1995), 40–54.

18. Letter from employees of Mutual Life to James Wadsworth, Dec. 24, 1923, Folder "Tax Reduction," Box 386, HR68A-H21.6, RG 233; "Administration Program," *Time*, November 26, 1923; "Income Tax Cuts of $323,000,000 Urged by Mellon," *New York Times*, November 12, 1923; Anne L. Alstott and Benjamin Novick, "War, Taxes, and Income Redistribution in the Twenties: The 1924 Veterans' Bonus and the Defeat of the Mellon Plan," 2006, Yale Law School, Public Law Working Paper no. 109; Quotation in M. Susan Murnane, "Selling Scientific Taxation: The Treasury Department's Campaign for Tax Reform in the 1920s," *Law & Social Inquiry* 29, no. 4 (2004): 819–856.

19. "Opposition Grows to Taxes Planned to Pay the Bonus," *New York Times*, February 13, 1922; Quotation in Jennifer D. Keene, *Doughboys, the Great War, and the Remaking of America* (Baltimore: Johns Hopkins University Press, 2001), 173.

20. "Business Agrees that Mellon Plan Means Prosperity," *New York Times*, December 30, 1923, 1; Murmane, "Selling Scientific Taxation," 832–836; Letter from Stanley Flint to Hon. Charles E. Fuller, December 17, 1923, Folder "Tax Reduction," Box 386, RG 233.

21. Address to Members' Council Luncheon, December 19, 1923; Letter from L. T. Canfield to Hon. Charles Fuller, January 2, 1924; Letter from Stewart Browne to U.S. Congress, December 20, 1923, Box 395, RG 233.

22. Quotation in "Democrats Draft Own Plan to Slash Small Taxes More," *Washington Post*, January 6, 1924; Letter From the American Paper and Pulp Association to Hon. Charles Fuller, December 28, 1923, Box 396, RG 233.

23. Letter from Charles Starr to Hon. Charles Fuller, January 2, 1924; Letter from John Levy to Hon. Celler, December 31, 1923; Letter from Chas M. Higgins to Emanuel Celler, December 31, 1923; Letter from J. W. Peele to Hon. Celler, December 31, 1923; Letter from Veterans from Cleveland to Hon. Theo Burton, undated, Box 395, RG 233; "Bonus-Or-Tax-Slash Question Divides Members of Congress," *Christian Science Monitor*, November 15, 1923, 2.

24. "Chicago Floods Congress with Mellon Tax Plea," *Chicago Daily Tribune*, December 25, 1923; "Garner Calls Mellon Tax "Conspiracy of Interests," *Chicago Daily Tribune*, December 31, 1923; "Legion Chief Replies in Support of Bonus," *New York Times*, January 7, 1924; "Copeland's Views on Bonus Hissed," *New York Times*, January 13, 1924, 16; "William Jennings Bryan Calls Mellon 'A Party Dictator,'" *New York Times*, May 11, 1924, 22; "Legion Urges Bonus and Tax Cut Also," *New York Times*, December 9, 1923; "Disputes Mellon on Bonus," *New York Times*, December 11, 1923, 4; "Mellon Tax Rates Will Go to Senate," *New York Times*, March 26, 1924, 1.

25. "Coolidge Assails but Signs Tax Bill as Better Than Existing War-Time Law," *New York Times*, June 3, 1924, 1; "Mellon Denounces Tax Bill

Agreed To," *New York Times*, May 23, 1924; Roy G. Blakey, "Revenue Act of 1924," *American Economic Review* 14, no. 3 (1924): 475–504; Keene, *Doughboys*, 174.

26. Milton L. Ready, "The Southern Tariff Association" (MA thesis, University of Houston, 1966); Letter from J. A. Arnold to Winston, January 9, 1925, Folder "Tax (General)," January–March 1925, Box 163, RG 56; "Obituaries: James Asbury Arnold," *Chicago Tribune*, July 31 1948; Christopher Loomis, "The Politics of Uncertainty: Lobbyists and Propaganda in Early Twentieth-Century America," *Journal of Policy History* 21, no. 2 (2009): 187–213; Kevin Motl, "Under the Influence: The Texas Business Men's Association and the Campaign Against Reform, 1906–1915," *Southwestern Historical Quarterly*, 109 (4): 495–529; Elna C. Green, "From Antisuffragism to Anti-Communism: The Conservative Career of Ida M. Darden," *The Journal of Southern History* 65, no. 2 (1999): 287–316; Murnane, "Selling Scientific Taxation," 843–844; Letter from John Kirby to Wilson Compton, September 27, 1920, Folder 24, Box 23, JKP.

27. "Bankers to Demand Full Mellon Plan," *Washington Post*, August 18, 1924; Letter from R. A. Crawford to Andrew W. Mellon, November 12, 1925, Entry 191, Box 164; Letter from M. A. Vincentelli to Andrew W. Mellon, June 16, 1925; Letter from J. A. Arnold to Andrew Mellon, May 17, 1925, Entry 191, Box 163, RG 56.

28. Robert E. Gilbert, "Calvin Coolidge's Tragic Presidency: The Political Effects of Bereavement and Depression," *Journal of American Studies* 39, no. 1 (2005): 87–109; Isaac W. Martin, "The Social Origins of the Texas Club Movement, 1924–1925," *Journal of Policy History*, 25, no. 3 (2013): 404–421.

29. "Tax Clubs—A New Factor in Tax Revision," *Literary Digest*, November 21, 1925, 68; Letter from R. A. Crawford to Honorable W. R. Green, September 25, 1925, Folder 69A, Box 365, RG 233; Murnane, "Selling Scientific Taxation," 847–848; "Outlining the Purposes and Methods, and Reviewing the Work of the American Taxpayers League," August, 1, 1927, JCSP; American Bankers' League, "Iowa Tax Clubs before House Ways and Means Committee," October 25, 1925; Letter from J. S. Rice et al. to Andrew W. Mellon, November 15, 1924, Entry 191,

Box 193, RG 56; Isaac W. Martin, *Rich People's Movement: Grassroots Campaign to Untax the One Percent* (New York: Oxford University Press, 2013), 90–110.

30. Quotation in Murray, "Bureaucracy and Bi-partisanship in Taxation," 223; "Address by Carter Glass," attached to a letter from James A. Arnold to G. B. Winston, July 15, 1925, Folder "Glass," Box 6, RG 56; Quotation in "Prophet," *Time*, June 22, 1925, 15; Evans C. Johnson, *Oscar W. Underwood: A Political Biography* (Baton Rouge: Louisiana State University Press, 1980).

31. "Law in Making," *Time*, November 2, 1925, 12; "Tax Clubs: A New Factor in Tax Revision," *Literary Digest*, November 21, 1925, 68; Quotation in Murnane, "Selling Scientific Taxation," 849.

32. Brownlee, *Federal Taxation*, 76–77; Letter from L. Hoover to W. R. Green, February 7, 1927, Folder 69A, Box 365, RG 233; "Elections," *Time*, November 15, 1926; Roy G. Blakey, "The Revenue Act of 1926," *American Economic Review* 16, no. 3 (1926): 401–425.

33. "Frick Will Leaves $117,300,000 in Gifts for Public Benefit," *New York Times*, December 7, 1919, 1; Susan Murnane, "Andrew Mellon's Unsuccessful Attempt to Repeal Estate Taxes," Tax History Project, online, August 22, 2005; Albert W. Atwood, *The Mind of the Millionaire* (New York: Harpers and Brothers, 1926).

34. Mellon, *Taxation*, 18; Quotation in Randolph Paul, *Taxation in the United States* (Boston: Little Brown, 1954), 137; "Mellon Declares High Estate Taxes 'Economic Suicide,'" *New York Times*, April 3, 1924; "Inheritance Tax Calls Socialistic," *New York Times*, June 5, 1925; "Supports Coolidge on Inheritance Tax," *New York Times*, February 21, 1925.

35. "Business on Record for Tax Reforms," *New York Times*, June 22, 1925; "Governors to Make Death Tax Protest," *New York Times*, October 12, 1925.

36. Murnane, "Andrew Mellon," 616–621; "Inheritance Tax," American Taxpayers League, June 27, 1927, Bulletin no. 64-A, Folder 17, Box 16, JSCP; Resolution signed by a majority of members of the Lower House of the Texas Legislature, Folder 69A, Box 365, RG 233; "Organize to Fight Federal Estate Tax," *New York Times*, September 11, 1927; "Bankers to Fight Federal Estate Tax," *New York Times*, September 4, 1927.

37. Christopher Loomis, "The Politics of Uncertainty"; *Socialism in Our Tax system*, American Taxpayers League, Bulletin no. 45–A, July 18, 1927, Folder 17, Box 16, JCSP; "Why We Are Opposed to a Federal Estate (Inheritance) Tax," American Taxpayers League, July 2, 1927, Folder 17, Box 16, JCSP.

38. *Inheritance Tax*, special report, American Taxpayers League, December 15, 1927; "A Popular Hallucination," *Council Bluffs Nonpareil*, December, 20, 1927; "The House and the Inheritance Tax," *Arkansas Democrat*, December 15, 1927; "Green's Nomination Silences Foe of Estate Tax Repeal," *Baltimore Sun*, February 21, 1928. "High Hatting," *Council Bluffs*, December 7, 1927, Folder 18, Box 16, JCSP.

39. National Council of State Legislatures, undated, Folder 19, Box 16, JSCP; "When Lobbying Gets Dangerous," *St. Louis Post-Dispatch*, December 7, 1927; Letter from Marvin L. Arnold, secretary of the California Taxation Improvement Association, to Mr. J. A. Arnold, April 3, 1928; "To All Taxpayers," American Taxpayers League, July, 13, 1928, JCSP; Roy G. Blakey, "The Revenue Act of 1928," *American Economic Review* 18, no. 3 (1928): 429–448, Folder 20, Box 16, JCSP.

40. "Parade for Tax Cuts," *New York Times*, December 8, 1929; Douglas A. Irwin, *Peddling Protectionism: Smoot-Hawley and the Great Depression* (Princeton: Princeton University Press, 2012).

41. E. E. Schattschneider, *Politics, Pressures, and the Tariff: A Study of Free Private Enterprise in Pressure Politics, as Shown in the 1929–1930 Revision of the Tariff* (New York: Prentice-Hall, 1935), 38–39; Ellis Hawley, "Herbert Hoover, the Commerce Secretariat, and the Vision of an Associative State," *Journal of American History* 61, no. 1 (1974): 116–140.

42. Jean Heffer, *La Grande Dépression: Les Etats-Unis en crise (1929–1933)* (Paris: Gallimard, 1991); Jordan Schwarz, *The Interregnum of Despair: Hoover, Congress, and the Depression* (Urbana: University of Illinois Press, 1970); Keene, *Doughboys*, 179–204.

43. Approvals of five-year tax program, Folder 24, Box 16, JCSP; Letter from J. A. Arnold to J. S. Cullinan, January 27, 1932, Folder 29, Box 16, JCSP;

Proposed radio program, July 14, 1931, American Taxpayers League, Folder 6, Box 17, JCSP; *Handbook on Taxation*, June 14, 1932, American Taxpayers League, Folder 31, Box 16, JCSP; Letter to all taxpayers by L. O. Broussard, president, June 1, 1931, Folder 25, Box 16, JCSP; "Radio Forum to Analyze Nation's Tax Problems," *New York Times*, November 29, 1931.

44. *Federal Income Tax of Individuals—Graduated Levies*, Bulletin no. 93, January 2, 1929, American Taxpayers League, Folder 19, Box 16, JCSP; two examples are culled from memorandum of the American Taxpayers League, January 23, 1929, Folder 23, Box 16, JCSP; "W. L. Mellon Listed as Tax Lobby Donor," *New York Times*, November 6, 1929.

45. Hon. Harold McGuin, "Our Government Can Not Last Under the Present Tax System," March 16, 1932, American Taxpayers League, Folder 30, Box 16, JSCP; Memorandum of meeting held in New York, March 23, 1932, American Taxpayers League, Folder 30, Box 16, JSCP; Letter from George W. Rossetter to Hon. George W. Lindsay, June, 9, 1932, Folder "Tax Reduction," Box 402, RG 233.

46. "Urge Platform Pledge for Cut in Tax Burdens," *Chicago Daily Tribune*, June, 15, 1932; "Taxpayers Unite!," Taxpayers Union, Folder 31, Box 16, JCSP; "Wadsworth Demands 25% Tax Reduction," *New York Times*, August 4, 1932; Edward Digby Baltzell, *The Protestant Establishment: Aristocracy and Caste in America* (New Haven: Yale University Press), 233–234.

47. "Demand Sales Levy Plank; Farmers Call for Help," *Chicago Herald*, June, 15, 1932; Letter from J. A. Arnold to J. C. Cullinan, June 9, 1931, Folder 25, Box 16, JCSP; Petition of Defenders of America, Defenders of American Tax Relief Association; Petition sent to Representative David J. Lewis, January 7, 1932, Folder "Tax Reduction," Box 401, RG 233; "F. W. Sargent Urges Nation-Wide Thrift," *New York Times*, June 16, 1932.

48. "The Cabinet: Since Hamilton," *Time*, February 4, 1929; "Depression Reaches Washington," *Time*, April 6, 1931; "Impertinent! Scandalous!," *Time*, November 26, 1934; "Twelve Ways to Dodge the Income Tax," *The New Republic*, May 29, 1935, 74–75.

5. The Bread-and-Circus Democracy

1. Letter from Arthur Page to the Honorable Hugh Gibson, November 8, 1940, Folder Correspondence 1940, Box 7, AWP; Karen Miller Russell, "Corporate Public Relations and Democracy: Arthur W. Page and the FCC, 1935–1941," 2007 (unpublished paper in author's possession).

2. W. Elliot Brownlee, *Federal Taxation in America: A Short History* (Cambridge: Cambridge University Press, 1996), 81–106; Mark Leff, *The Limits of Symbolic Reform: The New Deal and Taxation, 1933–1939* (Cambridge: Cambridge University Press, 1984); Joseph J. Thorndike, *Their Fair Share: Taxing the Rich in the Age of FDR* (Washington D.C.: Urban Institute Press, 2013); "Harvest Campaigns—Taxpayers, Organize!," *New York American*, February 23, 1935, Folder 5, Box 17, JCSP; Ira Katznelson, *Fear Itself: The New Deal and the Origins of our Time* (New York: Liveright Publishing Corporation, 2013).

3. Letter from William H. Stayton to the members of our Former Executive Committee, letter no. 4, August 13, 1934, Folder 21, Box 13, JCSP; Alan Brinkley, *Voices of Protest, Huey Long, Father Coughlin and the Great Depression* (New York: Alfred Knopf, 1982).

4. Colin Gordon, *New Deals: Business, Labor, and Politics, 1920–1935* (New York: Cambridge University Press, 1994), 280–305; Robert Burk, *The Corporate State and the Broker State: The Du Ponts and American National Politics, 1925–1940* (Cambridge, MA: Harvard University Press, 1990), 40–41; Brownlee, *Federal Taxation*, 89; David Beito, *Taxpayers in Revolt: Tax Resistance during the Great Depression* (Chapel Hill: University of North Carolina Press, 1989), 140–141; Jason Scott Smith, *Building New Deal Liberalism: The Political Economy of Public Works, 1933–1956* (Cambridge: Cambridge University Press, 2006), 62–69.

5. Michael Perino, *The Hellhound of Wall Street: How Ferdinand Pecora's Investigation of the Great Crash Forever Changed American Finance* (New York: Penguin Press 2009); "Morgan Paid No Income Tax for the Years 1931 and 1932," *New York Times*, May 24, 1933, 1; "War without Profit," *Time*, December 24, 1934; Roy Blakey and Gladys Blakey, "The Two Federal Revenue Acts of 1940," *American Economic Review* 30, no. 4 (1940): 727–729.

6. Leff, *Limit of Symbolic Reform*, 61–68.

7. David Farber, *Everybody Ought to Be Rich: The Life and Times of John J. Raskob* (New York: Oxford University Press, 2013); George Wolfskill, *The Revolt of the Conservatives: A History of the American Liberty League, 1934–1940* (Boston: Houghton Mifflin, 1962); Frederik Randolph, "The American Liberty League 1933–1940," *American Historical Review* 56, no. 1 (1950): 19–33; Kim Philipps-Fein, *Invisible Hands: The Making of the Conservative Movement from the New Deal to Reagan* (New York: W. W. Norton, 2009), 10–13.

8. Wendy L. Wall, *Inventing the "American Way": The Politics of Consensus from the New Deal to the Civil Rights Movement* (New York: Oxford University Press, 2008): 48–62; Richard S. Tedlow, "The National Association of Manufacturers and Public Relations during the New Deal," *Business History Review* 50 (1976): 25–45; W. J. Pat Enright, "They Got What They Ordered!," *Pittsburgh Sun Telegraph*, January, 3, 1934.

9. Quoted in Katherine S. Newman and Elisabeth S. Jacobs, *Who Cares? Public Ambivalence and Government Activism from the New Deal to the Second Gilded Age* (Princeton: Princeton University Press, 2010), 19.

10. Letter from Walt Disney to Robert L. Doughton, February 28, 1935, Folder "HR 74," Box 454, RG 233; Marjorie Kornhauser, "Shaping Public Opinion and the Law: How a 'Common Man' Law Ended a Rich Man's Law," *Law and Contemporary Problems* 73 (2009): 123–147.

11. Arthur Krock, "In Washington: Bacon Maintains Lone Fight on Tax 'Pink Slip,'" *New York Times*, February 21, 1935, 18; "Pink Slip Repeal . . . A Beginning," The Sentinels of the Republic, June 1935, Bulletin no. 1; "The Story of the Sentinels," The Sentinels of the Republic, Bulletin no. 1, June 1935, 2, Folder "Sentinels," Box 1, ALP.

12. Petition sent to the Committee on Ways and Means, February 6, 1935, Folder "Correspondence File," Box 386, 74th Congress, HR 74 A-F391, RG 233; The Sentinels of the Republic, "Suggested Form of Resolution to be Adopted by Organizations Supporting the Sentinels of the Republic 'Pink Slip' Repeal," File "Sentinels 3," Box 6, ALP.

13. Letter from Watson Eastman to Robert L. Doughton, February 12, 1935; Letter from John Fetzen to Robert Doughton, February 12, 1935;

Letter from Harry Cooper to Louis Ludlow, February 5, 1935; Letter to Chairman Robert Doughton, February 18, 1935, Letter from the Philadelphia Board of Trade to Congress, February 18, 1935, Folder "HR 74," Box 454, RG 233.

14. Letter from H. A. Osborne to Robert Doughton, February 18, 1935, Folder "Revenue Act, January 1935 to February 1935," RG 233; Letter from Stuart Perry to Robert Doughton, February 22, 1935, Folder "Revenue Act–February 22," Box 387, RG 233.

15. Beito, *Taxpayers in Revolt*, 60–80; Jim Fisher, *The Lindbergh Case* (New Brunswick: Rutgers University Press, 1987); Letter sent to Hon. Richard J. Welch, January, 29, 1935; Letter from H. B. Canby to Robert Doughton, February 22, 1935; Letter from H. B. Canby to Robert Doughton, February 22, 1935; Letter from Webb Hackert to Hatton W. Summers, February 5, 1935, Folder "Revenue Act, January 1935 to February 1935," Box 454, RG 233.

16. *Congressional Record*, 79th Congress, 2307; Letter from Mrs. Cutler B. Downer to Robert Doughton, February 18, 1935, Folder "Revenue Act, January 1935 to February 1935," RG 233; Letter from Illiminati to Congress, March 7, 1935, Folder HR 74, Box 454, RG 233.

17. "The Fiscal Nudes," *Chicago Daily Tribune*, reprinted in *Washington Post*, March 8, 1935, 8; H. I. Philips, "Once Overs," *Washington Post*, January 18, 1935, 9; Alan Havig, *Fred Allen's Radio Comedy* (Philadelphia: Temple University Press, 1989).

18. *Congressional Record*, 79th Congress, 1st Session, 1935, 2640–2641; Letter sent to Robert Doughton, March 12, 1935, Folder HR 74, Box 454, RG 233.

19. Letter sent to Robert Doughton, March 12, 1935, Folder HR 74, Box 454, RG 233.

20. Morton Keller, *In Defense of Yesterday: James M. Beck and the Politics of Conservatism 1861–1936* (Cambridge, MA: Harvard University Press, 1958); James M. Beck, *Our Wonderland of Bureaucracy: A Study of the Growth of Bureaucracy in the Federal Government, and Its Destructive Effect upon the Constitution* (New York: The MacMillan Company, 1932), 251.

21. Harvey O' Connor, *Mellon's Millions: The Biography of a Fortune: The Life and Times of Andrew W. Mellon* (New York: The John Day Company, 1933); Thomas O. Shepard, "Dodging Taxes with Mellon," *The Nation* 140, no. 3645 (1935): 564–566; Robert H. Jackson, "The Rich Get Richer," *The New Republic*, August 28, 1935.

22. "Chamber Opens War Tax Plan," *New York Times*, July 12, 1935, 8; Walter Lambert, "New Deal Revenue Act," (PhD dissertation, University of Texas, 1970), 189–192; *Proposed Taxation of Individual and Corporate Income, Inheritances, and Gifts: Hearings before the Ways and Means Committee*, 74th Congress, 1st Session (Washington, D.C.: U.S. Government Printing Office, 1935), 245–253.

23. "100 Civic Groups Fight Passage of Huge Tax Bill," *Chicago Daily News*, August, 6, 1935; " 'Soak Thrifty' " Foes Gird to Fight Bill," *Chicago Herald and Examiner*, August 6, 1935; "Suggested Tax Program," American Taxpayers League, October 7, 1935; "Cause and Effect of Destructive Taxes," Bulletin no. 150, December 16, 1935, American Taxpayers League, JSCP; "John H. Kirby Starts Fight on New Deal," *The Houston Press*, August 6, 1935; Letter from J. A. Arnold to J. S. Cullinan, July, 31, 1935, Folder 5, Box 17, JCSP; Beito, *Taxpayers in Revolt*, 1–34; "Tax Relief Clubs," June 10, 1935, American Taxpayers League, Folder 5, Box 17, JCSP; "Bombshell Aimed at Federal Extravagance Exploded by Federal Life President," *American Insurance Digest and Insurance Monitor*, June 15, 1935; Letter from J. S. Cullinan to W. H. Stayton, December 30, 1935, Box 13, Folder 22, JSCP.

24. Letter from J. A. Arnold to Mr. J. S. Cullinan, March 11, 1935, Folder 4, Box 17, JCSP; "Taxpayers' Battle on Reckless Waste: Protest Over 'Unlimited Spending,' " *New York American*, March 6, 1935; "The President's Tax Program," American Liberty League, Folder 4, Box 17, JCSP; Gary Gerstle, *American Crucible: Race and Nation in the Twentieth Century* (Princeton: Princeton University Press, 2001), 128–162.

25. "Liberty League," *Newsweek*, December 7, 1935, 11–12; Wolfskill, *The Revolt of the Conservatives*, 62–63; Farber, *Everybody Ought to Be*

Rich, 242–262; Randolph, "The American Liberty League 1933–1940," 19–33.

26. Donald R. Kennon and Rebecca M. Rogers, *The Committee on Ways and Means: A Bicentennial History 1789–1989* (Washington D.C.: U.S. Government Printing Office, 1990), 293.

27. Christopher Finan, *Alfred E. Smith, The Happy Warrior* (New York: Hill & Wang, 2003); Letter from J. A. Arnold to J. S. Cullinan, January 2, 1936, Folder 5, Box 17, JCSP.

28. Raoul Desvernine, *Democratic Despotism* (New York, Dodd, Mead, and Company, 1936); Letter from J. A. Arnold to J. S. Cullinan, January, 2, 1936, Folder 5, Box 17, JCSP; "Fomenting Class Hatred," September 15, 1936, *American Liberty League Bulletin*, vol. 2, number 2, JSCP.

29. Theodore Sky, *To Provide for the General Welfare: A History of the Federal Spending Power* (Newark: University of Delaware Press, 2003), 306–311; Jean Choate, *Disputed Grounds: Farm Groups That Opposed the New Deal Agriculture Programs* (New York: McFarland, 2002); "Capital Stock Tax Declared Unconstitutional," May 1, 1936, American Taxpayers League, Folder 7, Box 17, JCSP.

30. Brinkley, *End of Reform*, 292–293; Adolph A. Berle Jr. and Gardiner C. Means, *The Modern Corporation and Private Property* (New York, Macmillan Co., 1933).

31. Naomi R. Lamoreaux, *The Great Merger Movement in American Business, 1895–1904* (New York: Cambridge University Press, 1985); Steven A. Bank, *From Sword to Shield: The Transformation of the Corporate Income Tax, 1861 to Present* (New York: Oxford University Press, 2010); Ajay Mehrotra, "The Story of the Corporate Reorganization Provisions: From 'Purely Paper' to Corporate Welfare," in Steven A. Bank and Kirk J. Stark, *Business Tax Stories* (2005), 41; Ralph E. Helper, "Taxation: Income Tax: Exempt Reorganizations: When Is a Reorganization Bona Fide under the Rule of *Gregory v. Helvering?*," *Michigan Law Review* 37, no. 4 (1939): 679–680; Assaf Likhovski "The Duke and the Lady: *Helvering v. Gregory* and the History of Tax Avoidance Adjudication," *Cardozo Law Review* 25, no. 1 (2004).

32. Republican Congressional Committee, *Tax Regimentation Tried by New Deal* (Washington, D.C., 1936); "Dividends Opposed by Sloan," *New York Times*, June 12, 1936, 33; Folder "Wealth Act," Box 32, RHJP; Quotation in Bank, *Corporate Managers*, 207.

33. Steven A. Bank, "Corporate Managers, Agency Costs, and the Rise of Double Taxation," *William & Mary Law Review* 44, no. 167 (2002): 167–261; Ellis Hawley, *The New Deal and the Problem of Monopoly* (New York: Fordham University Press, 1995); "Industrial Stockholders Threatened by the New Tax Proposal, June 27, 1935," National Association of Manufacturers, Folder 22, Box 13, JSCP.

34. Clyde Weed, *The Nemesis of Reform: The Republican Party during the New Deal* (New York: Columbia University Press, 1994); "Taxation— and the Day of Reckoning," Address by Governor Alfred M. Landon in Buffalo, N.Y., August, 26, 1936; "National Affairs: Taxes and Truth," *Time*, September 14, 1936; Majorie E. Kornhauser, "Remembering the 'Forgotten Man' (and Woman): Hidden Taxes and the 1936 Election," *Studies in the History of Tax Law*, Tax Law History Conference 2008, J. Tiley, ed., Hart Publishing Ltd., 2010 (available at SSRN: http://ssrn .com/abstract=1159747).

35. *Have you been fooled? Soak the Rich Taxes Really Soak the Poor: A Few Little-known Facts about Taxation by Deception* (Washington, D.C., 1936); Daniel A. Reed, *Tax Regimentation Tried by New Deal* (Washington, D.C., 1936).

36. Catherine Rymph, *Republican Women: Feminism and Conservatism from Suffrage through the Rise of the New Right* (Chapel Hill: University of North Carolina Press, 2006), 62–66; Quotation in Meg Jacobs, *Pocketbook Politics: Economic Citizenship in Twentieth-Century America* (Princeton: Princeton University Press, 2005), 152; *American Liberty League Bulletin*, vol. 2, no. 2, September 15, 1936; *Tax Facts*, Folder "American Liberty League, Tax Facts," 1936, IRWC.

37. Rymph, *Republican Women*, 55–60; Michelle M. Nickerson, *Mothers of Conservatism: Women and the Postwar Right* (Princeton: Princeton University Press, 2012), 19; June Melby Benowitz, *Days of Discontent:*

American Women and Right-Wing Politics, 1933–1945 (Dekalb: Northern Illinois University Press, 2002), 12–19.

38. Republican Senatorial and Congressional Committee, *Another "New Deal," Attempt to Deceive the Taxpayers* (Washington, D.C., 1936); Republican Congressional Committee, *Debts That Are Forced Upon Us: Contracted by Braintrusters, We or Posterity Must Pay Them* (Washington, D.C., 1936); Philipps-Fein, *Invisible Hands*, 20–21.

39. Quotation in Wall, *Inventing the "American Way,"* 56; Quotation in Brinkley, *The End of Reform*, 56; Hawley, *The New Deal and the Problem of Monopoly*, 345–359.

40. "Brookings Figure," *Time*, December, 20, 1937; M. Slade Kendrick, *The Undistributed Profits Tax* (Washington, D.C.: Brookings Institution, 1937); Folder 13, Taxation, Box 18, FSP.

41. Chamber of Commerce of the State of New York, October 7, 1937; Letter from James Stewart to Hon. Eugene J. Keogh, November 16, 1937, Folder HR, A75-H19.7, Box 413, RG 233; Quotation in Bank, *Corporate Managers*, 236.

42. Quotation in Jacobs, *Pocketbook Politics*, 164; Letter from the California Wool Growers Association to congressmen, November, 17, 1938, Folder "Processes Taxes," Box 433, RG 233.

43. Quotation in Bank, *Corporate Managers*, 249–250.

44. Felix Belair, "An Assuring Tone," *New York Times*, February 18, 1939; Arthur Krock, "Business Appeasement Now Up to the President," *New York Times*, February 26, 1939; Paul, *Taxation in the United States*, 214–216; John W. Hanes, "We Face a Test of our Common Sense," *New York Times*, May 22, 1938; Charles Oscar Hardy, "Liberalism in the Modern State: The Philosophy of Henry Simons," *Journal of Political Economy* 56, no. 4 (1948): 305–314; Angus Burgin, *The Great Persuasion: Reinventing Free Markets since the Depression* (Cambridge, MA: Harvard University Press, 2012), 38–40; Henry C. Simons, *Personal Income Taxation: The Definition of Income as a Problem of Fiscal Policy* (Chicago: University of Chicago Press, 1938).

45. Samuel Pettengill, *Jefferson, the Forgotten Man* (New York: America's Future, Inc., 1939), 200, 221.

46. *Needed Now: Capacity for Leadership, Courage to Lead,* A Pamphlet by the Committee for Constitutional Government, Folder "Committee for Constitutional Government," IRWC; Richard Polenberg, "The National Committee to Uphold Constitutional Government, 1937–1941," *Journal of American History* 52, no. 3 (1965): 582–598; James Arnold, *The Desire to Own* (Washington, D.C.: Press of B. S. Adams, 1938), 24; "Address of Mr. Robert B. Dresser," Houston, Texas, May 14, 1953, Committee for Constitutional Government, IRWC.

47. Quotation in Bank, *"Corporate Managers,"* 256.

48. "Repeal the 16th Amendment—Put Idle Dollars and Idle Men to Work," Tax Information Series no. 1, August 15, 1939; "Labor's Stake in the Tax Battle," Tax Information Series no. 3, October 15, 1939; "The Woman Pays and Pays," Tax Information Series no. 4, November 1, 1939; "The Woman Pays and Pays," Tax Information Series no. 4, November 1, 1939, Folder "American Taxpayers Association," IRWC; "Taxes Hit New High—Where Are We Going to Get the Money," Tax Information Series no. 6, September 16, 1940, IRWC.

49. Moss Hart and George S. Kaufman, *You Can't Take It With You* (1936), 21; Marquis Childs, "They Hate Roosevelt," *Harper's,* May 1936, 634–642; Quotation in "Week in Business: Sentinel Spies Pink Tax Slip Sees Red," *Time,* February 16, 1935, 34; Gordon, *New Deals,* 285; American Taxpayers' League, Annual report of Mr. L. O. Broussard, January 16, 1935, Folder 7, Box 17, JCSP.

6. FROM THE KITCHEN TO THE CAPITAL?

1. "Tax Revolt Report," March 10, 1959; "Start of the 1959 Tax Revolt," March 19, 1959; "Ritzville Petition Against More taxes Gathering Signers," February 18, 1959, Folder "Revolt Ritzville," Box 9, JWCP; Jane Sanders, *Cold War on the Campus: Academic Freedom at the University of Washington, 1949–1964* (Seattle: University of Washington Press, 1979); Ronald E. Magden, "The Schuddakopf Case, 1954–1958: Tacoma Public Schools and Anticommunism," *Pacific Northwest Quarterly* 89, no. 1 (1997/98): 4–11; Bill Boni, "Adams Backs 'Tax Revolt,'" *The Spokesman Review* February 18, 1959, Folder "Revolt Ritzville," Box 9, JWCP;

Eckard V. Troy, "The Right Side of the 1960s: The Origins of the John
Birch Society in the Pacific Northwest," *Oregon Historical Quarterly*,
105, no. 2 (2004): 260–283.

2. "Petition for Redress from the Burden of Excessive Taxation," Folder
"Revolt Ritzville," Box 9, JWCP; W. Eliott Brownlee, *Federal Taxation
in America: A Short History* (New York: Cambridge University Press
2004), 107–121; Julian Zelizer, *Taxing America: Wilbur D. Mills, Congress, and the State 1945–1975* (New York: Cambridge University Press,
1998); Richard Hofstadter, *Paranoid Style in American Politics* (New
York: Alfred A. Knopf, 1965); Ira Katznelson, "Public Policy and the
Middle-Class Racial Divide after the Second World War," in *Social
Contracts Under Stress: The Middle Classes of American Europe, and
Japan at the Turn of the Century*, ed. Olivier Zunz, Leonard Schoppa,
and Nobuhiro Hiwatari (New York: Russell Sage Foundation, 2002),
157–178.

3. Sara Diamond, *Roads to Dominion: Right-Wing Movements and Political Power in the United States* (New York: Guilford Press, 1995);
Lisa McGirr, *Suburban Warriors: The Origins of the New American
Right* (Princeton: Princeton University Press, 2001); Michelle Nickerson, *Mothers of Conservatism: Women and the Postwar Right* (Princeton: Princeton University Press, 2012); "They're Not Giving Up," *Seattle Post Intelligencer*, May 5, 1959, Folder "Revolt Ritzville," Box 9,
JWCP.

4. "Socialistic Textbooks Provided for Armed Forces," Tax Information
Series no. 79, November 12, 1946, Folder "American Taxpayers Association," IRWC; Carolyn Jones, "Mass-Based Income Taxation: Creating a Taxpaying Culture, 1940–1952," in *Funding the Modern American State, 1941–1995: The Rise and Fall of the Era of Easy Finance*, ed.
W. Elliot Brownlee (New York: Cambridge University Press, 1996),
107–147; Mark H. Leff, "The Politics of Sacrifice on the American
Home Front in World War II," *Journal of American History* 77 (1991):
1296–318.

5. George E. Lent, "Excess-Profits Taxation in the United States," *Journal
of Political Economy* 59 (1951): 481–497; Steven A. Bank, Kirk J. Stark,

and Joseph J. Thorndike, *War and Taxes* (Washington, D.C.: Urban Institute, 2008), 63–81; Samuel B. Pettengill, *Smoke Screen* (New York: Southern Publishers, 1940); "A New Shot in the Arm—25 Billions More Debt 'On Order,'" Tax Information Series no. 8, October 15, 1940; "It is Time for Clear Thinking," Tax Information Series no. 9, November 18, 1940, Folder "American Taxpayers Association," IRWC.

6. Brownlee, *Federal Taxation*, 108–119; Robert Westbrook, *Why We Fought: Forging American Obligations in World War II* (Washington, D.C.: Smithsonian Books, 2004); James Sparrow, *Warfare State: World War II Americans and the Age of Big Government* (New York: Cambridge University Press, 2011), 127–132.

7. Richard Polenberg, "The National Committee to Uphold Constitutional Government 1937–1941," *Journal of American History* 52 (1965): 582–598; "Progress Report on Repeal of 16th Amendment," Tax Information Series no. 11, May, 1, 1941, Folder "American Taxpayers Association," IRWC.

8. For the survey, 230 persons were interviewed in Baltimore and Minneapolis from August 7 to August 20, 1942. All were employees in establishments where the payroll deduction plan for war bond purchases was in effect; "Attitudes toward Payroll Deductions: The Proposed Withholding Tax and Increased Social Security," Data Prepared by Mr. Friedman, Special Report no. 20, Office of War Information, Bureau of Intelligence, Folder Preliminary Results of Office of War Information, Box 22 of 66, RG 56; Meg Jacobs, *Pocketbook Politics. Economic Citizenship in Twentieth-Century America*, (Princeton: Princeton University Press, 2005), 200–201; Angus Burgin, *The Great Persuasion: Reinventing Free Markets since the Depression* (Cambridge, MA: Harvard University Press, 2012), 164–165.

9. Editorial, *Life*, April 26, 1943, 22; Patrick D. Reagan, "The Withholding Tax, Beardsley Ruml, and Modern American Policy," *Prologue* 24 (1992): 19–31.

10. "Ruml Plan Backed by State Chamber," *New York Times*, September 11, 1942; "Miss Donlon Backs Ruml Plan," *New York Times*, February 3, 1943; Petition sent to Honorable S. Otis Bland, March 12, 1943; Petition

of citizens of Dutchess County, New York State, Various Subjects, Box 501, Committee Papers, RG 233.

11. Letter from the Buffalo Fur Merchants sent to the Honorable Walter G. Andrews, January 18, 1943; Resolution adopted January 20, 1943, Various Subjects, Box 501, Committee Papers, RG 233.

12. Mirit Eyal-Cohen, "When American Small Business Hit the Jackpot: Taxes, Politics, and the History of Organization Choice in the 1950s," *Pittsburgh Tax Review* 6, no. 20 (2009): 1–61; "Profit into Loss," *Time*, January, 24, 1944.

13. "Miss Kellems Defends Her Action in Refusing to Pay Income Tax," *The Bridgeport Telegram*, January 21, 1944; "U.S. to Assess Penalties in One-Woman Tax Strike," *The Chicago Sun*, January 21, 1944, Folder "Tax Strike 1944," Box 62, VKP.

14. Olivier Burtin, "A One-Woman Army" (master's degree, Institut d'études politiques, Paris, 2011); Carolyn C. Jones, "Vivien Kellems and the Folkways of Taxation," in *Total War and the Law: The American Home Front in World War Two*, ed. Daniel R. Ernst and Victor Jew (Westport, CO: Praeger, 2002), 121–148.

15. "Miss Kellems Defies Government to Act," *New York Times*, January 21, 1944; Quotation in "U.S. to Assess Penalties in One-Woman Tax Strike," *The Chicago Sun*, January 21, 1944; "Vivien Kellems Rebuts Charge by Morgenthau," *Herald Tribune*, January 21, 1944; Quotation in "U.S. to Assess Penalties in One-Woman Tax Strike," *The Chicago Sun*, January 21, 1944, Folder "Tax Strike 1944," Box 62, VKP.

16. "Two More States Approve Program to Limit Federal Taxing Power," Tax Information Series no. 50, March, 30, 1944, Folder "American Taxpayers Association," IRWC; "The Controversy of the Month: Should the Federal Taxing Power Be Limited?," *Congressional Digest* 23, no. 11 (1944): 259–288; "Rumley Indicted for Holding Data," *New York Times*, October 3, 1944, 13; "House Group PAC Opens PAC Inquiry Here," *New York Times*, November 13, 1944, 25; Committee for Constitutional Government, "A Ceiling on the Power to Destroy You by Taxation," "Campaign to Repeal 16th Amendment Is Gaining Speed!," Tax Information Series no. 51; "Repeal of the 16th Amendment Will Insure

Sound Postwar Tax Policies," January 6, 1945, Tax Information Series no. 63, Folder "American Taxpayers Association," IRWC; Edward A. Morrow, "Corporate Tax Cut Urged by Hancock," *New York Times*, August 9, 1944, 21.

17. Talk by the Secretary on the American Taxpayers, March 15 1944, "Income Tax Problem," Secondary Draft, January 10, 1944, Folder G4–1/44–4, "Questions and Answers on Tax Simplification," January 4, 1944, RG 56; James Sparrow, " "Buying Our Boys Back": The Mass Foundations of Fiscal Citizenship in World War II," *Journal of Policy history* 20, no. 2 (2008): 264–286.

18. Mark R. Wilson, "The Advantages of Obscurity: World War II Tax Carry-Back Provisions and the Normalization of Corporate Welfare," in *What's Good for Business: Business and Politics since World War II*, ed. Julian Zelizer and Kim Philipps-Fein (New York: Oxford University Press, 2012), 16–44; Carl S. Shoup, "The Revenue Act of 1945," *Political Science Quarterly* 60 (1945): 487; Beardsley Ruml, "Taxes for Revenue Are Obsolete," *American Affairs* 8, no. 1 (1946): 35–39.

19. Quotation in Elna C. Green, "From Antisuffragism to Anti-Communism: The Conservative Career of Ida M. Darden," *Journal of Southern History* 65, no. 2 (1999): 309; Robert Griffith, "Dwight D. Eisenhower and the Corporate Commonwealth," *American Historical Review* 87, no. 1 (1982): 87–122.

20. Andrew J. Dunar, *The Truman Scandals and the Politics of Morality* (Columbia: University of Missouri Press, 1984), 96–120; Catherine Rymph, *Republican Women: Feminism and Conservatism from Suffrage through the Rise of the New Right* (Chapel Hill: University of North Carolina Press, 2006), 119–120.

21. *Cedar Rapids Gazette*, February 13, 1948, Folder "Columnists on Tax Case," Box 32, VKP.

22. Letter from Mrs. Pearl Bussey to *Meet the Press*, May 25, 1948; Letter from (Miss) Catherine A. Maue to Vivien Kellems, May 24, 1948; Letter from Walter Marquart to Vivien Kellems, May 22, 1948; Letter from Joseph T. Craig to Vivien Kellems, May 27, 1948; Letter from Chauncey H. Whitcher to Vivien Kellems, May 27, 1948; Letter from R. M. Kelley

to Vivien Kellems, May 28, 1948, Folder "Tax Fan Letters Meet the Press Program," Box 32, VKP.

23. Doug Rossinow. *The Politics of Authenticity: Liberalism, Christianity, and the New Left in America* (New York: Columbia University Press, 1998); Margaret T. McGehee, "Disturbing the Peace: 'Lost Boundaries Pinky,' and Censorship in Atlanta, Georgia, 1949–1952," *Cinema Journal* 46, no. 1 (2006): 44; Jill Quadagno, *The Color of Welfare: How Racism Undermined the War on Poverty* (New York: Oxford University Press, 1994); Larry DeWitt, "The Decision to Exclude Agricultural and Domestic Workers from the 1935 Social Security Act," *Social Security Bulletin* 70, no. 4 (2010): 49–68.

24. The sixteen women were Carolyn Abney, Winifred Furth, Dorothy Whelan, Celest Clemens, Mary Hicks, R. B. Lothrop, Louise Littlejohn, Dorothy Martin, Eileen Pelz, Joy Quinn, Constance Key Wood, Mozelle Warren, Anita McNatt, Janie Pitts, and Eleanor Bradford. One could add Abney's mother-in-law, Virginia Abney, and Martin's sister-in-law, Etheldra Spangler, and Pelz's mother-in-law, Rubye Pelz; Gail K. Beil, "The Marshall Housewives Rebellion," unpublished paper (in author's possession); Bill Moyers, "Journalism & Democracy," *The Nation*, May 7, 2001.

25. *American Magazine*, December 1951, 112; *Newsweek*, August 20, 1951, 27.

26. "Marshal Housewives Continue Fight Against Household Tax," *Dallas Texas News*, March 29, 1952; "Housewives Fighting Tax Collection," *American Press*, Lake Charles, LA, May 27, 1953; "Housewife Loses Long Tax Revolt," *New York Times*, January 5, 1954; "Can't Make Collectors of Us, Wives Argue," *Chicago Tribune*, May 27, 1953, Folder "Marshall Housewives," Box 37, VKP.

27. Quotation in "Texas Housewives to Press Social Security Case," *Reading Eagle*, July 1, 1952; Ellen Schrecker, *Many are the Crimes: McCarthyism in America* (Princeton: Princeton University Press, 1998), 91–99; "Household Help: Social Security Tax Adds New Complication in Hiring Home Help," *Wall St. Journal*, March 22, 1955, 1; Ruby Clayton McKee, "Marshall Housewives Continue Fight Against Household Tax," *Dallas Texas News*, March 29, 1952; Robert F. Lof-

tus, "Revenue Agents to Visit Social Security 'Striker," *Long Island Press*, March 15, 1952.

28. Tom Buckley, "Just Plain H. L. Hunt," *Esquire*, January 1967, 64–69, 140–154; Letter from Vivien Kellems to Blaisdell, July 25, 1952, Folder "Liberty Belles, Inc., California, 1953," Box 37; Bess M. Wilson, "Liberty Belle U.S. Rally to Attack Federal Abuse of Citizens, Constitutional Violations," *Los Angeles Times*, November 18, 1951; Florence Farrell, "Liberty Belles Present Program in El Segundo," *El Segundo Herald*, May 1, 1952, Folder "Liberty Belles clippings, 1952," Box 61. VKP.

29. Folder "Power of Women, Publicity Plan"; Folder "Power of Women, and Photographs"; Letter from Allegra Taylor to Mrs Fred Griesel, April 15, 1952, Folder "Minute Women, 1952," Box 35, VKP.

30. Robert Dresser, "Socialism and the Federal Estate and Gift Taxes," April 25, 1952, Folder "Committee for Constitutional Government," IRWC; "The Sixteenth Amendment (Income Tax) Is on the Way Out," Tax Information Series, no. 103, November 10, 1950, Folder "American Taxpayers Association," IRWC; The eight states were Iowa, Florida, Kansas, Maine, Montana, Nevada, New Mexico, and Utah; Isaac William Martin, "Redistributing toward the Rich: Strategic Policy Crafting in the Campaign to Repeal the Sixteenth Amendment 1938–1958," *American Journal of Sociology* 116, 1 (2010): 19–21; Molly C. Michelmore, *Tax and Spend: The Welfare State, Tax Politics, and the Limits of American Liberalism* (Philadelphia: University of Pennsylvania Press, 2012).

31. Vivien Kellems to Mr. Horace W. Peters, August 27, 1953, Folder "Tax Exempt Status," Box 37, VKP; "Liberty Belles Battle over Primary Backing," *Los Angeles Times*, March 7, 1952; "Liberty Belles Protest on Werdel Move Grows," *Los Angeles Times*, May 8, 1952; "Liberty Belles Widen Rift on Werdel Slate," *Los Angeles Times*, May 9, 1952; "Leader Quits Liberty Belles in New Dispute," *Los Angeles Times*, May 20, 1952; "Minutes of the Liberty Belles Board of Directors," April 7, September 18, December 2, 1952, February 7, March 10, 1953, Folder "Liberty Belles, Inc. Minutebook, 1952," Box 37, VKP.

32. Dennis Lythgoe, *Let' Em Holler: A Political Biography of J. Bracken Lee* (Salt Lake City: Utah, 1982); Frank Jonas and Garth Jones, "J. Bracken Lee and the Public Service in Utah," *Western Political Quarterly* 10, no.

4 (1957): 911–925; *Washington Post*, October 9, 1955; *Milwaukee Journal*, October 12, 1955, Newspaper Clippings, Folder Taxes-General, Box 1, JLBP; Donald T. Critchlow, *Phyllis Schlafly and Grassroots Conservatism: A Woman's Crusade* (Princeton: Princeton University Press, 2005), 84–87.

33. Quotation in George B. Russell and J. Bracken Lee, *The Taxpayers' Champion* (New York: Robert Speller & Sons, 1961), 98–99; "The Man at the Wheel," *Time*, April 24, 1950, 28; Joe Alex Morris, "The Stubbornest Man in Utah," *Saturday Evening Post*, May 6, 1950, 124–126; Don Eddy, "Lone Wolf of Utah," *American Magazine*, May 1950, 24–25; Richard L. Williams, "Politician without a Future," *Life*, May 1, 1950, 109–110, 113–116; Newspaper Clippings, Folder "Taxes-General," Box 1, JLBP.

34. Letter from J. S. Kimmel to J. Bracken Lee, October 13, 1954; Letter from J. Bracken Lee to Fellow Americans, October 16, 1955, Series Correspondence, Folder 2, Box 77, JLBP.

35. Letter from Roland Wise to J. Lee Bracken, Series Correspondence, Folder 2, Box 77, JLBP; "Tax Warning Goes to Utah Governor," *New York Times*, October 8, 1955."Utah's Governor to Battle Taxes," *New York Times*, January 7, 1956.

36. Burgin, *The Great Persuasion*, 123–151; Nickerson, *Mothers of Conservatism*, 143–148; Jennifer Burns, *Goddess of the Market: Ayn Rand and the American Right* (New York: Oxford University Press, 2009).

37. Vivien Kellems, *Toil, Taxes, and Trouble* (New York: E. P. Dutton & Co, 1952), 63–63, 81–82, 152; Letter from secretary to Miss Kellems, August 19, 1958; "Breakdown of Sales," letter from Vivien Kellems to General Bonner Fellers, October 7, 1958, Folder "Toil, Taxes and Trouble, Sales Report," Box 39, VKP; Letter from Edward A. Rumley to Vivien Kellems, October 28, 1952, Folder "Toil, Taxes and Trouble, Reviews 1952–1953," Box 60, VKP; Philipps-Fein, *Invisible Hands*, 81–86.

38. U.S. Senate Judiciary Subcommittee, Hearings Before a Subcommittee of the Committee of the Judiciary of the United States Senate, 84th Congress, 2nd Session, "Proposing an Amendment to the Constitution

of the United States Relative to Taxes on Incomes, Inheritances and Gifts," April 25, 1956 (Washington, D.C.: U.S. Government Printing Office, 1956), 80; Nickerson, *Mothers of Conservatism*, 143; Isaac W. Martin, *Rich People's Movement: Grassroots Campaign to Untax the One Percent* (New York: Oxford University Press, 2013).

39. Vivien Kellems, "Is the Fair Deal Destroying Individual Responsibility?," Folder "Town Meeting," Box 30, VKP; Jerome Beatty, "Woman on the Warpath," *The Reader's Digest*, August 1952, Box 57, VKP; Frank Chodorov, *The Income Tax: Root of All Evil* (New York: Devin-Adair, 1954); John T. Flynn, "Federal Politicians Use Income Tax to Arrogate Powers," *American Progress* 3, no. 1 (1957): 4; John Moser, *Right Turn: John T. Flynn and the Transformation of American Liberalism* (New York: New York University Press, 2005).

40. *Monthly Tax Features* 3, no. 7 (July–August 1959), 1, IRWC; Jeff Roche, "Cowboy conservatism," in *Conservatism in the Sixties*, ed. David Farber, Jeff Roche (New York: Peter Lang Publisher, 2003), 80–81.

41. Heather Hendershot, *What's Fair on the Air? Cold War Right-Wing Broadcasting and the Public Interest* (Chicago: University of Chicago Press, 2011).

42. T. Coleman Andrews, American Challenge Publication, Distributed Tax Rebellion Committee, Folder "Tax Rebellion Committee, (hdqtrs. Fresno, Calif.)"; "Why the Income Tax is Bad." Exclusive Interview with T. Coleman Andrews," *U.S. News World Report*, May 25, 1956, 62–73.

43. "Propose to Repeal Income Tax Law," *American Progress* 1, no. 5, May 1955, 28; James L. Potts, "The Relation of the Income Tax to Democracy in the United States," *Western Political Quarterly* 10, no. 4 (1957): 911–925; Arthur Kemp, "Economy in Government Efficiency and Reduced Functions," *The Tax Digest* 36, no. 2 (February 1958): 27; Folder "California Taxpayers' Association," IRWC.

44. *Monthly Tax Features* 3, no. 7 (July–August 1959): 1, IRWC; Pamphlet "Abolish the Tax and the Form," 1958, Folder "Organization to Repeal Federal Income Taxes," IRWC.

45. Mary Brennan, *Turning Right in the Sixties: The Conservative Capture of the GOP* (Chapel Hill: University of North Carolina Press, 1995); Quotation in Philipps-Fein, *Invisible Hands*, 82, 84; "Letter to the Tax-payers," *American Progress* 4, no. 1 (Fall–Winter 1957–1958): 30; "Taxation: The Hidden Tyrant," Address Published in *American Progress* 4, no. 2 (Spring Edition, 1958): 44–46.

46. Matthew Lassiter, *The Silent Majority: Suburban Politics in the Sunbelt South* (Princeton: Princeton University Press, 2006); Kevin Kruse, *White Flight: Atlanta and the Making of Modern Conservatism* (Princeton: Princeton University Press, 2006); Jason Morgan Ward, *Defending White Democracy: The Making of a Segregationist Movement and the Remaking of Racial Politics, 1936–1965* (Chapel Hill: University of North Carolina Press, 2011); all examples are culled from Camille Walsh, *Racial Taxation: School Finance and "Taxpayer Citizenship 1869–1973* (book manuscript, to be published).

47. John Andrew, *Power to Destroy: The Political Uses of the IRS from Kennedy to Nixon* (Chicago: Ivan R. Dee, 2002), 25; *Special* 6, (March 25,1963), Life Line Foundation, Folder "Ideological Material, Historian's File," Box 78, Entire File "Official Use Only," 1975, RG 58; Critchlow, *The Conservative Ascendancy*, 223.

48. "California T(ax) Parties," *American Progress* 7, no. 4 (September–October 1962): 2–7; "California T Parties Score Hit," *American Progress* 7, no. 5 (November–December 1962): 6–10; Lisa McGirr, *Suburban Warriors: The Origins of the New American Right* (Princeton: Princeton University Press, 2001); Philipps-Fein, *Invisible Hands*, 140; Norman E. Nygaard, *Walter Knott: Twentieth Century Pioneer* (Grand Rapids, MI: Zondervan Publishing House, 1965).

49. "Who is Willis E. Stone?" n.d., Folder "Stone Willis Emerson," Box 1; Letter from Willis Stone to Dan Hanson, September 28, 1957, Folder "Hanson, Dan," Box 6, WSP.

50. "Liberty This Is The Issue," *American Progress* 7, no. 7 (May–June 1962): 8; Willis E. Stone, "1964—Year of Decision," *Freedom Magazine* (January–February 1964): 9, 1; Nickerson, *Mothers of Conservatism*, 143–144; Rick Perlstein, *Before the Storm: Barry Goldwater and*

the *Unmaking of the American Consensus* (New York: Hill & Wang, 2001); Donald Critchlow, *Phyllis Schlafly and Grassroots Conservatism* (Princeton: Princeton University Press, 2006), 137–162; Kurt Schuppara, "Barry Goldwater and the Southern California Conservatism: Ideology, Image and Myth in the 1964 California Republican Presidential Primary," *Southern California Quarterly* 74 (1992): 227–298.

51. Philipps-Fein, *Invisible Hands*, 136; Letter from Gordon Reed to Vivien Kellems, September 30, 1964, Folder "Republican State Headquarters 1964," Box 39, VKP; "G.O.P. Presses Vivien Kellems to End Goldwater Broadcasts," *New York Times*, September 27, 1964; Vivien Kellems, Social Security Speech, September 18, 1964, Folder "Speeches 1964," Box 40, VKP.

52. "Operation Street Scene 1965," *Freedom Magazine* 10, no. 2 (March–April 1965): 7; *Taxpayers' Power!* 1, no. 1 (March 18, 1968), Box "Taxpayers Power" (Formerly *American Liberty Crusader*), IRWC; Willis E. Stone, "Propectus: Organization Plan of Local Liberty Amendment Committees," October 9, 1967, Folder 8, Box 4, WSP.

53. Critchlow, *The Conservative Ascendancy*, 224; Quotation in Mary Rich Brogan, "Next 'Bout: Women Versus Uncle Sam," Folder "Marshall Housewives, 1952," Box 37, VKP; Ronald Reagan, with Richard Hubler, *Where's the Rest of Me? The Ronald Reagan Story* (New York: Duell, Sloan and Pearce, 1965), 16.

7. THE TYRANNY OF THE "INFERNAL REVENUE SERVICE"

1. Kim Philipps-Fein, *Invisible Hands: The Making of the Conservative Movement from the New Deal to Reagan* (New York: W.W. Norton, 2009), 182–183; Quotation from Jack Kemp, "You and Your Taxes," April 1977, 7, Folder 5, "Taxes 1975–1977," Box 134, JkP; Molly C. Michelmore, *Tax and Spend: The Welfare State, Tax Politics, and the Limits of American Liberalism* (Philadelphia: University of Pennsylvania Press, 2012), 47–71; Edward C. Burks, "Rep. Kemp's Play May Make Old No. 15 Taxpayers No. 1," *New York Times*, May 23, 1978, 1.

2. Judith Stein, *Pivotal Decade: How the United States Traded Factories for Finance in the Seventies* (New Haven: Yale University Press, 2010); Quotation in Thomas Byrne Edsall and Mary D. Edsall, *Chain Reaction: The Impact of Race, Rights, and Taxes on American Politics* (New York: Norton, 1992), 132.

3. Christopher Capozzola, "It Makes You Want To Believe in the Country: Celebrating the Bicentennial in an Age of Limits," in *America in the Seventies*, ed. Beth Bailey and David Farber (Lawrence: Kansas University Press, 2004), 29–49; "Operation Tax Rebellion," Sacramento Invaded by Tax Rebels, Undated, Folder "Tax Rebellion Committee of L.A.," ns, IRWC.

4. Lisa McGirr, *Suburban Warriors: The Origins of the New American Right* (Princeton: Princeton University Press, 2001); Kurt Schuppara, *Triumph of the Right: The Rise of the California Conservative Movement. 1945–1996* (Armonk, NY: M. E. Sharpe, 1998); Martin A. Larson, "The IRS and the Welfare State," *Tax Strike News*, January 1978, 3, Folder "Tax Strike News," IRWC; Matthew D. Lassiter, "Inventing Family Values," in *Rightward Bound: Making America Conservatives in the 1970s*, ed. Bruce J. Schulman and Julian E. Zelizer (Cambridge, MA: Harvard University Press 2008), 13–28; Martin A. Larson, *The Great Tax Fraud: How the Federal Government Favors the Rich and Exploits the Masses* (New York: Devin-Adair, 1968).

5. Quotation from Gerry Clark, "Tyranny Can Triumph if Good Men Do Nothing," Folder PAT, Box "Parents and Taxpayers," IRWC.

6. *Parents and Taxpayers, Freedom Issue* 8, no. 4 (June–July 1973), Folder PAT, RWC.

7. Quotation in "IRS Vs Hutchinson—Government vs. Citizen," Box "Parents and Taxpayers," IRWC; Jim Wood, "America's Newest Mini-Martyr: A Running Battle with the IRS," *San Francisco Examiner*, February, 25, 1973.

8. Jim Scott, "Conception and Birth of This Nation Was Due to a Tax Rebellion: A Tax Rebellion Can Now Save This Nation," Tax Rebellion Committee, Undated, Folder "Tax Rebellion Committee (hdqtrs. Fresno,

Calif.),” IRWC; *IRS Historical Fact Book: A Chronology, 1646–1992,* IRS Historical Studies (Washington D.C.: U.S. Government Printing Office, 1993), 181–185.

9. Letter from Jim Scott to the Editor, May, 1971; Letter from Jim Scott to Mr. Robert W. Schafer, Assistant Regional Counsel, IRS, May 31, 1972; Miranda Pamphlet, Undated, Folder “Tax Rebellion Committee (hdqtrs. Fresno, Calif.),” IRWC; Michael Flamm, *Law and Order: Street Crime, Civil Unrest, and the Crisis of Liberalism* (New York: Columbia University Press, 2005).

10. Letter from Jim Scott to the editor, May, 1971, Folder “Tax Rebellion Committee (hdqtrs Fresno, Calif.),” IRWC.

11. Tom Anderson, *Foreword*, 1968, Tax Rebellion Committee of L.A., *T.R.U.E. News* 1, no. 3 (1973): 3, Folder “T.R.U.E.,” IRWC; Willard A. Heaps, *Taxation U.S.A.* (New York: Seabury Press, 1971), 159–163; McGirr, *Suburban Warriors*, 217–262.

12. “TAX EXPO’73 KEEP YOUR MONEY GREEN, AND YOUR FLAG—RED, WHITE AND BLUE!,” Folder “Tax Rebellion Committee (hdqtrs. Fresno, Calif.),” IRWC; Jill Lepore, *The Whites of their Eyes: The Tea Party’s Revolution and the Battle over American History* (Princeton: Princeton University Press, 2010), 112.

13. T.R.U.E. Tea Party Seminar and Tax Seminar, December 1972, Folder “Parents and Taxpayers,” IRWC; Quotation in Kurt Schuparra, *Triumph of the Right: The Rise of the California Conservative Movement 1945–1966* (Armonk, NY: M. E. Sharpe, 1998), 145; Ronald Reagan, “Why Not Cut the Income Tax?,” *Washington Post*, October 12, 1976.

14. William A. Link. *Righteous Warrior: Jesse Helms and the Rise of Modern Conservatism* (New York: St. Martin’s Press, 2008), 131–167; from an editorial by Senator Jesse N. Helms, North Carolina, *Parents and Taxpayers* 2, no. 11 (1974), 4, Folder “Parents and Taxpayers,” IRWC.

15. Beth Bailey, “She ‘Can Bring Home the Bacon’: Negotiating Gender in the 1970s,” in *America in the Seventies*, ed. Beth Bailey and David Farber, 107–128; Quotation in Peggy Constantine, “Single Taxpayers Fight for Equal Rates,” *Buffalo Evening News*, Saturday, March 10, 1973, B-18;

Ida Walters, "Lonely Causes: At 77, Vivien Kellems Looks Ahead to Years of Battling the IRS," *Wall Street Journal*, January 7, 1974; Gwen Gibson, "A Connecticut Yankee in Tax Court," *Los Angeles Times*, September 30, 1971; Prudence Brown, "Single Woman Fights the System," *Newsday Business*, Folder "Connecticut, 1971–1972," Box 59, VKP.

16. Edward J. McCaffery, *Taxing Women* (Chicago: University of Chicago Press, 1997), 29–57; Alice Kessler-Harris, *In Pursuit of Equity: Women, Men, and the Quest for Economic Citizenship* (Oxford: Oxford University Press, 2001), 170–202; "Open Letter from Vivien Kellems to Secretary John Connally," *Washington Post*, March 11, 1971, Folder "Editorial," Box 59, VKP.

17. Robert Waters, "McCarthy Goes to Bat for Vivien," *Hartford Courant*, June 4, 1969.

18. Vivien Kellems to "Dear Browbeaten, Discriminated Against, and Impoverished Taxpayer," Folder "1969–1971 Tax," Box 42, VKP; Letter from Vivien Kellems to my "Dear Frustrated, Single Taxpayer," undated, Folder "Singles Tax Materials, 1969–1971," Box 43, VKP; Robert Waters, "Vivien's Tax Bill Loses in Senate Vote by 66–25," *Hartford Courant*, December 11, 1969; U.S. Congress, Senate Committee on Finance, *Tax Reform Act of 1969*, September 26, 29, 30, Oct. 1, 2, 1969, 91st Congress, 1st Session (Washington, D.C.: Government Printing Office, 1969), 4875–4891; "Singles Rebel Against 'Penalty': New Tea Party Brews Over Tax Inequity," *The Evening Times* [NJ], March 8, 1972; "Vivien Says Tax Rate Vote Moral Victory," *Hartford Courant*, December 12, 1969, Folder "New Jersey, 1972," Box 59, VKP.

19. Beggy Price, "She Refuses to Pay 'Tax for Being Single,'" *Chicago Today American*, May 22, 1969, Folder "Clippings, Taxes, 1969–1970," Box 58, VKP; Barbara Carlson, "Vivien's Protest Is Becoming a National Movement," *Hartford Courant*, April 17, 1969; "Congressmen Encourage Vivien," *Hartford Courant*, April 22, 1969; House Committee on Ways and Means, *Tax Treatment of Single Persons*, 15–16; Robert Waters, "Vivien Vows Jail before Ending," *Hartford Courant*, March 25, 1971; *Congressional Record—Senate*, February 18, 1971, 3037–3038; Rob-

ert Waters, "Vivien Holds Capitol Steps Press Conference on Tax Bill," *Hartford Courant*, February 19, 1971; "'True Grit' Spinster Presses Tax Attack," *Augusta Chronicle*, March 25, 1971, Folder "Georgia, 1971," Box 59, VKP.

20. Susan Trento, *The Power House: Robert Keith Fray and the Selling of Access and Influence in Washington* (New York: St. Martin's Press, 1992); Karen Miller, *The Voice of Business: Hill & Knowlton and Postwar Public Relations* (Chapel Hill: University of North Carolina Press, 1999); Quotation in Peggy Constantine, "Single Taxpayers Fight for Equal Rates," *Buffalo Evening News*, March 10, 1973, B-18; Sylvia Porter, "Single Tax Fighters Show Gains," *Herald Rutland*, August 27, 1971.

21. Mary E., "Single Tax Fighters Show Gans," *St. Paul Pioneer Press*, March, 22, 1971.

22. House Committee on Ways and Means, *Tax Treatment of Single Persons*; U.S. Congress, House Committee on Ways and Means, *General Tax Reform*, March 23, 1973, 93rd Congress, 1st Session, 2945–3001; "Single Taxpayers Renew Their Fight to Equalize Taxes," *New York Times*, January 8, 1975; Lee Spencer, "The 'Singles' Tax," *Chicago Tribune*, April 29, 1976; Clarence Petersen, "Pay an Estimated 20% More: Singles Protest 'Unfair' Income Taxes," *Chicago Tribune*, February 7, 1974; Robert Waters, "Tax Bout Lost by Miss Kellems," *Hartford Courant*, July 26, 1974.

23. "Vivien Sees Wilbur Mills as Her 'Biggest Obstacle,'" *Naugatuck News*, March 25, 1971, Folder "Connecticut, 1971–1972"; Kathryn Kolkhorst, "Miss Kellems Blames Mills for Tax Delay," *New Haven Journal Courier*, October 15, 1973, Folder "Connecticut, 1973," Box 59, VKP; House Committee on Ways and Means, *General Tax Reform*, 2953; Herbert Stein, "The Fiscal Revolution in America, Part II: 1964–1994" in *Funding the Modern American State*, ed. W. Elliot Brownlee (Cambridge: Cambridge University Press, 1996), 194–286; John Chamberlain, "These Days," *Dublin* [GA] *Courier-Herald*, September 3, 1969; Lynn Sherr, "Unwed Taxpayers, 28 Million, Claim It's Discrimination," *Macon Telegraph and News*, April 12, 1970, Folder "Clippings, Taxes, 1969–1970," Box 58, VKP.

24. Bill Ryan, "Viv Has 'A Lovely Time' at IRS Meeting," *Hartford Times*, December 30, 1970; Ida Walters, "Lonely Causes: At 77, Vivien Kellems Looks Ahead to Years of Battling the IRS," *The Wall Street Journal*, January 7, 1974; Gwen Gibson, "A Connecticut Yankee in Tax Court," *Los Angeles Times*, September 30, 1971, 16, Folder "Connecticut," Box 59, VKP.

25. Quotation in Jeannette Smyth, "Airing Tax Grievances," *Washington Post*, April, 12, 1972, C-3; John Barron, "Tyranny in the Internal Revenue Service," *Reader's Digest*, August 1967; John Barron, "Time for Reform in the IRS," *Reader's Digest*, September 1968, 47–56; John Barron, "The Tragic Case of John J. Hafer and the IRS," *Reader's Digest*, January 1969, 53–58.

26. Jim Wood, "America's Newest Mini-Martyr: A Running Battle with the IRS," *San Francisco Examiner*, February, 25, 1973; John A. Andrew, *The Political Uses of the IRS from Kennedy to Nixon* (Chicago: Ivan R. Dee, 2002); *Newsweek*, Special Edition on the "Troubled American," 6 (October 1969): 60; Jefferson Cowie, *Stayin' Alive: The 1970s and the Last Days of the Working Class* (New York: New Press 2010), 1–19; John Barron, "Time for Reform in the IRS," *Reader's Digest*, September 1968, 47–53.

27. David C. Johnson, "Donald C. Alexander, 87, Who Resisted Nixon at I.R.S., Is Dead," *New York Times*, February 8, 2009, A-19; "The Nation: Keeping a Little List at the IRS," *Time*, August 13, 1973; Andrew, *Power to Destroy*, 278–280.

28. Ibid, 296–313.

29. Zelizer, *Taxing America*, 353; "The Fall of Chairman Wilbur Mills," *Time*, December 16, 1974; Brian Balogh, *Chain Reaction: Expert Debate and Public Participation in American Commercial Nuclear Power, 1945–1975* (New York: Cambridge University Press, 1991); *Let's Bring Uncle Sam, Parents and Taxpayers* 10, no. 3 (July 1976): 3, Folder "Parents and Taxpayers," IRWC; United States Taxpayers Union pamphlet, 1975, Folder USTU, IRWC.

30. Jude Wanniski, *The Way the World Works* (Washington, D.C.: Regnery Publishing, 1978); Philipps-Fein, *Invisible Hands*, 180–188; Monica

Prasad, "The Popular Origins of Neoliberalism in the Reagan Tax Cut of 1981," *Journal of Policy History* 24, no. 2 (2012): 351–383; Seymour Zucker, "The Fallacy of Slashing Taxes without Cutting Spending," *Business Week* August 7, 1982, 62.

31. Angus Burgin, *The Great Persuasion: Reinventing Free Markets since the Depression* (Cambridge, MA: Harvard University Press, 2012), 152–185; Daniel T. Rodgers, *Age of Fracture* (Cambridge, MA: Harvard University Press, 2011), 50–55.

32. Philipps-Fein, *Invisible Hands*, 192–198; Cathie J. Martin, *Shifting the Burden: The Struggle Over Growth and Corporate Taxation* (Chicago: University of Chicago Press, 1991), 116, 117–118; Mark S. Mizruchi, *The Fracturing of the American Corporate Elite* (Cambridge, MA: Harvard University Press, 2013).

33. Irvin Molotsky, "Norman B. Ture, Architect of the 1981 Tax Cut, Dies at 74," *New York Times*, August 13, 1997; Rodgers, *Age of Fracture*, 51–54; Robert M. Collins, *More: The Politics of Growth in Postwar United States* (New York: Oxford University Press, 2000).

34. Jude Wanniski, "It's Time to Cut Taxes," *Wall Street Journal*, December 11, 1974, 18; Jude Wanniski, "Should a GOP Scrooge Shoot St. Nick? The Two Santa Claus Theory," *National Observer*, March 6, 1976; Jude Wanniski, "Taxes and the Kennedy Gamble," *Wall Street Journal*, September 23, 1976; Jack Kemp, "Business Has a Great Deal at Stake," March 1978, 3–4, Folder "Taxes and Taxation.Kemp-Roth Tax Reduction Bills 1978," Box 134, JkP.

35. Monica Prasad, "The Popular Origins of Neoliberalism in the Reagan Tax Cut of 1981," *Journal of Policy History* 24, no. 3: 351–83; J. Craig Jenkins and Craig M. Eckert, "The Right Turn in Economic Policy: Business Elites and the New Conservative Economics," *Sociological Forum* 15, no. 2 (2000): 307–338; Don Critchlow, *Phyllis Schlafly and Grassroots Conservatism: A Woman's Crusade* (Princeton: Princeton University Press, 2007).

36. Howard Jarvis, *I'm Mad as Hell* (New York: Time Books, 1979); David O. Sears and Jack Citrin, *Tax Revolt: Something for Nothing in California* (Cambridge, MA: Harvard University Press, 1985); Clarence Lo,

Small Property versus Big Government (Berkeley: University of California Press, 1990); Phyllis Schlafly Radio Network, CBS, May 14, 1976, *Spectrum*, Folder 5, "Taxes 1975–1977," Box 134, JKP

37. Daniel A. Smith, "Howard Jarvis, Populist Entrepreneur: Reevaluating the Causes of Proposition 13," *Social Science History* 23, no. 2 (1999): 173–210; Isaac W. Martin, *The Permanent Tax Revolt: How the Property Tax Transformed American Politics* (Stanford, CA: Stanford University Press, 2008).

38. Herman Turk, "Imageries of Social Control," *Urban Life* 8 (1979): 335–358.

39. Quotation in Isaac W. Martin, "The Campaign for Federal Tax Limitation and the Reagan Revolution," paper presented at the Social Science History Association in 2011 (in author's hands).

40. Quotation in Cody White, "Rising from the Ashes: The Impact of Proposition 13 on Public Libraries in California," *Libraries & the Cultural Record* 46, no. 4 (2011): 350; Quotation in Sally Quinn, "Proposition Man: Howard Jarvis, the Tax Fighter, Is Riding High on Number 13," *Washington Post*, June 29, 1978, B1.

41. Letter from Howard Jarvis to "Dear Fellow Taxpayer," undated, Folder "American Tax Reduction Movement," IRWC; Milton Friedman, "The Message from California," *Newsweek*, June 19, 1978, 26.

42. Paul Gann to "Dear Citizen," n.d. (1981?), Folder "National Taxpayers' Union", IRWC; Lo, *Small Property versus Big Government*, 178–194; Martin, "The Campaign for Federal Tax Limitation and the Reagan Revolution."

43. Philips-Fein, *Invisible Hands*, 234.

44. Kenneth T. Andrews, "Movement-Countermovement Dynamics and the Emergence of New Institutions: The Case of 'White Flight' Schools in Mississippi," *Social Forces* 80, no. 3 (2002): 911–936; Joseph Crespino, *In Search of Another Country: Mississippi and the Conservative Counterrevolution* (Princeton: Princeton University Press, 2007), 237–266.

45. U.S. Department of the Treasury, Internal Revenue Service, "Proposed Revenue Procedure on Tax-Exempt Schools," 3; Statement of Jerome

Kurtz, commissioner of internal revenue before the Subcommittee on Oversight of the House Committee on Ways and Means, Historian's Book, Box 38, RG 58.

46. Kenneth T. Andrews, *Freedom Is a Constant Struggle: The Mississippi Civil Rights Movement and Its Legacy* (Chicago: University of Chicago Press, 2004); Charles M. Payne, *I've Got the Light of Freedom: The Organizing Tradition and the Mississippi Freedom Struggle* (Berkeley: University of California Press, 1995).

47. Quotation in Joseph Crespino, "Civil Rights and the Religious Right," in *Rightward Bound*, 103.

48. Jack Kemp, "An American Renaissance," February 3, 1979, Folder 7 "Taxes and Taxation. Kemp-Roth Notebook," Box 90, JkP; Edward C. Burks, "Rep. Kemp's Play Can Make Old No. 15 Taxpayers' No. 1," *New York Times*, May 23, 1978, 20; Norman C. Miller, "Tax-Cut Plan Gives GOP a New Issue—And a New Face," *Wall Street Journal*, September 19, 1978, 1; Jack Kemp, "Why Corporate Taxes Should Be Slashed," *Human Events*, May 17, 1975, Folder 5, Box 134, JkP; "Jack Kemp Rated 'Tops' by National Taxpayers Union," Folder "Advertising," Box 205, JkP; "Tax Revolt Gains Stream," *Tax Strike News*, March 1978, 1, Folder "Tax Strike News," IRWC.

49. "Death and Taxes Are Inevitable," Pamphlet of the American Tax Reduction Movement, Folder "American Tax Reduction Movement," IRWC.

50. *Dollars and Sense*, February 1979, 4; April–May 1979, 5; September 1978, 1; Lo, *Small Property versus Big Government*, 178–194; Letter from NTU to members, Undated, Folder "National Taxpayers Union," IRWC.

51. Lewis Uhler, *A Taxpayer's Guide to Survival: Constitutional Tax Limitation* (National Tax Limitation Committee, 1979).

52. Howell Raines, "President's Reported Tax Cut Plan Attacked by Reagan as 'Gimmick,'" *New York Times*, June 20, 1980; "The Candidate's Money Policies," *New York Times*, October 31, 1980.

53. Phillips-Fein, *Invisible Hands*, 236–262; Critchlow, *The Conservative Ascendancy*, 173–183; Crespino, *In Search of Another Country*, 258; "36

Billion Tax Cut is Urged by Reagan and GOP Leaders," *New York Times*, June 26, 1980.

54. Quotation in Statement from Terry Oakes, Folder "Tax Rebellion Committee," IRWC; Jude Wanniski, "The No. 1 Problem," *New York Times*, February 27, 1980, A-27; James Q. Wilson, "A Guide to Reagan Country," *Commentary* (1967), 37.

8. Tea Parties All Over Again?

1. Quotation in "Reagan Making His Big Pitch," *Time*, June 10, 1985.
2. Bruce Schulman, *The Seventies: The Great Shift in American Culture, Society, and Politics* (New York: Da Capo Press, 2001); Daniel Rodgers, *Age of Fracture* (Cambridge, MA: Harvard University Press, 2012); Quotation in Molly C. Michelmore, *Tax and Spend: The Welfare State, Tax Politics, and the Limits of American Liberalism* (Philadelphia: University of Pennsylvania Press, 2012), 135; George Gilder, *Wealth and Poverty* (New York: Basic Books, 1981).
3. Remarks of the president at reception with representatives of the business community, September 15, 1981, Folder "Thank-You Reception—Tax Package (1)," JBF; W. Eliott Brownlee and C. Eugene Steuerle, "Taxation," in W. Eliott Brownlee and C. Eugene Steuerle, *The Reagan Presidency: Pragmatic Conservatism and Its Legacies* (Lawrence: Kansas University Press, 2003), 155–181.
4. Jeffrey H. Birnbaum and Alan S. Murray, *Showdown at Gucci Gulch: Lawmakers, Lobbyists and the Unlikely Triumph of Tax Reform* (New York: Vintage Books, 1987); Cathie J. Martin, *Shifting the Burden: The Struggle over Growth and Corporate Taxation* (Chicago: Chicago University Press, 1991); Quotation In Monica Prasad, "The Popular Origins of Neoliberalism in the Reagan Tax Cut of 1981," *Journal of Policy History* 24, no. 3 (2012): 369–370; Quotation in Ed Magnuson, David Beckwith, and Neil MacNeil "Bye Bye Balanced Budget," *Time*, November 16, 1981; Quotation in George J. Church, Laurence I. Barrett, and David Beckwith, "Challenge to Change: Reagan Calls for an End to Spendthrift Big Government," *Time*, March 2, 1981; Quotation in Schulman, *The Seventies*, 236.

5. Michelmore, *Tax and Spend*, 137–149; Ella Howard, *Homeless: Poverty and Urban Place in Urban America* (Philadelphia: University of Pennsylvania Press, 2013), 201–209.

6. Quotation in Patrick J. Akard, "Corporate Mobilization and Political Power: The Transformation of American Economic Policy in the 1970s." *American Sociological Review* 57, no. 5 (1992): 608; Sheldon D. Pollack, *Refinancing America: The Republican Antitax Agenda* (Albany: State University of New York Press, 2003), 60–62; Martin, *Shifting the Burden*, 118–124; Marisa Chappell, *The War on Welfare: Family, Poverty, and Politics in Modern America* (Philadelphia: University of Pennsylvania Press, 2010), 199–241.

7. Pollack, *Refinancing America*, 57–62; Michelmore, *Tax and Spend*, 137–141; Isaac W. Martin, "The Campaign for Federal Tax Limitation and the Reagan Revolution," paper presented at the Social Science History Association in 2011 (in author's hands).

8. Joseph Crespino, *In Search of Another Country: Mississippi and the Conservative Counterrevolution* (Princeton: Princeton University Press 2007), 257–258.

9. Quotation in "In Major Shift, IRS Is Now Neutral on Bias," *New York Times*, January 10, 1982; Glenn Fowler, "Tax-Exempt Ruling Draws Protest," *Anchorage Daily News*, January 10, 1982; Lee Lescaze and John Berry, "President Defends His Policies," *Washington Post*, January 20, 1982, A-1; Linda Hilbun, "Tax Break for Biased Private Schools Rapped," *Memphis Press-Scimitar*, January 9, 1982.

10. Statement of Edward C. Schmults before the Senate Finance Committee, February 1, 1982, Historian's Book, Box 38, RG 58; "Groups Decry Government Move in Bob Jones Case," *The News*, January 10, 1982; "Ex IRS Aides Assail School Bias Exemption Shift," *New York Times*, January 12, 1982; "Tax Policy: Congressmen to Challenge Decision," Daily Report for Executives, January 11, 1982, RG 58; "Editorial," *The Seattle Times*, January, 12, 1982; "Subsidizing Discrimination," *The Boston Globe*, January 12, 1982, 14; Richard Cohen, "Ronald Crow," *Washington Post*, January 12, 1982.

11. "NAACP Will Ask to Prosecute Bias Suits," *The Minneapolis Tribune*, January 12 1982; "Storm Brews Over BJU Case," *The News*,

January 12, 1982; "We're not Racist, Just Unusual," *Chicago Tribune*, January 17, 1982; "A Touchy Turnaround on Private Schools," *U.S. News and World Report*, January 25, 1982; "Reagan Policies 'Aid Racists, Urban League Leader Says,'" *Chicago Tribune*, January 21, 1982; Anthony Lewis, "Shucks, It's Only the Law," *New York Times*, January 21, 1982, A-23; Quotation in Walter Isaac, Douglas Brew, and Jeanne Saddler, "Pirouetting on Civil Rights," *Time*, January 25, 1982.

12. Lee Lescaze, "Reagan Submits Bill Denying Tax Breaks to Segregated Schools," *Washington Post*, January 19, 1982, A-1; Quotation in Gilbert Lewthwaite, "Tax Shift on Schools Is Sought," *The Sun*, January 19, 1982, 1; "Reagan Deepens Doubts about His Stand on Racism," *The Philadelphia Inquirer*, January 20, 1982; "Reagan: Kill Tax Break for Race-Biased Schools," *Detroit Free Press*, January 13, 1982; "Reagan, in Shift, Will Seek to Deny Tax-Exemption to Biased Schools," *The Philadelphia Inquirer*, January 13, 1985; "Reagan Says He'll Ask Law Taxing Segregated Schools," *The Boston Globe*, January 13, 1982, A-1; "News in Brief," *The Philadelphia Inquirer*, January 16, 1982, A-3; "Bob Jones University and Racial Discrimination," *Good Morning America*, Jan. 21, 1982, transcript, Historian's Book, Box 38, RG 58.

13. Letter from Bill Barr to Jay Wilkinson et al., May, 9, 1983, Folder "Bob Jones Bill," WBF; Letter from Bob Jones III to Fred E. Fielding, December 27, 1983, Folder "JGR/Bob Jones University Decision" (1 of 2), Box 6.

14. Bernard Reed, "Gordon Kahl (Shooting Of)," in *The Encyclopedia of Arkansas: History & Culture* (http://encyclopediaofarkansas.net/encyclopedia/entry-detail.aspx?entryID=5483); Catherine McNicol Stock, *Rural Radicals: From Bacon's Rebellion to the Oklahoma City Bombing* (New York: Random House, 1996), 171–174; Quotation in "Shootout in a Sleepy Hamlet," *Time*, June 13, 1983.

15. Quotation in "Dakota Dragnet," *Time*, February 28, 1983.

16. "Tax Protester Gets Fine, Jail Sentence," *Eugene Register-Guard*, June 19, 1982; "Garden Grove: Tax Resistance Group Now Meets in Warehouse," *Los Angeles Times*, February 25,1985; Lisa McGirr, *Suburban*

Warriors: The Origins of the New American Right (Princeton: Princeton University Press, 2002).

17. Otto Friedrich, David Beckwith, and Adam Zagorin, "Cheating by the Millions," *Time*, March 28, 1983.

18. Schulman, *The Seventies*, 218.

19. Richard A. Viguerie, "An Open Letter to President Reagan," *Conservative Digest* (1982): 46–47; Richard A. Viguerie, *The New Right: We're Ready to Lead* (Falls Church, VA: Viguerie, 1981); Kim Philipps-Fein, *Invisible Hands: The Making of the Conservative Movement from the New Deal to Reagan* (New York: W. W. Norton, 2009), 213–218; Paul Weyrich, "The White House, the Elections, the Right," *Conservative Digest* (1982): 45; Quotation in Donald T. Critchlow, *The Conservative Ascendancy: How the GOP Right Made Political History* (Cambridge, MA: Harvard University Press, 2007), 201.

20. Donald Regan, *For the Record: From Wall Street to Washington* (New York: St Marin's Press, 1988); Edwin Meese III, *With Reagan: The Inside Story* (Washington, D.C.: Regnery Gateway, 1992), 142–147; Quotation in Martin, *Shifting the Burden*, 140.

21. Gil Troy, *Morning in America: How Ronald Reagan Invented the 1980s* (Princeton: Princeton University Press, 2005).

22. "Remark of the President to Citizens Group, May, 29, 1985," Folder "Mainline Protestant Group on Tax Reform (Packet)," JDH.

23. "Tax Reform for an American Opportunity Society," *Police Federation News*, March–April 1985, Folder 6, Box 98, JkP; Quotation in Brownlee, *Federal Taxation in America*, 160; Pollack, *Refinancing America*, 65–66; Jack Kemp, "Prospects for Tax Reform," Folder 11, Box 98, JkP.

24. Quotation in "Reagan Making His Big Pitch," *Time*, June 10, 1985; Quotation in Brownlee, *Federal Taxation in America*, 166; Quotation in "The Making of a Miracle," *Time*, August 25, 1986.

25. "The President's Pro-Family Tax Proposals," Folder "Christian Media-Tax Reform Aug. 1, 1985," CAF; Bill Mattox, "Tax Reform and the Family: An Analysis of President Reagan's Tax Reform Proposal," Family

Research Council of America, July 1985, Folder "Christian Media," CAF.

26. Joe Klein, "The Power Broker," *Time*, July 14, 2011, 26–28.

27. America's Tax Plan, Talking Points, 5, no. 8 (May 31, 1985), Folder "Christian Media—Tax Reform, August 1, 1985," CAF; "FAIR TAXES NOW: A Coalition for American Tax Reform, Plan of Operations, June 18, 1985," Folder "Americans for Tax Reform," CAF; Martin, *Shifting the Burden*, 171, 192–193.

28. "Rep. Jack Kemp Hails 'Most Historic Tax Reform since 1923 for American Entrepreneurs and Small Business Community,'" Folder "Taxes and Taxation," Box 98, JkP; "Death and Taxes," presidential radio talk, May 10, 1986, Folder "Radio Address, Death and Taxes," Box 264, Speechwriting Office of Research Office, Records Series I, Speeches, RRPL; Quotation in Brownlee, *Federal Taxation in America*, 165.

29. Ella Howard, *Homeless: Poverty and Place in Urban America* (Philadelphia: University of Pennsylvania Press, 2013), 204–209; Marjorie Kornhauser, "Legitimacy and the Right of Revolution: The Role of Tax Protests and Anti-Tax Rhetoric in America," *Buffalo Law Review* 50, no. 3 (2002): 819–930.

30. Quotation in "GOP: Tax Limitation Amendment May Hinder Overhaul," *USA Today*, March 20, 1996; Quotation in Pollack, *Refinancing America*, 82–83.

31. Donald T. Critchlow, *The Conservative Ascendancy: How the GOP Right Made Political History* (Cambridge, MA: Harvard University Press, 2007), 246–248; Alice O' Connor, *Poverty Knowledge: Social Science, Social Policy, and the Poor in Twentieth-Century U.S. History* (Princeton: Princeton University Press, 2001), 284–295.

32. Dan Goodgame, "The Point of No Return," *Time*, April 17, 1995; Quotation in Pollack, *Refinancing America*, 71.

33. Robert Hall and Alvin Rabushka, *The Flat Tax* (Washington, D.C.: Hoover Institution Press, 1995); Quotation in Marjorie Kornhauser, "Equality, Liberty and a Fair Income Tax," *Fordham Urban Law Journal* 23 (1995): 612.

34. Quotation in Brownlee, *Federal Taxation in America*, 206; Carolyn Lochhead, "Elimination of Tax Code Gaining Favor," *San Francisco Chronicle*, July 24, 1995.

35. Pollack, *Refinancing America*, 92.

36. Allison Mitchell and Katharine Seelye, "State of the Union Response: In New Unity, GOP Seeks Tax Cuts," *New York Times*, January 20, 1999; Trova Heffernan, *The Impact of Jennifer Dunn* (Washington, D.C.: Legacy Project, 2008); Matthew A. Wasniewski, *Women in Congress: 1917–2006* (Washington, D.C.: Government Printing Office, 2006), 701–703; Ralph Thomas, "Jennifer Dunn, Who Inspired Face of Today's State GOP, Dies at 66," *The Seattle Times*, September 6, 2007; Neil Modie and Chris McGann, "Jennifer Dunn, 1941–2007: Tireless Advocate for State's Interests," *Seattle Post-Intelligencer*, September 6, 2007; David Postman, "Jennifer Dunn's Son up for King County Council Seat," *The Seattle Times*, January 26, 2005; Danny Westneat, "Race and Gender at Play in GOP Leadership Spots—Jennifer Dunn Appealing to Party to Place Women in Key Roles," *The Seattle Times*, November 17, 1998.

37. Joshua Green, "Meet Mr. Death," *The American Prospect*, December 19, 2001; Larry M. Bartels, "Homer Gets a Tax Cut: Inequality and Public Policy in the American Mind," *Prospective on Politics* 3 (2005): 15–31; George Cooper, "A Voluntary Tax? New Perspectives on Sophisticated Estate Tax Avoidance," *Columbia Law Review* 77, no. 16 (1977): 78–105; Quotation in Alex Halpern Levy, *Rhetoric and Reason in the Estate Tax Repeal Debate* (master's degree, Wesleyan College, 2008), 83.

38. Michael Graetz, Ian Shapiro, *Death by a Thousand Cuts: The Fight over Taxing Inherited Wealth* (Princeton: Princeton University Press, 2005), 12–22.

39. Quotation in Levy, *Rhetoric and Reason*, 88; Quotation in Graetz and Shapiro, *Death by a Thousand Cuts*, 81; Quotation in Levy, *Rhetoric and Reason*, 95; Graetz and Shapiro, *Death by a Thousand Cuts*, 168; Jim Grote, "Taxation without Respiration: Economic Liberty and Political Equality," *Business Ethics Quarterly* 13, no. 4 (2003): 581–590.

40. Richard W. Stevenson, "A Nation Challenged: The Economy; Bush Wants More Tax Cuts in Efforts to Help Economy," *New York Times*, October 6, 2001; Daniel Kadlec, "Kill the Estate Tax," *Time*, August 14, 2000.

41. Quotation in David Frum, *The Right Man: The Surprise Presidency of George W. Bush* (New York: Random House, 2003), 50; Jack Kemp, "We Can Afford a Much Bigger Tax Cut," *New York Times*, February 21, 2001, A-19; David E. Rosenbaum, "Republicans in New Tactic, Offer Increase in Tax Breaks," *New York Times*, March, 15, 2001, A-22; Heidi Glenn, "Armey Defends Bigger Tax Cut," *Tax Notes Today* 49–2 (2001): 2; "The Non-taxpaying Classes," *Wall Street Journal*, November 20, 2002.

42. Milton Friedman, "What Every American Wants," *Wall Street Journal*, January 19, 2003; Quotation in Ronnee Schreiber, *Righting Feminism: Conservative Women & American Politics* (New York: Oxford University Press, 2008), 92.

43. David E. Rosenbaum, "A Tax Cut Without End," *New York Times*, May 23, 2003; Paul Krugman, *Fuzzy Math: The Essential Guide to the Bush Tax Plan* (New York: W. W. Norton Company, 2001); see Brownlee, *Federal Taxation in America*, 241; Steven A. Bank, Kirk J. Stark, and Joseph J. Thorndike, *War and Taxes* (Washington, D.C.: Urban Institute Press, 2008), 145–165.

44. Jimmy Carter, "1970s Saw a Tea Party-like Wave," *USA Today*, September 29, 2010; Theda Skocpol and Vanessa Williamson, *The Tea Party and the Remaking of Republican Conservatism* (New York: Oxford University Press, 2012), 33.

45. Liz Robbins, "Protesters Air Views on Government Spending at Tax Day Parties Across U.S.," *New York Times*, April 16, 2009, A-16; Quotation in Ronald P. Formisano, *The Tea Party* (Baltimore: Johns Hopkins University Press, 2012), 7.

46. Skocpol and Williamson, *The Tea Party*, 22, 104; Kate Zernike and Jennifer Steinhauser, "A Power Again in Congress Years after He Left It," *New York Times*, November 15, 2010, A-1, A-16. Skocpol and Williamson, *The Tea Party*, 105.

47. Kate Zenike and Megan Thee-Brenan, "Polls Find Tea Party Backers Wealthier and More Educated," *New York Times*, April 14, 2010, A-1, A-12.
48. Skocpol and Williamson, *The Tea Party*, 37, 131.
49. Willard Cleon Skousen, *The 5000 Year Leap: The 28 Ideas That Changed the World* (Washington, D.C.: National Center for Constitutional Studies, 1981); Jeffrey Rosen, "Radical Constitutionalism," *New York Times Magazine*, November 28, 2010; Quotation in Jill Lepore, *The Whites of Their Eyes: The Tea Party's Revolution and the Battle over American History* (Princeton: Princeton University Press, 2010), 4.
50. Joseph Farah, *The Tea Party Manifesto: A Vision for an American Rebirth* (Washington, D.C.: WND Books, 2010), 106; Jill Lepore, *The Whites of Their Eyes*, 44; Skocpol and Williamson, *The Tea Party*, 31.
51. Quotation in Kate Zernike, *Boiling Mad: Inside Tea Party America* (New York: Times Books/Henry Holt and Co., 2010), 65.
52. Warren Buffet, "Stop Coddling the Super-Rich," *New York Times*, August 14, 2011, A-21; Quotation in "AACF challenges the Buffet Rule," January 29, 2012 (http://accf.org/press-release/accf-challenges-the-buffett-rule).

Epilogue

1. Quotation in Alfred E. Young, *The Shoemaker and the Tea Party: Memory and the American Revolution* (Boston: Beacon Press, 1999), 187; Jill Lepore, *The Whites of Their Eyes: The Tea Party's Revolution over American History* (Princeton: Princeton University Press, 2010).
2. Jude Wanniski, "Taxes and a Two-Santa Theory," *National Observer*, March 6, 1976; Larry Bartels, *Unequal Democracy: The Political Economy of the New Gilded Age* (Princeton: Princeton University Press, 2008); Romain Huret, *Katrina, 2005. L'ouragan, l'Etat et les pauvres* (Paris: Editions de l'Ecole des hautes études en sciences sociales, 2010).
3. Richard T. Ely, *Taxation in American States and Cities* (New York: T. Y. Crowell, 1888), 14.

4. Matthew Lassiter, "Political History beyond the Red-Blue Divide, *Journal of American History* 98, no. 3 (2011): 764; Donald T. Critchlow, "Rethinking American Conservatism: Toward a New Narrative," *Journal of American History* 98 (2011): 752; Lisa McGirr, "Now That Historians Know So Much about the Right, How Should We Best Approach the Study of Conservatism?," *Journal of American History* 98 (2011): 770; Jefferson Cowie and Nick Salvatore, "The Long Exception: Rethinking the Place of the New Deal in American History," *International Labor and Working-Class History* 74 (2008): 3–32.

5. Tanina Rostain, Milton C. Regan Jr., *Confidence Games: Lawyers, Accountants, and the Tax Shelter Industry* (MIT Press forthcoming); Liam Murphy and Thomas Nagel, *The Myth of Ownership: Taxes and Justice* (New York: Oxford University Press, 2002).

6. Olivier Zunz, *Philanthropy in America: A History* (Princeton University Press, 2012).

7. Charles C. Tilly, "War Making and State Making as Organizing Crime," in *Bringing the State Back In*, ed. Peter Evans, Dietrich Rueschmeyer, and Theda Skocpol (Cambridge: Cambridge University Press, 1985), 169–186.

8. Glenn W. Fisher, *The Worst Tax? A History of Property Tax in America* (Lawrence: University of Kansas Press, 1996); Isaac William Martin, Ajay K. Mehrotra, and Monica Prased, "The Thunder of History: The Origins and Development of the New Fiscal Sociology," in *The New Fiscal Sociology: Taxation in Comparative and Historical Perspective*, ed. Isaac William Martin, Ajay K. Mehrotra, and Monica Prasad (Cambridge: Cambridge University Press, 2009), 1–27; Romain Huret, "All Again in the Family? Political History and the Challenge of Social History," *Journal of Policy History* 21, no. 3, (2009): 239–263.

9. Jefferson Cowie, *Stayin' Alive: The 1970s and the Last Days of the Working Class* (New York: 2010); Judith Stein, *Pivotal Decade: How the United States Traded Factories for Finance in the Seventies* (New Haven: Yale University Press, 2010); Natasha Zaretsky, *No Direction Home: The American Family and the Fear of National Decline 1968–1980* (Chapel Hill: University of North Carolina Press, 2007); Jacob S. Hacker, *The*

Great Risk Shift: The New Economic Security and the Decline of the American Dream (New York: Oxford University Press, 2008); Daniel T. Rodgers, *Age of Fracture* (Cambridge, MA: Harvard University Press, 2011); Julia C. Ott, *When Wall Street Met Main Street: The Quest for an Investor's Democracy* (Cambridge, MA: Harvard University Press, 2011); Donald R. Hickey, *The War of 1812: A Forgotten Conflict* (Urbana: University of Illinois Press, 1990), 120.

ACKNOWLEDGMENTS

American Tax Resisters started many years ago in the South of France. While traveling to Aix-en-Provence for my military stint, I wondered, after reading Paul Auster's *Leviathan* (1992), why Americans had such a complex relationship with their federal government. It took me almost twenty years to focus on tax resistance as the main narrative of my broader reflection on American antistatism. Along the way, I met so many people who helped me that it would take me another book to thank them all.

First and foremost, this book has been written at a time of crisis in higher education in France. I've been very lucky to benefit from a grant from the Institut universitaire de France for five years, and without it, all research trips for this book would never have been possible. I would like to thank the Centre national de la recherche scientifique, the University of Lyon 2, the Ecole normale supérieure of Lyon and the Ecole des hautes études en sciences sociales (EHESS) of Paris. In France, all members of the Centre d'études nord-américaines of the EHESS deserve particular acknowledgment for their generosity and their insight. Between 2005 and 2009 I gave presentations on the chapters in this book and strongly benefited from all participants' astute ideas and critiques, especially Camille Amat, Nicolas Barreyre, Jean Heffer, Pap Ndiaye, Yann Philippe, Alexandre Rios-Bordes, Cecile Vidal, and François Weil. In Lyon, I'm grateful to thank Brigitte Esnault for her patience with all the red tape, Gilles Christoph, Jean Kempf, Alix Meyer, Marie Plassart, Renaud Payre, Gilles Pollet, Sabine Remanofsky, Jean Solchany, Jean-Claude Zanccharini, and of, course, Barbara and Vincent Michelot for the couch, wine, and *aligot*.

Earlier versions of this work were presented at conferences of the American Historical Association, the Business History Conference, the Institute for Policy History, the Organization of American Historians, the Social Science History Association, and the Center for European Studies at Harvard. For generous readings and critiques of the manuscript, I am immensely grateful to Dominique Ané, John Angell, Brian Balogh, Beth Bailey, Richard Bensel, Alan Brinkley, W. Elliot Brownlee, Olivier Burtin, Dan Carpenter, Christophe Charle, Don Critchlow, Martin Daunton, Nicolas Delalande, Andrew Diamond, Olivier Dard, Robin Einhorn, Eric Foner, Gary Gerstle, Daniel Geary, Christian Ingrao, Richard John, James Kloppenberg, Mathieu Leimgruber, Isaac Martin, Joseph McCartin, James McMurtry, Ajay Mehrotra, Jennifer Merchant, Evangeline Morphos, Bill Novak, Peter Onuf, Richard John, Caroline Rolland-Diamond, Stephen Sawyer, Randy Sparks, Jim Sparrow, Alexis Spire, Jennie Sutton, Maurizio Vaudagna, Jean-Christian Vinel, Mark Wilson, Julian Zelizer, and Olivier Zunz. I also would like to thank all the archivists who helped to find little-known material, especially Lucas Clawson, William H. Davis, Linda Hall, Richard McCulley, Matthew Harris, David Ross, Teresa Tomkins-Walsh, and Roy Wilson. The two anonymous readers of the manuscript also considerably helped me to frame my arguments.

As I was looking for a publisher, David Armitage wisely advised me to send my manuscript to Joyce Seltzer. During lunch in an Indian restaurant, he also gave me another sagacious piece of advice: stop discovering new archives and finish the book. I met Joyce in a small Japanese establishment in New York, and since then have enjoyed every moment of our collaboration. Brian Distelberg at Harvard University Press and Angela DeFini and Kimberly Giambattisto at Westchester Publishing Services provided vital support in the book's final stages. My friends (so many to mention—thank you all) always supported my project and always listened to me, even when I was talking about taxes and tariffs. Special thanks to the wise guys from Tunisia and Corsica. My sisters and brother—Anne-France, Nathalie, Sandra, and Stéphane—deserve special acknowledgment for their love and support over the years. A million thanks also to the young generation: Géraldine, Jennifer, Ophélia, and Rodolphe, and to my great "in-laws," Anne Devine and Michel Giordano.

Last but not least, I dedicate this book to my parents, Annick Huret and Antonio Agomeri, for always telling me to enjoy the beauty of the days gone by. And, of course, to my wonderful boys—Emilien, Melvil, and Raphaël—and to my wife, Ariane Boissy, *per la dolce della vita* from Nice to New York.

INDEX

Abney, Carolyn, 189, 190, 206. *See also* Marshall housewives
Abzug, Bella, 225
Agricultural Adjustment Act, 143, 146, 157
Aid to Families with Dependent Children, 244, 245. *See also* Welfare
Aldrich, Nelson W., 100
Alexander, Donald Crichton, 224, 225
Allen, Fred, 151
Aluminum Company of America, 132
America First Committee, 176
American Association of Christian Schools, 235
American Automobile Association, 121
American Bankers Association, 130
American Bar Association, 119
American Conservative Union, 232, 233, 234, 263
American Constitutional League, 118
American Council for Capital Formation, 256, 273
American Enterprise Institute, 228
American Farm Bureau, 121
American Federal of Labor, 96
American Institute of Certified Public Accountants, 166, 251
American Legion, 120, 124, 145
American Liberty League, 142, 143, 145, 152–156, 159, 162
American Paper and Pulp Association, 123
American Revolution, 2, 3, 46, 80, 216, 231, 253, 268
Americans for Democratic Action, 247
Americans for Tax Reform, 255, 256

American Social Science Association, 56, 74
American Sugar Refining Company, 93, 102
American Taxpayers Association, 168, 169 175, 176, 177, 178, 183, 192. *See also* American Taxpayers League
American Taxpayers League, 126, 127, 131, 136, 140, 145, 146, 154, 155, 157, 168, 169. *See also* American Taxpayers Association
American Tax Reduction Movement, 231, 236, 237
American Tobacco Company, 102
Andrews, Thomas Coleman, 193, 199
Anticommunism, 7, 54, 58, 59, 117, 156, 199, 203, 251
Anti-Income Tax Association, 40–43
Archer, William Reynolds Jr. "Bill," 258, 264
Armey, Richard K. "Dick," 259, 260, 265, 268
Arnold, James, 126, 127, 131, 135, 154, 156, 169, 185
Arthur, Chester A., 47, 65
Association against the Prohibition Amendment, 142
Association of Concerned Taxpayers, 212
Astor, William Backhouse, 13, 14, 18, 25, 41
AT&T, 141
Atwell, William H., 191
Atwood, Albert W., 130
Avery, Sewell Lee, 203